D0906066

INNOVATION

Also by Peter Ackroyd

Fiction

The Canterbury Tales: A Retelling

The Trial of Elizabeth Cree

The Last Testament of Oscar Wilde

Chatterton

First Light

English Music

Dan Leno and the Limehouse Golem

Milton in America

The Plato Papers

The Clerkenwell Tales

The Lambs of London

The Fall of Troy

The Casebook of Victor Frankenstein

The Death of King Arthur

Nonfiction

The Collection: Journalism, Reviews, Essays, Short Stories, Lectures
(edited by Thomas Wright)

London Under: The Secret History Beneath the Streets

Dressing Up: Transvestism and Drag: The History of an Obsession

London: The Biography

Albion: The Origins of the English Imagination

Thames: Sacred River

Venice: Pure City

T. S. Eliot

Dickens

Blake

The Life of Thomas More

Shakespeare

Chaucer

J. M. W. Turner

Newton

Poe: A Life Cut Short

Foundation: The History of England from Its Earliest Beginnings to the Tudors

Tudors: The History of England from Henry VIII to Elizabeth I

Rebellion: The History of England from James I to the Glorious Revolution

Revolution: The History of England from the Battle of the Boyne to the Battle of Waterloo

Dominion: The History of England from the Battle of Waterloo to Victoria's Diamond Jubilee

Peter Ackroyd

THE HISTORY OF ENGLAND

VOLUME VI

INNOVATION

ST. MARTIN'S PRESS
NEW YORK

First published in the United States by St. Martin's Press, an imprint of St. Martin's Publishing Group

www.stmartins.com

Library of Congress Cataloging-in-Publication Data

Names: Ackroyd, Peter, 1949– author.
Title: Innovation / Peter Ackroyd.
Description: First U.S. edition. | New York : St. Martin's Press, 2021. | Series: The history of England ; 6 | Includes bibliographical references and index.
Identifiers: LCCN 2021017799 | ISBN 9781250003669 (hardcover) | ISBN 9781250135544 (ebook)
Subjects: LCSH: Great Britain—History—20th century.
Classification: LCC DA566 .A25 2021 | DDC 942.082—dc23
LC record available at https://lccn.loc.gov/2021017799

Originally published in Great Britain by Picador, an imprint of Pan Macmillan

First U.S. Edition: 2021

10 9 8 7 6 5 4 3 2 1

Contents

List of illustrations

20. The Suez Canal in October 1956 (John Frost Newspapers / Alamy Stock Photo)
21. Harold Wilson (Popperfoto / Contributor)
22. The premiere of John Osborne's *Look Back in Anger* (Frank Pocklington / Stringer)
23. Mary Quant (Trinity Mirror / Mirrorpix / Alamy Stock Photo)
24. The 1966 World Cup final (Trinity Mirror / Mirrorpix / Alamy Stock Photo)
25. The Beatles (Keystone Press / Alamy Stock Photo)
26. The queen watching television in 1969 (Joan Williams / Shutterstock)
27. A British family watching television in the 1970s (Homer Sykes / Alamy Stock Photo)
28. The three-day week (J. Wilds / Stringer)
29. The miners' strike of 1984 (Manchester Daily Express / Contributor)
30. Margaret Thatcher (peter jordan / Alamy Stock Photo)
31. Princess Diana (Tim Graham / Contributor)
32. Tony Blair (Dan White / Alamy Stock Photo)
33. The Millennium Dome (Trinity Mirror / Mirrorpix / Alamy Stock Photo)

Acknowledgements

I would like to thank my research assistants, Murrough O"Brien and Thomas Wright, for their invaluable assistance in the preparation of this volume.

1

The sun never rises

The greatest shock of the Second Boer War was not the protracted and bloody guerrilla warfare, but the wretched condition of the British troops.* The conscripts were malnourished and sickly, their morale low. After the war was over in 1902, an inquiry revealed that 16,000 servicemen had died of disease, due to poor rations and constitutional weakness. Many of the English soldiers had been press-ganged by penury, but around 60 per cent of the volunteers had been rejected as unfit for service. This finding prompted further investigations into the 'deterioration of certain classes of the population', though they came at least fifty years too late.

Investigations into the military conduct of the war were equally disturbing. It had taken almost half a million British troops to subdue a Boer population similar to that of Brighton, at a cost of £250 million. The publication of these inquiries prompted the government to create a Committee of Imperial Defence to coordinate the armed forces, and stemmed the tide of English jingoism. In 1900, during the triumphant opening phase of the war, a wave

* This is a history of England, rather than of Britain. However, British institutions, such as the British army, navy, government, monarchy and empire, are constantly referred to in this book, as they are inextricably bound up with England's history. For the same reason, certain events which took place in the wider United Kingdom are also covered.

of imperialist enthusiasm had carried the Conservative and Liberal Unionist coalition to power at the so-called 'khaki election'. The Tory-dominated coalition secured a large majority over the Liberals, defying the 'swing of the pendulum' law of British politics.

As the war continued, those who had previously felt imperial pride expressed disappointment and shame. The working classes even declared their admiration for the Boer rebels. 'What's the good of talking about the Empire on which the sun never sets,' one Londoner put it, 'when the sun never rises on our court?' By the end of the decade, patriotic platitudes concerning the 'Great Empire' provoked laughter.

Were the British army's deficiencies symptomatic of a wider national degeneration? In the nineteenth century, many people had believed that English enterprise and integrity had helped to bring order to the distant territories and diverse cultures of the British Empire; at the beginning of the new century, they no longer believed these boasts. After the Boer War, it was customary for politicians to speak of the 'consolidation' or 'integration' of existing colonies, dominions and 'spheres of economic influence'. It was thought that strengthening political and economic ties within the empire was crucial if England were to survive as a great power, at a time when Germany, Japan and the United States of America were flourishing.

Some politicians argued that the creation of a system of 'self-governing dominions' within the empire was the only way to secure unity, given the limited capacity of British troops and increasing nationalist sentiment in territories under British control. In the late nineteenth century, India's educated elite had developed political theories based on the principle of 'representative national institutions'. In Ireland, popular support for 'Home Rule' had been paramount for decades, and anti-English sentiment became more intense.

Similar criticism could be heard in England. The burning of thousands of Boer homes and farms by British troops, and the construction of 8,000 'concentration camps' to house the evicted Boers, provoked outrage, and when around 20,000 women and children died in the camps, the anger grew. Then news reached England that the government had allowed 50,000 Chinese labourers to work in South African mines for paltry wages and in appalling living conditions. On the opposition benches, Liberal politicians took up the cry of 'Chinese slavery'. Imperial expansion had been justified by the argument that Britain was bestowing civilization on 'primitive' societies. At the end of the nineteenth century, the English viceroy of India had boasted of importing 'the rule of justice' to the country, along with 'peace and order and good government'. But in the wake of the Boer War, many observers regarded Britain's 'civilizing mission' as an excuse for exploitation.

After 1900, the English were also forced to confront their economy's diminishing international status. In the Victorian era, English manufacturers had dominated world trade. A combination of technological innovation and cheap labour had allowed goods to be produced inexpensively in England; the availability and expansion of imperial markets, as well as mastery of the seas, had ensured they could be safely sold around the world. Meanwhile, Britain's colonies had commissioned elaborate engineering projects from English firms, with money borrowed from the City of London. The United Kingdom had been responsible for a third of the world's manufacturing in the 1870s, but in the early 1900s this figure fell to 10 per cent.

England could no longer claim to be the 'workshop of the world' – that title was now contested by Germany and the United States, which had been strengthened by unification in the second half of the nineteenth century and had developed modern production methods during recent wars. By 1900 the United States produced more coal and iron than England, while Germany's mining technology, electrical engineering and chemical industries were superior. Part of England's problem was that it had industrialized long before its rivals, and neither the government nor the representatives of capital and labour had the vision or the will to reinvigorate the manufacturing sector. England was technologically sclerotic, unable to add to its imperial territories and shut out from many international markets by the tariffs of foreign governments. Her staple export industries of iron, wool, shipbuilding and coal had entered their senescence. To compound the problem of declining exports, England was increasingly dependent on foreign imports. After 1900 there was a balance-of-payments deficit, with more money leaving the country than coming in. Over the next fourteen years, economic growth halved.

At the beginning of 1901, *The Annual Register* described the outlook for England as 'full of misgivings'. A few weeks later, on 22 January, the nation's anxiety was compounded when Queen Victoria died. As the news spread across the country, church bells tolled, theatrical performances were abandoned and traffic halted, as people poured onto the streets. For many, despair was coupled with bewilderment. It is sometimes said by foreign observers that monarchism is the religion of the English, yet by no means everyone in the country was a believer: the novelist Arnold Bennett thought that Londoners 'were not, on the whole, deeply moved, whatever journalists may say'.

All the commentators agreed, however, that the queen's death marked a transition in the country's history. 'We are less secure of our position,' announced *The Times*. 'Our impetus' as a 'nation may be spent'. Soon after Victoria's death, the passing of the ethos of Victorianism was also predicted. In his parliamentary address, the Tory leader of the Commons, Arthur James Balfour, announced 'the end of a great epoch'.

It was not long before another pillar of the Victorian establishment fell. In July 1902, Lord Salisbury resigned as prime minister on the grounds of bad health, his gargantuan weight placing an inordinate strain on his legs and heart. Ever since the split of the Liberal party over Irish Home Rule in 1886 and the defection of the Liberal Unionists to the Conservatives, the Tory grandee had controlled political life, holding office for all but three of those sixteen years. A Tory aristocrat of the old school, he abhorred the democratic tendencies of the modern age, seeing his party's mission as representing the landed 'governing' class and maintaining the status quo in their interest. 'Whatever happens will be for the worse,' was his most famous political pronouncement, 'and therefore it is in our interest that as little should happen as possible.' Some observers saw, in the manner of Salisbury's passing in the following year, an omen of the imminent collapse of the British Empire; others regarded his death as confirmation that the Victorian era had ended.

Nevertheless, Conservatives in the Salisbury mould endeavoured to deny the demise of the old order. To Tories, the Victorian verities, including laissez-faire economics and politics and the centrality to national life of the aristocracy, the crown, the Anglican Church and the empire, were sacred. Though the Liberals represented the commercial and Nonconformist sections of the English population, an influential aristocratic element within them was even more passionately committed to free-market capitalism than its rival party.

The passivity within the two parties reflected the inertia in the political system. The 'first-past-the-post' system of British elections made it virtually impossible for a new party to achieve an electoral victory. As a consequence, the Tories and the Liberals had shared power for decades. The right to vote was limited to males who paid an annual rent of £10 or owned land worth the same amount, which meant that 40 per cent of English males, as well as the entire female population, were excluded from the franchise. Since MPs were unpaid, only the wealthiest men could afford to stand for election to the Commons. Once elected, MPs devised legislative proposals that were modified or rejected by an unelected, Tory-dominated House of Lords, before being submitted to the monarch for approval. In addition to being the head of Britain's church, army and aristocracy and one of its biggest landowners, the ostensibly 'constitutional' monarch actually enjoyed extensive executive powers known as the 'royal prerogative', which included the freedom to dismiss and appoint prime ministers.

In contrast to the English politicians, the country's intellectuals celebrated the end of Victorianism, and eagerly devised plans for a brave new world. H. G. Wells compared Queen Victoria to a 'great paper-weight that for half a century [had] sat upon men's minds . . . when she was removed their ideas began to blow about all over the place haphazardly'. Radicals such as Wells used 'Victorian' as a pejorative term; a fairer, more rational era was coming. The Liberal economist J. A. Hobson remarked on the way increasing numbers of people suddenly appeared 'possessed by the duty and desire to put the very questions which their parents thought shocking, and to insist upon plain intelligible answers'. What is the role of the state? What is the purpose of the empire? Why should women and the working classes be excluded from the electoral process? And what are the causes and cures of economic and social inequality?

Attempts to answer these questions produced a plethora of political and cultural movements. Socialist, anarchist and feminist groups were founded, while trade unions flourished. Some intellectuals turned to religious philosophies such as theosophy, or took up single-issue political causes including anti-vivisection and anti-vaccination. Many reformers looked to science to point the way to a brighter future. While different radicals promoted different means, the Fabian socialist Beatrice Webb believed they were all working towards the same end: 'The whole nation', she wrote, is 'sliding towards Social Democracy'.

The men who replaced the falling giants of the Victorian establishment did not quite match their stature. Victoria was succeeded by her eldest son Edward who, at the age of almost sixty, 'got his innings at last', in the words of the young Tory MP Winston Churchill. Born in 1841, Edward had a distinctly nineteenth-century appearance, with a thick moustache and rotund figure. He had a taste for cigars, women, gossip, jokes and military uniforms, but his greatest passion was food. The tone of his reign was set when his coronation had to be delayed as a result of an illness brought on by overindulgence. The new king's conspicuous consumption was a source of embarrassment to the court, at a time when a large percentage of his subjects lived in poverty.

Edward was also animated by the conviviality, energy and exuberance that was characteristic of the Victorian era. Eyewitness accounts describe him as 'roaring like a bull' as he vented the 'hereditary Hanoverian spleen'. Many of his political views also marked him out as a man of the previous century. In imperial affairs he deplored the idea of granting autonomy to the colonies. Yet compared to his fervently Tory mother, Edward was more neutral in party-political terms, and less inclined to interfere in the affairs of government and parliament. On the other hand, the new king was eager to exercise a decisive influence over the government's diplomacy. As the speaker of a variety of continental languages and as a man who prided himself on being a 'good European', he was better qualified than most modern English monarchs to do so.

Victoria had not been amused by the hedonistic lifestyle of her eldest son, yet Edward's amiability, elegant dressing and fondness for public appearances gained him numerous admirers. When his coronation eventually took place, it was enthusiastically celebrated, and he remained a popular king throughout his reign. The author J. B. Priestley, who grew up in the 'Edwardian age', recalled the enthusiasm the monarch inspired throughout the country, and believed Edward to be the most popular English king since Charles II. The overwhelmingly right-wing English newspapers presented the king as an icon through whom they could enjoy vicarious power and pleasure.

Like the succession to the throne, succession to the office of prime minister was a family affair. When Lord Salisbury retired in 1902, there was no election; instead he appointed his nephew, Arthur Balfour, as premier. This was by no means the first occasion on which Salisbury had promoted a relative within his government, and nothing better illustrates the hegemony of England's aristocratic governing caste, or the essential identity of the Conservative party.

Balfour offered a striking contrast to the king whose government he led, with his languid posture and subtle intelligence. His most famous publication was a philosophical tract called *A Defence of Philosophic Doubt*, and his taste for philosophic inquiry was accompanied by a genius for rhetoric. Yet this mastery of the parliamentary medium often made it difficult for others to identify his message. Balfour never appeared to advocate or condemn a point of view; instead of proposing a course of action, he preferred to analyse all possible options until none seemed viable. As a patrician Tory he had little interest in altering the status quo, yet there was something idiosyncratic about his suspicion of all forms of political passion. It was as though he was petrified by the prospect of anarchy, and he laboured to keep it at a distance through irony, oratory and even coercion. As chief secretary for Ireland in the 1880s he had been known as 'Bloody Balfour' for his draconian policies. 'To allow' the Home Rulers to 'win', he had said, 'is simply to give up civilisation . . . and authority'. Balfour regularly defended Conservative 'values', but he felt no enthusiasm for any specific political issue. Politics was an art to be pursued for its own sake rather than a means of getting things done.

Many of Balfour's critics dismissed the prime minister as effete and ineffectual, while others lamented his lack of interest in the people he governed. It was said that he had never read a newspaper in his life. With little interest in the 'lower orders', and nothing but contempt for a middle class 'unfit' for anything 'besides manufacturing', the Tory prime minister epitomized the hauteur of the governing aristocratic elite. Was this the leader to face the challenges of a new era?

2

Home sweet home

Beyond the palace and parliament lay numberless streets of newly built houses. They were semi-detached or detached two-storey red-brick buildings, with slate roofs and bow windows, timber frames, casement windows and small front gardens. Peering over the hedges that protected the privacy of these new homes, the passer-by could discern carefully arranged window displays behind lace curtains. In their tidiness, cleanliness and air of modest comfort, the homes of the 'suburbs' seemed to proclaim a prosperous and content population. During Edward's reign, the suburban population exploded: in 1910, there were almost a million people living in 'outer London'.

The new houses were given names like 'Fairview', or 'The Laurels' – the name of the home of the archetypal suburbanite Charles Pooter, hero of George and Weedon Grossmith's late-Victorian classic, *The Diary of a Nobody*. They were typically clustered in squares or along truncated streets. Nearby there would be a park, a bowls or tennis club and a row of shops. Men in dark suits and bowler hats would leave the houses for work, umbrella in hand; young mothers would push perambulators, and boys from the grocer's and newsagent's would make their deliveries. Few children could be heard playing in the streets. This was the deep consciousness of 'middle England'.

The suburbs were characterized by a removal from the commercial and industrial concerns of urban centres. Pervaded by a spirit of rural and romantic make-believe, with their tree-lined streets and patches of grass, they formed cityless cities for those who could afford to escape the tumultuous streets of the centre. The more leafy and spacious the suburb, the higher the house prices and the higher the percentage of owner-occupiers. A house in the green south London suburb of Balham cost over £1,000 to buy or 12 shillings a week to rent, prices that only the middle classes could afford.

At the lower end of the suburban cohort were skilled craftsmen and artisans, who had authority at work and were addressed by their 'betters' as 'Mr' rather than just by their surnames. This group also included shopkeepers, tradesmen, publicans, teachers, boarding-house keepers and small-scale merchants. They generally rented houses in the 'inner suburbs' and sometimes kept a servant – a necessity in the labour-intensive Edwardian home, as well as a status symbol to demonstrate that they were a level above semi-skilled or unskilled factory workers or labourers. Members of the lowest of the 'servant-keeping classes' felt too superior to mix with the working people in the public house but could not afford to frequent middle-class restaurants. In fact, they often struggled to maintain their social status, which was everything in Edwardian England – slipping down the scale and moving from the inner suburbs to the inner city was perceived as tragic and irreversible. Bankruptcy, loss of employment and the sickness or death of a family member might be the cause of this misfortune.

Clerks in city offices were more secure in their social position; so too were civil servants, bookkeepers and assistant managers, who earned between £300 and £700 a year. Such people kept two or more servants and could afford to buy houses in inner suburbs, such as Chorlton and Withington just outside Manchester. Yet more leafy outer suburban areas were beyond their means, though not their aspirations. The most attractive and genteel suburbs were colonized by the upper middle classes – manufacturers and wholesalers, along with the accountants, architects, solicitors, barristers, doctors, vets, bankers, actuaries and surveyors who comprised the professional classes. As the nineteenth century had progressed, they had become increasingly powerful and well-organized, with the creation of associations for each occupation. They could afford to keep several servants and privately educate their children. After schooling, boys would often take up the same professions as their fathers; girls were encouraged to become shorthand writers or governesses while they awaited marriage.

Suburbanites could commute to work in the city along the recently established transport links, which included electric trams and omnibuses, as well as overground and underground trains. Balham, for example, was connected to the City of London via underground stations at Kennington and Stockwell, and Didsbury was connected to Manchester Central Station by an overland train. Trams were the cheapest way to travel, with special 'workman's fares' for early-morning journeys allowing passengers to travel up to ten miles for a penny. Yet precisely because trams were popular with workers, the middle class tended to shun them and instead take the train.

Whenever a new train station was built just outside a city, estate agents' offices would emerge nearby, offering land to speculators, construction firms and private buyers. In 1907, Golders Green in north London was connected to the City by the Charing Cross, Euston and Hampstead Railway; immediately afterwards, the armies of builders arrived. 'All day long', remarked a local paper in 1910, 'there is a continuous hammering which reminds one of distant thunder', as the tiled, gabled and half-timbered 'semis' grew up around the station, the railway line and the roads. There was no development plan and local authority control was virtually non-existent, so the houses were built close together to maximize profits. It was a sprawl that failed to take into consideration either the quality of life of the new inhabitants or the preservation of the countryside. By 1914 it was impossible to believe that Golders Green had been full of trees and hedges only a decade before.

The unrelenting development of these outer cities gave the impression that the English population was also expanding. Yet the low-density housing of the suburbs, in contrast with the high blocks of flats on the Continent and the older terraces in English cities, revealed a different demographic trend. The new houses suited England's relatively ageing population. For the first time on record, the increase in England's population slowed during the Edwardian period. Between 1900 and 1910 the birth rate decreased from thirty-six to twenty-four per 1,000 population; it was only the declining death rate and increasing immigration into the country that kept the population growing.

Declining birth and death rates meant that England was no longer the young, vigorous country it had been at the beginning of Victoria's reign. In 1841 half of the population had been under twenty, but by 1914 the figure was less than a third. This development provoked further concerns about the robustness of the nation, while increasing immigration prompted xenophobia, with many complaining that England was 'falling to the Irish and the Jews'. Popular anxiety over the racial 'deterioration' and 'adulteration' of the supposedly Anglo-Saxon English would inform the 1905 Aliens Act, which was introduced by the Tories to reduce immigration into Britain from outside the empire.

The keynotes of suburban life were privacy, domesticity and respectability. The privet hedge at the front of the semi-detached houses and their fenced back gardens ensured that the suburban family's 'home sweet home' became their castle. Suburbanites could live undisturbed by their neighbours, with whom they might exchange no more than a few words. And yet everyone was aware of their social and economic status – the size of one's house and its presentation proclaimed one's ranking. The most affluent families set the standards to which all denizens of a suburb aspired: 'keeping up with the Joneses', a phrase coined in 1913, was the aim of suburban life. Everyone in a suburb was also aware of a neighbour's transgressions from genteel standards of morality, such as an unwanted pregnancy. A group-monitored respectability pervaded these outer cities, and the word 'respectable' became synonymous with the suburban middle class.

The aspirational character of middle-class suburbanites offered an obvious subject for literary caricature. 'We live our unreal, stupid little lives,' a suburban character comments in a story by the upper-middle-class author Saki, 'and persuade ourselves that we really are untrammelled men and women leading a reasonable existence.' Other authors mocked the supposedly unsophisticated cultural societies such as drama, singing, art and flower arranging that proliferated in the new neighbourhoods, together with the tennis, bowls and golf clubs that monopolized so much of the suburbanite's leisure time. The suburbs themselves were also denigrated and denounced. In his 1910 novel *Howards End*, E. M. Forster described a stain of 'red rust' spreading out into the countryside around London.

Some intellectuals championed suburbia. The radical Liberal MP Charles Masterman predicted that the suburbs would become the major urban form of the twentieth century, replacing the countryside as the breeding ground of a new 'English yeomanry'. Animated by the Victorian values of self-help, laissez-faire and individualism, it was believed that suburbanites were distinguished by their drive, ambition, worldliness and agnosticism. The suburban middle class was also on the rise as a political force. Partially enfranchised by the reform acts of the 1860s and 1880s and then fully enfranchised in 1918, their electoral choices would determine who governed England throughout the twentieth century. In acknowledgement of the growing power of that class, the 1911 census made the occupation of the male head of the household, rather than the land he owned or his family connections, the main criterion of social position.

Yet the new population had its limitations. Neither political consciousness nor a sense of solidarity could flourish in the suburbs, where private interests took precedence over public concerns. In the absence of a strong community spirit and a compelling code of public ethics, religious observance also declined. It was not that atheism was spreading among suburbanites; it was just that they dedicated their time to their families, to leisure activities and to spending money. Sundays in the suburbs were spent playing golf, tennis and bowls rather than going to church. Most members of the middle class remained Christian in their outlook, but they increasingly did not feel the need to affirm this by attending church. Their indifference to the established Church of England set the tone for the entire nation, and for the coming century. While the Anglican Church would continue to influence English culture in the decades ahead, its popular appeal and political power would be severely diminished.

3

The lie of the land

Beyond the suburbs lay the old villages of rural England, whose decay was constantly lamented. Over 1 million English people still worked the land, but they represented a dwindling percentage of the workforce. In 1851 a quarter of English males were agricultural labourers, but by 1911 the figure fell below 5 per cent. England was now an overwhelmingly urban nation, with over three-quarters of the population living in towns and cities – a development that alarmed those who believed that the health of the English people was threatened by urban living.

Rural labourers lived in six main areas of the country – the grazing counties of the north-west, north-east and south-west, and the arable counties of East Anglia, the Midlands and the south-east. The agricultural depression of the late nineteenth century had ravaged the arable sector. In 1870 arable goods had accounted for half of the national agricultural produce, but by 1914 that figure had fallen below 20 per cent. Improvements in transport and preservation allowed producers as far away as New Zealand to export their goods to England; half of all food consumed in the country was imported.

Wages for those who worked the land were low at the start of Edward's reign. The average pay for a sixty-five-hour week was around 12 shillings, a sum which the social reformer Benjamin

Seebohm Rowntree described as 'insufficient to maintain a family of average size in a state of merely physical efficiency'. Rural wages would increase by 3 per cent between 1900 and 1912, well behind the general 15 per cent increase in the cost of living over the same period. Where possible, agricultural labourers would rear their own animals for slaughter and cultivate their own allotments.

The English peasantry owned none of the land it cultivated. After the enclosures of the previous centuries, almost every rural acre belonged to private aristocratic landlords. Even in Ireland, where great swathes of the land had been appropriated by the British from the native Catholic population in the sixteenth and seventeenth centuries, the situation was more favourable to agricultural labourers, after the 1903 Wyndham Land (Purchase) Act offered subsidies to tenants who wanted to purchase land from landlords. Agricultural labour in Edwardian England was often characterized as cheerless toil for someone else's benefit, while living conditions for the peasantry were frequently desperate. It is hardly surprising that so many labourers either joined unions and agitated for an improvement in their lot or left the land for towns and cities. With the country population decreasing, the traditional rural way of life, with its ancient trades, crafts and pastimes, slowly died out. Village festivals became less frequent and public houses shut down, while bread and meat were now bought from the baker's and butcher's vans that came from the nearest town.

On their journeys to England's cities, emigrant rural workers would often meet wealthy townspeople travelling in the opposite direction by motor car. Upper-middle-class Edwardians decided to move to the country in order to return to the 'simpler' way of life that had been evoked in the works of such Victorian writers as John Ruskin. The magazine *Country Life*, founded at the end of the 1890s, exerted an even larger influence, with its promises of 'peace, plenty and quiet' for the 'country-loving businessman'. Nostalgia for a largely imaginary version of traditional rural life would be a prominent feature of the urban middle-class imagination throughout the twentieth century. The more country life was destroyed, the greater influence the ideal of that traditional life exercised on the English psyche.

While rich city folk often claimed to love traditional rural life, they were not prepared to forgo modern comfort. Instead of renovating the dilapidated cottages left vacant by the city-bound peasants, they generally built their own 'cottagey' homes replete with modern conveniences. Numerous 'riverside' housing developments sprang up along the Thames, with regular railway services allowing their inhabitants to commute to the City. The new houses were in the countryside but not of it. The sounds of a piano or a tennis party would issue from them; city talk now filled the country lanes.

When the rural workers arrived in a city, they found streets upon streets of indistinguishable houses and shops. The majority of the working-class men who inhabited inner cities were semi-skilled or unskilled labourers employed in factories or in the construction industry for a weekly wage. Others, still lower down the social and economic scale, assumed more precarious occupations, such as scavenger, knife grinder or hawker. According to the 1911 census, the leading occupational category for working-class men and women in England was domestic service, with some one and a quarter million people employed as servants. The number of people in domestic work reinforced the Conservative idea of England as an 'organic' hierarchical society in which everyone had a place and knew it.

Working-class people who were not live-in domestics often resided in the 'two-up, two-down' terraced city houses constructed during Victoria's reign. These cheaply built 'workers' cottages' were poorly insulated and lacked running water, though many were now lit by gas. Family life centred on the ground-floor room at the back of the house, which served as a kitchen and living room. The front room downstairs displayed the family's best furniture and was used only on special occasions. There was a small garden at the back with an outdoor toilet; the garden could be used to grow vegetables or as a yard where work tools might be stored.

Just under half of the working classes were officially classified as impoverished. While the national income increased by 20 per cent over Edward's reign, real wages dropped by around 6 per cent. When working husbands failed to bring in enough money to cover their family's needs, their wives were forced to pawn the family's possessions. In the first decade of the new century there were 700 pawn shops within ten miles of the City of London.

The ever-present fear of the working class was the penury that might come as a consequence of unemployment, ill health, a wage cut or injury at work. When the rent on a terraced house could no longer be paid, a once respectable family had to look for accommodation among the crowded and squalid slums of the 'residuum'. It is thought that 35,000 people were homeless in London in 1910. They tramped the streets during the night and waited by the gates of the public parks until they opened, when they fell asleep on the benches. The workhouses offered little in the way of refuge. Their occupants would earn meagre meals by picking oakum and breaking stones all day, like prisoners – and any negligence could be punished by imprisonment.

The working classes were often described by middle-class observers as a different race – stunted, sickly, violent, exhausted and addicted to stimulants such as tobacco and alcohol. But while drink was condemned by genteel reformers as the 'curse of the working classes', drinkers often referred to it as 'the shortest way out of the slums'. Religion was not one of the preferred stimulants of the 'masses' – less than 15 per cent of the urban working class regularly attended religious services. Some clergymen were concerned that the workers were regressing to paganism, while more acute observers believed they had never fully converted to Christianity in the first place. It may be significant that the denominations that retained some of their working-class allegiance combined an other-worldly ethos with an interest in earthly, political concerns. Keir Hardie, who had become the first ever 'Labour' MP in 1892, was an ardent Nonconformist who declared that 'the only way to serve God is by serving humanity'. The Anglican Church, meanwhile, was regarded with indifference by the workers, hardly surprising given its reputation as 'the Tory Party at prayer'.

4

Plates in the air

Poor wages, fear of penury and conspicuous social and economic inequality made the workers anxious and angry. In a country where there was segregation at public baths between working people and the 'higher classes', class hostility was inevitable. In 1900 the Labour Representation Committee (LRC) was established by socialist bodies including the Fabians and the Independent Labour Party (ILP), along with various trade unionists who were determined to secure their legal status and right to strike. The general aim of the union-backed LRC (or the Labour party, as it would be called from 1906) was to further working-class interests in the Commons, by sponsoring parliamentary representatives who would, in Keir Hardie's words, form 'a distinct Labour group . . . and cooperate with any party promoting legislation in the direct interests of labour'. It conceived a programme of 'gradualist' socialism, designed to improve Britain's existing economic, social and political system. Reform, rather than revolution, was its purpose.

The parliamentary rise of 'Labour', and the electoral challenge it posed to the Liberal party, are striking in the history of twentieth-century politics. As early as 1901, the Fabian Sidney Webb argued that the emergence of a party of labour threatened the Liberal party's status as 'the political organ of the progressive instinct' and as the main opposition to the Tories. Yet in the five years following its formation, 'Labour' was merely a parliamentary pressure group, with no aspirations to challenging the Liberals. It had only two MPs, one of whom was the redoubtable Hardie, known for wearing a cloth cap in parliament rather than the customary silk top hat. The sight of him at Westminster was a shock to many: 'A Republic,' wrote one journalist, 'has insinuated itself in the folds of a monarchy.' Hardie was lambasted by the overwhelmingly Conservative newspapers for his republican views. From the back benches, he advocated increasing as well as graduating income tax (which only 7 per cent of the population currently paid) to subsidize a programme of social reforms, designed to improve the conditions of the working class.

For the moment, no one listened to the voice of Labour. Balfour's administration, which lasted from 1902 to 1905, showed little interest in introducing social legislation, while the idea of raising taxes was abhorrent to most Tories. Nevertheless the government did pass the 1903 Unemployed Workmen Act, which at least acknowledged that the state ought to address the problem of unemployment. The government's most ambitious piece of domestic legislation was the 1902 Education Act, which provided funds, from local ratepayers, for denominational religious instruction; it also united the voluntary elementary schools run by the Anglican and Catholic churches with those administered by school boards. But the act provoked outrage on the Liberal benches. It was discriminatory against Nonconformists, they claimed, since it was predominantly Anglican schools that were to be subsidized by rates.

While the Education Act proved controversial, the political cause célèbre of Balfour's tenure was protectionism. In 1902 a group of Liberal Unionists and Conservatives tried to persuade his government to impose tariffs on all imports coming into Britain from outside the empire. Their proposals effectively called for the end of laissez-faire economics and free trade – two of the great Victorian verities. The Liberal party united in opposition to the proposal, on the grounds that unfettered competition was natural, moral and patriotic.

The debate not only drew a clear dividing line between the two parties, it also split the Conservative and Liberal Unionist coalition. Many Conservatives had sympathy with the arguments of the free-trade Liberals, and even more believed that the status quo should not be disturbed. How, they asked, could such a radical idea emerge from within a Tory-dominated coalition, whose central aim was to *conserve* things as they were, and to perpetuate the power the party had enjoyed at Westminster for almost two decades?

The answer was simple: Joseph Chamberlain, the colonial secretary and Liberal Unionist leader, whose conversion to Tariff Reform guaranteed it would become the great issue of the day. Chamberlain, as the young Tory Winston Churchill commented, 'was the one who made the weather' – in the cabinet, in Westminster and in the country. The charismatic man with the monocle and the orchid in his buttonhole had been 'Made in Birmingham'. Imbued with the confidence of a city that had experienced extraordinary material and technological progress during the industrial revolution, this former screw manufacturer was truculent, practical, energetic and ambitious. He was an emblem of Birmingham's thriving commercial aristocracy – he had been mayor of the city in the 1870s and had improved its infrastructure through the implementation of a programme of 'municipal socialism'.

Given Chamberlain's character and background, it is unsurprising that not all Tories celebrated his defection to their side of the House in 1886, in protest at the Liberal government's Irish Home Rule Bill. The old party of the landed governing class and the Anglican Church ought not, some Tories believed, to ally itself with manufacturers and dissenters, especially when they were as radical, flashy and potentially divisive as Chamberlain. Yet he proved to be a great electoral asset to what became the Unionist Alliance. His Liberal Unionist group contributed seventy-one MPs to the coalition after the 1895 election, while the policies he pursued as colonial secretary from that date had been immensely popular. Chamberlain was a zealous imperialist who believed 'that the British race is the greatest of the governing races that the world has ever seen'. His plan for the empire was the knitting together of 'kindred races' for 'similar objects'; in particular, he aimed to strengthen the 'bonds' linking Britain, Canada and America in a 'Greater Britain'. Yet unifying and integrating the empire were not enough to satisfy Chamberlain; he dreamed of expanding its frontiers. His aggressive policies had helped provoke the conflict with the Boers, which became known as 'Joe's War'. In the early days of the military campaign he had basked in the triumphs of the British troops, which helped secure a decisive electoral victory for the Unionist Alliance in 1900.

The speeches and journalism Chamberlain produced during the election campaign were peppered with slogans. 'Every seat lost to the government,' he had declared, 'is a seat sold to the Boers.' Chamberlain believed that subtlety of argument was inappropriate for the twentieth century: 'in politics', he would say, 'you must paint with a broad brush'. His ability to speak directly to the voting lower middle class and the business classes, through simple language and the modern media, made Chamberlain unique among the coalition ranks. He was, in Churchill's phrase, 'the man the masses knew'. While some Tories, and most Liberals, accused him of lowering the standard of public life with his 'demagoguery', the party hierarchy was forced to tolerate him.

With jingoism apparently dead following the debacle of the Boer War, and with the Liberal opposition gaining momentum, Chamberlain needed another popular cry. Besides, he was nearing seventy and itching for one last adventure. That adventure might also advance his ultimate ambition – the leadership of a Unionist government and the country. An acute interpreter of the spirit of the age, Chamberlain sensed that businessmen and the lower middle classes were slowly coming to the conclusion that free competition was a Victorian truism. It was this intuition that inspired Chamberlain's Tariff Reform programme.

Chamberlain presented his plans to the cabinet in 1902. Some of his colleagues were persuaded by his argument that tariffs would protect British industry from foreign competition, but others were openly hostile. Balfour decided that he could not afford to lose the support of Chamberlain's critics by backing the plan. The government's official position was expressed in a characteristic Balfourian equivocation – Tariff Reform was desirable but impractical at the present time. Yet Chamberlain was not a man to wait. In May 1903, he defied Balfour by publicizing his proposals in a startling speech in Birmingham, insisting that England's free trade policies, and the tariffs imposed by other nations on English goods, were destroying the country's industry. 'Sugar is gone; silk has gone; iron is threatened; wool is threatened; cotton will go! How long are you going to stand it?' Only the imposition of tariffs on goods coming into England from outside the empire could arrest the country's economic decline and preserve English jobs: 'Tariff Reform', ran his new slogan, 'Means Work for All'. Tariffs would, in addition, further the two causes closest to his heart – imperialism and social reform. They would bind the vast empire closer together, as a single economic, political and military unit, and raise government revenue which could be spent on domestic legislation. 'The foreigner' would thus pay for social reform, rather than the English taxpayer.

Chamberlain's panacea for England's difficulties was well received by his audience. Some Unionist MPs praised the programme as an ambitious bid both to revamp Disraelian 'one-nation Toryism' and to revive the empire as a popular and party-political issue. But Balfour was dismayed. There was now intense pressure on him to join the side of either protectionism or free trade, yet his cabinet and party were divided on the issue. In the end, Balfour could not bring himself to choose sides and permitted members of his cabinet to make up their own minds. He also formulated an ambiguous piece of legislation that aimed to appease both factions within his party – 'retaliatory' tariffs were introduced on countries who had anti-British tariffs in place; protectionist measures would thereby promote free trade.

The only problem with this characteristic solution was that it satisfied neither faction. The prime minister's reluctance to dictate an official line to his cabinet, meanwhile, was interpreted as a dereliction of his duty as leader. Representatives of both sides of the argument resigned from the cabinet, with Chamberlain declaring that he would leave the government in order to take his protectionist gospel to the country. Instead of confronting Chamberlain, Balfour told him that if he managed to convert the majority of the electorate, the coalition would back the Tariff Reform programme at the next election.

The episode undermined Balfour's authority within his party and the Commons, where the Liberals were vociferous in their criticism. He believed in protectionism, they claimed, but knew the policy was unpopular, and had therefore sacrificed his most talented minister, and his own convictions, to pragmatic considerations. Balfour's government was now bereft of an ambitious policy, as well as of its principal source of energy and ideas. Remarkably, Balfour managed to keep the plates spinning for a couple of years, but in November 1905 his fatally weakened government finally resigned. This may have been a ruse to expose divisions within the Liberal shadow cabinet, since it was now incumbent on them to form a government. If that is so, the ruse was a failure. Although he did not command the allegiance of all senior members of his party, the Liberal leader Sir Henry Campbell-Bannerman succeeded in forming a Liberal government and led his party united into a general election in January 1906, from which it emerged victorious. Five years into the post-Victorian era, the indolent patrician prime minister had been exposed and forced out of Downing Street; he would never lead the country again.

5

The most powerful thing

A sense of insecurity, as well as impotence, had pervaded Balfour's administration. This was nowhere more obvious than in foreign affairs. With its economy languishing, its empire overstretched and its population growth slowing, Britain was no longer the pre-eminent world power, capable of confronting simultaneous challenges on many fronts. Some British people even wondered whether the country was strong enough to face a single threat.

The most likely menace was believed to come from Germany. That country's burgeoning industrial might, its vast land army, the imperialist dreams of its Kaiser and its expanding navy inspired anxiety among the English. Admiral Tirpitz's Navy Bill of 1900 specifically aimed to establish a fleet 'of such strength that, even for the mightiest naval power, a war with Germany would involve such risks as to jeopardise its own supremacy'. This was interpreted as a thinly veiled threat to Britain. The Foreign Office declared that Germany 'appeared to be aiming at political hegemony and maritime ascendency, threatening the independence of her neighbours and ultimately the existence of England'.

Conservative English newspapers urged the government to respond by building bigger and better battleships, and by 1905 a large portion of the English population agreed. The navy was the pride of a country that was celebrating the centenary of the Battle of Trafalgar; by protecting trade routes and imperial borders, it guaranteed England's prosperity as well as her security. Balfour's government responded to popular demand by commissioning HMS *Dreadnought*, a vast battleship that was launched by King Edward at Portsmouth in 1906. Described by one English admiral as 'the most powerful thing in the world', it caused a popular sensation. But the United States, Japan and Germany soon joined in the game of battleships, and the press demanded that the government should win the international arms race.

But even if victory in that race were possible, would it secure the prize of peace? For however many dreadnoughts England stock-piled, it could no longer command the waves unaided. The country's isolation from continental affairs had once been described by English politicians as 'splendid'; it allowed England to concentrate on global affairs and expand its empire. But with that empire now overstretched, and with England's economy diminished, isolation had become perilous. It was imperative that England now build European alliances, but the country had few friends on the Continent. The widespread distaste for its actions during the Boer War had further alienated potential allies. What had been the point of oppressing the free farmers of the volk apart from a lust for South African gold? The infamous conflict had lent credence to long-standing French suspicions regarding *la perfide Albion*; the possibility of an Anglo-French alliance seemed remote.

Nevertheless, King Edward was determined to improve relations between England and its closest neighbour. He understood the danger of England's isolated position, and preferred the French to the Germans. His state visit to France in 1903 helped create the atmosphere in which an historic 'Entente Cordiale' was signed the following year. That agreement, based on mutual suspicion of Germany, marked the end of centuries of Anglo-French distrust. Meanwhile, Edward's half-hearted attempts to forge more amicable links with the Germans came to nothing. The king soon fell out with the German emperor, and railed against 'lying' German officials; the Kaiser branded the English 'degenerate'.

Germany soon put the Entente Cordiale to the test by opposing France's bid to control Morocco. She sent a cruiser to the region, ostensibly to protect her economic interests but actually as a military challenge. To German indignation, England stood by her new partner and the Anglo-French alliance was strengthened. The Kaiser accused England of 'pursuing an anti-German policy all over the world', while anti-German sentiment spread in England. As H. G. Wells wrote in his novel *Mr Britling Sees it Through* (1916), 'the world-wide clash of British and German interests' became 'facts in the consciousness of Englishmen . . . A whole generation was brought up in the threat of German war.'

England also looked beyond Europe's borders for allies. Chamberlain continued to advocate the union of Britain and the United States in a 'Greater Britain' that would dominate the world economy and police the globe. While that appeared unlikely, a strong diplomatic friendship between the countries was a more realistic proposition. Ever since the 1890s, matches had been made between American heiresses and English aristocrats, while the historical and linguistic links that supposedly bound the two countries were celebrated. An agreement was eventually reached, involving a concession by Britain to America's demands in Alaska and the Caribbean. England had been forced to recognize the new reality of the United States' economic and naval pre-eminence. Yet neither these alliances, nor the manufacture of dreadnoughts, could quell concerns about England's capacity to defend herself. Many felt that the martial might of the country was bound up with its racial and moral strength; both were now believed to be sadly lacking.

Another emblem of England's anxiety was the Boy Scout Movement. Its founder, Lieutenant General Robert Baden-Powell, had taken part in the Boer War, and knew first-hand the alarming condition of the British troops. Convinced that the British Empire was in a state of decline, he was determined to halt the process. The shadow of imperial and racial catastrophe hangs over every page of his book *Scouting for Boys*, which became a bestseller in 1908. The book inspired the spontaneous creation of 'Scout Patrols' throughout England; there were over 100,000 scouts by 1910. The boys were organized by 'masters', many of whom were ex-soldiers; they encouraged the scouts to become fitter, more resilient and resourceful, through an emphasis on outdoor activities and survival skills. 'Through Scouting, sickly, weak and barrel-chested boys would', Baden-Powell declared, 'be trained in the traits of manhood.' With their army-style uniforms, ranks, flag ceremonies and troop inspections, the scouts formed an unofficial youth army. Their motto was 'Be prepared'.

6

Demands for reform

The Liberals won the 1906 election with a huge majority. The Unionist coalition lost more than half of its 400 seats, with Balfour and many members of the cabinet among the casualties. Three hundred and ninety-seven Liberals were returned to the Commons, where the party held 241 more seats than their rivals. It was one of the most spectacular defeats in Conservative history; after twenty years of dominance, many Tories found it difficult to accept. Yet Balfour was stoical in defeat. As the election results had come in, he murmured: 'These things *will* happen.'

During the election campaign, the Liberals had attacked the Unionist coalition's record, and in particular the Boer War. They had also denounced Chamberlain's protectionist plans, arguing that tariffs would increase the price of imported food. By accepting this argument, the electorate ensured that laissez-faire doctrine would continue to determine economic policy, perhaps to the detriment of a manufacturing sector in urgent need of reinvigoration. The 1906 election was therefore a protest vote. The electorate passed the severest possible judgement not only on the Unionist Alliance, but also on the Tories and on Toryism. Voters had decided that the party was not fit to face the challenges of the new century, and that the 'governing class' it represented was unworthy of power. It is suggestive that half of those returned to the Commons in 1906 were new MPs, very few of whom came from the landed gentry.

Balfour's immediate concerns involved returning to the Commons and maintaining his own position. He achieved his first aim by means of a safe seat, but the second proved more problematic. Many Tories blamed his leadership for the election defeat. Leo Maxse, the editor of the right-wing *National Review*, thought Balfour had 'fallen into complete disrepute outside the Commons'. To add to Balfour's problems, the vast majority of Conservatives and Liberal Unionist MPs returned to the Commons in 1906 were pro-protectionist. This left him at the head of an alliance whose principal policy he did not altogether support; he was also vulnerable to a leadership challenge from Chamberlain. At the age of seventy, however, the dynamo of the Unionist Alliance was finally slowing down. Soon after the election, Chamberlain suffered a stroke and was forced to retire from public life. For the moment, Balfour was unchallenged as leader.

Balfour's inept leadership and Chamberlain's retirement were not the only reasons for the pessimism in the Tory party. The Conservative privy counsellor Sir James Fergusson had been defeated at the election by a working-class trade unionist, and such losses seemed to presage a difficult time. 'The Old Conservative Party has gone forever,' one party veteran lamented. The Labour party was identified as the primary cause of the electoral rout, as well as the greatest cause for future concern: 'The Labour Movement and Organisation', one Tory politician commented, 'has been of incomparably greater importance than anything else'. Balfour agreed, hearing in the results 'a faint echo of the same revolutionary movement which has produced massacres in St. Petersburg, riots in Vienna and socialist processions in Berlin'.

Labour's share of seats had increased sharply, from two to twenty-nine. Their success was facilitated by the secret Liberal–Labour pact of 1903, according to which each party allowed representatives of the other to stand unchallenged in selected constituencies. The two parties were united in their commitment to anti-militarism, free trade and social reform, though there were obvious differences in outlook. The Liberals aspired to represent the whole country, whereas Labour's aim was to further the cause of the working class and the unions. Labour MPs also advocated far more extensive social reform than most Liberals.

By making the 1903 pact the Liberals bought the support of a small group of Labour MPs, at a time when a landslide victory for them seemed impossible. They were about the rise of Labour as an independent parliamentary force, and a party that might one day monopolize the votes of the less affluent electorate. 'We are keenly in sympathy with the representatives of Labour,' Campbell-Bannerman remarked. 'We have too few of them in the House.' It was a short-term calculation which had long-term consequences. The pact helped to establish Labour as a major party which could rival the Liberals for the anti-Tory vote among the progressive middle classes. Yet the risks were not only on the Liberals' side. There was a danger that Labour would lose its distinct identity and eventually be absorbed into the Liberal party, whose extreme radical wing espoused views on social reform that were similar to its own.

Among the new intake of Labour MPs were the eloquent Scot Ramsay MacDonald, and the methodical Yorkshireman Philip Snowden. Both of these working-class men had former links with the Liberal party, while MacDonald had been one of the main architects of the Lib–Lab pact. Although the pair declared their support for socialism, it was a parliamentary, Christian and non-revolutionary variety. Like most Labour MPs, they were part of a generation of newly literate working- and lower-middle-class men. Their intellectual influences were British writers such as Thomas Carlyle, John Ruskin and Charles Dickens, rather than Karl Marx. After establishing himself as one of the leaders of parliamentary Labour, MacDonald was determined that it should develop into a serious Westminster party rather than a trade union pressure group. The party might, he believed, one day displace the Liberals as the main electoral alternative to the Tories. Arthur Henderson, a self-educated Methodist and erstwhile Liberal sympathizer, joined MacDonald, Snowden and Keir Hardie in the Commons. Henderson's rise from prominent unionist to Labour MP is emblematic of the key factor in Labour's success: the decision of the unions to turn to politics to secure the legislative gains they had made.

The new Labour MPs were earnest, studious and often teetotal. Yet despite their distinctly un-revolutionary nature, their arrival in the Commons caused consternation among orthodox Tories. What would King Edward make of their uncouth appearance when he opened parliament? Advanced intellectuals and optimistic reformers welcomed the advent of the new men, and in doing so offered further evidence of the cultural divide in England between those who wanted to shore up the Victorian establishment and those who hoped to build a more egalitarian country from its ruins.

The success of politicians who preached socialism indicated that attitudes to state intervention were changing. Socialism implied the reorganization of society and the economy for the benefit of the whole community, rather than in the interests of an elite. Previously associated with the hated Poor Law, compulsory education and restrictions on alcohol consumption, the state was increasingly seen in a kindlier light. People gradually began to think of themselves as stakeholders in the nation.

The publication of various sociological studies into poverty showed that it could no longer be blamed on the immorality of the poor. It was seen instead as a consequence of social and economic circumstances beyond their control. The radical Edwardian intelligentsia established poverty as a fact that had to be acknowledged by the government and addressed by the state. After their interventions, few people believed that poverty could be eradicated through the efforts of individuals, municipal boards and voluntary organizations. Even *The Times* now spoke of the inevitability of increased reform and a degree of wealth redistribution managed by government. Many people looked to the new Liberal administration to reduce poverty, and to implement an ambitious programme of domestic legislation. But were the Liberals up to the task? After all, Victorian Liberalism had been built on a creed of non-interference.

To judge by the Liberals' election campaign, the party was neither capable of, nor interested in, introducing extensive legislation. The Liberal leader – the portly, canny and likeable Scot Campbell-Bannerman (or C-B as he preferred to be known) – had based the campaign on the traditional Gladstonian platform of 'peace, retrenchment and reform'. Rather than outlining an innovative and detailed programme, most Liberal electioneering had concentrated on criticizing Balfour's government. That had also been C-B's strong suit during his seven years as opposition leader. When he faced the subtle and patrician Balfour across the dispatch box in the Commons, it seemed, as one journalist put it, as if 'a stout, amiable City man' had been 'called upon to face, with nothing better than a walking stick, a lithe fencer with a nimble rapier'. C-B was often effective and invariably imperturbable, which irritated Balfour enormously.

C-B had employed negative electioneering tactics out of necessity as well as choice. He led a fractious and disunited party, which could only come together in criticism of the opposition. When Balfour forced the Liberals to form a government at the end of 1905, the pro-imperialist faction of the party, which included such prominent MPs as Herbert Henry Asquith and Sir Edward Grey, tried to pack C-B off to the Lords, thereby assuming control in the Commons. C-B punctured the rebellion by offering the rebels key positions in his cabinet, on the condition that they drop their demands. They agreed, and backed his vague and anodyne election programme.

Disunity within the Liberal Party was an expression of the disparate character of the elements that comprised it. Nonconformists featured prominently, as did commercialists and industrialists; yet it also contained aristocratic Whigs, as well as radicals such as John Burns, the son of a washerwoman. The party had traditionally protected the rights of Nonconformists against attacks from the established church; it also defended commerce and industry against the landed interest. It was difficult, however, to formulate a coherent programme that might satisfy all of the factions within the party. Historically, the Liberals had preferred to advocate a series of single 'causes', such as Irish Home Rule, yet the danger of this tactic was that it made them seem a party of protest. The bonds linking its disparate elements might also one day be loosened, or some of those elements might switch their allegiance. Joseph Chamberlain's defection from the Liberal benches to the Tory side of the House suggested that the party ought not, for instance, count on the undying loyalty of self-made Nonconformist businessmen.

At the beginning of 1906, however, Liberal supporters were in confident mood. Their 400 MPs took their places in the new parliament, behind a talented front bench that reflected the broad church of Liberalism. The three former 'imperialist' rebels sat alongside radical and Nonconformist MPs, while several cabinet members had titles. In early debates of the parliament, C-B overpowered Balfour: 'The right honourable gentleman', he declared, 'has learned nothing. He comes back to this new Commons with the . . . same frivolous way of dealing with great questions. He little knows the temper of the new House . . . Let us get to business.'

'Business' included the implementation of social legislation that, while modest in scope and impact, represented a significant improvement on the efforts of Balfour's administration. Free school meals were provided for every child, should local authorities apply for them; the power and legal status of the unions were reinforced by the Trade Disputes Act (1906); and the 1906 Workmen's Compensation Act gave compensation to those injured at work. Abroad, C-B's administration granted self-government to the Boers in the Transvaal Colony, closing an unhappy chapter of English history.

7

The Terrible Twins

On 3 April 1908, C-B stepped down as premier, exhausted by overwork and immobilized by a series of heart attacks. He died a couple of weeks afterwards, still resident in Downing Street. A competent successor was waiting in the wings, in Herbert Henry Asquith. Despite his earlier interest in rebellion, Asquith had been loyal to C-B as chancellor of the Exchequer, while also demonstrating his administrative ability. Asquith's 'mind', Churchill commented, 'opened and shut smoothly and exactly like the breech of a gun', a portrait that captured something of Asquith's nonchalant efficiency. His nonchalance was also suggested by his nickname 'Squiffy', which alluded to his habit of drinking heavily, even when there was political business to be conducted. He was in his element at a country house party, where he might enjoy cards and the companionship of attractive young women, or in a London club in the company of aristocrats.

The heart of the English establishment was a curious place to find a man of Asquith's background. He came from a radical Nonconformist family in Yorkshire that had made its fortune in wool, and had been orphaned at an early age. Yet his difficult and puritanical middle-class upbringing, which instilled in him an unshakeable self-belief, had been complemented by an establishment education in the south of England. He had taken the traditional routes into government, via Oxford and the Inns of Court, acquiring at the first a consciousness of effortless superiority and at the second the ability to destroy the arguments of others. In the late 1880s, while his legal career flourished, Asquith became a Liberal MP and rose effortlessly within the party; in 1892 he served as home secretary under Gladstone.

Though Asquith made memorable speeches from the front bench, it was often difficult to remember the message behind his stylish rhetoric. He rivalled Balfour as a master of the art of elegant equivocation, and nor was obfuscation the only thing the pair had in common. 'Asquith does not inspire men with great passions,' one journalist commented, while even Asquith's wife described him as a 'cold hard unsympathetic man loved by none'. There was also a Balfourian indolence, dilatoriness and aloofness about the new Liberal prime minister. He rarely came to cabinet meetings fully prepared, but instead considered questions as they were raised. The aristocratic establishment was able to perpetuate itself by absorbing and fashioning members of the new, wealthy and powerful middle class who were willing to conform to its rules. Asquith would renounce his Nonconformism, for example, and convert to the Anglican tradition. He also decided to marry the daughter of a baronet, the eccentric society 'wit' Margot Tennant.

Asquith's establishment views did not equip him to implement extensive and radical social reform, yet they did enable him to conciliate the diverse ideological elements in his party. In his convoluted orations, he struck a fine balance between competing Liberal creeds and factions. He would criticize the 'misdirected and paralysing activity of the state' in one breath, but acknowledge the 'needs and services which could not be safely left to the unregulated forces of supply and demand' with the next. He presided over the motley characters in his cabinet as a chairman rather than as an autocrat. The Whiggish faction of the party was represented by Reginald McKenna and a large group of earls and lords; the Gladstonian element by John Morley. The radical Liberal wing was pleased that Burns retained his position as president of the Local Government Board, while Nonconformists were delighted that the Welshman David Lloyd George had taken over from Asquith at the Exchequer. The most unexpected decision Asquith made was in appointing the former Tory MP Winston Churchill to the Board of Trade. These last two appointments of men with a passion for social reform and inordinate ambition and energy appeared promising to progressives.

Lloyd George, the son of a farmer, was brought up as a Welsh-speaker and ardent chapelgoer. It was there, as much as in the London courts he attended as a solicitor, that he learned the rhetorical tricks that established him as the greatest orator of the age. He acquired the skill of presenting complex issues as clear-cut struggles between right and wrong. He could be lofty and lyrical or pointed and precise, according to the character or mood of his audience, which made him equally persuasive in a tête-à-tête in the Commons' smoking room, in a cabinet meeting or in front of an audience of thousands.

Lloyd George did not attend university but educated himself, reading widely in literature and political theory. He was drawn to the question of land ownership, since his links were with rural Wales. Though the landscape of his political imagination was pre-industrial, he had no arguments with industrialists, businessmen or with the accumulation of capital, and no interest in socialism. In his youth he had been attracted to Liberalism by Joseph Chamberlain's programme of social reform. 'Our Joe' was an inspiration and a kindred spirit, yet the young Welshman would soon identify Chamberlain's fatal flaws – the monomania and dogmatism that manifested themselves in his obsessive opposition to Irish Home Rule. When Chamberlain left Gladstone's Liberal party over its Irish policy, Lloyd George remained on Gladstone's side. It would not be the last time that his pragmatism overcame his principles.

In the Commons, Lloyd George came to public notice as the most eloquent opponent of the Boer War, attacking the 'racial arrogance' that sustained imperialism. It was not that he wished to disband the empire, rather that he wanted to refashion it as a federation of autonomous states. He demonstrated an affinity with C-B, who, on assuming office, rewarded his disciple by appointing him to the Board of Trade. Lloyd George's greatest achievement in that capacity was averting a national railway strike. Drawing on all his charm and verbal dexterity, he had brokered a deal between the unions and the railway companies, who had previously been irreconcilable adversaries. Even the *Daily Mail* had been impressed by

Lloyd George's ministerial record, and welcomed the radical MP's appointment as chancellor: 'he has proved in office that he possesses in exceptional measure . . . practical business capacity . . . initiative, and large open-mindedness'. This irrepressible man of action, an eloquent Machiavelli with no establishment allegiances, would dominate Westminster politics for the next fifteen years.

Conservative journalists were not so enthusiastic about Churchill's elevation to the presidency of the Board of Trade. A few years previously he had abandoned the Tory party, his natural political home, crossing the floor in protest against growing support for protectionism within the Unionist Alliance. According to the *National Review*, Churchill's act of 'treachery' was typical of 'a soldier of fortune who has never pretended to be animated by any motive beyond a desire for his own advancement'. The accusation of egotism would be repeated throughout Churchill's career, along with the related charges of political grandstanding and of an addiction to power. Civil servants complained that Churchill was unpunctual, prey to sudden enthusiasms, and enthralled by extravagant ideas and fine phrases. He was a free and fiery spirit who inspired admiration and mistrust in equal measure. Allies hailed him as a genius, while his enemies regarded him as unbalanced and unscrupulous.

Although the Tory press highlighted Churchill's pragmatism, he was not without principles. He was genuinely committed to social reform, just as his father, Lord Randolph, had been. He had found Balfour's party reactionary and inhospitable; the Liberals welcomed him as one who could help them improve the conditions of the working classes. It was a shared commitment to social reform – as well as shared ambition – that brought Lloyd George and Churchill together inside Asquith's government. The pair understood that a new period of political history had opened, in which the 'condition of the people' was the dominant issue. Both men were convinced that extensive reform was the context for future progress and social stability. Both also believed that domestic legislation offered the Liberals the opportunity of outmanoeuvring the Labour party and checking the spread of socialism.

'The Terrible Twins', as the Tory press dubbed them, were responsible for introducing a slew of social legislation and significantly increasing the portion of government expenditure devoted to social services. Churchill was instrumental in passing the Trade Boards Bill, which set down minimum wage criteria, and in setting up the labour exchanges that increased labour mobility. Lloyd George, meanwhile, was the driving force behind the 1908 Children Act, which protected minors from dangerous trades and abuse, and the Old Age Pensions Act (1908), which awarded non-contributory pensions to men over seventy who earned less than £31 a year. The 1910 Education Act, which aimed to provide youths with a choice of employment, was also Lloyd George's proposal, as was the Mental Deficiency Act of 1913, which moved the mentally ill from poor-houses and prisons to specialized institutions. Finally, and most famously, Lloyd George introduced the National Insurance Act of 1911, the first ever piece of health and unemployment insurance legislation.

When the first groups of elderly men came to collect their pensions, one post office worker recalled that 'tears of joy would run down the cheeks of some, and they would say . . . "God Bless that Lord (sic) George"'. The popular elevation of the proudly plebeian chancellor to the status of a lord suggests that the Victorian spirit of deference was not yet dead, but the new legislation represented a twentieth- rather than a nineteenth-century response to England's social ills. Promoted by politicians and civil servants with professional rather than patrician backgrounds, it laid the foundation for the future welfare state by guaranteeing minimum standards for a portion of the population. It thereby granted people their rights as citizens, and welcomed them, in the contemporary phrase, 'to the common table of the nation'. It is hardly surprising that the programme was described as a form of socialistic 'New Liberalism', or that it inspired enthusiasm among students and the young intelligentsia. The rising generation believed that Lloyd George and Churchill had gone some way to satisfying their demand for social justice.

Lloyd George and Churchill probably went as far as the Tory-dominated House of Lords and the laissez-faire ideology of many Liberals would allow them. There was also Asquith's caution to overcome. While the prime minister assented to most of their policies, he prided himself on never being 'pushed along against [my] will . . . by energetic colleagues'. Whenever he regarded a proposal as too risky, Asquith's conservative instincts prompted him to apply 'the brake'. In private, Lloyd George complained to Churchill about his 'aimlessness'.

Yet it was also possible that danger could come from activity. That was one of the lessons that Asquith might have drawn from the controversy provoked by the 'People's Budget' of 1909. Lloyd George's budget was informed by the principle of the redistribution of wealth, a radical notion that had been alien to most Victorians. It aimed to fund the government's extensive social welfare programmes with a graduated tax on high incomes and by taxing land through various measures, including a 20 per cent tax on any unearned increment of land values. The chancellor justified these unprecedented peacetime demands on wealth by calling it 'a war budget . . . for raising money to wage implacable warfare against poverty and squalidness'. The proposed taxes would not affect middle-class salary earners or the majority of industrialists, whom Lloyd George identified as the Liberals' natural constituency. Once again the chancellor was trying to quell social unrest and outflank Labour, whose MPs could only applaud him. If the price was to alienate the landed gentry, it was one Lloyd George was happy to pay.

Others were not so happy. The Liberal party grandee Lord Rosebery dismissed Lloyd George's proposals as 'tyrannical and socialistic'. Here was a call for the establishment to close ranks, regardless of party allegiance, and the Tory party was not slow in responding. Even the new breed of Conservative MPs, recruited from the wealthy business classes, denounced the budget as unjust. Stanley Baldwin spoke, in one of his first Commons speeches, of the excessive expenditure the aristocracy would have to undertake if the budget were passed. The atmosphere in the Commons had not been as tense since the debates on the 1832 Reform Act.

The atmosphere in the Tory-dominated Lords, meanwhile, was one of defiance mingled with dread. It threw out the People's Budget and a constitutional impasse ensued, damaging confidence in the political system. Terrified by the possible ramifications, King Edward tried to arrange a deal behind the scenes, yet even the monarch's efforts were in vain. The Tory peers justified their intransigence by arguing that the budget lacked an electoral mandate – an indication that Balfour believed they would win a general election.

The Terrible Twins welcomed the opportunity of taking the New Liberal case to the people, and Asquith assented to their demands for an election in early 1910. Lloyd George and Churchill directed the Liberal campaign with customary vigour. They formed the 'Budget League' and coordinated the activities of Liberal newspaper editors. They also used the latest technology, sending vans to remote areas of the country with speakers fixed to them so that their words could be broadcast in the highlands and lowlands. The struggle between the lower and the upper house was characterized as one of social democracy against inherited privilege. It was also cast as a war between an increasingly middle-class Commons, where the Liberals were dominant, and a patrician and Tory House of Lords. Lloyd George was determined to create a division between the middle class and the upper class; he would gain the allegiance of the former for his party, and unite every class below the aristocracy by identifying it as their common enemy. In his public speeches he described the unelected peers as 'five hundred men chosen at random from among the unemployed'.

This language of class war appalled the establishment, with King Edward branding Lloyd George's statements 'improper' and 'insidious'. According to a Tory MP, the chancellor 'set the fashion for attacking rich men because they were rich'. Yet the patrician Churchill was also responsible for introducing egalitarian and meritocratic ideas into Edwardian political discourse. 'We do not only ask today, "How much have you got?"' he declared, 'we also ask, "How did you get it? Did you earn it by yourself, or has it just been left to you by others?"' Churchill even advocated the abolition of the Lords, on the grounds that the Tories would always find a way of controlling the upper house.

Yet the omens were not good for Churchill and Lloyd George. The Tory party was able to mobilize its vastly superior financial and propaganda resources. *The Times* and the *Daily Mail* instructed the electorate to reject the Liberals and instead to back the Chamberlainite Tariff Reform as a means of funding social reform without raising taxes. The lower middle class seem to have been convinced by these arguments, while the suburban middle classes found Lloyd

George's class war rhetoric too socialistic. In the event, the Liberals lost 123 seats in the election, nearly all of which were taken by the Tories, but they returned to office courtesy of the support of the Irish Parliamentary Party and the burgeoning Labour party, which claimed forty seats.

The challenge of passing the 'People's Budget' was now infinitely more difficult for the Liberal government; expediting the 'wide programme of reconstruction' that Lloyd George and Churchill had outlined during the election campaign was unthinkable for a minority administration. A friend of Asquith's remembered how he 'wandered about utterly wretched and restless' in the days following the election, yet somehow the prime minister muddled through. However disappointing the election results were, he believed they gave his government a popular mandate for the budget. The best way to force the Tory peers to back down, he suggested, was for Edward to threaten to create enough new Liberal peers to ensure the budget's safe passage. Although this proposal was not unprecedented, the king thought it 'simply disgusting'. Like many members of the establishment, Edward believed the government was now controlled by an Irish party that planned to emasculate the upper house in order to force through a Home Rule bill. He decided to try to negotiate once again with Balfour and the Tory peers; when discussions led nowhere, however, he reluctantly acceded to Asquith's demands with a proviso: he would threaten to create a crowd of new Liberal peers if the Lords continued to reject the budget, but only after two general elections had confirmed public opinion on the issue.

Asquith also pressed the king on a related matter – the introduction of legislation to alter the Lords' power of veto. Once again, in the absence of a viable alternative, Edward reluctantly agreed. Asquith's decision to pursue the reform of the Lords was no doubt instigated by pressure from the Irish MPs, yet his party had long desired to reduce the powers of the upper house. On his arrival in Downing Street in 1906, C-B had spoken of his desire to 'clip the wings' of the peers, and Lloyd George had been eager to carry out the threat of his old mentor for some time. To the chancellor, the upper chamber was not so much the 'watchdog of the constitution' as 'Mr Balfour's poodle'.

Edward's willingness to create Liberal peers proved persuasive, and the Lords eventually let the People's Budget through with a few amendments. The Tory peers remained recalcitrant, however, on the proposals to restrict their powers, and demanded another election on the issue. One was called in December 1910, but it produced a virtually identical result to the January contest. Asquith once again claimed a popular mandate for his proposals and the new king George V, who had succeeded his father in May, saw no choice but to threaten the upper house with the creation of new Liberal peers in order to force through the reforms.

The government introduced a Parliament Act, which removed the right of the Lords to veto money bills and limited its veto over other acts. It passed through the Commons and a long debate in the Lords was followed by a narrow victory for the government. Balfour and his allies in the Lords had surprised many by backing down at the last moment in the face of the king's threat. As a result, the Tory and Unionist 'die-hards', an influential aristocratic faction within the alliance, accused their leader and his allies of betrayal.

The passing of the Parliament Act, and the People's Budget before it, constituted an extraordinary victory for the Liberal party. After a two-year struggle, a radical budget and revolutionary constitutional bill had been passed, despite the opposition of the Tory party and the landed establishment. The supremacy of the lower house had been formally established, and the status of unelected hereditary peers had been diminished. One of the provisions of the Parliament Act was that MPs received a salary; politics became a career, open to men from the professional classes, rather than a gentlemanly hobby. A significant step had been taken towards full parliamentary democracy.

Yet victory had come at a price. The Liberal government had lost its majority and was dependent on Irish support for its survival. That backing was dependent on the introduction of a Home Rule bill that was bound to be controversial. Moreover, the struggle had roused the anger of the 'die-hard' Tories, who had much of the aristocratic establishment behind them. 'When the king wants loyal men,' one of them commented after the Lords vote, 'he will find us ready to die for him. He may want us. For the House of Lords today voted for revolution.'

8

What happened to the gentry?

In the announcement of the Lords vote, the Tory 'die-hards' sensed the demise of the landed gentry's political pre-eminence. After the 1906 election, neither the Commons nor the cabinet was dominated by the territorial aristocracy. The five lawyers who sat on Asquith's front bench attested to the new power of the professional classes. Following the introduction of MPs' salaries in 1911, their political influence would increase. In local politics, too, the power of the landed interest had diminished. While Justices of the Peace, Lords Lieutenant and high sheriffs still tended to be drawn from the gentry, they could no longer determine local government elections, and they rarely stood as candidates themselves. It was the burgeoning middle class who now dominated in the English counties. As the state extended in scope and power, country society retreated. Now that local politics demanded administrative competence, how could it be regarded as an aspect of *noblesse oblige*?

Outside the political sphere, the territorial aristocracy had been declining for decades. In 1873 the publication of an official inquiry into English landownership had revealed that all of England was owned by less than 5 per cent of its population. This finding appalled the increasingly powerful middle classes, and landed privilege was attacked on several fronts. The gentry's patronage in the professions was significantly reduced when the purchasing of army positions and ecclesiastical benefices was prohibited by law, and examinations were made compulsory. Open competition for places in the legal professions and the civil service soon followed; the amateurish aristocratic ethos that pervaded these occupations had been dispelled by the beginning of the new century.

The late-nineteenth-century agricultural depression further weakened the gentry. The value of land was the same in 1910 as it had been in 1880, during which period rents had fallen by around 40 per cent in the south and east of England. And then there were the death duties imposed by Liberal governments, and denounced by Lady Bracknell in Oscar Wilde's *The Importance of Being Earnest* (1895): 'Between the duties expected of one during one's lifetime, and the duties exacted from one after one's death,' she declared, 'land has ceased to be either a profit or a pleasure. It gives one position, and prevents one from keeping it up.' Many of the gentry decided to sell off their estates as a result. The additional land taxes that were introduced as part of the 'People's Budget' led to the closure of even more country houses – an unprecedented 800,000 estates were put on the market between 1909 and 1914. Yet even before this surge in sales, the age in which the 'great house' had dominated the countryside had come to an end.

The demise of the landed gentry did not eliminate the aristocracy as a whole. After 1890, spectacularly wealthy members of the middle class had been permitted to enter the peerage. In the late nineteenth century the amalgamation of small, family-owned businesses had created corporations whose owners became almost unimaginably rich. Brewers, cotton and metal magnates were now as wealthy as landowners, and they demanded recognition from the establishment. Among the new Edwardian peers, representatives of finance, industry and commerce were dominant.

Many older aristocrats disapproved of the arrival of the new men, with some dismissing them as 'plutocrats'. They had, it was said, made their money as a result of Victorian commercial and imperial expansion, and now had no other interest than in spending it ostentatiously. *Punch* magazine caricatured the group as vulgar, ignorant, greedy and obsessed with golf and motor cars. The gentry feared the plutocrats might 'adulterate' their caste, fears that were sometimes informed by anti-Semitism; the Tory 'die-hard' Lord

Willoughby de Broke lamented the 'contamination' of old English stock by 'cosmopolitan' and 'Levantine' finance. The anxiety, however, was prompted largely by unadulterated snobbery. 'The rushing flood of ill-gotten gold has overflown its banks and polluted the crystal river of unreproved enjoyment,' remarked a member of the Russell family. Existing members of the elite criticized new recruits as a means of displaying their pedigree, and disguising the fact their ancestors had also once been social climbers. Other aristocrats believed that upper-class society had been shrewd in swallowing the new millionaires, just as it had assimilated middle-class politicians such as Asquith and Baldwin. Had society not done so, these 'keen-witted, pushing, clever and energetic' men might, in Lady Dorothy Nevill's view, have overthrown the social order.

The recently minted nobles, however, had no intention of dismantling the gentry. They acquired the landed estates that were coming onto the market, married into the gentry and supported the Tories. The nouveau riche press barons all sided with the old party of land, the crown and the Church, and that party's power in the country was vastly extended through newspapers such as the *Daily Mail*. As one historian of the aristocracy, F. M. L. Thompson, observed, 'The old order concentrated on the preservation of the power of property, manipulating the machinery of political democracy through mass ignorance, prejudice and apathy to delay the spread of social equality . . . for as long as possible.'

Like the Tory party, the City of London became an emblem of the marriage of convenience between the old and new aristocracies. Many of the gentry invested the money they had made from the sale of their lands in stocks and shares, sometimes following the advice of recently ennobled financiers. Over the Edwardian era, the value of their investments rose much faster than inflation. Younger members of the older aristocratic families even entered the City as stockbrokers, conferring 'respectability' on a profession previously regarded as middle class. Here was a thoroughly English revolution – a great change had taken place in society so that its fundamental structure might remain the same.

9

Car crazy

'On Sunday morning, along the Kennington Road,' Charlie Chaplin recalled of his early-twentieth-century adolescence, 'one could see a smart pony and trap outside a house, ready to take a vaudevillian for a ten-mile drive as far as Merton or Norwood.' In 1900 horses were the most common means of travel and the roads were relatively uncrowded, with railways carrying livestock as well as long-distance travellers. Within a decade, however, transport had changed rapidly, in every sense of the word.

The horses were first overtaken by bicycles with inflated tyres, which had been invented in the late 1880s by John Boyd Dunlop. The new tyres made bicycles far more comfortable to ride, and by 1900 'cyclemania' was everywhere. Its leading lights were seen riding in the parks, the men in suits and boaters, the ladies sporting loose knickerbockers under their billowy dresses. At first cyclists were barred from Hyde Park, and confined to the less fashionable public gardens. Conservative aristocrats objected to the sight of unchaperoned ladies racing up and down Rotten Row in revealing knickerbockers, yet soon cyclists infiltrated every part of the city.

The press spread fears about the effects of prolonged cycling. Overenthusiastic cyclists might develop 'bicycle hump' by leaning too long over the handlebars; acute cases of 'bicycle foot' and even 'bicycle face' were reported. Since some of the cheaper bicycles were difficult to steer and had only rudimentary brakes, falling off was a more tangible danger, yet this did not stop intrepid cyclists from speeding around, regardless of safety.

In 1901 bicycles were the fastest means of transport on the roads, but they enjoyed supremacy for only the shortest of spells. Both bikes and horses were soon surpassed by motor cars, which could travel over 20 miles per hour by 1903. These petrol-driven automobiles had replaced the slow and unreliable steam-powered vehicles of the late nineteenth century. The driver of the early Edwardian motor car sat on a high box, just like a coachman, behind a windscreen if that optional extra had been purchased. If there was no windscreen, he or she ran the risk of being propelled forward over the front of the car whenever they braked too abruptly. Sometimes mischievous children would try to provoke an accident by throwing their caps into the path of oncoming vehicles. The motor car travelled on the left side of the road and overtook bicycles by pulling out to the right, a manoeuvre often accompanied by accidents and arguments. As only the wealthiest could afford automobiles – which cost hundreds of pounds to buy and hundreds per year to run – early drivers often looked down on cyclists, referring to them as 'cads on casters'.

Some aristocratic motorists had an equally condescending attitude to the law. When Lord Portsmouth was stopped for exceeding the speed limit, he was belligerent: 'I have been one of the chief magistrates of the county for some years,' he told the constable, 'and I have never heard of such an absurd thing as speeding. If I were you I should not take this any further.' Other members of the old caste declined to pay the steep fines on the grounds that restricted speed limits were 'un-English'. Drivers stopped by the police usually claimed to have been travelling under the speed limit; others tried to bribe the representatives of the law. When these tactics failed, the motorist would be hauled before the local magistrate. Among those charged with speeding in the period was the prime minister, Arthur Balfour. Such was Balfour's notoriety on the roads that, when the Motor Car Act of 1903 was discussed in parliament, one humorous MP proposed that the 20-mile-per-hour speed limit in the legislation should not apply to him.

Motor cars became a symbol of the threat the urban world posed to the countryside. At weekends, the automobiles of affluent city dwellers piled up beside wayside inns. To local villagers, motorists looked like people from another world. They wore heavy leather or fur-lined suits and coats, cloth caps with ear flaps and rubber 'ponchos' in inclement weather. They were startling manifestations of the new spirit of the age.

In a country where class antagonism was increasing, it is not surprising that cars were seen as an emblem of England's 'idle rich'. During the debates over the 1903 Motor Car Act, one MP described driving as 'an amusement which is indulged in principally by wealthy people' and urged the Balfour administration to prove that it was not 'a government of the rich, for the rich and by the rich' by punishing aristocratic lawbreakers. Wealthy drivers ought to be taxed and made to contribute to the maintenance of country roads, and they should be forced to pass a test.

Such drivers may have been an unpopular minority but they were a formidable one. Lord Northcliffe, a fanatical early motorist, furthered the drivers' cause in his newspapers. *The Times* described motor cars as 'no mere article of luxury or amusement for a small minority'; they were instead a means of transport with potential to 'serve the public' and to become a 'key English industry' in the future. As part of its pro-motorist initiative, the newspaper attempted to distinguish blue-blooded drivers from the nouveau riche whose behaviour was blamed for the public outcry. 'The number of owners and drivers of motor cars who are not gentlemen,' the paper commented, 'would seem to be unduly large. There is no turning a cad into a gentleman.' The debate surrounding motorists was informed by contemporary anxieties concerning the 'dilution' of the gentry. The irony was that Northcliffe, the man responsible for this anti-plutocrat propaganda, had himself only recently been ennobled.

Those who supported the motorists claimed that reports concerning the number of accidents caused by vehicles were wildly exaggerated. They were part of a nationwide 'motor car panic', which was in part an attack on wealth and privilege. Yet the criticisms of dangerous drivers continued, largely because the facts supported the critics. In 1909 motor cars caused 373 accidents in Britain, but in 1914 there were 1,329 – though the rise was largely owing to the increasing use of the vehicles.

As they became an increasingly familiar sight on English roads, the 'motor car panic' died down. The press no longer exaggerated the incidence of minor accidents, and the government welcomed automobiles as a new source of revenue. Motor cars gradually became accepted in the same way that bicycles had been. Private cars were joined on the streets of London by taxis or 'hackney carriages', and jostled for space with hansoms, bicycles, electric and horse-drawn trams, and open-topped omnibuses. It is hard to think of another period of English history when so many different types of vehicle sped along the capital's roads, or when London's streets witnessed such mayhem.

The absence of transport management was partially remedied when the Liberal government introduced its Town Planning Act in 1909. Yet the pandemonium on the streets could no more be restrained by legislation than could suburban sprawl. The proliferation of motor cars and the sudden expansion of the suburbs were both expressions of the spirit of a speed-obsessed and restless age. The same spirit informed the numerous social reforms passed in quick succession by the Liberal government, as well as England's breathless participation in an international arms race. Everything seemed faster following the death of Victoria and the decline of Victorianism, including thought and perhaps even time itself. The culture of the period might be compared to a new motor car, uncertain of its destination but intent on arriving in record time.

10

Little hammers in their muffs

King Edward VII had died unexpectedly, in the middle of the constitutional crisis and after a mere nine years on the throne. The apparently hearty sixty-eight-year-old had been ill for months, and a life of overindulgence had weakened his constitution. Yet as his ailments had not been widely reported, his death in May 1910 seemed sudden.

Asquith spoke for many of his countrymen when he described himself as 'stunned' by the news of Edward's death. Outside Buckingham Palace the crowds stood silent, and 400,000 people visited the king's coffin in Westminster Hall in two days. The organizers of the funeral wanted the proceedings to be as democratic as possible, so the wealthier classes were forced to queue along with everyone else to pay their last respects. Here was testimony to how England had changed since Victoria's funeral less than a decade before; the tolerant and relaxed Edward had seemed far more accessible to his subjects than his mother had been. The newspapers celebrated the late king as 'a very average typical Englishman in his tastes and habits', while omitting to mention that he was not at all average in his indulgence of those tastes. Edward was the first English monarch to be presented to his subjects as 'ordinary'. He was also one of the first stars of an emerging personality culture, created by the increasingly influential popular press. This may explain why, in the words of one cabinet member, 'the feeling of grief and sense of *personal* loss' in the country were 'deeper and keener than when the Queen died'. Yet the public outpouring of emotion was an expression of fear for the future as well as of sadness. 'At home things seemed to be going from bad to worse,' remarked one Tory MP.

The new king, George, was 'heart-broken and overwhelmed' by the death of the man whom he called 'the best of fathers'. As a youth, Edward's second son had trained as a naval officer, but on the death of his elder brother towards the end of Victoria's reign he had become second in line to the throne, and his naval career had come to an abrupt end. Marriage, children, a crash course in constitutional history and tours of the empire followed, though George did not enjoy either of the latter pursuits, being as averse to foreign food as he was uninterested in books.

Short in stature and knock-kneed, George was a modest and devoted family man. His naval training had moulded his character. Although he lived like a conservative country squire, he thought and talked like a naval officer, with a booming gruff voice and a fondness for salty humour. He had inherited his father's blue eyes and fair hair but lacked Edward's Falstaffian figure, energy and bonhomie, as well as his passionate interest in high society and continental diplomacy. Within weeks of his ascent to the throne, George had the luxurious decor of Buckingham Palace toned down; he also decided to keep lavish public banquets to a minimum, since they did not agree with his poor digestion. George was intent on restoring the atmosphere of simplicity, earnestness and domesticity that had characterized the English court in the reign of his grandmother. While the king's air of melancholy was sometimes dissipated on public occasions and while he could be explosive in private, he never acted impulsively. To the outside world, it seemed that the private and reserved king dedicated his time to hunting and stamp collecting. Yet his passion for those pursuits revealed a single-mindedness as well as a desire for order.

The history lessons George had received in his youth could not have prepared him for the political crisis that he faced after his coronation. Asquith had urged the new king to threaten the Tory-dominated Lords with the creation of new Liberal peers if they did not pass the bill that would restrict their powers. If George refused to do so, the prime minister would resign and go to the country. As a natural Tory, George had an instinctive dislike of the Liberal government; he hated that 'damned fellow' Lloyd George and regarded Asquith as 'not quite a gentleman'. Yet against his instincts, he acceded to his prime minister's demand; siding with 'the peers against the people' had seemed too dangerous in a nation increasingly exercised by inequality. In retrospect, George believed he had made a grave error, and blamed Asquith for exploiting his inexperience.

The early years of George's reign would be both testing and fiery. Between 1910 and 1914, England's society and economy seemed to be on the point of collapse, while the population was described as seething with unrest. The minority Liberal government – and the political system as a whole – appeared impotent in the face of new challenges and progressive demands. 'In 1910,' wrote the historian George Dangerfield in *The Strange Death of Liberal England* (1935), 'the fires long smouldering in the English spirit suddenly flared up, so that by the end of 1913 Liberal England was reduced to ashes.'

The first of the social and political conflagrations identified by Dangerfield came in the form of industrial action, which spread across the country after 1910. *The Times* described the strikes as 'of an unexampled character' in their extent and intensity. Throughout England, groups of workers downed tools. Most were protesting for better working conditions, while some were demanding an increase in wages, which had declined sharply in real terms. The failure of the 'New Liberal' social reforms to substantially reduce the incidence of poverty was also a source of discontent. 'Some magical allurement,' commented Ramsay MacDonald, seemed to 'seize the Labour world' as 1910 progressed. Without warning, hundreds of women factory workers in London stopped work and poured onto the streets. There the strikers shouted, sang and encouraged other workers to join the protest.

In 1911 the strikes proliferated and intensified. Protests overwhelmed the ports, the mines and the railways. 'More works are being closed down every day,' wrote Austen Chamberlain, son of Joseph and leader of the protectionist wing of the Unionist Alliance.

'More trains are being taken off the railways. The whole machinery of national life is slowly stopping.' Asquith used a similar metaphor when he spoke of the 'severe strain upon the whole social and political machine'. It seemed that society and the economy, which in normal times worked independently of government control, were in danger of breaking down. The vast majority of trade unionists and Labour MPs did not want to replace the machine with another, socialist model, but they did want the government to ensure it apportioned a higher percentage of profits to the workers. State intervention should, MacDonald argued, be in the interest of the general community. Yet many Liberals felt this would represent a categorical rejection of laissez-faire politics and economics; it would also encourage the idea that wealth ought to be redistributed along with profits, through increased progressive taxation on incomes, on property and on assets, or even through direct redistributive socialist legislation. While the 'People's Budget' had made steps in a reformist direction, Lloyd George had intended it as a defence against socialism, rather than as a promotion of that 'illiberal' ideology.

Asquith's government had to improvise a response to the strikes, and without the benefit of a parliamentary majority. They tried various strategies, which enjoyed varying degrees of failure. Churchill, who had been promoted to home secretary in 1910, tried to force the strikers back to work by sending in the army to confront them. In Liverpool, riots broke out and the troops fired on protesters, killing two men. King George thought the situation 'more like revolution than a strike' and felt the government's response should be more draconian. The English establishment was beginning to panic.

When Labour MPs attacked government coercion, Asquith tried passing legislation. One government-sponsored bill guaranteed a minimum wage to the miners, while another granted unions the right to establish funds for political purposes. Yet it was not enough to appease the strikers, including those who worked on the railways. In 1911 the government decided to play its best card and sent Lloyd George to broker a deal between the railway workers and their employers. The chancellor was famous as a 'man of the people', and posed as their 'champion'. 'He plays upon men round a table,' Asquith's secretary wrote, 'like the chords of a musical instrument

. . . until a real harmony is struck.' Lloyd George's verbal dexterity had its effect and an agreement was reached, though he could not repeat his success the following year, when he was unable to reconcile the striking dockers and their employers. After that failure, the government retreated from direct involvement in industrial disputes, and the strikes continued with increasing intensity. More than a thousand protests now took place annually, and involved over a million and a half workers – eight times the number who had gone on strike in each year of Edward's reign.

In the long term, the consequences of these strikes were beneficial for both the unions and for the working class generally. Union membership swelled, becoming twice as high in 1914 as it had been in 1906, while working-class consciousness was encouraged. Along with the rise of the Labour party, the strikes gave a clear indication to the government and ruling class that the low place allotted to workers in Victorian England was unacceptable to the labourers of the new century. They demanded a greater share of the fruits of their labour, and were prepared to take action if denied it.

The second social and political fire of the period was ignited by women campaigning for the right to vote. Ever since the middle of the nineteenth century, women's suffrage movements had demanded an extension of the franchise, in the hope that this would lead to an improvement in their parlous situation. Middle-class women could not take degrees or practise professions in Victorian England, while pay in the few occupations they were permitted to enter was grossly unequal. Working-class women were either employed in factories as manual labourers with limited rights or stayed at home, where they might bear as many as ten children.

Demands for the female vote were denied by a late-Victorian establishment that feared the beginning of the end of male hegemony. The Edwardian establishment was equally unsympathetic to the suffragist cause. Nevertheless, women's participation in the political process did increase in the early twentieth century. Women were now permitted to serve on local councils, vote in local elections and even become mayors. The rationale for allowing women to participate in local government was that it dealt with purely domestic affairs, women's 'natural sphere'. By the end of Edward's reign, middle-class women also had much better access to higher education (despite still being unable to graduate) and to certain categories of employment, such as teaching and nursing.

Many so-called 'go-ahead women' began to complain about their limited professional opportunities, as well as unequal marriage rights and their lack of sexual freedom. Burgeoning female confidence was expressed through their widespread pursuit of dynamic new sports such as tennis, roller skating and cycling, and through new female fashions. Angles and curves were 'out', while loose-hanging and straighter garments were 'in'; violent colours replaced demurer shades. One male journalist remarked: 'In Victorian England woman was a symbol of innocence, a creature with pretty, kitten-like ways, but having no relevance to the business of the world. Today she is emerging into sex consciousness and beating at the bars of circumstance.'

It is unsurprising that the suffragist movement grew in the Edwardian era or that it became more radical in character. In 1903 the accomplished orator Emmeline Pankhurst, along with her daughters Christabel and Sylvia, established the Women's Social and Political Union. The WSPU differed from previous suffragist organizations. 'We resolved to limit our membership exclusively to women,' Pankhurst declared, 'to keep ourselves absolutely free from party affiliation, and to be satisfied with nothing but action. "Deeds, not words" was our motto.' When the *Daily Mail* derisively dubbed WSPU members 'suffragettes', they confidently appropriated and altered the term, pronouncing it 'suffra*gets*', to emphasize their determination to obtain the vote. What the suffragettes wanted to 'get' was not a vote for every woman, regardless of class and property, since this was also denied to men. Instead they demanded that their sex ceased to be a disqualification for the franchise. Votes on the same terms as men would enfranchise only middle-class female householders, but establishing the principle of votes for women was the key issue.

By the time of George's coronation in 1910, the resources of the WSPU had grown rapidly, while the number of sister suffrage societies had proliferated. Yet the growing strength of the movement did not result in greater parliamentary influence. A succession of private member's bills relating to female enfranchisement were introduced around this time but failed to make their way through the Commons. Some backbenchers openly mocked the idea of women voting, while the leading politicians of the day were divided on the issue. Asquith believed that women's 'sphere was not the turmoil and dust of politics, but the circle of social and domestic life'. His wife and daughter, who as aristocrats did not require the vote to wield political influence, shared his contempt for 'petticoat politics', and physically restrained suffragette protesters who attempted to approach him. The king, too, dismissed the suffragettes as 'dreadful women'. On the other hand, Balfour and Lloyd George expressed guarded sympathy for the cause, while some Labour MPs championed it – despite the ambivalent official response of their party.

Since the members of the Commons were unresponsive to their cause, the suffragettes decided to challenge them directly. They began interrupting political meetings with questions, and they attempted to disrupt sittings of parliament. On 18 November 1910, thousands of suffragettes marched on Parliament Square, where they were met with police resistance. Churchill had instructed officers to keep the protesters away from parliament by any means, an order that led to scores of women being hit, pushed and arrested. The Pankhursts were put on trial for incitement to riot, but ended up turning the proceedings into a dissection of the government's incoherent opposition to women's suffrage. The events of 'Black Friday' and its aftermath inspired support for the campaigners throughout the country.

From 1911 onwards, the suffragette movement became more militant. Activists set postboxes alight, chained themselves to railings, broke the windows of shops and male clubs, destroyed public flower beds and slashed cushions on trains. They also wrote graffiti on public buildings and vandalized paintings that depicted women as objects of male desire. Not all suffragists advocated these tactics, yet Pankhurst was convinced that violence was the only option. From 1913 suffragettes also carried out arson attacks, setting light to some 350 buildings over eighteen months in a carefully organized campaign. Leading suffragettes supplied instructions and flammable material to the incendiaries, who manufactured crude bombs and left them in prominent public places. Some of the devices failed to explode, but others damaged buildings, including Lloyd George's house.

On 4 June 1913, Emily Davison provided the campaign with its most potent symbol. Striding out onto the race track during the Epsom Derby, she was knocked down by an oncoming horse belonging to King George and died in hospital four days later. Some historians suggest that Davison intended to pin a suffragette banner onto the animal, but there is a strong possibility that she was intent on martyrdom. 'To re-enact the tragedy of Calvary for generations yet unborn,' Davison had written in a newspaper article, 'is the last consummate sacrifice of the Militant.' Immediately after Davison's death, the suffragettes claimed her as a martyr; over 50,000 sympathizers attended her funeral.

The weak Liberal government once again found itself in unknown territory; as before, its instinct was to respond with coercion. Asquith imprisoned approximately one thousand suffragettes, while denying them the status of political prisoners. This prompted many of the incarcerated women to go on hunger strike. Fearing that they might die in prison and be applauded as martyrs, the government insisted they be strapped to chairs and fed via tubes inserted into the nose and throat before reaching the stomach.

The treatment of the suffragette prisoners caused public outrage. In the Commons the recently elected Labour MP George Lansbury told Asquith: 'You are beneath contempt . . . you will go down in history as the man who tortured innocent women.' The prime minister responded to criticism with legislation, just as he had done during the recent strikes. He introduced a bill which put an end to force-feeding in prison, and allowed enfeebled hunger strikers to be temporarily released in order to recover their health at home, before resuming their sentences. The bill became known as the 'Cat and Mouse Act', after the cat's fondness of toying with its prey, and the Liberals accompanied it with a counter-propaganda campaign. They caricatured the suffragettes as a small group of wealthy and unbalanced eccentrics intent on subverting law and order, rather than a mass movement with a popular political agenda.

Some historians argue that the government's response was effective in the short term: the suffragette campaign decreased in militancy in the early months of 1914. Yet government repression had undoubtedly roused public sympathy for the suffragettes; it also gave their cause invaluable publicity. From a modern perspective, it is the brutality of the Liberal government that is conspicuous, along with its myopia. 'Those who read the history of the movement,' Emmeline Pankhurst predicted, 'will wonder at the blindness that led the Government to obstinately resist so simple and so obvious a measure of justice.'

11

The Orange card

Male supremacism informed the government's repressive response to the suffragette movement. Yet it may have also been prompted by the fact that the campaign took place at a time of unprecedented social chaos, during which Asquith's minority administration felt under siege. Between 1910 and 1914, industrial action was evident throughout the country, and in 1912 the third political fire of the period broke out in Ireland.

Ireland was nominally amalgamated with England in the United Kingdom of Great Britain and Ireland, yet it had been treated as a de facto colony by Britain for centuries. A union between the countries had been established in 1800, after the United Irishmen Rebellion against British overlordship had been brutally suppressed, with members of Ireland's independent parliament bribed to support the Act of Union. The parliament in Dublin was dissolved, and thereafter Ireland's elected politicians sat in Westminster. The British continued to govern the country through the Lord Lieutenant in Dublin Castle.

Neither the 1800 Act of Union nor the British colonial administration rested on popular Irish consent, and nor was the British government's record in Ireland in the nineteenth century by any measure exemplary. It took Britain three decades to fulfil its promise of repealing the penal laws that discriminated against the majority

Catholic population. The government's response to the Irish potato blight of the 1840s, which caused around 1 million Irish people to die of starvation or disease and another million to emigrate, was incompetent and indifferent when it was not cruel. In the first half of the nineteenth century, the majority of the Irish population had supported Daniel O'Connell's movement to repeal the union, and in its second half they had consistently returned to Westminster MPs who campaigned for Irish Home Rule.

After the 1910 election, the minority Asquith government was dependent on the votes of the Irish Parliamentary Party (IPP), led by John Redmond. As a price for the party's support, Redmond insisted on autonomy for Ireland within the Union through the establishment of a Dublin parliament to deal with 'local' matters. The Liberal government agreed to the proposal, for principled as well as pragmatic reasons. The party had been committed to granting Home Rule to the Irish ever since its leader Gladstone had been converted to the cause in 1885 and allied his party with the IPP. Gladstone's two attempts to pass Home Rule legislation in 1886 and 1893 had been sabotaged by the Tory-dominated Lords, but as the 1911 Parliament Act had deprived the House of Lords of its power of veto, implementing Home Rule might now be easier. In 1912 Asquith announced the government's plan to introduce a third Home Rule Bill.

Yet Protestant Unionists in Ireland, along with a handful of Unionist Alliance MPs at Westminster, strenuously opposed the proposed legislation, arguing that Home Rule would allow Ireland's Catholic majority to oppress them. Resistance was especially strong in the four north-eastern counties of Ulster that had majority-Protestant populations. These Ulster Protestants defended the Union, which maintained their hold on local economic and political power, and informed their cultural and religious identity. Some of them were descended from the English and Scottish settlers who had come to Ulster following the sixteenth- and seventeenth-century British colonization of the region, when land had been appropriated in order to establish a Protestant Ascendancy.

The Ulster Unionist MPs had a forceful and charismatic leader in Edward Carson, whose hatred of Home Rule was fanatical. Yet what gave Protestant Unionism influence at Westminster was support from the Tory party. The alliance of Toryism and Ulster Unionism dated back to 1886 when the Tories had opposed Gladstonian Home Rule, despite having previously favoured self-government for Ireland. In order to bring down the Liberal government, the Tories had decided, in the words of Randolph Churchill, that 'The Orange card was the one to play', a reference to the 'Orange Order' that had been founded in Ulster in 1795 to defend the region's Protestant Ascendancy. The Tories had played that card repeatedly in the years that followed. In the 1890s they had opposed Gladstone's second Home Rule Bill and established an official alliance with Ulster Unionist MPs and peers. In the early twentieth century, the association had been strengthened. Amidst fears of imperial decline provoked by the Boer War, the idea of granting Ireland any degree of autonomy had become abhorrent to many Tories: the 'root objection', as Austen Chamberlain put it, was the idea that Ireland as a nation might one day leave the Union and the empire, thereby undermining them. The Tories were, moreover, in a fragile political position after defeat at the 1906 election and the 1911 Parliament Act. Divided over Tariff Reform, bereft of compelling ideas and deprived of the Lords' veto, they were eager for a popular cry behind which to unite. Once more the temptation to play the Orange card proved irresistible, though the consequence was the increase of sectarian division in Ireland.

It is no coincidence that a staunch Unionist of Ulster Scots ancestry had around this time become prominent within the Tory party. The rapid ascent of the self-educated and self-made businessman Andrew Bonar Law can be attributed in part to his fervent Unionism, yet it was also a reward for his striking interventions in the Commons. According to one Tory MP, Law's forthright parliamentary style was 'like the hammering of a skilled riveter, every blow hitting the nail on the head'. It was, as Asquith noted, also an entirely new style in its use of insults and sarcasm: Law dismissed the Liberal cabinet as a 'gaggle of gamblers' and 'swine'. Such combative rhetoric identified him as heir to Joseph Chamberlain, as did his protectionist views and enthusiasm for the empire, of which he believed Ireland to be an integral part.

The middle-class Law was himself the target of insults. Asquith referred to him as 'the gilded tradesman', while some aristocratic

Tories found his manner disconcerting: 'I felt,' remarked one, 'as if I were being addressed by my highly educated carpenter.' In this new era, wealthy businessmen – even those who, like Law, had no English roots and adhered to Nonconformist beliefs – became the leading figures in the party of old England. Joseph Chamberlain had been the 'trailblazer', to use a contemporary term, with Law and others following in his path. The new era for the party began in earnest in 1911, when a beleaguered Balfour resigned the Tory leadership and Law replaced him. The witty English patrician had been superseded by a tough-talking, middle-class and teetotal Ulster Scot. If the appointment caused dismay among Tory aristocrats, it also provoked anxiety on the Liberal front bench: 'The fools,' remarked Lloyd George, 'have stumbled on their best man by accident.'

Law's elevation to the Tory leadership hardened the party's opposition to Irish Home Rule. The new leader's father had been a Presbyterian minister in Ulster, and he was proud of his membership of the Protestant denomination that held power in the four north-eastern counties of Ulster. They were a 'homogeneous people', he declared, who had a 'right' to participate in the Union. One of his first acts as leader was to rename the Conservative and Liberal Unionist party as the 'Unionists', an indication that Ulster Unionism was now integral to the party's identity. He also struck up a close relationship with Edward Carson, who ensured that his Unionist MPs and peers took the Tory whip. While Law and Carson were zealots in the Ulster Protestant cause, the marriage of their groups was one of convenience. The Tory party offered the Ulster Unionists help in maintaining their ascendancy in north-east Ulster, while the Ulster Unionists were a weapon the Tories could employ against the Liberals and their proposed Third Home Rule Bill.

Law opposed Asquith's Home Rule proposals with characteristic vigour. He declared that forcing a Home Rule bill 'through the back door' of the 1911 Parliament Act had no popular mandate – an election on the issue must be called. Law believed the Tories could win that contest against a fragile Liberal government by appealing to the traditionally anti-Irish British electorate. Asquith had no appetite for another election, so he ignored Law and introduced his Home Rule Bill, without making any special provision for the north-eastern Protestant minority. If the bill reached the statute book the Ulster Protestants would have to participate in an autonomous Dublin parliament, which would replace some of the old British colonial administration. The absence of any clause in the bill relating to the Ulster Protestants suggested that Asquith and Redmond underestimated the ferocity of Ulster Unionist and Tory opposition.

After the bill was introduced, Law excited popular Unionist anger outside parliament. In a series of public speeches in England and north-east Ireland, he declared that he could 'imagine no length of resistance to which Ulster will not go, in which I shall not be ready to support them'. If that was not clear enough, he added: 'We shall use any means . . . Even if the Home Rule Bill passes through the Commons . . . there are things stronger than parliamentary majorities.' This was fighting talk. For the first time since the seventeenth century, a British politician was openly inciting extra-parliamentary violence against the elected government of the United Kingdom. Nor was Law alone in making incendiary statements. Carson vowed that Unionists would 'break every law' if the bill were passed, while Tory MPs and 'die-hard' peers spoke of Ulster's 'moral right to resist'. Such inflammatory rhetoric provoked consternation among the Liberals. Asquith condemned Law's statements as 'a complete grammar of anarchy', while Churchill said the Tories were determined 'to govern the country whether in office or in opposition'; as they now lacked the Lords' 'veto of privilege', they would do so through the 'veto of violence'. Law attempted to use the royal veto, by which the English monarch could refuse royal assent to parliamentary bills. But King George, annoyed by Unionist intransigence, declined to exercise the veto, and nor would he dissolve parliament to force an election.

In truth, the Unionists in north-east Ulster needed little incitement from Law to rebel against Asquith's bill. In 1912 the paramilitary Ulster Volunteers were established, and the following year these volunteers were organized into the Ulster Volunteer Force (UVF). Membership was limited to 100,000 men prepared to 'defend' the four north-eastern counties from Home Rule, with force if necessary. In 1914 they collaborated with the Ulster Unionist Council in an operation which saw 25,000 rifles smuggled into the north-east of Ireland from the German Empire. The British government did nothing to stop the gunrunning, and a new, militaristic chapter opened in Irish politics.

In response to the establishment of the Ulster Volunteers, Irish nationalists from organizations such as the Gaelic League, the Ancient Order of Hibernians, the political party Sinn Féin and the Irish Republican Brotherhood formed the Irish Volunteers. While some Protestants joined, the majority of recruits were Catholic. Irish nationalism, and even Irish separatism, had flourished in the previous two decades among people disenchanted by the failure of conventional politicians to deliver Home Rule. The principal aim of the Volunteers was 'to secure and maintain the rights and liberties common to the whole people of Ireland . . . without distinction of creed, politics or social grade'. Their manifesto implied that, if all else failed, those rights and liberties could be maintained by arms. In July 1914, 1,500 rifles were brought from Germany into Howth, near Dublin, for the Irish Volunteers, whose membership had swelled to 200,000 people.

In the meantime, the Third Home Rule Bill slowly worked its way through the Commons, but was then rejected by the Lords. According to the 1911 Parliament Act, a bill could only become law without the consent of the Lords if it passed three times through the Commons in successive parliaments. This guaranteed its passage would be prolonged, and Law made sure there would be many additional delays along the way. Law and Carson also used the interval to foment Unionist rebellion, and to threaten the Liberal government with armed rebellion once again. 'Do you plan to hurl the full majesty and power of the law,' Law asked Asquith, 'supported on the bayonets of the British Army, against a million Ulstermen marching under the Union Flag and singing 'God Save The King'? Would the Army hold? Would the British people – would the Crown – stand for such a slaughter?'

While Asquith was not prepared to send the army into the north-east of Ireland to impose Home Rule, he did look to the armed forces for help in opposing the UVF. In March 1914, British intelligence reported that the Ulster Protestant organization was about to seize ammunition from various army buildings; there were even rumours of an imminent coup in Ulster and of a march on Dublin. The Liberal government issued an order for partial mobilization to the officers at the Curragh Camp in Kildare, the largest British army base in Ireland, yet many of them refused and threatened to resign in protest. Some soldiers believed that Irish Home Rule might undermine Britain's Protestant empire, while others acted on the instigation of military officials in London with links to Law. The Unionist leader approved of their rebellion, arguing that all British citizens had the right to choose sides in what was effectively a civil war.

The so-called 'Curragh Mutiny' was the first time the British army had refused to follow a government order since the seventeenth century. An appalled King George thought the reputation of his army tarnished; the entire system of British governance in Ireland seemed on the point of collapse. The Liberal administration chose not to reprimand the mutineers, preferring to pretend that the affair had never happened. It was now obvious that Home Rule would not be implemented in the four north-eastern counties. The Ulster Unionists drew the moral that they were untouchable, while the Irish Volunteers concluded that they needed more weapons, since the British army would defend neither them nor the Liberal government's Home Rule Bill.

Asquith and Redmond finally realized that the Tory-backed Unionists in Ulster were not bluffing. They would have to seek a compromise over the terms of Home Rule. Behind-the-scenes negotiations took place between Law, Carson, Asquith and Redmond. The prime minister raised the possible exclusion of the four Protestant-majority counties of north-east Ulster from the Home Rule Bill, but Carson insisted that the two Ulster counties with small nationalist majorities should also be exempt. Redmond rejected this notion and threatened to remove the IPP's support from the government if it were pursued. A stalemate followed. With the Home Rule Bill almost on the statute book, Ireland was on the brink of bloody civil war.

But even though the Home Rule Bill did become law in the summer of 1914, no rifles were fired in Ulster. The sudden outbreak of war on the Continent drew the attention of all parties away from Ireland. The implementation of the bill was officially postponed until the end of the European conflict, with Asquith assuring the Unionists that he would consider amending it before it went into full effect. In return the Unionists agreed to postpone arguments over Ireland in the interests of national unity. The prime minister congratulated himself on his narrow escape: 'the one bright spot,' he commented in the summer of 1914, 'was the settlement of Irish civil strife'. But strife in Ireland had merely been postponed.

12

The black sun

To many Liberals, the summer of 1914 seemed gloomy and forbidding. 'I see not a patch of blue sky,' the MP John Morley commented, alluding to the gloomy clouds over Ireland. To the east, the prospect of international strife had been growing steadily. After 1906 England had grown closer to France, with mutual fear and envy of Germany strengthening the entente. Germany, the Continent's flourishing economic and military power, responded by investing so heavily in her navy that she almost caught up with Britain. Portions of the right-wing English press and population demanded the construction of yet more dreadnought battleships: 'We want eight, and we won't wait!' was their rallying cry. Lloyd George argued that building a further four dreadnoughts would be sufficient, but the foreign secretary Edward Grey disagreed and Asquith commissioned a further eight battleships.

Germany's allies, Austria-Hungary and Italy, also increased their spending on armaments. The Italians threatened British ascendancy in the Mediterranean by building a fleet of new battleships. England now faced an uninviting choice between falling behind in the arms race, bankrupting herself by constructing more dreadnoughts, negotiating a non-aggression pact with Germany, or agreeing to French requests for the coordination of a continental defence strategy. She chose the last option, drawing up military plans with her entente partner that included their response to aggression from an unnamed third power, which could only be Germany. Anglo-German relations, meanwhile, failed to improve even after the death of the anti-German King Edward. The problem was that most people in the English government and ruling class shared the prejudices of their former king: Grey called Germany 'our worst enemy and our greatest danger'. The Kaiser and the German establishment had similar views of the English, and it is unsurprising that talks between the two countries broke down. Germany wanted England to agree to the expansion of its navy and to promise neutrality in the case of a continental conflict, whereas England was only prepared to offer colonial concessions.

Britain, which still thought of itself primarily as a global power, became increasingly embroiled in the European argument, in large part out of fear that her empire was overstretched. Although Britain was part of an island off the Continent, it could not remain aloof from it because of its proximity; besides, the country now lacked the military and economic resources to maintain her empire without French assistance. After the Boer War, where the British army's strength was uncertain and its navy no longer supreme, diplomatic isolation from the Continent would be perilous.

The 1907 Anglo-Russian convention was further acknowledgement of this reality. Since Russia was, like Britain, already allied with France, the three empires now formed a Triple Alliance, a counterweight to the alliance between Germany and Austria-Hungary. But the Kaiser dismissed this talk of balance as a smokescreen for a traditional anti-German Franco-British policy; in his mind, the Triple Alliance was simply another attempt to encircle Germany. Some English people questioned the anti-German premise of Britain's balance of power strategy, and thought Grey was being too aggressive. Others regarded it as an inherently unstable tactic that might entangle Britain in a continental war.

The balance of power would only succeed, critics said, if there was a genuine equilibrium between the two sides, and if all the parties involved were committed to maintaining it. This was a remote possibility. The Ottoman Empire was crumbling; European nationalism was on the rise, particularly in the Balkans; Germany was determined to rival Britain as a naval as well as imperial power; and there was the constant possibility of international disagreements breaking out along the colonial borders of the European nations. Africa had provided a release valve for potential antagonism in the late nineteenth century, its vast lands and resources affording all the continental powers the chance to satisfy their economic and military ambitions. But Africa had been almost entirely carved up and plundered by Britain, France, Germany, Belgium, Italy and Portugal, and the colonizers now stared at each other suspiciously across the continent's internal frontiers.

The hardest test of the balance of power came on 28 June 1914, when Archduke Franz Ferdinand of Austria, heir to the Austro-Hungarian throne, was assassinated in Sarajevo by a nationalist Bosnian Serb. There had been assassinations of equally powerful figures before; this time none of those involved seemed determined to resolve the situation. Austria-Hungary felt threatened by Balkan nationalism and Russian ambitions in the area. Too weak to stand alone, they asked the Germans if they would support a declaration of war against Serbia, even if Russia were to stand by its Serbian allies. The Germans, who also feared Russian influence in the Balkans, were convinced that they would have to confront Russia at some point; it would be easier to do so sooner rather than later, given Russia's long-term rearmament plans. So Germany offered Austria-Hungary a blank cheque, and war on Serbia was declared. Now the other pieces fell into place. The Russians, calculating that France would support them, mobilized their forces against Austria-Hungary in support of Serbia; Germany responded by declaring war against Russia. France, which had been fearful of a German invasion ever since its 1871 conquest of French territory, now mobilized in support of Russia.

Britain was the only major European power yet to make a move. Germany was convinced the British would not enter the struggle, and the mood of the Liberal cabinet was, according to Churchill, 'overwhelmingly pacific'. In contrast, Law, leader of the Unionist opposition, was in a belligerent mood. He warned Asquith that 'it would be fatal to the honour and security' of the country 'to hesitate in supporting France and Russia.' Imperceptibly, yet inevitably, the cabinet came round to Law's view; the momentum of events seemed to be moving Britain inexorably towards continental war. 'We are all adrift,' Churchill commented, 'in a kind of dull cataleptic trance.'

On 3 August 1914, Germany declared war on France; the following day, Germany invaded Belgium. The Liberal administration condemned the violation of the neutrality of a continental country, and declared war on Germany in support of Belgium, and in order to aid her French and Russian allies. The government now believed it had little choice but to confront the country that Britain had identified as the greatest threat to her security and prosperity. Germany had to be stopped.

The government's declaration was made in the confidence that war would be over in a matter of weeks, an optimism shared by all the belligerents. Britain's fleet, which stood ready in the North Sea, was still superior to that of Germany, and it was believed that the Triple Alliance troops would sandwich Germany and Austria-Hungary with quick assaults from west and east. The extensive territories of the British Empire would, it was thought, provide an almost limitless supply of soldiers. For these reasons, Grey assured the Commons: 'we shall suffer little more in war than if we [stood] aside.' Churchill was certain the effects of the conflict would not be felt in England itself, where it would be 'business as usual'.

Grey and Churchill were not the only politicians buoyed up by optimism. Only weeks previously, Lansbury, Hardie and Henderson had publicly denounced all 'capitalist' and 'imperialist' wars; yet now the Labour leadership followed the government line, with the exception of MacDonald, who resigned the chairmanship of the party on pacifist principle. Law and the Unionists offered Asquith's government unhesitating support for the declaration of war and announced the end of active opposition in the Commons, as well as in Unionist Ulster. King George was also cheered by the declaration of war, and would become strongly anti-German over the coming months, despite his numerous German titles and family ties. In fact, he would soon disguise the Teutonic ancestry of the royal family by changing its name from Saxe-Coburg and Gotha to Windsor.

A mood of patriotism swept through England for the first time since the early months of the Boer War. It was mingled with relief that the country was defending a neutral neighbouring country from unprovoked aggression, rather than attacking farmers for gain. When the newspaper boys announced that war had been declared, people rushed out of shops and houses to cheer. Horatio Bottomley's popular magazine *John Bull* set the tone, with its headline 'The Dawn of Britain's Greatest Glory'. Radical intellectuals were enthusiastic about an ideological crusade against 'Prussian militarism'. Many progressives hoped the conflict would offer an opportunity to bury the failed political, economic and social culture of the nineteenth century, and to build something better. Was it the end of one age and the beginning of another? The politicians, the people and the intelligentsia displayed the naivety of a generation with no experience of European war. For those born in the second half of the nineteenth century, conflict meant engagements at a safe distance from Britain's shores against significantly weaker forces. The last time the country had fought on the Continent had been during the Napoleonic era, a period that belonged to ancient history. Thus blindly, and with overweening confidence and eagerness, England entered a conflict that would become the first ever world war.

On one side stood Germany and Austria-Hungary, the 'Central Powers', which were eventually supported by the Ottoman Empire. On the other was the Triple Alliance of Britain, France and Russia, who were dubbed 'the Allies' and who were joined by the Italians. As the combatants moved towards Belgium, many sang their national anthems, the patriotism and optimism of the moment blending to produce a euphoric mood. Those who lived through the following years of agony and terror would remember the songs of the men who marched to the Western Front; some died with those songs still on their lips.

Countless British soldiers would be among the dead. In the first week of August, an Expeditionary Force of six British infantry divisions and one cavalry division was assembled. The plan was to send them to Belgium to support the French army. The newly appointed secretary of war, Lord Kitchener, a veteran of the anti-Boer campaign, believed that Belgium was too dangerous as a theatre of war. The French staff officers, and their allies among the British military hierarchy, overcame Kitchener's concerns, but events would bear out his view. The decision to send its forces to Belgium deprived

Britain of its tactical independence, committing the country to fight side by side with its French ally for the duration of the war.

Kitchener was even more concerned about troop numbers than he was about strategy. Being a great naval power, and the landlord of a vast and vastly populated empire, Britain did not believe it required anything like as large a standing army as other European nations. 'Did you consider when you went headlong into a war like this,' Kitchener asked the cabinet, 'that you were without an army? Did you not realize the war was likely to last for years and require tens of thousands of soldiers?' He was soon permitted to ask for volunteers among the male adult population.

Buoyed up by the feeling 'that war was a glorious affair and the British always won', as one soldier put it, a million men made their way to English recruiting stations, some of them walking for miles through the night. The slogans on the recruitment posters urged the population to respond to Kitchener's call: 'Your Country needs YOU', 'Women of England! Do your duty! Send your man *Today* to join our Glorious Army' and 'Daddy, what did you do in the war?' After being given a few weeks' training, the volunteers would line up in villages and towns and then march to the nearest train station, cheered along the way by those who remained. The train would take the men to military centres in England, from which they would soon be dispatched to the Western Front.

The fighting in that area, which became known as 'The Battle of the Frontiers', provided a salutary lesson. On 23 August 1914, the British engaged in their first major action, alongside the French at Mons in Belgium. The jubilant German army, which had just conquered Brussels, outnumbered the Allies three to one. In these difficult circumstances the British fought well, but they could not halt the German advance. The news of the Allied retreat, according to *The Times*, 'broke like a thunderbolt' back home in England. Questions were asked about the preparedness of the troops. The soldiers had been trained and equipped for an old-style imperial campaign, but were they ready for modern continental warfare? They had plenty of rifles but what about machine guns, hand grenades and telephones?

The Germans drove the Franco-British back mile after mile, a manoeuvre that became known as the 'Great Retreat'. As the Allies withdrew from the towns and villages of northern France, they left behind them piles of dead bodies. The corpses of their own men were left behind, the retreating armies having no time to bury them. The conquering Germans killed or deported thousands of French and Belgian civilians, countless women and children among them, sometimes hanging the naked corpses up in butcher's shops. Their conduct inspired the 'great terror' among civilians and prompted relentless anti-German propaganda in England. As a result, Germans were attacked on English streets and German shops and homes were looted, while many Germans were interned in camps for enemy aliens.

Well-executed Franco-British rearguard actions slowed the advance of the Germans, who halted east of Paris. When the belligerents confronted each other again at the Battle of the Marne in early September, the Allies emerged victorious. It was now the turn of the Germans to retreat, in the so-called 'Race to the Sea'. The two sides engaged in offensives and counteroffensives as they moved through Picardy, Artois and Flanders. Ypres was recaptured by the Allies, who hoped to push the Germans back further, but their advance was halted. A decisive victory now appeared unlikely for either side. Their aim became to retreat no further, rather than to overwhelm the enemy.

The visible symbols of the stalemate were the elaborate rows of trenches the antagonists now dug opposite each other; they zigzagged down France from the Channel to the border with neutral Switzerland. These trench systems would eventually reach a total length of 25,000 miles. In between the opposing trenches lay a mine-filled 'no man's land', an area exposed to machine-gun fire, mortars, flamethrowers, shells and a new weapon of death, the poison-gas canister. The killing was done at a distance by high-tech weapons, as the waves of men were fed to a vast killing machine. Any attempt to attack the enemy's trenches was doomed to failure. If advancing soldiers miraculously managed to dodge the bullets, the mines and the gas canisters, they would have to breach a wall of barbed wire before confronting an enemy of vast numerical superiority.

When they were not engaging in futile attacks, the opposing forces sheltered in their trenches, exhausted and depressed by battle, disease, the falling temperatures of autumn and the death of their comrades. Some soldiers also suffered from 'shell shock' which left them in a state of helpless panic, unable to walk or talk, and prey to hysteria and insomnia. In the early months of the conflict, army doctors said such men were suffering from nerves or had weak constitutions, yet the disease became part of a new pathology of war. Life in the trenches was uncomfortable, anxious and restless. The noise of the constant gunfire and heavy shelling, mingled with the cries of maimed or dying men, was unbearable.

The soldiers realized that it was now a war of attrition, to use a coined phrase. 'We have got to stick it longer than the other side,' as one captain put it, 'and go on producing men, and material until they cry quits.' But who knew how long and how many deaths it might take to grind out a bloody victory? Given the type of warfare in which the antagonists were now engaged, and the huge industrial resources commanded by the Germans, it was likely the struggle would be prolonged and the death toll unprecedented. What had happened to the short, sweet war the government had predicted?

To make matters worse, the expected war at sea had not begun, since the Germans refused to engage the British navy and preferred to pick off British cruisers with their U-boats. When a German mine destroyed a British battleship, the commander-in-chief ordered the British fleet to retreat out of danger to the coast of Ireland. There was little progress either on the Eastern Front, where the battle was far more mobile than in the cratered killing fields of the west. The Russians quickly invaded East Prussia, while Austria-Hungary lost almost a million men in an offensive in the Carpathians. But the mood of optimism among the Allies stalled when the Germans forced the Russians back over their own borders, and Turkey decided to support the Central Powers.

English enthusiasm for war was further dampened as autumn turned to winter. Newspaper reports of deaths and casualties at first provoked pity and fear, then numb resignation. Soon so many soldiers were dying that there was no room in the papers to list all of the names. Across England, women and children dressed in mourning. Soldiers on crutches or in wheelchairs, returned from the front, became a common sight. As the optimism of the early days of the war evaporated, many intellectuals began to fear a German victory. Where was England's legendary strength and pluck? By Christmas few believed the war would soon be over, and there was little surprise among the population when Kitchener requested further volunteers. Over the coming months, an additional million and a half men would enlist.

Kitchener had correctly predicted the difficulty and duration of the war; yet he was often wrong about military tactics. The commander of the British Expeditionary Force, Sir John French, thought the secretary of war incompetent and sometimes 'mad'; few now had faith in his Western Front tactics. In early 1915 the First Lord of the Admiralty, Winston Churchill, made a proposal which was intended to revitalize Britain's strategy. Waging war on an entirely new front, far from Germany's sphere of influence, would, Churchill told the cabinet, open up the war. And if the new front were to be at sea, then the horrific casualties of trench warfare would be avoided. Churchill suggested an 'amphibious operation', using ships and soldiers, on a strip of water called the Dardanelles, which separated Europe from Asia and which was under Ottoman control. If the straits were secured, reinforcements could be sent by the British and French to the Russians; Allied troops could also land in the area and capture Constantinople. The defeat of the Ottomans would materially weaken the Central Powers and in addition would help to protect the British Suez Canal.

Lloyd George liked the proposal, but Asquith was sceptical; Kitchener wavered, then agreed. Many of the plan's supporters laboured under the illusion that the Turks were constitutionally weak. Churchill initially regarded the attack as a difficult operation, requiring a large force on the ground, yet Kitchener convinced him the navy could succeed virtually alone. But when the British and French began their assault on the Dardanelles in mid-March, Churchill received one of the greatest shocks of his career. The Allied navy was scuppered by Turkish mines, and the Turks repulsed its efforts to invade their territory. Another landing of British, French and colonial troops was attempted at the end of April, with the same result. While the Allied soldiers remained on the beaches, the Turks dug trenches that were as impenetrable as those of their German allies. When the Allied ammunition ran low, the attack was called off. One hundred and twenty thousand British soldiers had died, were wounded or went missing. When Churchill heard the news, he was distraught at the failure and loss of life.

After the debacle, the English press turned on the Liberal government and the British military high command. The war was being mismanaged; the troops needed reinforcements, different tactics and better equipment. Above all, greater supplies of high-explosive heavy artillery should immediately be sent to the Western Front. *The Times* and the *Daily Mail* campaigned for more shells. Lord Northcliffe, who owned both papers, backed up Lloyd George's call for the establishment of a munitions department with himself at its head.

Meanwhile, opposition in the Commons was unconstrained over the 'shells scandal'. Law openly attacked the government for the first time since the declaration of war. For its part, the Irish Parliamentary Party saw little reason to sustain the Liberal administration, now that Home Rule had reached the statute book. When Redmond withdrew his support, Asquith's government was at the point of collapse. Grey had been proved wrong about the duration of the conflict, Churchill about the navy's strength during the Dardanelles campaign and Kitchener about strategy. The only cabinet minister to have emerged with credit was Lloyd George, who had brokered a deal between the trade unions and business leaders. The unions had agreed to the dilution of labour through the introduction of a quarter of a million women, as well as unskilled or semi-skilled men, into factories and offices. In return, the chancellor had assured the unions that this would be a temporary wartime measure; he also promised that industrial profits would be controlled, an unprecedented concession to secure union support. In other ways, too, Lloyd George had shown a willingness to intervene in the wartime economy, in contradiction of his Liberal principles. He had imposed import duties, increased taxes, shored up the City banks, allowed the national debt to grow, and taken over factories that failed to meet their munitions quotas.

As the chancellor's reputation rose, Asquith's fell. Lloyd George seemed to display the initiative the prime minister lacked, and the chancellor's friends in the press emphasized the contrast. The papers criticized Asquith's reluctance to wield the considerable powers the war had bestowed on the state and mentioned his addiction to brandy. Friends claimed the drink cleared Asquith's mind, yet the sight of a prime minister supine and sodden in the House did not inspire confidence, in either Fleet Street or the country. To journalists 'Squiffy' seemed as though he had survived into an age in which his skills of conciliation and his instinctive caution were no longer relevant. A twentieth-century world war demanded a different kind of statesman. The future belonged to men like Lloyd George who were capable of decisive, improvised action as well as striking public gestures, and who could reach a vast public through the press. With Northcliffe on his side, the chancellor appeared irresistible.

After consulting Northcliffe and his potential partners on the opposition benches, Lloyd George declared, 'We must have a coalition.' As a pragmatist, he saw the advantages of a government based on a loose affiliation of parties, personalities and ideas. It would give him freedom for manoeuvre, without the constraints of the Liberal party's hierarchy or its traditional creed. He was rooted in Nonconformist Liberalism, but sensed that it was a dwindling political force. Law's Unionists, for their part, had no desire to assume sole responsibility for the military failures abroad, or for the hardship of the population at home. It seemed likely that conscription and food rationing might soon have to be introduced, and they believed that the people were more likely to accept these measures from a coalition than a Tory-Unionist government.

Lloyd George's timing was impeccable. The public was weary of the stories of endless, senseless slaughter and martial failures, and close to hysteria after the recent appearance of German Zeppelins in the sky over London. With the population anxious for a change of fortune and direction, and with support in the Commons and Fleet Street for a Liberal administration wearing thin, Asquith reluctantly assented to the proposal for a coalition and the Liberal government came to an end in May 1915.

Asquith would lead the coalition, but he was leader in name only. He came to cabinet meetings with few proposals, and usually concluded them by postponing a decision. Lloyd George, the real leader, was given sole responsibility for the home front, coordinating all aspects of social and economic policy as minister of munitions. The influence of Asquith's friends in the cabinet was diluted by the presence of the leading Unionists – Law, Balfour, Austen Chamberlain and Edward Carson. Arthur Henderson, who had taken over as Labour leader from MacDonald, became minister for education, and two other Labour MPs joined the coalition in the coming months. The presence of the Labour men gave the cabinet a genuinely 'national' appearance and also changed its social composition. The appointments suggested that Labour was no longer merely a protest party but a movement which was ready for office. Within the military hierarchy there was also a change of personnel. Churchill was demoted to chancellor of the Duchy of Lancaster, partly because of the Dardanelles fiasco but also to appease Law, who regarded the Tory renegade as an unbalanced maverick.

The new government was faced with the old problems – the absence of a convincing military strategy, the lack of manpower and equipment at the front, and the need to reorganize the economy and society in accordance with the demands of war. These last two challenges were ably met by Lloyd George, who hired a staff of businessmen to ensure that ever-increasing quantities of shells, tanks and machine guns were sent to the soldiers. During Lloyd George's command of the ministry, the production of medium guns rose by 380 per cent and of heavy guns by 1,200 per cent. The munitions minister also appointed 'controllers' of shipping, food production, coal and labour, all of whom were experts in these sectors. His new breed of administrators extended the role of the state to all spheres of the economy and to countless aspects of civilian life. They took over factories, imposing strict regulations and new production procedures; they introduced industrial conscription and increased labour mobility. At the same time they placated the unions by reducing working hours, improving working conditions and keeping wages high. Lloyd George had no difficulty in convincing the Unionists in the cabinet that such concessions were necessary; Law understood that the unions were 'the only thing between us and anarchy'.

Lloyd George and his men controlled the production and distribution of food, metals and chemical products. They also directed large amounts of state money to scientific and technological research, and to the study of management and production processes. Central government now seemed to control everything. Bureaucracy was expanded, with efficiency the aim; public expenditure increased rapidly, together with the amount of money collected from direct taxation. The number of citizens who paid income tax rose from 1 million to 8 million, while those who earned more paid more, with steeply progressive taxation imposed and accepted.

Here was an economic, social and political revolution. The newspapers spoke of 'war socialism' and a transformation in government, with businessmen and professionals supplanting wealthy, privately educated public servants. For the first time in history, many members of the lower middle and working classes felt appreciated and rewarded: wages rose, poverty was reduced, and the Labour movement was recognized as a vital part of the economy and society. And what was true for men was equally true for women, who entered the workforce in large numbers, especially in the newly created munitions factories. English women felt that they were participating not only in a great patriotic struggle but also in a national enterprise that was more egalitarian than anything they had previously experienced. The nation was starting to resemble a genuine community, based on the principle of the general good. 'England has broken with her past,' commented the historian W. H. Dawson, 'and when the day of peace arrives we shall be confronted by an altogether altered situation.'

13

Forced to fight

Coalition policies produced positive results on the home front, but there were only failures abroad. After the Dardanelles debacle, plans to open up a new Eastern Front were abandoned; with no prospect of a naval engagement imminent, the government and the military command saw the Western Front as the only viable option – except that it was not viable at all. Since the French had aided the British in the Dardanelles, Kitchener felt bound to support them in their plans for an autumn advance against the Germans. The Battle of Loos was the biggest British attack of 1915, and one of the least successful. Little or no ground was gained, at the cost of the lives of 50,000 British men. The only evidence that 'some of the divisions actually reached the enemy's trenches', reported one official during the battle, was that 'their bodies can be seen on the barbed wire'.

After the carnage, Kitchener's calls for volunteers became more frequent and hysterical. Yet when his appeals failed to inspire an enthusiastic response, Asquith was forced to contemplate the introduction of conscription. Both he and Balfour loathed the idea, while Lloyd George and Law favoured it – a vivid illustration of the division between the 'old' and the 'new' men inside the cabinet. The new men thought conscription would show Britain's allies and enemies that they 'meant business'. 'The fight must be to the finish,' declared Lloyd George, whose primary war aim was to destroy the

'German menace'. Yet Asquith, who hated the 'horrible' war and whose eldest son was fighting in the trenches, appeared intent on an accommodation with Germany.

The dearth of volunteers, and pressure from members of the cabinet, eventually compelled Asquith into action over conscription. Yet even now he acted with customary circumspection. His Military Service Bill of January 1916 imposed compulsory service on bachelors and childless widowers, while excluding married men. By taking this middle course, Asquith managed to conciliate most of his divided cabinet. A few months later, however, events dictated that compulsory service be extended to married men, and Asquith altered the Military Service Bill accordingly. Through the extension of conscription the state assumed control over the life and death of the entire male adult population; 'Kitchener's Army' of volunteers was replaced by men forced to fight. It also resulted in the removal of able-bodied men from the factories at home and their replacement by women and less sturdy men.

Conscription was not extended to Ireland, a clear indication of that country's uncertain status within the United Kingdom. The government realized that the Irish would not accept the forced recruitment of all adult males to defend either the Union or the British Empire; while the irony of conscripting Irishmen to liberate the 'small Catholic nation' of Belgium from a militaristic aggressor was obvious. An overwhelming majority of Irish Parliamentary Party MPs at Westminster had, in fact, voted against the Military Service Bill. Thousands of Irishmen, Catholics as well as Protestants, had come forward to fight following the declaration of war in August 1914; but volunteering for a 'short and glorious' war in 1914 was one thing, conscription imposed by the British government in 1916 another.

The IPP leader John Redmond had encouraged members of the Irish Volunteers to enlist in 1914, with the argument that their sacrifice would make the implementation of the Liberal Home Rule Bill more likely. While the majority of Volunteers had answered Redmond's call to arms, around 12,000 refused. These men had lost faith in the British government's willingness, or ability, to deliver on its promises of Irish self-government; in any case, they wanted far more autonomy than had been pledged in the Home Rule Bill.

They believed that the world war offered them a unique opportunity of realizing their dream of an independent Irish Republic: 'England's difficulty', they said, 'is Ireland's opportunity.'

On Monday, 24 April 1916, a small group of these Irish Volunteers, along with some soldiers of the Irish Citizen Army, staged an uprising in Dublin. They captured a number of official buildings, including the General Post Office, over which they raised the flag of the Irish Republic. Patrick Pearse, one of the rebel leaders, read out a 'Proclamation of the Irish Republic' to passing Dubliners. He declared 'the right of the people of Ireland to the ownership of Ireland', and added that the new republic would 'guarantee religious and civil liberty, equal rights and equal opportunities'.

Pearse called for his fellow Irishmen and women to rise up, yet very few Dubliners showed any interest in doing so. Some felt the rebellion unnecessary with the Home Rule Bill already on the statute book, however uncertain its implementation date. Others considered it an act of questionable opportunism when almost 200,000 Irishmen were fighting at the front. Nearly everyone in Dublin thought the insurrection was doomed to failure. Differences of opinion among the Irish Volunteers had resulted in the participation of just 1,500 men, and the abandonment of plans for a nationwide uprising in favour of one confined to Dublin. The rebels also lacked an adequate supply of arms, after the British navy intercepted a ship carrying German weapons to Dublin.

The British government decided that bullets and bombs would be more effective than a blockade of the Dublin GPO. Heavy artillery was fired from a battery in Trinity College and from a patrol vessel on the Liffey, reducing the square mile around the Post Office to rubble. After a few days of bombardment and bloody street fighting, which saw the death of 200 combatants and 250 civilians, the rebels surrendered. Westminster's rule in Ireland was restored and martial law was introduced, with military personnel taking control of the government of the country. Almost 200 rebels faced courts martial that were later deemed illegal, because they were held in secret and conducted by men who had suppressed the uprising. Ninety insurgents were sentenced to death; fifteen of these men had their sentences confirmed, including several men who had neither led the uprising nor been responsible for any deaths. The executions were carried out by firing squad in the first weeks of May 1916.

Edward Carson applauded the government's draconian response. He told the Commons the rebellion 'ought to be put down with courage and determination, and with an example which would prevent a revival'. Redmond also initially supported the executions, though he later became concerned that they would undermine popular support for constitutional nationalism and urged Asquith to stop the shooting. The prime minister eventually agreed that a 'large number' of executions might 'sow the seeds of lasting trouble' and ordered that they should cease.

Yet the damage had been done. Nationalist opinion in Ireland was becoming radicalized. 'Changed, changed utterly,' wrote the poet W. B. Yeats in his poem 'Easter, 1916'. 'A terrible beauty is born.' The executed men were elevated to the status of martyrs by an Irish population that had been indifferent, ambivalent or hostile to the uprising itself. Some Irish people were stirred by the inhumanity of the executions, others by the rebels' 'sacrifice'. The bombardment of Dublin, news of atrocities committed by the British troops during the uprising and the summary justice of British officials after it, inspired aversion to British colonial rule in Ireland. The spectre of conscription also roused nationalist opinion. An unpopular, apparently futile and largely symbolic revolution had succeeded in awakening Irish opinion. The ultranationalist political party Sinn Féin would soon reap the electoral benefits of radicalization; they, rather than the IPP, now represented the nationalist cause.

The executions also outraged progressive opinion in England. One Liberal MP demanded that no more Irish people be put to death without a civic trial; another called for the prosecution of those who first imported arms to Ireland – the Ulster Unionists, with the tacit consent of the Tory Unionists, since it was the arrival of guns that had prompted the Irish Volunteers to arm in 1914. Asquith responded to the criticism by asking Lloyd George to arrange a deal between the Unionists and the IPP that would lead to the immediate implementation of Home Rule. Using all his charm and cunning, Lloyd George succeeded in persuading Redmond, Carson and Balfour to sign up to a plan that would exclude six counties of Ulster for the duration of war, with the promise to review the situation after hostilities had ceased. But the deal broke down when the 'die-hard' Tories in the cabinet demanded the permanent exclusion of the six counties, and Law withdrew from the negotiations. In the absence of a compromise in his cabinet, Asquith felt powerless to do anything; nothing, therefore, was done. Ireland was still ruled from Westminster, and nationalist feeling in the country continued to increase.

During the Easter Rising, word reached England that the eastern offensive of the Russians had collapsed. News from elsewhere was no better. At the end of May, German warships attacked the British Grand Fleet off the North Sea coast of Denmark's Jutland Peninsula. Although the German ship *Lützow* received twenty-four direct hits, it still managed to sink British ships including HMS *Invincible*, killing over 6,000 British seamen. When news of the deaths reached England, people were shocked and bewildered. In the immediate aftermath of the battle, the Kaiser boasted that 'the spell of Trafalgar is broken', yet it was not as simple as that. A full analysis of the battle revealed that the Germans had also sustained serious losses; moreover, they had failed to achieve the twin aims of their mission – access to the United Kingdom and the Atlantic, and the crippling of the British fleet. Henceforth Germany would concentrate on submarine attacks against shipping in, or close to, British waters, a strategy that would have momentous consequences for the outcome of the war.

Meanwhile, on the Western Front, relentless inconclusive battles undermined the belligerents. The number of dead and wounded could not be comprehended, let alone endured. On the first day of the Battle of the Somme (1 July 1916), there were nearly 60,000 British casualties, with almost 20,000 men killed – the heaviest losses for a single combat in the army's history. 'By the end of the day,' wrote the poet Edmund Blunden, 'both sides had seen, in a sad scrawl of broken earth and murdered men, no road. No thoroughfare. Neither had won, nor could win, the War.' The battle, lasting for more than four months, achieved nothing. The Allies advanced about six miles into German-occupied territory, but the Germans dug in and defended their new position. The price of the meagre advance? Over 350,000 British casualties, and over a million on all sides, in what was the bloodiest battle in history. No wonder the Somme became a symbol of the mud, blood and futility that characterized war in the West, or that English troops referred to it as 'The Great F*** Up'.

The endless slaughter prompted English soldiers to ask why they were fighting. The French were defending their homeland, but that wasn't the case for the British. Combatants also questioned the competence of Britain's military hierarchy. Were their current tactics productive of anything other than carnage, as German machine guns mowed down row after row of attacking British privates?

Criticism of the army elite was sometimes couched in the language of intergenerational antagonism, but more often it was informed by class conflict. The author J. B. Priestley, who was shot, bombed and poisoned by gas on the Western Front, deplored the fact that 'The British Army never saw itself as a citizens' army [but] behaved as if a small gentlemanly officer class still had to make soldiers out of under-gardener's runaway sons and slum lads . . . The traditions of an officer class killed most of my friends.' The class antagonism experienced by the soldiers would be a prominent feature in the post-war political and social environment.

The writings of authors of the lieutenant and captain class contain powerful criticisms of the war, as well as vivid evocations of life on the Western Front. In Wilfred Owen's verse innocent soldiers die, 'guttering' and 'choking', for empty patriotic slogans such as *Dulce et decorum est pro patria mori* ('How sweet and honourable it is to die for one's country'). In the pages of Robert Graves's autobiography *Good-Bye to All That* (1929), the voices of the privates rise up again from no man's land: 'Not cowards, sir. Willing enough. But we're all f—ing dead.'

Lloyd George was appalled by the lack of military progress and determined to take a more prominent role in deciding strategy. His opportunity came in the summer of 1916, when HMS *Hampshire* was sunk by a German mine and Kitchener was among the drowned soldiers. On taking over as war secretary he fired off countless directives to the generals, in defiance of their objection to 'civilian interference'; he also dismissed his Liberal colleagues' proposal for a negotiated peace. Despite his new responsibilities, Lloyd George had energy left over to plot behind the scenes, frequently briefing the press about Asquith's lack of vision, energy and flair.

In the autumn of 1916 the war secretary informed his political allies that reorganization was essential. He proposed a small war council 'free from the "dead hand" of Asquith's inertia', which he would lead himself. The prime minister was dismayed, and rejected the plan. Before making his next move, Lloyd George consulted Law and Carson, who appeared inclined to support him rather than Asquith; their reaction emboldened him to resign. Over the coming weeks, there was much discussion between Lloyd George, Asquith and the Unionists, but when no compromise could be found, Asquith saw no alternative but to resign. Law was asked to form a government but declined to do so since the Liberals would not serve in it. The king then turned to Lloyd George.

The king accused Lloyd George of behaving like a blackmailer during the controversy, while Churchill said he effectively seized power. While these are exaggerations, Lloyd George undoubtedly displayed ruthlessness and certainly bears the main responsibility for forcing out Asquith. On leaving Downing Street, Asquith compared himself to Job, the Old Testament patriarch who endures appalling suffering through no fault of his own. The English public's reaction was sympathetic to a departing prime minister who had recently lost his eldest son in the war. Yet most people probably shared the view of Douglas Haig, the commander of the British forces: 'I am personally very sorry for poor old Squiff. However, I expect more action and less talk is needed now.'

Most Liberal MPs tried to comfort Asquith in his distress, as did the party's rank and file in London and the south of England. The Liberals now became the official opposition to Lloyd George's coalition, though they were reluctant to oppose the conduct of a war which they themselves had begun. They were united only by a devotion to laissez-faire economics and a dislike, in Asquith's phrase, of the new prime minister's 'incurable defects of character'. The Nonconformist and provincial sections of the Liberal membership, however, supported Lloyd George, as did a handful of Liberal MPs, including Churchill. More Liberal MPs would join the coalition in time.

The Liberal party thus split, just as it had done thirty years previously over Irish Home Rule. On this occasion, however, the schism would be fatal. Unlike Gladstone's party of the 1880s, Asquith's Liberals lacked a coherent political credo and a secure social base. Nonconformism no longer provided a popular political ideology, and the causes of free trade, laissez-faire economics and Irish Home Rule were now immaterial. The key economic and social struggle of the first half of the twentieth century was between capital and labour, and neither side looked to the Liberal party as its champion. For the workers, Labour was the new lodestar, while the representatives of capital and industrial wealth increasingly looked to the Tories. But the party of old England was also changing in response to the changing times, absorbing and promoting new men with new ideas, such as Law and Baldwin. They had far greater financial resources than the Liberals, too, and better links with the social elite and the press. Moreover, the British electoral system encouraged division between two main parties with contrasting creeds. A third, smaller party, with a more fluid identity, would always be under-represented in parliament.

With the exception of Lloyd George himself, Liberals did not appear in the new coalition's war cabinet. The Unionists also dominated the wider administration, with Balfour at the Foreign Office and Carson at the Admiralty. Law now led the Commons, and the veteran Tory Lord Curzon the Lords. Lloyd George aside, the only indication the government was a 'national coalition', rather than a Unionist administration, was the presence of Labour's Henderson in the war cabinet. Lloyd George was now, in effect, a president without a party. He deftly presided over the cabinet and oversaw the various ministries of government, to which he appointed his friends from the business world.

This system gave Lloyd George absolute control over home affairs, and considerable influence over the conduct of the war. 'He pulled the levers,' one government official wrote, 'and the traffic moved in Westminster, in Fleet Street, in party offices, in town and village halls, in polling booths.' Churchill, who joined the government as minister of munitions, was enthusiastic about Lloyd George's despotism, while leading Unionists accepted the situation because it gave them influence without responsibility. 'If the remarkable, unscrupulous little man wants to be a dictator,' commented Balfour, 'let him be.' Over the ensuing months, Law and Lloyd George would form a successful working partnership, despite the striking contrast in their characters.

The king was among the many people who accused Lloyd George of mendacity, and nor was that the monarch's only complaint about his new prime minister. Lloyd George regularly neglected to reply to his letters and often failed to appear when summoned to Buckingham Palace. The man who had risen in politics through his own merits had nothing but contempt for hereditary monarchy; he took pleasure in treating the king 'abominably', to use George V's own term. Here was another wartime revolution – a middle-class politician intimidating the king. Lloyd George's reputation as a 'man of the people' was also enhanced when he recruited three ministers from the Labour party to the coalition.

Lloyd George described his government as a 'win the war' coalition. He used the terrors on the battlefields of France as an argument for continuing the conflict, declaring that the 'perpetrators' must be 'punished'. His message was faithfully broadcast by his old ally Lord Northcliffe and by Max Aitken, the owner of the *Daily Express*. Aitken, who had been instrumental in the removal of Asquith from office, would soon be elevated to the peerage as Lord Beaverbrook and appointed the coalition's minister of information. Lloyd George's propaganda efforts largely ensured that the country, however uneasily, still supported the war.

The prime minister, however, was eager to increase the war's popularity by delivering a 'knock-out blow'. He believed no mission was impossible – British troops could capture Jerusalem, help the Italians defeat Austria-Hungary or even gain the elusive breakthrough in France. In order to achieve that last aim, Lloyd George removed Britain's largely incompetent military high command and placed the army under the authority of Robert Nivelle, a French general. Yet the next major engagement, at Arras in April 1917, was no more decisive and no less bloody than the battles preceding it.

In the same month, however, an incident took place that was to prove decisive in determining the outcome of the war. Over the previous few months Germany had conducted indiscriminate submarine attacks on any ships entering British waters, in an attempt to blockade Britain and starve her population into submission. The strategy resulted in the sinking of several vessels from the United States. The Americans were so incensed by the attacks that, on 16 April, they declared war on Germany. It was hoped that the United States might tip the scales in the Allies' favour, though it would be months before American men and supplies reached the Western Front.

But as one ally was gained, another was lost. In Russia, the starved and weary population brought down Tsar Nicholas II, in what became known as the February Revolution, and a provisional government assumed power in his place. At first, Lloyd George welcomed the fall of the House of Romanov, and the opportunity to present the war as a moral struggle between the liberal 'democratic' Allies and the autocratic Central Powers. Yet Russia's new government turned out to be unenthusiastic about a military crusade and proposed a peace with no annexations and indemnities.

Lloyd George's strategy suffered a further blow in April, when the revolutionary Bolshevik leader Lenin arrived in Petrograd, in a train laid on by the Germans, to denounce the imperialist war. 'The war,' he declared, 'is being waged for the division of colonies and the robbery of foreign territory; thieves have fallen out . . . to identify the interests of the thieves with the interests of the nation is an unconscionable bourgeois lie.' It was a view that won wide acceptance in Russia, and also among the hungry working classes of Europe. Lenin's Bolsheviks would become increasingly powerful over the coming months, and in November they would storm Petrograd's Winter Palace, the seat of Russia's government, and establish a 'Soviet republic'. As head of the first ever socialist state, Lenin would end Russia's involvement in the war by signing a treaty with Germany.

As the revolution unfolded in Russia there was no change on the Western Front. While the imminent arrival of thousands of American soldiers appeared to increase Field Marshal Sir Douglas Haig's confidence, it also prompted him to attempt to finish the job before the Americans reached France, no doubt in order to claim more glory for himself. Haig now believed the British could retake Ypres, march on to the Belgian coast and precipitate the fall of the German front. Lloyd George cautioned him against hubris and hastiness, but Haig silenced the doubters in the government and another bloody battle began, this time at Passchendaele, in July 1917. When the first British assault failed, Haig did not call off the operation, as he had promised; he remained convinced of a 'tremendous' breakthrough.

The battle persisted through August, September and October, with no breakthrough. The unseasonably early rains, and the volume of weapons and horses dragged over the terrain, turned the battlefield into a deadly morass in which thousands of soldiers drowned. During the 'Battle of the Mud' there were around 300,000 casualties on both sides, and once more the sacrifice of the Allied soldiers achieved little or nothing. Although Passchendaele was eventually taken in November, by a Canadian corps, there was no decisive victory.

By the closing months of 1917 there was no prospect of victory in sight. Because of the German submarine blockade, supplies of wheat in England were running low and compulsory rationing was introduced. The terrifying Zeppelins once more appeared in the London skies, where they were joined by Gotha aeroplanes. As the German aircraft rained down bombs on the English capital, 300,000 of its inhabitants took refuge in the Underground every night. Calls for a negotiated settlement with Germany could now be heard among the people; the campaigners for peace were now as vociferous as the propagandists for war. Numerous Labour supporters wanted to follow Soviet Russia and sign a treaty with the Germans, while Henderson resigned from the coalition in protest at its lack of engagement with European socialism. Even Unionist support for the war appeared to be waning; one leading light of the party warned that 'prolongation will spell ruin for the civilised world'.

As the war entered its fourth calendar year, there was no enthusiasm for it in England. Events in the spring of 1918 only darkened the mood. The German army, reinforced by soldiers transferred from the Eastern Front as a result of its treaty with Russia, decided to embark on a major offensive to take advantage of its numerical superiority before soldiers from the United States joined the Allies. General Ludendorff's plan was to break through the opposition and then attack its trenches from behind. It enjoyed an excellent start, when the Germans overwhelmed the British at the Somme and advanced forty miles towards Paris. For the retreating Allies, the situation was desperate.

With American reinforcements still some weeks away, Lloyd George urgently needed more men. His war cabinet decided to impose conscription on Ireland, promising the nationalists the immediate implementation of Home Rule in return. But few Irish people believed Lloyd George's promise, and many were outraged that he had made Home Rule dependent on the acceptance of compulsory military service. Nationalist opinion was inflamed: leading Sinn Féin politicians, along with the hierarchy of the Irish Catholic Church, pledged themselves 'to one another to resist conscription by the most effective means at our disposal'. Undaunted, Lloyd George passed the new conscription law, and arrested many of the Sinn Féin politicians on trumped-up charges of collusion with Germany. The arrests only served to further galvanize support for nationalism in Ireland, while attempts by the British administration to implement the conscription law were unsuccessful.

Although there were no reinforcements from Ireland, the Allies managed to survive on the Western Front until the American soldiers started to arrive in the early summer of 1918. Around one and a half million United States troops landed in France, with 10,000 men sent to the Allied front every day. Reinforced by the American contingents, the Allies began a counteroffensive which would see the Germans retreat over all the ground they had taken in the spring. On the first day of the Battle of Amiens in August, a day Ludendorff called 'the black day of the German Army', the Allied forces advanced seven miles.

As the Germans were pressed back across France, news reached them that Turkish forces had collapsed in the east, giving the Allies an open road into Austria-Hungary. German soldiers began to surrender and desert en masse, while a German population facing starvation called for the end of the war. Politicians in Germany realized the war was lost. The German generals also reluctantly admitted defeat, but refused to take responsibility for it, thereby propagating the myth that the politicians had 'stabbed them in the back' by forcing them to sue for peace. The Kaiser abdicated and a

German Republic was proclaimed, while Austria-Hungary disintegrated into numerous individual states.

On 11 November 1918, the German generals signed the Armistice. This agreement ended a global conflict that had lasted over four years, claimed around 18 million lives and left 23 million people seriously wounded, with millions more ill and homeless. The war also put unprecedented strain on the economic, social and cultural fabric of participating countries, as the example of Russia demonstrated. One English soldier, who was lucky enough to return from the front, described the war as 'the suicide of Western civilization'.

14

The regiment of women

The war had offered abundant evidence that women were neither naturally passive nor destined by their sex to be 'angels in the house'. During the conflict they had also demonstrated their fitness for 'men's work' – by 1918 female workers were visible in shops and offices, on trams and trains, and in banks and schools. Women now went down mines, drove vehicles and worked on the land. They were employed in the civil service as well as in factories, while hundreds of thousands worked in government-run armaments plants. Many female munitions workers had left their family homes to live in lodgings or purpose-built hostels near the factories, becoming physically and economically independent from their parents or employers. While their earnings lagged far behind those of their male counterparts, women now earned on average twice as much as they had before the war period. For the first time in history, lower-middle-class and working-class women – the unmarried as well as the married – had money in their pockets.

During the war almost 60,000 women also volunteered to serve in the Women's Army Auxiliary Corps. They were employed as clerks, mechanics, nurses and munitions workers at home, or sent to the Western Front to work as cooks and medical personnel. The Corps was directed by the physician Mona Chalmers Watson, who believed it represented 'an advance of the women's movement' that softened the frontiers of gender. The 'war-working type of woman' appeared on the home front, sporting cropped hair, overalls and boots. Given the nature of their work, and the wartime fabric shortages, their attire had to be plain and practical. Frilly Edwardian dresses were replaced by short skirts, trousers or shorts. Along with the new jobs, clothes and freedom came a new confidence, which bred a determination never to return to the old dispensation.

The male establishment was fulsome in its praise of the women's war effort. 'How could we have carried on the war without them?' Asquith remarked. 'Short of actually bearing arms in the field, there is hardly a service . . . in which women have not been as active and as efficient as men.' The former prime minister now declared himself a convert to the cause of women's enfranchisement. As the fighting came to an end, many politicians agreed that granting women the vote might be a 'fitting recognition' of their contribution to the war. In private they admitted to other, more pragmatic reasons for extending the franchise: 'As the atmosphere after the conclusion of the war cannot be calm,' remarked one Liberal peer, there might be a return to pre-war suffragette agitation 'if the grant of the vote is refused'. When a law conceding the vote to women over thirty reached the statute book in 1918, the victory belonged to the suffragettes who had campaigned before the war as well as to the women who had served during it.

The 1918 Representation of the People Act enfranchised over 8 million women, yet it was hardly a fitting recognition of women's great wartime contribution, let alone an adequate response to suffragette calls for electoral equality. Under the terms of the act younger women were still denied the vote. As for parity with men, it preserved the gender gap by enfranchising all men over twenty-one years of age and all servicemen over nineteen, regardless of property qualification. In contrast, women over thirty received the vote only if they were either a member or married to a member of the Local Government Register, a property owner or a graduate voting in a university constituency. The extension of the male franchise added over 5 million men to the electorate, and meant that women accounted for approximately 35 per cent of all voters, despite outnumbering men by almost 2 million.

The 1918 Representation of the People Act set the tone of

post-war legislation relating to women. New laws promised great steps forward, but equality remained distant. As a result of the 1919 Sexual Disqualification Act and the Employment of Women, Young Persons, and Children Act 1920, women could no longer be sacked because of their sex, while they were also permitted to become MPs, university students, architects and lawyers. Yet they were still barred from Cambridge University and the Stock Exchange, while their entry into medical professions was severely restricted.

One of the biggest blows to the cause of female equality was the dismissal of 750,000 women who had worked in factories on the home front, which left the proportion of females in employment lower than it had been before the war. The 1918 Restoration of Pre-War Practices Act effectively re-established women as second-class workers, much to the relief of the overwhelmingly male trade unions who were anxious to secure work for male members returning from the front. Many on the left preached equality, but only for men. Labour was still a masculine party, despite the fact that work was no longer an exclusively male preserve. Some Labour MPs joined Unionists and right-wing male journalists in blaming the widespread male unemployment of the early Twenties on women. Few now spoke of women as the 'saviours of the nation'.

During the Twenties, the attacks on women's independence continued. Legislation specifically aimed at women tended to identify them as wives and mothers by concentrating on maternity or widowhood. A marriage bar was also introduced in professions such as the civil service and teaching, which meant that the many women who had been employed in these sectors in wartime now had to choose between work and marriage, with the implicit encouragement to select the latter.

Yet veteran feminists were on hand to protect the younger generation of women from the propaganda. The British author Rebecca West explained to her young 'sisters' that 'the woman who does not realize that by reason of her sex she lives in a beleaguered city, is a fool who deserves to lose (as she certainly will) all the privileges that have been won for her by her more robustly minded sisters'. Guided by the old guard, many young women were able to lead confident and independent lives, despite the male establishment. The self-assurance of the young women of the decade seemed so radical to contemporaries that they were given a new name: 'flappers'. In the Victorian era, a flapper had been a child prostitute; in Edwardian England it was applied to young women who enjoyed the latest dances. The post-war flapper came to denote a young, zesty and sexually confident girl. By the early Twenties the term would imply all of these elements, and more – youth, unconventionality, impetuousness, independence, sexual heterodoxy, hedonism, confidence, high-spiritedness, a passion for fashion and the mimicking of masculinity.

The word 'flapper' was uttered by middle-aged men in a tone of stern disapproval. In a public lecture, one physician, Dr R. Murray-Leslie, condemned 'the social butterfly type . . . the frivolous, irresponsible, undisciplined, scantily clad, jazzing "flapper"'. Yet demographics were against these male critics, since women now outnumbered men, especially among the younger sections of the population. The spirit of the age also favoured the flappers. In the Twenties young people were determined to drink and dance away the searing memories of war, while the old men who had brought about the carnage were to be laughed at, lambasted or ignored. Young women proudly appropriated the word flapper, using it to describe themselves and their sisters.

Some flappers came from the lower middle classes. Secretaries, waitresses, journalists, receptionists, teachers and shop assistants worked hard by day and caroused by night. Many of these 'career girls' were able to maintain independence from their families. Even if most could not afford to live away from their parents, they insisted on having a key to let themselves in after a 'night on the tiles'. Yet it was mainly upper-middle-class or upper-class flappers who attracted the eye of novelists and journalists in the Twenties. Nina Blount, the daughter of a wealthy colonel in Evelyn Waugh's novel *Vile Bodies* (1930), offers a glorious archetype. On being asked if she'd 'mind' being seduced, she replies 'not as much as all that'. The sexual experience following this exchange was probably unsatisfactory, to judge by a comment Nina makes later in the novel: 'All this fuss about sleeping together. For physical pleasure, I'd sooner go to my dentist any day.'

Sex was a favourite topic of conversation among flappers. 'We talk of everything,' wrote a young woman in *Eve* magazine, 'we do not rule out one single emotion or experience as being impossible or improper.' Feminism informed and animated such behaviour. In the Twenties feminists encouraged their sisters to use birth control as a way to obtain freedom from birthing, domestic responsibility and lack of money. Contraceptives also offered women the chance to explore their impulses, tastes and capacity for pleasure. The intellectual Dora Russell described sex as 'a thing of dignity, beauty and delight' for women – 'even without children, even without marriage', physical satisfaction was possible for all. The most influential propagandist of the period was Marie Stopes. She established a birth control clinic in London, and disseminated knowledge of contraception through her book *Married Love*, a bestseller on its publication in 1918. Stopes encouraged women to see themselves as more than 'the passive instrument of man's need', and to explore sexual pleasure as something of 'supreme value in itself'.

This was a revolution without an articulated aim or ideology, yet the flappers were, in their own style, practical feminists. It was absolutely outrageous, according to some journalists, that a young, unchaperoned woman should be seen in public with a young man, let alone meet him in private. Meanwhile, the consequences of liaisons among the unmarried were too horrifying to be named: the newspapers referred to the increasing numbers of unmarried women who became pregnant as being in 'a certain condition'. Fathers lectured their daughters on the dangers of lechery, drunkenness and stopping out late. Girls were warned that a quarter of London taxis participated in the slave trade; they had no handles on the inside, so passengers could not escape.

Ignoring the propaganda, the flappers strutted on the nocturnal streets of England's cities, looking for places to dance. Upper- and upper-middle-class girls would be dropped off at classes in hotels or private houses by a chaperone or chauffeur, while those lower down the social scale would walk or take the tram or bus to lessons at the town hall. To a piano accompaniment, the teacher would help them master the steps of the dance currently in vogue. The jive, the one-step, the Black Bottom, the Lindy Hop, the shimmy, the Varsity Drag and the fast foxtrot all enjoyed brief popularity during the decade; from 1925 everyone was doing the Charleston, described by an outraged newspaper as 'freakish, degenerate, negroid'.

Most of the new dances came from the United States, and were characterized by vigour, gaiety and informality. Unlike the pre-war waltzes, everyone could do the Black Bottom, however they were dressed and wherever they happened to be. They were democratic dances for an age of burgeoning democracy. Some of the new steps had been imported by American soldiers, who had stayed in England after the end of the war; others featured in the American films that were shown in cinemas across the country. They were known as 'rag dances' because they were accompanied by ragtime piano tunes, or by the music that would come to define the decade – jazz. The word 'jazz' – a Creole euphemism for sex – covered a multitude of musical forms with syncopated rhythm, intermittent improvisation and an air of freedom and exultation. From its opening in 1919, the Palais de Danse in London's Hammersmith hosted American jazz groups such as the Original Dixieland Jazz Band. Outside of London, the purpose-built dance halls would arrive a little later.

Flappers also danced the night away at private parties. An upper-class hostess would invite friends round, often at only a few hours' notice, and after dinner the guests danced to ragtime music. If there were no musicians available a gramophone would suffice, since they had become much cheaper and more compact; in the absence of a gramophone, a wireless would do. Chaperones, known as 'dancing mothers', or more colloquially as 'alarm clocks' and 'fire extinguishers', would keep an eye on proceedings.

The other great dancing venues of the period were the night-clubs, which opened across London despite being regularly persecuted under the 1914 Defence of the Realm Act. The act, which had given wartime government extensive powers over society and culture, allowed the government to shut down places of entertainment should they be used for 'immoral' purposes. This gave nightclubs an air of illegality, which was enhanced by reports of the drug-fuelled orgies that supposedly took place inside them. The flappers who congregated at underground clubs such as the frequently raided '43' on Soho's Gerrard Street would mingle with aristocratic bohemians, the criminal elite, Oxbridge undergraduates and sports personalities. This establishment was run by the redoubtable Irishwoman Kate Meyrick, until she was caught serving intoxicating liquor without a licence and sent to prison for six months. Undaunted, she opened the Silver Slipper after her release, a club famous for its glass dance floor.

Other forms of pleasure available to flappers at clubs included cocktails and cigarettes. It was the first time women had smoked cigarettes in public, and the flappers flaunted their freedom by using ostentatiously long cigarette holders. Cocktails were regarded by many as the most romantic expression of modern life; Martinis, Manhattans, Bronxes and White Ladies all took their turn as the drink of choice. Some nightclubs also offered a new form of entertainment called 'cabaret', which consisted of floor shows featuring music, dance and song, with the performers either on stage or moving between the tables.

It would have been impossible to perform the dances favoured by the flappers, or to engage in other pursuits such as tennis, cycling and riding pillion on a motorcycle, in the laces, buttons and hoops that had impeded women's breathing and movement before the war. Simplicity, lightness and comfort were all, with Coco Chanel's 'little black dress' of 1926 emblematic of the period. Along with simplicity came inexpensiveness: dresses could be sewn at home from a single yard of fabric, and if the fabric was rayon, or 'artificial silk', the saving was all the greater.

For the first time in history, women aspired to boyish figures, with straight waists, flat chests and slender thighs, hips and buttocks. Achieving the desired androgynous physique was not easy for some, and many flappers turned to diets, massage, swimming and exercises, while others relied on clothes to suggest boyish slenderness. Where corsets had once accentuated the bust, breasts were now flattened by tight bodices or brassieres. Waists were eliminated, along with hips, by dresses that were straight, loose and cylindrical, and by baggy trousers. In donning trousers, some flappers wanted to allude to the uniforms factory women had worn during the war; it was a way of celebrating social and political emancipation. They also used clothes to proclaim their pleasure in sex and fleshliness. Flapper dresses, often dipping low at the front and back, were sleeveless and short; their skirts inched up the legs as the decade progressed.

'In times of war and social upheaval,' commented one fashion expert, 'the tendency for women to cut off their hair seems almost to be irresistible.' The bobs and the crops were often topped by the fashion sensation of the decade – the cloche hat spawned scores of imitations, and helmet-like hats appeared in shops everywhere. Some flappers preferred to wear them so low that the brim covered their eyebrows, but those who put on make-up raised the brims to show off the kohl and mascara around their eyes. Through such cosmetic means these women would achieve the desired look for a particular evening: 'ethereal' and 'starved' were among the most popular. Flappers who preferred a mischievous 'little-girl' pose painted their lips in a 'cupid's bow' shape. Their widespread application of make-up was another audacious gesture; before the war cosmetics had been generally associated with whores and actresses.

Along with fashions in clothes came fashions in language. To express approval, a flapper might call something 'jazz', 'the bee's knees' or 'the cat's meow'; disapprobation was indicated by epithets such as 'Victorian', 'stuffy' and 'junk'. Boring men were 'pillow cases', and young men any girl could 'borrow' for the evening were 'umbrellas'. Women eager for experience were admiringly known as 'biscuits', but if a girl stole a friend's boyfriend she became a 'strike-breaker'. In such epithets and phrases, we can hear an echo of the confidence and irreverence of the young women of post-war England.

15

The clock stops

Failure to grant electoral equality to women was not the only limitation of the 1918 Representation of the People Act. It also stopped short of establishing the principle of 'one man, one vote' in the constituency of residence – around one and a half million middle-class men enjoyed an extra vote, because of their ability to vote in university constituencies or in constituencies where their businesses operated. Neither did it introduce any proportional representation into the electoral system, but instead maintained the first-past-the-post formula, which strongly favoured the more established parties. The continued use of this system created widespread disillusionment among English voters. What was the point of voting for one's preferred party in a constituency where it had no chance of winning?

Yet despite these defects, the 1918 Representation of the People Act was a revolutionary piece of legislation, tripling the electorate to around 21 million. It gave the majority of working-class men a stake in society by granting them the vote for the first time. Like the enfranchisement of women over the age of thirty, the granting of the vote to working-class men was regarded by some politicians as a reward for the enormous contribution these men had made to the war effort, both at home and on the Western Front. It was also an acknowledgement of the status and power that Labour and the unions had achieved during the war, and a pragmatic concession from a political establishment that feared a return to pre-war industrial unrest.

The consequences of enfranchising 14 million women and working-class men would soon be evident; Lloyd George called a general election immediately after the armistice. Officially he sought a popular mandate to negotiate a lasting post-war international settlement, and to implement a programme of social and economic reconstruction. Yet there were also political reasons for calling an election. Lloyd George wanted to capitalize on his reputation as 'The Man Who Won the War' and as the prime minister who could, in Churchill's phrase, 'get things done'. The only problem was that he no longer had a strong and united party behind him. Only half of the Liberal MPs in the 1918 Commons backed him, the others standing by Asquith in principled but hopeless opposition. The prime minister also lacked a coherent political credo – traditional Liberalism had been exploded by the experience of war.

But the celebrated political fixer soon came up with a solution: a continuation of the national coalition, in peacetime, under his leadership. Lloyd George believed the traditional battle lines between the parties had become obscured during the war, events having blunted the divisiveness of debates surrounding free trade and protection, jingoism and anti-imperialism, state intervention and private enterprise. He hoped that consensus politics had replaced the old tribal and class- or interest-based politics and that he would emerge as a presidential figure with cross-party appeal. The Unionists signed up to his plan, partly because Lloyd George was unassailable. The party lacked a leader with the prime minister's popular appeal and doubted its ability to appeal to newly enfranchised working-class voters. Moreover, some Tories sensed the opportunity of destroying the Liberal party by driving a wedge between the coalition Liberals and the 'Squiffites'.

The Labour party declined the invitation to remain in the coalition, preferring to work alone. The addition of a great swathe of the working class to the electorate gave them confidence, as did the doubling of the party membership to 3 million during the war, and the enhanced status and size of the unions, which now comprised 8 million members. The increase in subscriptions gave the party the resources to expand its National Executive and establish a network of branches throughout the country. The party's recent experience of government, together with the demise of the Liberals, inspired optimism throughout its ranks, as did the fact that a socialist economy had been established during the war and accepted by the population.

Labour also believed it could exploit the radicalism that was sweeping across England after the war. People wanted to build a new and better society, and were determined that a capitalist or imperialistic conflict should never break out again. According to George Orwell: 'After that unspeakable idiotic mess you couldn't go on regarding society as something eternal and unquestionable . . . You knew it was just a balls-up.' A similar attitude may have prompted people to protest and riot during the 1919 Peace Day celebrations, which had been organized by the government to encourage national unity. In Luton a crowd stormed and burned down the town hall. The leaders of the nation were perturbed. As one senior courtier, Lord Esher, remarked, 'The Monarchy and its cost will now have to be justified in the eyes of a war-worn and hungry proletariat, endowed with a huge preponderance of voting power.'

Labour felt emboldened to formulate radical policy proposals, including the nationalization of the railways, the workers' control of industry and a capital levy to eliminate the national debt. Since working-class men had been conscripted to fight the war, trade unionists and Labour MPs argued that the 'accumulated wealth' of the middle and upper classes should be 'conscripted to defray the financial liability incurred by the conflict'. The party also decided to adopt an overtly socialist creed, which would clearly distinguish it from its Liberal rivals. In its revised constitution of 1918, it pledged 'to the workers by hand or by brain the full fruits of their industry and the most equitable distribution thereof . . . upon the basis of common ownership of the means of production and control of each industry and service'.

The reference to 'workers by brain' suggests an attempt by Labour to attract the middle classes and the intelligentsia that had been drawn to the reforming Liberal administrations before the war. The adoption of socialism as the official Labour doctrine manifests a desire to distance the party from the unions and to broaden its social appeal; socialism was an international, supra-class creed rather than a working-class or trade unionist one. Ramsay MacDonald advocated nebulous and gradualist socialism that was tailored to appeal to 'the middle section' radicalized by the war, whose 'nucleus is the intelligent artisan and the intellectual well-to-do'. Yet Labour's espousal of socialism, however cautious, left it open to attack from the centre and the right. In the run-up to the 1918 election, Lloyd George's friends in the conservative press raised the spectre of a Labour-sponsored socialist revolution, while the prime minister claimed that 'The Labour Party is being run by the extreme pacifist, Bolshevik group.' But Labour was not intimidated into abandoning its endorsement of socialism; it was convinced that the centre ground of politics had shifted to the left.

The national coalition won the election by an enormous margin, with Unionist and Liberal candidates who received a letter of endorsement from Lloyd George and Law claiming over 500 seats out of 700. To add to the prime minister's delight, MacDonald lost his seat – evidence that Lloyd George's anti-pacifist jibes had been effective. The result was an expression of the population's overwhelming gratitude for his wartime heroics and an endorsement of his plans to rebuild the country. The election had been won through promises of a better future, and the electorate's belief that Lloyd George and his Unionist allies could fulfil them. Young Unionist candidates, such as Neville Chamberlain (the second son of Joseph, and half-brother of Austen), secured their seats with the pledge to 'show gratitude to those who have fought and died for England, by making it a better place to live in'.

Although the results were a cause of celebration for Lloyd George, they might also have given him cause for concern. Labour had attracted strong support among the newly enfranchised working classes, increasing its share of the popular vote from 6 per cent to 21 per cent and polling almost two and a half million votes, but the first-past-the-post system ensured that this failed to translate into parliamentary gains. Nevertheless sixty MPs represented a significant increase on the forty the party had returned in 1910. Labour was now a powerful national force, and the largest single

British party of opposition. Meanwhile, virtually all the Irish constituencies outside the four Protestant-majority counties in north-east Ulster were won by the ultranationalist party Sinn Féin, which replaced the IPP as the official political voice of Ireland. Many of the elected Sinn Féin politicians were serving jail sentences; all the party's MPs declined to take up their seats in Westminster, refusing to take the oath to the British monarch or to recognize the right of a British parliament to intervene in Irish affairs. Instead the politicians set up their own parliament, the Dáil Éireann, in Dublin. Lloyd George's government would now have to answer an even more urgent 'Irish question' than the one with which Asquith's administration had grappled before the war.

The demise of the IPP also deprived the Liberals of their traditional support from the Irish benches, one of the reasons why the 1918 election results represented a death sentence for the Liberal party. The official 'Squiffite' Liberals won a mere thirty-six seats, with Asquith himself losing in East Fife, while the coalition Liberals amassed only 127 seats, making them the junior partner in a Unionist-dominated coalition. The Unionists, with 382 seats, had such a large majority in the Commons that they could, in theory, form a government without Lloyd George whenever they wished. Their dominance was reflected in the cabinet Lloyd George assembled: Law was Lord Privy Seal and leader of the House of Commons, Austen Chamberlain was chancellor, and Balfour was foreign secretary.

The Unionists had performed a brilliant manoeuvre. Under the aegis of a resplendent Liberal war hero, they had appealed to the new working-class electorate. They had also attracted a fair share of the women's vote, thereby establishing a strong relationship with the female electorate that would last throughout the twentieth century. The party had, moreover, exploited and exacerbated divisions in the Liberal party, while replacing it as the unofficial representative of business. Many of the 260 new MPs were self-made businessmen, and the overwhelming majority sat on Unionist benches. These new arrivals, who were famously described by Stanley Baldwin as 'hard-faced men who looked as if they had done very well out of the war', effectively replaced the aristocracy as the lifeblood of the Tory party. Only a dozen heirs to the peerage were elected at the 1918 election, while there were four aristocrats in the coalition's twenty-two-man cabinet. Lloyd George had hoped the election would herald the arrival of a new consensual coalition politics, but the parliament which assembled at the beginning of 1919 was as divided as ever. When the prime minister rose to address it, he saw 'the TUC on the one side and the Associated Chambers of Commerce on the other' – Labour represented the former, while the Unionists represented the latter. Who did the Liberals on the other benches represent?

Although he was now isolated at the head of a Unionist-dominated administration, things went well for Lloyd George at first. He established hegemony over his Unionist colleagues in the cabinet through a characteristic combination of flattery and bullying, and bypassed many of his ministers as he had done during the war. He also ignored parliament, preferring to deal with issues directly as they arose.

The battle to win the peace on the home front began well. An influenza epidemic, which had claimed over 200,000 British lives since the armistice, gradually abated. The English larder was slowly 'demobilized', with meat, sugar and butter coupons phased out. The political, social and industrial unrest feared by many in the government failed to materialize – the 1918 Representation of the People Act had satisfied the popular appetite for reform and the post-war economy was buoyant. The war had created a boom, with high government spending and inflation stimulating the manufacturing and agricultural sectors. The army of workers expanded with the return of men from the front, but they were absorbed into the growing economy, and unemployment rarely exceeded 1 million (though the 750,000 women dismissed from their positions to make way for the returning men were not included in the figures). The boom continued after the war, sustained by the lavish spending of people who had saved money during the conflict, and by the 'new men' who had made vast fortunes out of it. An insufficient supply of goods caused a rise in both prices and wages, which encouraged people to spend more, which further boosted wages and profits.

The extravagant spending of the population was matched by Lloyd George's government as it attempted to inaugurate its reconstruction projects. In 1918 it introduced an Education Act which raised the school leaving age to fourteen. The following year it passed a Housing Act, through which the state accepted responsibility for housing the working classes. So long as the economy was booming and neither business nor wealth felt oppressed by taxation, the Unionists allowed the prime minister to keep public spending high.

Lloyd George was optimistic that he could also succeed in international affairs. In January 1919, he went to Versailles, where the victorious Allies would dictate peace terms to the defeated Central Powers. The prime minister was confident that he could help orchestrate an enduring peace settlement that would be favourable to Britain. His aim was to remove the possibility of future German aggression without undermining her capacity to act as a counterweight to Soviet Russia on the Continent. So far as Britain's specific aims were concerned, much had been achieved prior to the conference. The German navy had been destroyed following the armistice, and the Allies had tacitly agreed to deprive Germany of her colonies and divide them up amongst themselves. In the event the British Empire would be extended by almost 2 million square miles in Africa, Palestine and Mesopotamia, incorporating 13 million new subjects. Lloyd George could afford to be magnanimous at Versailles.

He also aimed to maintain the close alliance with the United States formed during the latter stages of the war. To further that objective, he endorsed President Woodrow Wilson's fourteen-point plan as the basis for the peace settlement. One point of Wilson's proposal was national self-determination for European peoples who had formerly been part of the Ottoman and Austro-Hungarian empires. Wilson and Lloyd George hoped that the emerging nation states would become harmonious liberal democracies, strong enough to resist the economic and political influence of Russia and Germany. Two other points of Wilson's plan aimed to remove the potential causes of a future war. Armament reduction for all countries was proposed, along with the establishment of a 'general association of nations' for 'the purpose of affording mutual guarantees of political independence and territorial integrity to great and small nations alike'. It was hoped that this association would replace the inherently unstable balance of power diplomacy.

On the German question, Lloyd George supported American attempts to curb France's appetite for vengeance. The French were determined to reduce Germany's frontiers and make the country pay onerous reparations, while Britain and the United States insisted that Germany should be diminished but not devastated, lest this create the conditions for future international discord. When the French proposed taking the Rhineland from Germany and establishing it as an independent state they were rebuffed; and when they suggested an exorbitant figure for German reparations, Lloyd George forced them to accept that the final amount of compensation would be decided at a later date.

Britain and the United States may have acted as a brake over these issues, but the French exacted revenge on Germany in other ways. The peace settlement of June 1919, which became known as the Versailles Treaty, restored to France the Alsace-Lorraine region which had been lost to Germany forty years previously, and permitted French soldiers to occupy the mineral-rich Saar region of Germany. It also declared the German city of Danzig a free state. Under the terms of the treaty, Germany lost 13 per cent of its pre-war European territory and 10 per cent of its pre-war population, while the German army was reduced to 100,000 men and the navy to 15,000. Germany was also forced to sign a 'war guilt clause', accepting responsibility for all the loss and damage of the war. The German government regarded this clause as a violation of honour and a lie, while one German official called the treaty 'the continuation of the war by other means'. Over the next decade, the treaty's punitive terms would provide a focus for popular anger in Germany, which would be expressed in support for the ultranationalist Nazi party.

It was not only the Germans who regarded the Versailles Treaty as harsh. The Cambridge economist and Treasury representative John Maynard Keynes argued that reparations were unwise because European harmony and prosperity were dependent on a strong Germany. Lloyd George agreed, but he was unable to convince the French that a powerful Germany was compatible with their security. Press and public opinion in Britain were also against him, with the right-wing newspapers conducting a 'Make Germany Pay' and 'Hate the Huns' campaign, supported by the Unionists. As a result Lloyd George was compelled to sign a treaty which he knew to be 'greedy' and 'vindictive' in its treatment of Germany, and unlikely to lay the foundations for a lasting European peace.

Neither did the treaty's other clauses inspire much optimism among experienced observers. The numerous independent countries that emerged after the dismantling of the empires of the Central Powers, such as Yugoslavia and Czechoslovakia, had no democratic traditions of their own; they also contained various, and often antagonistic, ethnic nationalities with historical links to the great continental powers. As for universal disarmament, none of the Allies was serious about reducing its arsenals and nor did the treaty clarify how many weapons should be decommissioned. Meanwhile, the forty-eight-member League of Nations, which was established to uphold peace, lacked an army and a navy. In their absence how could it police Europe effectively? The authority of the association was also undermined when the United States decided against joining, a retreat into isolation that was also a blow to Lloyd George's diplomatic strategy. Since Britain lacked the military and economic capacity to supervise the globe alone, it required the assistance of the world's emerging superpower. In the absence of a transatlantic alliance, Britain would be weaker and more isolated. It is unsurprising that English diplomats returned from Versailles in pessimistic mood. 'If this was a war to make the world safe for democracy, it has failed,' commented Lord Eustace Percy. 'If it was a war to end war, it has left the future of the world more uncertain and more contentious.'

After signing the Versailles Treaty in June 1919, Lloyd George returned to an England barely recognizable from the one he had left. In the six months it had taken the Allies to share out the spoils of war, England's economic boom had lost its momentum. 'The whole thing came to an end, like the stopping of a clock,' remembered Charles Masterman. The underlying cause of the recession was the international competition faced by Britain's heavily indebted and technologically antiquated shipbuilding, coal and cotton industries. Meanwhile, the United States was enjoying the benefits of a technological revolution, based on automated machinery and new methods of management which ensured low-cost mass production. The native industries of India, Canada and South Africa were also flourishing. As British imports had not reached these imperial territories during the war, they had become self-sufficient. Engineering projects within the empire could now be carried out by local companies, and their products were more competitively priced. International demand for British produce was also affected by economic chaos on the Continent. How could the German people afford expensive British goods during the hyperinflation of the early Twenties?

Britain's staple industries had received substantial investment during the war, and this was followed by an avalanche of orders in the immediate post-armistice period. Eight million tons of shipping lost in the conflict had to be replaced, and the shipbuilding, steel and iron giants had expanded to meet the demand. Yet wartime investment and post-war demand disguised the inherent weakness of these industries, as well as the serious damage done to the economy by the conflict. The country's preoccupation with war had also offered the United States – which had been neutral from 1914 to 1917 – the opportunity to take over many of her customers. When government investment stopped, and the rush of post-war orders ended, Britain's industries found themselves with a stockpile of expensive goods that no one wanted to buy. Total British exports were 20 per cent lower than they had been before the war, and Britain's share of the world export market fell to 11 per cent, below that of the United States. To compound these problems, lavish post-war spending had stimulated inflation, and the government raised interest rates to keep prices under control. This discouraged borrowing and spending, and so reduced internal demand; it also meant that money borrowed in the low-interest boom time would have to be paid back at higher rates. In consequence, many banks were overextended and many businesses collapsed.

Britain's industrial activity and gross domestic product fell precipitately in 1920–21 and there was a sudden rise in unemployment. By the summer of 1921, unemployment in Britain exceeded 2 million (around 20 per cent of the working population). Long queues of men outside labour exchanges became a familiar sight in the old industrial centres of northern England. Among those waiting in line were many ex-soldiers, who came to the conclusion that the country they had fought for neither needed nor wanted them. 'If they'd told me in France that I should come back to this,' commented one former private, 'I wouldn't have believed it. Sometimes I wish to God the Germans had knocked me out.'

In a bid to avoid industrial and political unrest Lloyd George acted quickly, extending unemployment insurance in 1920 to all those who earned under five pounds per week. The following year he allowed the unemployed to continue to draw benefit beyond the maximum period allowed under the insurance scheme, as long as they could prove that they were genuinely seeking employment. The extension was necessary because people were now out of work for long periods. Yet Lloyd George's decisiveness could not prevent protests and industrial action. In 1921 the first Hunger March from London to Brighton was organized by the recently formed National Unemployed Workers' Movement. In 1920 and 1921 engineers, miners, railway workers, cotton spinners, shipyard workers and even the police went on strike for better job security and the maintenance of wages. In 1921 alone, 85 million working days were lost to industrial action.

The government feared that strikes might coalesce into one general strike that would bring the economy to a standstill. Lloyd George drew up plans for such an eventuality, which included the creation of a Defence Force of 75,000 men that would police the protests, run public transport and distribute food. The authorities were anxious. 'The people grow discontented,' remarked King George. 'Riot begets revolt and possibly revolution.' The elite had good reason to be fearful. The Soviet Workers' State inspired sympathy in the left-wing press, and communist movements seemed on the verge of achieving power in Italy and Germany. In 1920 a British Communist party was established, its very existence encouraging the belief that capitalism was on the verge of collapse. Most economists did not share this view, but many had lost faith in the system's power to improve living standards and reduce inequality.

Yet as the crisis continued into 1921, the prospect of a revolution receded. At the beginning of the year, the resolve of the strikers appeared to weaken; the government enfeebled it further through a combination of threats, empty promises and the offer of slightly higher wages and shorter hours. Lloyd George was in a strong bargaining position; high unemployment meant that no alternative employment was available to the striking workers – the choice was between accepting the employers' terms or semi-starvation on the dole. The prime minister had strengthened his position further at the end of 1920 by introducing an Emergency Powers Act: the coalition was now empowered to govern by decree should there be the threat of industrial action. In the circumstances, the strikers had little choice but to back down, and a general strike in support of the miners planned for 15 April was called off. The date became known as 'Black Friday', because many on the left regarded it as the last day on which a war against the capitalists and the government might have been fought and won.

Lloyd George emerged victorious from his battle with the Labour movement, but it was a pyrrhic victory. The alliance he had struck up with the unions during the war was broken beyond repair, and he could no longer pose as a 'man of the people'. What chance did he and his coalition Liberals have of luring working-class voters away from Labour, at a time when they were increasingly disappointed by the government's failure to deliver on its promise to build a 'fit country for heroes to live in'? While some progressive measures had been implemented, the most ambitious government projects were scaled down when the economic slump intervened. The 1919 Housing Act had offered local authorities the funds to build over 200,000 rental homes, yet when the slump arrived the building came to an abrupt halt with only half of the houses constructed.

In the middle of the slump, the coalition's Unionist majority reminded the prime minister that national debt stood at £8,000 million – forty times higher than it had been in 1914. To the Unionists the slump was an opportunity to reduce the debt through public spending cuts, though this would have the effect of increasing unemployment and reducing aggregate demand in the economy. The alternative of raising income tax further seemed illogical, since Unionists regarded the rich as the productive classes on whom the economy depended. Allying itself with the popular 'Anti-Waste' campaign, which espoused the creed of efficiency and economy in government, the Unionist party promoted an emergency austerity programme that served as cover for their ideological aim of reducing public spending and general state intervention. Bowing to pressure, Lloyd George created a committee of businessmen to decide where the cuts should be made. The chosen victims included education, health and pensions, with the cuts amounting to £85 million. Labour politicians were quick to point out the prime minister's hypocrisy: the man who posed as 'the people's champion' had made the working class pay the nation's debts.

16

England's Irish question

While industrial action continued in England, another crisis broke out in Ireland. In truth Ireland had been in a permanent state of crisis ever since the Home Rule emergency of 1912–14, with the Easter Rising of 1916 followed by the anti-conscription protests of 1918. In 1919, the Sinn Féin-dominated Dáil in Dublin proclaimed a second Irish Republic, independent from the United Kingdom. Britain refused to acknowledge either the Republic or the Dáil, and ostensibly still oversaw the administration of the country from Dublin Castle. Yet the Dáil proceeded to bypass Britain's colonial administration; they imposed taxes on the Irish people, directed local authorities and established their own courts of justice, police force and military, which was known as the Irish Republican Army (IRA).

This was a challenge to the empire, which at that point covered around a quarter of the earth's land and incorporated a quarter of the world's population. Yet the first two decades of the twentieth century had demonstrated that empire's vulnerability, as well as Britain's diminishing military and economic power. The Boer War and the Great War had severely tested the empire, while imperialism as an ideology was also under threat. The president of the United States had enshrined the principle of national self-determination in the Versailles Treaty, which encouraged many of Britain's imperial territories to demand more autonomy. Independence movements flourished in Burma and Egypt, as well as in Ireland.

In India the National Congress was gaining in popularity under the leadership of Mohandas Karamchand 'Mahatma' Gandhi, a former London lawyer who demanded dominion status for the country. The Government of India Act 1919 increased the involvement of native Indians in provincial councils, which were given greater powers. But it was not enough to convince the population of the legitimacy of continued British rule; social tensions remained high, and martial law was imposed. The consequences of this decision were immediate. On 13 April 1919, large numbers of Sikhs gathered in a garden in Amritsar to celebrate a religious festival and stage a political protest. Following the orders of Colonel Dyer, British troops covered the exits of the garden and opened fire on the unarmed crowd. According to the colonel, it was not 'a question of merely dispersing the crowd, but one of producing a sufficient moral effect from a military point of view' throughout India. Between 380 and 1,000 people were killed.

Dyer received praise from Tories in parliament and in the press for 'saving the Empire'. Although he was eventually dismissed from the army, a public collection for him raised £26,000. Anger at the killings spread throughout India. How could the English now claim to bring civilization to their 'benighted' subjects? In 1906 the British viceroy of India had spoken of 'subduing' the people of India, 'not to the law of the sword but to the rule of justice'; now those words sounded hollow. In the aftermath of the massacre, many more Indians decided to support the National Congress. The incident marked the beginning of the end of British rule.

It was within the context of an overstretched and anxious empire that events in Ireland unfolded. Ireland was nominally part of the United Kingdom; its proximity made it vital to England's security and prosperity. Unlike India, Egypt or Burma, the country had been under English influence since the twelfth century. Among those most concerned by the rise of Irish nationalism were the Unionists who dominated Lloyd George's government; during the Home Rule crisis of 1912–14 they had zealously defended the interests of Protestant Unionists in north-east Ulster, even at the risk of civil war. The Ulster Unionists now lived in a de facto Irish republic, governed from Dublin by men who were from a different political, ethnic and sectarian tradition. The administrative control of the new republic did not extend to the north-east of Ulster, where the presence of British forces remained high, but there was no guarantee the situation would not change.

The Irish nationalist movement was composed of diverse elements, with differing aims. Many in Sinn Féin espoused independence from Britain, to be secured by peaceful methods where possible. On the other hand, the recently formed IRA was ready to fight the British and defend the recently proclaimed republic by force. The army was led by Michael Collins, who had a genius for military strategy.

The power and reach of Britain's colonial administration was now diminished. Effective imperial government depended on the collaboration of the Irish population – on post office workers, tax collectors, local government officials and policemen – and the majority of them had voted for Sinn Féin. Judging that the time was now right to challenge British rule with force, the IRA declared war on the colonial government, thus beginning the 'War of Independence'. Collins had learned from the failed Easter Rising that defeating the British by conventional military means was unrealistic; his plan was instead to make imperial rule in Ireland impossible. The IRA embarked on a series of guerrilla attacks on the personnel of the British state, 'executing' eighteen members of the Irish police force towards the end of 1919. The campaign was facilitated by Irish collaborators within the imperial police force and intelligence agency, and by countless members of the population who shielded the nationalist gunmen.

The success of the IRA campaign convinced the British government that its grip on Ireland was loosening, and its response was brutal. Lloyd George declared Sinn Féin illegal, appointed a draconian Irish chief secretary and recruited British ex-soldiers to 'police' Ireland. The unemployed ex-soldiers were promised '£15 a week . . . plenty of girls and lashings to drink' as payment for destroying the IRA and quelling Irish nationalism. They formed a 'terror squad' and became known as the 'Black and Tans', a name that reflected the colour of their uniforms and recalled a breed of hunting hound. They proceeded to live up to their name by hunting down, kidnapping, torturing and executing suspects, raiding houses, looting shops and setting fire to entire villages.

The IRA responded by targeting the Black and Tans, while many civilians were caught in the crossfire. At Croke Park in Dublin on 21 November 1920, the Tans opened fire on a crowd watching a Gaelic football match. Twelve people were killed and sixty wounded on what became known as 'Bloody Sunday'. The British chief secretary claimed the forces had acted in self-defence, but it was in fact an act of revenge for the IRA's killing of twelve British intelligence agents and members of its forces earlier in the day.

The Croke Park massacre and other atrocities undermined any moral or legal authority the British might try to claim in Ireland. British brutality also inspired further popular support for nationalism, which undermined the numerical advantage the British forces enjoyed over the IRA. As reports of British cruelty reached England, and as the death toll rose to over 1,000 (in a population of only 3 million), the liberal English press and intelligentsia increasingly sympathized with Irish nationalism and condemned the 'terroristic' methods of the coalition, which now declared martial law. George Bernard Shaw, an Irish dramatist and intellectual with considerable popularity in England, drew a parallel between the Black and Tans terror and the Amritsar massacre, and some of the English elite agreed with this analysis. 'Things are being done in Ireland,' Asquith told parliament, 'which would disgrace the blackest annals of the lowest despotism in Europe.' 'Are you going to shoot all the people in Ireland?' King George asked Lloyd George. When the prime minister shook his head, the king continued, 'Well, then you must come to some agreement with them. This thing cannot go on.'

At first, Lloyd George had defended the Black and Tans as 'bravely' defending the 'civilisation' of a 'glorious' empire from the threat of 'terrorism'. Yet eventually he was forced to admit that 'mistakes' had been made by 'a certain number of undesirables'. He was also compelled to pursue a more constructive policy. He introduced a fourth Home Rule Bill, officially called the Government of Ireland Act, which was passed at the end of 1920. By the terms of the act, one Home Rule parliament was established in Dublin, and another in Belfast to oversee the six counties of Ulster with substantial Protestant populations. Representatives of these two bodies would meet in a Council of Ireland, while a reduced number of Irish MPs would continue to sit in Westminster. The country would continue to acknowledge the ultimate authority of the British monarch and his representative in Ireland, the Lord Lieutenant.

Unsurprisingly, this compromise satisfied none of the interested parties. The Irish nationalists did not recognize the Dublin Home Rule parliament and instead continued to convene the Dáil; the Ulster Unionists refused to acknowledge the Council of Ireland. The Unionists did, however, accept the new parliament in Belfast, despite their objection to Home Rule. Following the passing of the act, elections were held for both Home Rule parliaments. The Unionists won an 80 per cent majority in the 'six counties' in Ulster, while Sinn Féin claimed virtually every seat in the south. These results merely served to confirm the stalemate; they also exacerbated sectarian divisions, as violence spread throughout Ulster. Thousands of Catholics were forcibly evacuated from Belfast housing estates and anti-Catholic discrimination was common on the streets. The IRA, meanwhile, killed Protestant policemen in the 'six counties', while the Dáil decided to boycott trade between the 'north' and 'south'.

Yet some good came out of the elections. When King George travelled to Belfast to open the northern Home Rule parliament, he called for 'the end of strife amongst [Ireland's] people, whatever their race or creed'. The monarch's words were followed by a truce, along with talks in London for a peace treaty. The chances of finding a compromise solution remained slim – the nationalists demanded an independent republic for all Ireland, while the Tory-dominated coalition was determined to preserve the 'integrity of the Empire' as well as the interests of the Unionists of Ulster, who were once again threatening civil war. 'If you are unable to protect us from the machinations of Sinn Féin,' Carson warned the government, 'we will take the matter into our own hands. At all costs, and notwithstanding the consequences.'

Lloyd George offered the nationalist delegation dominion status for the twenty-six counties outside of the six counties of Ulster with substantial Protestant populations. The southern dominion, to be called the 'Irish Free State', would be self-governing and free from British forces; members of its parliament would, however, still swear an oath of allegiance to the British monarch as official head of state. The six counties in Ulster, meanwhile, were offered the right to remain part of the United Kingdom under the name 'Northern Ireland'. Privately, though, Lloyd George promised the nationalists that the boundary would be drawn in such a way that the six-county northern state would be politically and economically unworkable; Northern Ireland would, he implied, soon have to join the Irish Free State. The prime minister also confirmed his acceptance of a de facto united Irish dominion by officially designating the treaty a settlement 'between Great Britain and Ireland'.

Tempering these private promises with the threat of renewed hostilities, Lloyd George badgered and bullied the nationalist representatives into signing the treaty on 6 December 1921. Collins realized that it did not represent 'the ultimate freedom that all nations desire and develop to', yet believed it gave Ireland the 'freedom to achieve' that position. Most people in Ireland greeted the news that agreement had been reached with relief, yet the treaty's critics argued that it opened up the near certainty of partition. Éamon de Valera refused to take an oath of allegiance to the British king and resigned as Dáil president soon after; Sinn Féin split into pro- and anti-treaty factions. These two groupings would fight a civil war that would last for around a year and claim 2,000 lives – a bloody beginning for the new 'free' state.

Immediately after the signing of the treaty, the Ulster Unionists opted out of the Free State. The 'territory', 'province' or 'region' of Northern Ireland was thereby established, and the union to which England belonged became 'The United Kingdom of Great Britain and Northern Ireland'. As the civil war raged in the south, the Unionists consolidated their power within Northern Ireland. They shaped electoral constituencies to guarantee clear Protestant majorities, and passed a Special Powers Act that gave the Unionist police the power to search and imprison Catholics without trial. The question of where the boundary would be drawn remained undecided for the duration of the Irish Civil War. After that conflict had ended, the impoverished Irish Free State, now led by De Valera, officially accepted the treaty and renounced its claim to govern the two Catholic-nationalist majority 'Northern Irish' counties of Fermanagh and Tyrone. In return the British government cancelled Ireland's debts to the British Empire. The British Boundary Commission of 1925 would confirm Northern Ireland's status as a six-county state.

In the long term, the treaty and partition failed to solve England's 'Irish question'. Over the succeeding decades, Unionist-dominated Northern Ireland would oppress its Catholic population, creating resentment both north and south of the border. That border would become a focus for attacks by the IRA, whose aim was to end partition and expel British forces from Irish soil. The Irish Free State, meanwhile, would last for a mere fifteen years, after which the Dáil renounced Ireland's dominion status and proclaimed the sovereignty of 'Éire' under a new constitution.

In the days following the 1921 treaty, Lloyd George was praised by his Liberal coalition colleagues for breaking the ten-year stalemate in Ireland, and for ending decades of uncertainty over the country's constitutional status. Many on the right, meanwhile, looked forward to reaping the benefits of the new electoral dispensation, which ensured that a majority of Unionists would be returned to Westminster from Northern Ireland, while no Liberal-leaning Irish MPs from the south would sit in the Commons. Liberated from Irish issues, many Unionists started referring to themselves again as 'Conservatives' or 'Tories', and the old name of 'the Conservative party' was eventually restored.

Yet not everyone in the Conservative party welcomed the developments in Ireland. Fifty or so 'die-hard' Tory Unionists denounced the treaty as a betrayal of the Protestants living in the Irish Free State. They argued that a series of IRA terror attacks in Northern Ireland and London proved that Lloyd George had not settled the 'Irish question', openly criticizing the prime minister and attempting to turn their fellow Tories against him. While the majority of Tories continued to support Lloyd George, their enthusiasm for the coalition ebbed; when he started selling countless peerages and knighthoods for his own personal gain, it evaporated. 'Bronco Bill' Sutherland, an associate of the prime minister, would trawl London's clubs and offer plutocrats baronetcies for around £10,000. One hundred and thirty baronetcies were sold in this way, along with 26 peerages and almost 500 knighthoods.

All governments sold honours in this way, and the Tories happily took some of the proceeds. What irritated them was that most of the money went to Lloyd George's personal fund, since he was a politician without an official party. Besides, offering honours so indiscriminately made a mockery of a system designed to glorify and perpetuate the British ruling class, as well as the British Empire and the monarch who reigned over it. It is hardly surprising that George V accused his prime minister of 'debasing' the whole system, a charge that did not trouble the egalitarian Lloyd George. Yet many Conservatives took the king's view, and began looking among their own ranks for a potential replacement.

There was, however, time for one last adventure. Lloyd George attempted to gain popular backing for British military intervention in support of Greece in its struggle against a resurgent Turkey. The Turks showed no desire to provoke the British forces into war, and the incident served only to emphasize how isolated Britain was and how overstretched its empire had become. Stanley Baldwin, an MP rising rapidly through the Conservative ranks, denounced Lloyd George at a Tory party meeting as a 'terrible dynamic force' that might split the Tories. It was time for the Tories to break away from the coalition, form a government and then fight an election under their own leader and on their own platform.

Buoyed by a recent by-election victory and encouraged by continuing division among the Liberals, the majority of Conservative MPs agreed with Baldwin. They had had enough of 'the Welsh attorney' 'dictating' to their party. Yet Austen Chamberlain, who had recently become party leader when Law had retired owing to ill health, took a different view; a split within the Conservative party seemed possible. After the vote of no confidence in the coalition Chamberlain resigned from the cabinet, followed by Lloyd George. The news of the resignations improved Law's health significantly, and he took over the leadership of a caretaker Tory government. He would remain in power briefly while parliament was dissolved and a general election called.

When Lloyd George resigned, King George remarked that he would soon be prime minister again. Law and Asquith were too old to lead the country and MacDonald's opportunity had not yet come, while Churchill belonged to the coalition Liberals who had lost their raison d'être. Yet without a powerful party to support him, there would never be a return to Downing Street for Lloyd George. The Tories thus tethered the Liberal scapegoat, before leading him out into the wilderness.

17

Gay as you like

If events in Ireland suggested the empire was breaking up, strikes across England suggested that society was breaking down. Unrest, discontent and division pervaded the country, while memories of the carnage on the Western Front were still vivid. It is hardly surprising that social and cultural life in the Twenties was characterized by confusion, pessimism and disquietude, yet there were also signs of vitality and exhilaration. Many would describe the decade as a time during which youth rebelled against their elders and attempted to forget the past.

Along with the flappers, the most famous revellers of the period were the bohemian aristocratic sets known as the 'bright young things'. They largely comprised rich young hooligans from Oxbridge and the older public schools, along with their girlfriends and acquaintances. According to Evelyn Waugh's *Vile Bodies*, the novel that immortalized them, their chief purpose was to party: 'masked parties, savage parties, Victorian parties, Greek parties, Wild West parties, Russian parties, Circus parties, almost naked parties in St John's Wood, parties in ships and hotels and night clubs, in windmills and swimming baths'. This last gathering was the famous 'Bath and Bottle party' at St George's swimming baths in London, where flowers and rubber horses floated on water illuminated by coloured spotlights. The guests, dressed in dazzling swimming costumes, drank 'Bathwater Cocktails' and danced to the strains of a black jazz orchestra, sometimes hurling themselves into the pool.

At these parties the transgressive infantilism of the set was given full and eccentric expression. The elder brothers, cousins, uncles and fathers of the bright young things had reached adulthood before the war, and many were now maimed, scarred or dead. Why should the young generation follow in footsteps that had led to the mass grave of the Western Front? The defiance of the group was also tinged with guilt at having been too young to die beside their older relatives.

The parties tended to be informal, crammed, wild and noisy. Obscenity and excess were the keynotes, as partygoers enjoyed sex, gin and 'uppies' (cocaine). The young hooligans also partied at breakneck speed: 'they rush from one restaurant and party to another,' a contemporary noted, 'to a third and fourth in the course of an evening, and finish up with an early morning bathing party, transported at 60 mph to the swimming baths of Eton, or a race down the Great West Road.' The young hedonists zigzagged across country roads 'at high speed, under the influence of drink, in the hope, if there was a smash, that the case would be reported in the Sunday newspapers'.

The escapades of the young aristocrats were the hysterical last hurrah of that class. Having lost its grip on the Commons and its veto in the Lords, the aristocracy no longer dominated British politics. In economic terms, too, the caste was in decline. Taxes on land had been historically high during the war; after the armistice the Central Land-Owners Association demanded the exchequer repeal them. Yet the anti-establishment Lloyd George maintained the land tax, and almost 50 per cent of country houses and 8 million acres of land were put on the market between 1918 and 1922. Over the decade that followed, the atrophy continued. By the time the American-born Tory MP Henry 'Chips' Channon visited a number of the old great houses in the Thirties, he was overwhelmed by 'the feel and smell of decay, of aristocracy in extremis'. There had perhaps been no greater change at the summit of English society since the Norman Conquest.

While the aristocracy was diminished in political and economic terms, its members remained influential in the creation of society's crazes and fashions. Their influence was strong in the arts, where some of the set promoted 'modernism'. That artistic movement was characterized by a conscious rejection of classical styles, and an interest in forms and themes appropriate to an urbanized and industrialized society. The children of privilege promoted avant-garde trends in music and painting, such as jazz and cubism, while in literature they championed the radical innovations of the 'Bloomsbury Group'.

Virginia Woolf was Bloomsbury's best and boldest novelist. The stream-of-consciousness style she employed in *Mrs Dalloway* (1925) oscillates between direct and indirect speech, interior monologue and soliloquy. Like the bright young people, Woolf rebelled against the formal conventions and the ethos of the Edwardian period – a 'fatal age', according to her, 'when character disappeared'. Meanwhile, T. S. Eliot, an American associate of the Bloomsbury Group, dramatized the disintegration of Western civilization during the war in his long poem *The Waste Land* (1922). In its deep ambiguities and elisions, and in its fragmented form, Eliot's poem reflected the post-war period with all its anxieties, fears for the future and mournful memories. Many of the first readers of *The Waste Land* struggled to find meaning in its plethora of voices, styles, allusions and images, yet the poem was written to be uttered rather than understood. The bright young people heard the poem's plangent music and realized that its rhythms and melodies were more important than its 'meaning'.

Eliot occasionally attended parties organized by the bright young things, as did other Bloomsbury authors, such as Lytton Strachey. In newspaper interviews Strachey expressed sympathy with the set's 'struggle' against the older generation and its harmful 'taboos and restrictions'. His comments offer an insight into both the psychology of the bright young people, and the author's own modernist tract, *Eminent Victorians* (1918). Strachey's collection of biographical essays – or rather assassinations – had been written in the war, during which the author was a conscientious objector. Instead of writing the earnest, exhaustive and exhausting biographies favoured by the Edwardians and Victorians, Strachey penned short, sprightly and ironic portraits. His purpose was to attack his subject in 'unexpected places [and] shoot a sudden, revealing searchlight into obscure recesses'. To achieve those ends Strachey drew upon the psychoanalytical theories of Sigmund Freud. In *Eminent Victorians* Strachey poured scorn on the Victorian values of Christianity and imperial service that had been espoused by a generation of 'mouthing bungling hypocrites'. Those values had helped bring about the war, he implied, yet they were still being adhered to by the older generation.

Some of the bright young men also ridiculed pre-war ideas and ideals of masculinity. Beards, moustaches and pipes were discarded as outmoded emblems of male pomposity. The new men favoured clean-shaven faces, and brushed back their oiled hair. They sported outlandish, self-parodic costumes that were as far away as possible from Edwardian male seriousness. And, just as the flappers had appropriated masculine fashion, the bright young men purloined clothes traditionally associated with women: 'nowadays,' as one of them remarked, 'boys are *girlish*.' They wore wide trousers called 'Oxford bags', which billowed around the legs and came in light, bright shades. The suede shoes and high-necked pullovers favoured by the men likewise featured soft colours; they were the first males ever to don pink shirts. Their waistcoats were flamboyant and their evening dress was embellished with patterns. They wore attractive wristwatches and constantly consulted them with a flourish of the forearm. As a result, wristwatches became associated with effeminacy; men who did not meet acceptable standards of masculinity were referred to as 'terribly wristwatch' or as having 'a wristwatch accent'. An effeminate enunciation and vocabulary was cultivated by bright young men. 'My dear, how could you!' they would exclaim. Their effeminate argot was brought to the stage by Noël Coward, whose plays enjoyed success towards the end of the decade.

Some of the bright young men were effeminate, some were homosexual and some were both. Of American descent, Brian Christian de Claiborne Howard grew up despising his father and adoring his mother. Tall, pale, aloof and flamboyant, Howard swaggered his way from Eton and Christ Church college, Oxford, to the West End, leaving a trail of pink champagne bottles and quotable utterances in his wake. He planned spoof art exhibitions, elaborate practical jokes, and parties at which he would cut a dashing figure in cross-dress or historical costumes. Some of Howard's historical parties had themes such as 'Homosexual Lovers Through the Ages', a daring idea when the laws that had condemned Oscar Wilde to two years' hard labour were still on the statute book. Howard was a dandy like Wilde, and together they established the figure as a gay archetype. Evelyn Waugh admired Howard's 'dash and insolence', but others were less than enthralled by his self-centredness and melancholy. As the years passed, he became increasingly morose, like so many of the bright young people. He wallowed in lost youthful promise and in the fading of his gilded youth, like a goldfish in a emptying pool.

And indeed, even at the height of their gay abandon, melancholy pervaded the hedonistic parties of the age. When their infantile indulgences began to pall, these spoiled children were paralysed by tedium. 'Bored young faces' peer out at us from the pages of Waugh's *Vile Bodies*, emanating a 'sense of desolation, of uncertainty, of futility'. Another novelist, Richard Aldington, detected the same air of despondency: 'all night the restless feet stamped . . . and the joyless rejoiced without joy; and at dawn, when the wind breathed an immense sigh . . . You could almost hear the rattle of the bones in this macabre pageant.' The image of the desolate dawn was commonplace in eyewitness accounts of parties, suggesting a foreboding for the future as well as an inability to dance away the memory of the recent conflict. It is telling that Waugh's portrait of the group, *Vile Bodies*, ends on the battlefield of a future war.

18

Labour at the summit

Lloyd George's fall from power was followed by a decisive Conservative victory at the 1922 election. According to some commentators, Law won the election for the simple reason that he was not Lloyd George. 'A drummer boy is an asset in battle,' the taciturn Tory leader told voters during the campaign, 'but he and his drum are a nuisance in peacetime.' British voters agreed; their desire was for the 'tranquillity' and 'stability' Law promised. According to Stanley Baldwin, now elevated to the Exchequer, the electorate also voted for honesty, a quality Lloyd George signally lacked.

In fact, it was more complicated. The election result was a rebellion made in the shadow of the war. Four years after the armistice, the conflict and its consequences were still the central issues of politics, and the Tories won the election by proposing to govern as though it had never happened. Law declared that he would give free scope to the initiative and enterprise of the people, by reining in the power of the state. His call for minimum interference by the government heralded the end of 'war socialism', and of Lloyd George's ambitious plans to rebuild a better country. The Tories also claimed victory courtesy of the new electoral dispensation in Ireland and the bias of a voting system which inflated their 38 per cent of the popular vote into 56 per cent of the parliamentary seats.

Yet despite its secure majority, the government lacked strength and stability. Austen Chamberlain declined to join Law's government, along with various other 'Conservative coalitionists'. Meanwhile, Law's health was failing, and he resigned after only a few months in office. Who would replace the man Asquith had dubbed 'The Unknown Prime Minister'? Lord Curzon was regarded by many as the heir apparent. The patrician peer had been foreign secretary since 1919, and he had held office under both Balfour and Salisbury. With his experience, background and air of authority, Curzon believed himself to be destined for the leadership.

Yet the party of the old aristocracy overlooked the autocratic lord for Stanley Baldwin, the son of an iron and steel magnate, and a member of the Commons. The choice was a sign of the ascendancy of the lower house at Westminster and indicated how far power had shifted to the businessmen within the Tory party. Despite his relative inexperience, Baldwin had the confidence of the City and of the commercial sector. Tory grandees complained that their party was being vulgarized by the advent of the plutocracy Baldwin represented, but their caste no longer dominated the party or the country. With characteristic pragmatism and shrewdness, Baldwin acknowledged the aristocracy's cultural power by posing as a countrified businessman, yet it is notable that he promoted talented men from the middling rank. The most significant appointment in his first government was Neville Chamberlain as minister of health and then as chancellor of the Exchequer.

The Tories' decision to back a businessman rather than an aristocrat brought few benefits in the short term. Baldwin had been instrumental in bringing down Lloyd George and was consequently distrusted by the coalition Conservatives. And then, only six months into his premiership, the prime minister had a Damascene conversion to Joseph Chamberlain's controversial protectionist programme. Since Baldwin felt he required a popular mandate to implement such a radical proposal, he called an election. The inexperienced prime minister believed he could attract recently enfranchised voters with the arguments Joseph Chamberlain had elaborated two decades previously: if tariffs were imposed on imports coming from outside the empire, then trade would be boosted within it; this would protect jobs at home and revive England's ailing industries. It would also raise revenue without the need to increase taxes. At the same time, the embattled empire would be transformed into a single economic unit with free trade inside its frontiers.

A new generation of voters, however, showed little enthusiasm for the old Chamberlainite cocktail of economic reform, social legislation and imperialism. At the 1923 election, the Tories lost 86 Commons seats. Although they remained the largest party in parliament, they had failed to win a popular mandate for protectionism; with his flagship policy rejected, Baldwin was reluctant to form a government. Neville Chamberlain, faithful to Baldwin and to his father's memory, blamed the defeat on 'the new electorate', while Curzon attributed it to Baldwin's 'utter incompetence'. Yet Baldwin somehow survived as leader – the first of the many escapes that would characterize his career. That was partly due to a lack of alternative leadership candidates, but it was also because his espousal of protectionism and of 'Tory democracy' had positive side effects. It united the Conservative party and nudged the Tories towards the centre ground of politics. In an increasingly democratic era, that was an advantageous position for the party of privilege to occupy.

The real story of the 1922 and 1923 elections, however, was the rise of Labour. The party claimed 142 seats in 1922 (up 80 from the previous parliament), and 191 seats in 1923. This figure compared favourably to the 115 seats of a Liberal party which had recently reunited under Asquith's leadership, and was 70 seats short of the Conservatives' total. Over the two elections Labour established itself as the main opposition to the Tories – two decades after its formation, the party of the 'have-nots' was close to having power. Among the causes of Labour's ascent, the widespread radicalism in post-war Britain and the party's broad appeal to the working and lower middle classes who had been enfranchised in 1918 played a significant part.

Labour represented the newly enfranchised classes in a literal sense, filling the benches of the 1922 and 1923 parliaments with men from the working and lower middle classes. The arrival of the 'masses' at Westminster led to a marked change in its etiquette. Plainly dressed MPs from northern English (and Scottish) constituencies favoured an impassioned 'soapbox' style when denouncing unemployment or expressing solidarity with the underprivileged.

On one occasion the new men broke out into a loud rendition of the party's socialist anthem, 'The Red Flag', to the horror of the Speaker who suspended the session. The *Morning Post* condemned such 'Bolshevist frightfulness', while the Conservatives denounced the song as a 'hymn of hate'.

Yet along with these radical working-class MPs, a new breed of middle-class Labour politician entered the Commons. None of the Labour MPs elected in 1918 had attended public school, and only one had attended university; the overwhelming majority had been working men sponsored by the unions. But in the 1923 parliament, there were nine ex-public school and twenty-one university-educated Labour men, while the union-sponsored MPs were no longer in the majority. Some of the new recruits were middle-class intellectuals with links to the Fabians and the old Independent Labour Party, such as Clement Attlee, an Oxford graduate who had fought at Gallipoli. Others had only recently joined Labour from the Liberals, out of despair at the ineffectiveness of their old party. Labour was no longer the protest party of a single class or the parliamentary wing of the unions – it was starting to resemble the socialist working- and middle-class alliance that Ramsay MacDonald had envisaged after the war.

It is entirely fitting that the party now chose MacDonald, who had returned to the Commons in 1922, as its leader. He was a much better parliamentarian than his rival in the leadership contest, the union man John Clynes, and he was also a public orator of genius. His lyricism inspired comparisons with Lloyd George, as did his sharp political intelligence and instinct for survival. If Labour had always been a party of protest and practical politics, MacDonald was a master of both.

Yet despite these qualities, MacDonald had won the leadership contest only by the narrowest of margins, and the revolutionary wing of the party would soon complain about the moderate brand of evolutionist socialism he espoused as party leader. He believed that social progress could be made through parliament alone; British society, he argued, had an 'enormous capacity to resist change', because of the strength of its 'inherited habits, modes of thought and traditions'. This inherent inertia meant that change could only be gradual. MacDonald believed that Labour might permanently replace the Liberal party as the main opposition to the Conservatives; a socialist utopia could wait for another day.

The 191 seats Labour won at the 1923 election made it the largest party to espouse free trade. Since voters favoured that policy over Tory protectionism, Labour had, Asquith declared, earned the right to govern the country with the support of his pro-free-trade Liberal party. Privately, the Liberal leader was hopeful that a minority Labour government would soon mutate into a free-trade coalition that he might lead. The 'wild' and 'beggarly' men who sat beside MacDonald on the front bench were, Asquith felt, likely to bring down his feeble government. There was a sense among the political elite that a Labour administration was inevitable, and that it could not be tried under safer conditions. Baldwin and Chamberlain espoused this argument – a minority Labour government 'would be too weak to do much harm', the latter commented, 'but not too weak to get discredited'.

Even so, some prominent members of society were appalled by the idea of Labour governing the country. When the idea of a Labour administration was mooted, there was considerable nervousness over the prospect of a socialist 'power grab'. The City and the press echoed the establishment's fear and anger, and Asquith received 'appeals, threats and prayers from all parts to step in and save the country from the horrors of socialism and confiscation'. Yet in the end the Liberal leader and his Tory counterpart decided that their parties ought not to stand in the way of MacDonald's men, in case it provoked outrage in the country.

Would Labour accept what might turn out to be a poisoned chalice? Many in the movement advised against doing so, for fear that a minority government was bound to fail. Others warned that the party of idealistic socialism would be tainted by an inherently conservative political system. Yet MacDonald argued that it was only by accepting office that Labour could prove it was 'fit to govern'. They must, he said, demonstrate that they could work within the existing political framework. If they rejected the opportunity, they would risk losing all of the electoral gains they had made since the war. In the end, MacDonald's view prevailed.

And so Britain had its first ever Labour government, to the trepidation and astonishment of some party purists. One member of the new government remarked on the 'strange turn of Fortune's wheel' that had brought a 'starveling clerk' (MacDonald), a foundry labourer (Henderson) and 'Clynes the mill hand' to receive the seals of office from the king at Buckingham Palace, and George V himself was no less astonished: 'I wonder what Grandmama [Victoria] would have thought of a Labour Government,' he commented. Nevertheless, the king was impressed with the new prime minister who, he felt, 'wishes to do the right thing'. In fact, the apparently ill-matched pair struck up a friendship that would prove to be an enduring one. So far as King George was concerned, the 'socialist' MacDonald was an improvement on the discourteous Lloyd George and the 'indolent' Baldwin, while the Labour party was now much less of a menace to the crown, having expunged all traces of republicanism from its constitution in the early Twenties. As for MacDonald, the king's good opinion offered an entrée into society. In a development that perhaps did not bode well for harmony in the Labour party, some of MacDonald's backbenchers began to refer to their leader as 'Gentleman Mac'.

As a minority government, MacDonald's administration had no scope to introduce a radical social or economic programme, yet this may have suited the new prime minister's purposes. Although there was a majority of working-class men in the cabinet for the first time in history, MacDonald also selected various ex-Liberals and a number of aristocrats. He gave the key position of chancellor to Philip Snowden, who agreed with MacDonald that Labour should 'show the country we are not under the domination of the wild men'.

Accordingly, Snowden produced a budget in the Gladstonian rather than the socialist mould. He reduced food taxes and set aside money for the historic Wheatley Housing Act, by which half a million council houses would be built for low-paid workers. Yet the Labour chancellor was unwilling to increase the country's debt by using public spending to counteract unemployment, which remained stubbornly above 1 million. During one debate on the issue, the new minister of labour confessed that he could not 'produce rabbits out of a hat'.

Industrial action was an inevitable consequence of the parlous economic situation. The strikes forced Labour politicians to condemn as 'disloyal' and 'Communistic' protests with which they had formerly sympathized. They also had to refuse the demands of the very unions who funded them. Some trade unionists now openly defied the government; Ernest Bevin, leader of the Transport and General Workers' Union, refused to call off a strike when requested to do so by MacDonald, and there was also discontent among Labour backbenchers. Even middle-class MPs such as Attlee were disappointed by the party's failure to produce effective policies, and concerned by the disdain MacDonald displayed for some of his proletarian colleagues. Meanwhile, relations between the administration and Asquith's Liberals had also deteriorated, and without a majority in the Commons it was impossible to carry out parliamentary business.

Yet it was not internecine warfare or Asquith that brought down the government, but its supposed sympathy towards Soviet Russia. When MacDonald's administration signed a commercial treaty with the country and quashed the prosecution of a communist British journalist, there was shock and anger. But it was nothing compared to the furore that followed the publication of a letter from the Russian President of the Communist International, implicating the government in communist activities. The letter was a fairly obvious forgery, but following its publication in the *Daily Mail*, 'red peril' hysteria spread throughout the country. It was an early example of the domination of British democracy by the popular press, which would become even more pronounced over the course of the century. The controversy gave the Conservatives an opportunity to attack the weak government; MacDonald resigned, and an election was called.

The Conservatives were in a better position to fight an election in 1924 than they had been a year previously, with Baldwin's protectionist programme having united his party. Now the Tory leader made another astute move, dropping his unpopular Tariff Reform programme to deny the Liberals their traditional election cry of 'anti-protection'. He shrewdly declined to set out detailed policy proposals during the campaign, but instead concentrated on criticizing MacDonald and his ministers. With the help of their friends in the press, the Tories communicated a simple message to the electorate: 'a vote for Socialists is a vote for the Communists'.

At the election the Tories polled around 47 per cent of the

popular vote and gained 67 per cent of the seats in the Commons. Liberal voters had turned to the Tories in their thousands; Asquith's party lost 75 per cent of its seats and was reduced to a mere forty MPs, with the leader himself one of the casualties. Keynes predicted that the party would never again hold office but would instead become a political finishing school, supplying Labour with ideas and the Tories with ministers. Churchill would soon rejoin the Conservative party, retracing the steps he had made two decades previously. His desertion of the Liberal party was understandable. As an idealist intent on opposing socialism and promoting 'Tory democracy', it would have been pointless to remain. It was now obvious that the Liberals had no hope of challenging Labour as the main opposition party to the Tories: MacDonald's men had increased their share of the popular vote to 33 per cent.

The election finally delivered the political stability the Tories had promised voters after the fall of Lloyd George two years earlier. There had been three elections, three prime ministers and two leadership battles since then, but the political turbulence was stilled. Clear battle lines were now drawn between the Conservatives and Labour, who had between them obliterated the Liberals and nullified the influence of that party's mercurial genius Lloyd George. The two major parties were united under skilful leaders, both of whom had the experience of an unsuccessful term of government behind them. Given its superior resources, the backing of the press and the vagaries of the electoral system, it was inevitable that the Tory party would enjoy the larger share of power for the foreseeable future.

19

Where is the match?

Baldwin, now almost sixty, presented himself to the public as an unassuming country gentleman. On meeting him for the first time, few would have guessed that he came from a family with an industrial empire. The Tory leader would pause mid-sentence to take a long draw on his trademark pipe, a symbol of the Victorian rural world to which Baldwin constantly referred. In this bygone place, 'old gentlemen spent their days sitting on the handles of wheelbarrows smoking' while listening to 'the tinkle of the hammer on the anvil in the country smithy'. This was England before the strikes, the gas canisters and the disintegrating empire; a society in which everyone had a place and everyone knew what it was. Baldwin believed in the population's inherent love of the countryside and the domestic hearth. The English were, he thought, a nostalgic and conservative people, distinguished by the virtues of decency, modesty, justice and common sense.

'Master Stanley' claimed to have a second-class intellect, despite his education at Harrow and Cambridge. Yet first-class intellects, he claimed, were usually reluctant to follow instructions. Dangerous men of genius, such as Lloyd George, also made the mistake of believing they could solve problems through initiative. Far better to do nothing, the prime minister reckoned, or to cautiously react to events as they unfolded. The middle-class industrialist thus cast himself as the heir of Salisbury and Balfour; he provided a bridge between the plutocratic Tory party he led and the party of landed wealth over which his predecessors had presided.

When Baldwin took office, the king urged him to combat class war, but the Tory leader needed no urging. His vision of a harmonious England marked him out as a 'one-nation Tory' of the Disraelian school, while his Tariff Reform programme of 1923 demonstrated that he was also a 'Tory democrat' in the mode of Chamberlain and Randolph Churchill. He criticized Labour for exacerbating class division and struggle, while his party stood 'for the unity of the nation, and of all interests and classes within it'. He preferred to focus in speeches on potentially unifying issues, such as 'Englishness' or 'the countryside', rather than on controversial or divisive party-political matters. He also attempted to revive popular interest in the empire, and to associate his party with national institutions such as the monarchy and the Anglican Church. He had Baldwin's remarkable management skills, as well as that sense of timing which is indispensable to a successful politician. This self-effacing and ostentatiously average Englishman had known exactly when to strike Lloyd George, the pre-eminent politician of the age.

On entering Downing Street in 1924, Baldwin declared that his ambition was 'to bring about a unity of the nation', yet the nation he governed was characterized by class division. George Orwell would call England 'the most class-ridden country under the sun'. It was assumed that every aspect of an English person's character and life – his or her education, attire, health, opinions, pastimes, manners, aspirations, wages and pronunciation – depended on social position.

It was certainly true that the working classes were less healthy than people higher up the scale. When in work, they had to 'make do' with a low weekly cash wage out of which they paid rent. Moving above the crucial £250-per-year threshold and through the gradations of the middle class, monthly salaries were more common, along with the ownership of houses and motor cars and the employment of servants. In the final band were the upper classes who had a monopoly on the country's wealth. One per cent of the nation owned two-thirds of its assets.

Antagonism between the classes was acute and palpable. 'The upper class,' commented one Liberal MP, 'despise the working people: the middle class fear them.' The workers, with their collective bargaining power and readiness to strike, were a threat to those 'above' them. Manual workers appeared, to middle- and upper-class eyes, 'uncouth', 'filthy' and 'militant'; their wage 'demands' were seen as exorbitant, while the unemployment benefits that supported them when they were out of work seemed undeserved and costly.

There was also little solidarity between the upper and middle classes. Members of the upper class regarded the middling ranks as vulgar and insolent; their children were seldom permitted to play with 'such people', in case they picked up unfortunate habits. For their part, the middle classes were more critical of unearned upper-class wealth in the Twenties than perhaps at any other period in the century. The middling orders did, however, feel a residual awe for the waning aristocracy, and expressed this in an enthusiasm for the monarchy and the cultivation of upper-class accents. They also aspired to send their children to private schools, the 'engines of privilege' through which the upper class perpetuated their power. Meanwhile, both the middle and upper classes were resented by the workers. Baldwin was aware of 'a growing feeling of class consciousness' and a 'bitter antagonism running through the workshops, north and south, east and west', though he blamed it on the propaganda of the Labour party.

Class was not the only thing that divided the English – there was also the experience of the trenches. Those who had fought in the war and received scant reward for their suffering felt isolated from the rest of the population. 'All was not right with their spirit,' a journalist commented of working-class ex-privates. 'They were subject to queer moods, fits of depression alternating with a restless desire for pleasure . . . the daily newspapers have been filled with the record of dreadful crimes, of violence and passion . . . The murders of young women, the outrages upon little girls.' As usual, it was women who suffered the consequences of male alienation. As for the upper-middle-class and aristocratic officers, those who came home from the war found the old Edwardian guard still in charge of landed society, as though 'the great interruption' had never occurred.

Almost every facet of English life in the Twenties was marked by conflict between the generations. There was a sharp contrast between the regular church attendance of a portion of the older generation, for example, and the steep decline in churchgoing among the young. 'We are lukewarm in religion,' commented the young philosopher and radio broadcaster C. E. M. Joad, 'unimpressed by authority, distrustful of moral codes, and impatient of moral restraints.' Once more, the experience of war seems to have been decisive. Millions had prayed for peace, but their prayers had gone unanswered. What kind of God would sit by and watch such carnage? Besides, patriotic church ministers from all Christian denominations had encouraged the butchery; how could the young generation genuflect before them?

Baldwin's eldest son Oliver was one of the decade's angry young men. He had loathed his schooling at Eton, displaying a disdain for authority, discipline and tradition. Yet it was his experience of the Western Front that set him vehemently against 'the old men' who had 'betrayed the young'. After the war Baldwin urged his son to marry the daughter of one of his political allies, but Oliver told his father he was homosexual and moved in with his partner. In 1924, his struggle against his father was expressed in the most emphatic way imaginable when he stood as a Labour candidate at the general election.

If Baldwin was unable to unite his own family, how could he unify a divided country? Any serious attempt to heal national divisions would require more than soothing rhetoric. Yet transmuting words into deeds was not Baldwin's forte; he was better at setting the tone of government than he was at working out the finer points of policy. Nor were most MPs in his party enthusiastic about extending the role and power of central government. During the war the state had been omnipresent in the economy, but Conservatives believed those circumstances had been exceptional. In peacetime, the state's job was merely to 'hold the ring', allowing manufacturers to introduce their own innovations, employers to bargain with workers and the market to function. 'All the available evidence indicates,' one Tory commented, 'that State enterprise is inherently un-enterprising.' Another Conservative remarked that central government had its 'hand in all pockets and its rod on all backs'. Here we see the origins of the market-orientated, anti-state ideology that would dominate Conservative political and economic philosophy in the last quarter of the twentieth century.

Yet despite these unpromising foundations, Baldwin's government was more active than previous twentieth-century Tory administrations. That was partly due to the presence in the cabinet of the man Baldwin called 'the hundred-horsepower mind'. Although Churchill admitted to possessing a 'limited comprehension of technical matters', he had been rewarded with the exchequership by Baldwin. The prime minister hoped this onerous appointment would keep Churchill so busy that he would not interfere with other ministers; it was also intended to keep Churchill out of contact with the working classes, who had never forgiven him for sending troops to confront strikers during his time as Liberal home secretary.

In 1925 the chancellor made the momentous decision to return sterling to the gold standard, thereby linking the currency to Britain's gold reserves. During the war, exchange rate stability and currency convertibility had been abandoned, and Treasury notes had replaced gold coins, since the government had needed to print money to cover its extraordinary costs. But the inevitable consequence of increasing the amount of money in circulation was inflation. Wary of increasing prices, Lloyd George's coalition had announced that the gold standard would be restored in the mid-Twenties. Churchill, similarly concerned about the potential impact of inflation, decided that the economic conditions were right to fulfil this promise.

Yet in truth the 1925 Gold Standard Act was introduced for political rather than economic reasons. It drew a line under the years of war, intimating a return to the pre-1914 days of peace and plenty that Baldwin loved to evoke. Besides, the Treasury took the view that a failure to return to currency convertibility and exchange rate stability would 'suggest our nerve had failed'. Churchill decided to fix sterling's exchange value at the high pre-war rate of $4.86 – a lower exchange rate would imply that Britain's economy had been surpassed by America in the intervening decade, and that sterling could no longer 'look the dollar in the face'. Immediately after the passing of the act, the economic weather seemed favourable. Manufacturing production levels started rising slightly and unemployment began to fall. This gave Churchill the confidence to reduce supertax, to the delight of the plutocrats and gentry in his party. Yet he also increased public spending on education, health and housing, in accordance with his previous commitment to a 'New Liberal' social state and his current espousal of 'Tory democracy'.

Churchill was not the only cabinet member whose father had been a proponent of that 'one-nation' Tory creed. The new minister of health, Neville Chamberlain, was the son of Joseph, a Unionist famous for his commitment to domestic reform. 'He was a great social reformer,' Neville remarked of his father, 'and it was my observance of his deep sympathy with the working classes which inspired me with an ambition to do something in my turn.' Using the money Churchill made available to the health ministry – then responsible for housing, insurance, pensions and the poor law – the idealistic and indefatigable Chamberlain set about implementing welfare proposals directly inspired by his father's 'municipal socialism'. Over the next four years he introduced twenty-five acts that aimed 'to improve the conditions of the less fortunate'. He united health, insurance and poor law services under one umbrella, extended pensions and insurance, and greatly empowered local government. During the same period Chamberlain established himself as Baldwin's unofficial deputy; he also excelled in parliament, where his tenacious memory and grasp of policy detail inspired comparisons with Law.

The reserved and methodical Chamberlain admired, but did not entirely approve of, the flamboyant aristocrat over at the Exchequer. While the health minister admitted that Churchill was 'brilliant', his 'amorality', 'want of judgement' and 'furious advocacy of half-baked ideas' made him a 'very dangerous man'. Indeed, in many respects Churchill resembled Lloyd George, whom Chamberlain regarded as a false friend to the British nation, and the tempter of its electorate. For his part, Churchill was impressed by Chamberlain's proficiency but regarded him as narrow and unadventurous.

Yet while the pair were opposites in terms of character, they often worked in tandem on strategy. Together they also fostered an energetic and ambitious atmosphere within an otherwise undistinguished Tory cabinet. Enterprising policies were formulated, such as the establishment of a public Central Electricity Board to oversee electricity generation, distribution and investment. Although it was in effect a proposal for nationalization, the Tories preferred to call it 'rationalization'. The resulting 1926 Electricity (Supply) Act would unify 500 separate generating stations under a state monopoly, prompting a fourfold increase in electricity production over the next decade.

Another ambitious act of nationalization was the granting of a Royal Charter, in 1926, for the British Broadcasting Corporation. Run by a director general and a board of governors selected by the prime minister, and funded from licence fees paid by wireless owners, its news bulletins, weather forecasts, children's programmes, variety shows and coverage of national sporting events and state occasions soon reached every county of England. By the end of its first decade, the BBC would speak to people from every class, as technological advances reduced the price of the wireless.

Baldwin immediately grasped the possibilities offered by the new medium. With his clear syntax, crisp enunciation and evenness of tone, he became a master of the new art of broadcasting. It was said that he would take an audible drag on his pipe just before beginning a talk, so listeners would imagine him sitting next to them as they gathered around the wireless – the modern equivalent of the Victorian hearth. For the duration of Baldwin's broadcasts, England became the harmonious society that his words invoked.

The most significant bill passed by Baldwin's government was the 1928 Representation of the People (Equal Franchise) Act, which extended the franchise to all women over twenty-one, regardless of property ownership, and gave them electoral parity with men. It was a concession to the National Union of Women's Suffrage Societies, which vigorously campaigned for equality of voting rights throughout the Twenties. Although the bill was a cross-party measure, Baldwin convinced his party that the addition of almost 5 million women to the electorate would not be a threat to its re-election.

On the international as well as the domestic stage, Baldwin's utterances were often followed up by action. The British Empire Exhibition, which ran from 1924 to 1925 at Wembley in London, was a vast and expensive propaganda exercise. Crammed full of symbols promoting peace and unity within Britain's imperial territories, its official purpose was 'to strengthen bonds that bind Mother Country to her Sister States and Daughters'. Along with all the palaces dedicated to British engineering and artistic ingenuity, the military displays and the musical performances, there were pavilions in which each colony or dominion exhibited typical products and traditional artefacts. Visitors could traverse the entire globe in a few hours, via roads named after imperial heroes such as Sir Francis Drake. By displaying a powerful British 'mother country' at the centre of a vast empire, the exhibition also aimed to rekindle imperial pride among the English lower classes. This was not an easy task in a post-war period when imperialism was constantly attacked by intellectuals, and when separatist movements within the empire had enjoyed considerable success.

King George made a speech at the opening ceremony that was broadcast to an audience of over 10 million people, the first of many occasions on which the monarch used the medium to promote imperial unity. George expressed the hope that the exhibition would bring lasting benefits both to the empire and 'to mankind in general'. Concentrating on the former aim, the Tory government promoted self-government within the empire at the 1926 Imperial Conference of British Empire. The meeting reformulated the relationship between Britain, Canada, South Africa and the Irish Free State, defining these countries as 'autonomous Communities within the British Empire, equal in status, in no way subordinate one to another.' The imperial parliament no longer determined any aspect of the domestic or external affairs of these dominions, which were decided by their own elected bodies.

In 1926, a relatively liberal viceroy in India was appointed. Lord Irwin, who believed that India should eventually be given dominion status, quickly established a cordial relationship with Mahatma Gandhi. The Indian leader had recently been imprisoned on a charge of sedition, after coordinating a 'non-cooperation' campaign during which thousands of Indians boycotted British goods and institutions. Baldwin sensed that nationalism was becoming an irresistible force in India; the selection of Irwin as viceroy acknowledged the situation.

A powerful challenge to Baldwin's mission of conciliation would arrive soon enough. England's industrial and manufacturing sectors had long been in decline and exports had fallen further since the post-war slump. Churchill's decision to return to the gold standard had strengthened sterling and reduced import prices, but this made English exports even more expensive and harder to sell on international markets. In the country's heavily indebted and antiquated coal, shipbuilding, iron, steel and cotton industries, profits declined and workers were laid off. Arguments inevitably rose about the extent to which the state should intervene in the economy in order to protect industries and those who worked in them. The English population had been radicalized by the experience of war; so had the thinking of economists. John Maynard Keynes argued that the state should take an active role in the peacetime economy and that wages should be determined by a standard of equity rather than by the market. Meanwhile, Labour and the unions enjoyed increasing political power. In such a climate, the Tories could no longer argue that the laws of the market were sacrosanct.

Nevertheless, many producers were adamant that the only way to reduce export prices was to cut wages, while the unions argued that profits could be used to modernize the staple industries. In 1925 mine owners proposed wage reductions of around 13 per cent, and the miners' union called a strike. The Trades Union Congress was lukewarm about the industrial action but decided to support the miners, partly out of shame for its capitulation on 'Black Friday' four years previously and also in the hope that it might bring about a compromise: it would pressure the miners into accepting an accommodation if the prime minister could persuade the mine owners to reduce their demands. Baldwin, whose experience as an industrialist gave him an insight into the dispute, agreed to act as an 'honest broker' between the antagonists. While he blamed the 'stupid and discourteous' employers for bad management, he also criticized the restrictive practices of the workers. To the dismay of some in the Tory party, Baldwin averted the strike with the help of the TUC; he promised to subsidize the miners' wages for nine months, during which time a committee would explore ways of increasing the efficiency of the coal industry.

The report recommended reorganizing and partially nationalizing the industry in the long term, while cutting wages in the short term. The mine owners opposed the former recommendations and the miners rejected the latter, so the negotiations were back to square one. To the government's annoyance, the owners inflamed the situation by proposing increased working hours for the miners, as well as reduced pay. The miners responded by calling another strike, which the TUC was obliged to back. Despite the misgivings of many trade unionists, a 'general' strike of miners, railwaymen, transport workers, printers, dockers, ironworkers and steelworkers was announced. MacDonald and his supporters within the Labour party were dismayed, believing progress for the working man could best be achieved through parliament rather than by industrial action or widespread social protest. Baldwin was so horrified by the prospect of a general strike that he took to his bed. When he returned to the cabinet he found it divided between those who, like himself, favoured conciliation, and those who wanted to 'stand up' to the unions. Churchill was in the latter party, as was Chamberlain; their view prevailed.

The General Strike began at midnight on 3 May 1926. All union members in the specified trades ceased to work in support of the miners, at considerable cost to themselves and their families. With around 1.75 million workers striking, the economy might have come to a standstill. That it did not was due to the government's careful planning and the efforts of middle- and upper-class volunteers, who drove trains, delivered food and joined the ranks of the police. There were violent confrontations between the police and the strikers, especially in London and in northern cities. To Baldwin's distress, Churchill did his best to aggravate hostility, branding the strikers 'the enemy', demanding the 'unconditional surrender' of the 'subversives' and proposing to arm any soldiers who confronted them.

Yet despite the episodes of violent class conflict in the General Strike, it is also remembered for the amity displayed between the strikers and the police. In many areas of the country, striking workers helped the police officers deliver food, while elsewhere the opposing sides played football against each other. If this was class war, it was not the sort of bloody conflict that had characterized similar episodes on the Continent. The strike was also remembered with fondness by many middle- and upper-class volunteers as a break from routine. Privileged women enjoyed dressing and acting like members of the lower orders. By keeping the economy afloat during the strike, the volunteers were also determined to demonstrate a sense of patriotic duty.

The tendency of volunteers and later historians to highlight the lighter side of the strike obscures the sense of revolution that hung over the country. Baldwin was acutely aware of the threat. He condemned the strike as an anarchic and communist attack on parliamentary democracy and the liberties of the people, since the elected government had opposed the industrial action. The unelected unions, he claimed, were 'starving the country' in a bid to 'force parliament and the community to bend to its will'. Baldwin was in effect forcing the TUC to back down or rise up in rebellion. His arguments were repeatedly aired by the pro-government BBC and by the only national newspaper circulating in large numbers during the strike – the government's own *British Gazette*. One of the ironies of the episode was that strike action deprived the workers of what could have been their most effective ally – the press. The TUC could not convincingly answer Baldwin's accusations of lawlessness, and it lacked the stomach for revolution.

In private, the prime minister pressed for concessions from the unions and the mine owners. George V, meanwhile, publicly expressed sympathy for the miners: 'Try living on their wages, before you judge them.' Herbert Samuel, chair of the Royal Commission, then proposed a compromise – that the TUC accept his recommendations for wage cuts on the understanding that his suggestions for the long-term reorganization of the mining industry would be implemented. Weary of the struggle, now in its ninth day, the TUC agreed. Many of the strikers regarded this as unconditional surrender, yet they had no choice but to return to work. The government had won the class war; the workers had lost.

In the aftermath of the TUC's 'betrayal' of the miners, union membership fell sharply. It had become clear that the government could not be pressured by large-scale industrial action into forcing employers to make concessions to employees. After 1927, industrial disputes declined significantly, despite worsening economic conditions. There was a decisive shift of focus in the Labour movement, away from strike action and towards constitutional socialism. Parliament became the main theatre of the class struggle and the Labour party would be the beneficiary. Even so, the strike had demonstrated the power latent in a united working class. It is surely no coincidence that English employers would keep wages at higher levels than those of workers in other European countries.

The General Strike offered incontrovertible evidence, however, of entrenched class divisions in England. It also made a mockery of Baldwin's government's assertion that it would bridge the great divide. For while Baldwin had made conciliatory noises during the confrontation, he had deferred to the claims of the haves over the have-nots. He had also been either unwilling or unable fully to restrain Churchill. Armoured cars had been employed by the chancellor to supply food, while peace demonstrations had been violently broken up by the police. If Churchill's actions during the strike tarnished the government's reputation, within months it lay in ruins. In 1927 Baldwin introduced a Trade Disputes and Trade Unions Act that outlawed any industrial action aimed at 'coercing the government' or 'inflicting harm on the community'. It also banned all forms of 'intimidation' and abolished the unions' political levy. The bill marked the declaration of a new class war.

20

Get on, or get out

After the General Strike and the Trade Disputes Act, Baldwin now appeared to some contemporaries in a much more calculating light. Instead of reaching out to the working classes as a whole, he seemed to target a segment within their ranks: a group comprising workers who, in Chamberlain's phrase, had 'the will and desire to raise themselves to higher and better things'. At its upper end, this segment included the lower-middle-class people who began to acquire houses in the suburbs. These homes were not built by Baldwin's government but by private companies who made a healthy profit on the sale. While the government cap on rents made rented accommodation relatively cheap, it was not always a feasible option for the lower middle class, especially after the Tory administration stopped building council houses. Meanwhile, Churchill encouraged first-time buying by introducing tax-relief schemes for mortgage payments and by insulating lower-middle-class savings against inflation.

Baldwin's Conservatives aimed to create the illusion of a property-owning democracy. They could thereby divide the working and lower middle classes between respectable and rate-paying Tory-voting suburbanites, and slum- or council-house-dwelling socialist renters, and hoped to convert some of the latter into the former through relocation. Orwell spoke of a plot to turn a vast section of the population into 'Tories and "yes-men"', though naturally Baldwin described suburbanization in different terms: 'Nothing can be more touching, than to see how the working man and woman after generations in the towns will have their tiny bit of garden.'

The ownership of detached or semi-detached property was a badge of status and respectability. The assumption of unprecedented levels of debt in the form of long-term mortgages, meanwhile, forced suburbanites to focus on keeping their jobs. Neither class consciousness nor political activism could flourish. 'Get on or get out!' went contemporary Tory slogans. 'There's plenty of room at the top.' Baldwin's tactics during the General Strike encouraged suburbanites to fear the working classes, while Conservative propaganda depicted Labour MPs as advocates of totalitarian socialism, determined to destroy middle England.

Baldwin's genius was to claim the suburban lower middle class as the Tory's natural constituency – no previous Conservative leader had attempted to cultivate its support. By welcoming the middling ranks, Baldwin extended his party's electoral base and gave it a modern identity. After his second administration, the Tories were no longer exclusively the party of landed or commercial wealth; they were also the party of *Daily Mail* readers. The ideological links between these disparate groups included a dislike of high taxes, 'socialism' and the state, together with a vague but zealous nationalism. Once again, the Conservatives demonstrated their adaptability, and their understanding that superficial change was necessary if the fundamental social and economic order were to survive.

Despite suffering from fatigue, Baldwin was confident going into the general election of 1929. Although it was fought against a backdrop of rising unemployment and in the wake of the General Strike, the Tory leader hoped that those who had opposed the protest would vote Conservative, out of fear and gratitude. During the campaign the Tory party mobilized its superior financial resources and fell back on Law's old 'tranquillity' pitch. Posters of Baldwin, billed as 'THE MAN YOU CAN TRUST!' appeared throughout England, emblazoned with 'Safety First'. The slogan carried an implied warning about the revolutionary legislation a Labour government would introduce.

The Liberal party lacked a broad constituency and required a far more inspiring message. Lloyd George, who had finally replaced

Asquith as leader in 1926, came up with a campaign distinguished by audacity, radicalism and flair – precisely the qualities the party had lacked during its decade under 'Squiffy'. In the aftermath of the General Strike, Lloyd George had drawn on the ideas of John Maynard Keynes and developed an ambitious programme of public works. He now promoted that plan under the slogan 'We Can Conquer Unemployment'. Abandoning conventional economic wisdom, which saw unemployment as inevitable and held that if a government taxed and spent less, the population would have more, the Liberal leader argued that the government should borrow money to finance public works and increase employment. Since the programme was a rejection of laissez-faire economics, many Liberals met it with hostility and even incomprehension. They lacked Lloyd George's intuitive insight into economic affairs, as well as his sensitivity to changes in the spirit of the age. His economic judgement had been right when he had introduced bold 'socialistic' measures during the war; events in the Thirties would prove that he was also right to advocate public spending in 1929.

Not for the first time, British voters appeared more progressive than most MPs. They responded enthusiastically to Lloyd George's proposal, and his party secured a quarter of the popular vote at the 1929 election. Yet the bias of the electoral system towards the two main parties meant that this translated into less than 10 per cent of the parliamentary seats. For Lloyd George it was a pyrrhic victory in another sense – most of the Liberal MPs returned to the new parliament were traditional 'Squiffites', who condemned Lloyd George's economic ideas as dangerous. The remaining seats were split fairly evenly between the Tories and Labour, though the latter emerged as the largest party for the first time in history, returning 287 MPs. Compared to their performance in 1924 the Tories won 9 per cent less of the popular vote, but lost 37 per cent of their seats. Baldwin was astonished that an electorate he had enlarged by 8 million people had been so ungrateful. The right of the Tory party, meanwhile, now looked to replace him as leader, with the help of the press barons, Lord Rothermere and Lord Beaverbrook.

The election result proved that voters had accepted Labour as a credible parliamentary party, with enough experience and middle-class MPs to be entrusted with power. MacDonald also reaped the benefits of the failure of the General Strike. He had achieved his two great aims – replacing the Liberals as England's progressive party and making Labour 'electable'. Did he now possess the vision to articulate and advance bolder objectives?

Baldwin and Chamberlain thought it would be 'unsporting' not to offer Labour the chance to form a minority government, but their 'sporting' gesture concealed a pragmatic motive. Baldwin wanted to nip in the bud Churchill's plans for a coalition between the Tories and his old ally Lloyd George, while Chamberlain believed a minority Labour government would soon disappoint Labour supporters. King George was more than happy to send for his friend MacDonald; the Labour leader accepted the king's commission, having warned his backbenchers that he would 'stand no "monkeying"' from them as prime minister. He assembled a cabinet of moderate politicians, including five men with titles – there would be no question of a Labour government introducing a radical socialist programme. Yet there was something genuinely radical about one of MacDonald's appointments. Margaret Bondfield, a veteran suffragist, was selected as the new labour minister and became the first ever female cabinet minister. It was, as she declared, 'part of the great revolution in the position of women'.

21

Crash

At the end of the decade, an economic crisis enveloped the Western world. After the 1921 recession, the value of American stocks had increased by 500 per cent, largely because of unregulated investor speculation. But when the bubble burst in the autumn of 1929, with the value of stocks plummeting by 40 per cent, the majority of ordinary citizens paid the long-term price – in lost jobs, increased taxes and severely reduced public spending.

The Wall Street Crash was the prelude to the largest and longest economic depression of the twentieth century, which would reduce worldwide gross domestic product by 15 per cent and diminish international trade by half. American loans had buoyed up trade in the West, giving other countries the cash to buy goods from the United States; now the loans and the demand for American products dried up. After the autumn of 1929, international prices, income, profits, employment and tax revenues all collapsed. With fewer jobs and less money in circulation, aggregate domestic demand was too low to stimulate weakened Western economies. To compound the problem, sharp deflation encouraged those who had money to hold on to it.

England was ill-prepared for the economic maelstrom that came across the Atlantic. Sterling was chained both to the gold standard and to an unrealistically high exchange rate with the dollar, and the country's antiquated industries were in terminal decline. As England's exports had decreased by a quarter over the past two decades, its imports had increased by approximately the same amount, leaving it reliant on international trade. Little had been done by politicians to improve the situation since the last crash, either by modernizing England's declining industries or by rebalancing the economy through the creation of new ones. MPs expected market forces to provide a solution, but none was forthcoming. Over the next three years industrial production in England decreased by 23 per cent, export prices fell by 50 per cent and foreign trade plummeted by 60 per cent. As a result of the collapse in production and trade, unemployment rose by over 120 per cent during the same period. The picture was even darker in the regions dependent on the old industries. In the north-west, unemployment trebled in the early Thirties, while in the north-east over 70 per cent of adult men found themselves without work. The 'unemployment problem' now dominated politics and public debate.

Having been precipitated by one financial crisis, England's industrial depression was followed by another. Sterling was sold off rapidly on the international markets, and vast amounts of money were withdrawn from the City of London. Much of this had been invested for short-term profit, but the City had accepted it with the risks it entailed. English banks had themselves indulged in speculation for short-term profit, borrowing from French investors at a rate of 2 per cent and lending to Germans at four or five times that amount. While the party lasted City banks did extremely well, but how long could it continue? In 1931 foreign investors suddenly withdrew their money from London, and City banks found themselves owing over £700 million. The Bank of England permitted them to withdraw gold from its reserves while French and American banks lent them £50 million, yet neither move was enough to shore up confidence in the City or in sterling. Foreign governments continued to withdraw around two and a half million pounds' worth of gold deposits from the Bank of England every day.

The extent and impact of the 'Great Depression' was unprecedented; its causes and possible cures were a mystery to virtually all economists and politicians. Like the First World War, there appeared to be an inevitability about its unfolding. Nineteenth-century economic orthodoxy had held that markets would always expand and purchasing power would increase, but the events of the twentieth century had proved that to be false. Yet since no one had anticipated a restriction of demand, governments had no idea how to adapt to it. On the left, prophets of doom were predicting the imminent collapse of capitalism and Western society. Even the pragmatic MacDonald took the quasi-Marxist view that 'the system under which we live has broken down . . . as it was bound to'.

Labour's record during its early months in government did not inspire confidence in its ability to resolve complex problems. Its Coal Mines Act (1930) reduced working hours by just thirty minutes per day, and the miners felt betrayed. If Labour were merely a lesser evil to the Tories, how could the party claim to represent the workers? Labour's education bill, which tried to raise the school leaving age to fifteen, was voted down, as was its proposal for electoral reform. This act would have replaced first-past-the-post with the alternative vote system, as well as abolishing plural voting and the university constituencies, but the minority government lacked the seats in the Commons to pass the legislation. The party's one significant domestic achievement was its 1930 Housing Act, which initiated slum clearances and subsidized housebuilding.

As the industrial depression and financial crisis deepened in 1930 and 1931, a plethora of policies was advocated in parliament. Protectionism was once again espoused from the Tory benches, but this time under the euphemistic banner of 'Empire Free Trade'. The idea was that the colonies and dominions should be 'encouraged' to offer preferential tariffs on British goods, though it was not clear how they would be so persuaded. Some on the left meanwhile proposed a reduction of the retirement age to sixty, thus freeing up jobs for younger people; others, such as Ernest Bevin, advocated the devaluation of the currency.

Lloyd George argued that the depression made his public works programme even more urgent. He was right, but it would take Keynes another few years fully to explain the reasons. According to the economist's argument, published in 1936 under the title of *The General Theory of Unemployment, Interest and Money*, public works and the reduction of interest rates were the only means to keep people employed and the economy functioning when investment from the private sector was unavailable. 'Keynesian theory' would become economic orthodoxy in the late Thirties, but few politicians apart from Lloyd George entertained such ideas at the beginning of the decade.

Yet one young Labour MP was thinking along Keynesian lines at that time. A member of the Economic Advisory Council created by MacDonald in 1930, Oswald Mosley advised the government to adopt an ambitious programme. Two hundred million pounds should be spent on extensive public works, the availability of credit ought to be increased, tariffs should be introduced and early retirement should be encouraged. Much of the banking and industrial sectors would have to be brought under state control, while a government body would 'rationalize' manufacturing, offer advice and oversee research. The crisis, Mosley said, had presented Labour with a unique opportunity to remodel the economy along centralized lines.

This was all too radical for Philip Snowden. The Labour chancellor was too attached to free trade and balanced budgets to approve such plans, while MacDonald did not have the imagination or the desire to overrule him. Despite styling themselves as 'socialists', neither Snowden nor MacDonald believed there was an effective alternative to the capitalist system; at most that ideology might be adjusted in the interest of workers, though even modest improvements would have to wait for more propitious economic circumstances. Besides, the pair were politicians, not economists, and it was their overriding aim to demonstrate Labour's credibility to the electorate; the promotion of extravagant economic schemes that were unlikely to pass through parliament would not further that. It was far better to err on the side of safety and try to consolidate the electoral gains Labour had made under their leadership.

The rejection of Mosley's proposal deprived Labour of his ideas and dynamism; he resigned before he could be expelled from the party for challenging the leadership. It also left the administration with no alternative but to fall back on the old economic orthodoxies, and on the idea of cross-party cooperation. After consulting the other party leaders and financial experts in the City and the Treasury, Snowden decided against significantly raising taxes or borrowing money, instead resolving to reduce government spending. The chancellor then created two committees to advise him on where the cuts should come. Expenditure on unemployment insurance made up a substantial segment of public spending and had risen from £12 million in 1928 to £125 million in 1932. It was inevitable that Snowden's committees would recommend that unemployment relief be cut. In the event, they suggested total cuts of £96 million, in order to 'save' the country from a £120 million deficit, with most of the savings coming from a 20 per cent reduction in unemployment benefit.

The alarmist nature of the committee reports encouraged the further flight of investment from the City. The Treasury told the government that its inability to balance the budget was the problem, and urged it to implement the recommended cuts. The national debt was, they claimed, undermining international confidence in England's ability to maintain its currency at its high valuation. If there were a run on the pound, the Bank of England's reserves would not be sufficient to maintain the all-important gold standard. 'To go off the gold standard,' one banker said, 'for a nation that depends so much on its credit would be a major disaster.' Like the navy or the empire, the gold standard was a symbol of the country's robustness; leaving it would be to renounce its status as a great power.

Over the ensuing days City experts and Treasury officials attempted to frighten the Labour government – sterling might, they warned, go under any day. After a few meetings, Snowden and MacDonald were thoroughly alarmed. Both were persuaded that anarchy would result if foreign confidence in sterling were not restored quickly and the gold standard maintained; both were convinced that reducing government expenditure on unemployment was the key to resolving the financial crisis. In accepting these arguments, Snowden and MacDonald also accepted Labour's responsibility not just for solving the crisis but also for provoking it.

MacDonald told his cabinet he was 'absolutely satisfied' that economies on unemployment insurance payments were the only way to shore up confidence. Yet how could Labour ministers implement a policy that was, as MacDonald himself admitted, a 'negation of everything that the party stood for'? After an intense debate, half of the cabinet ministers declared themselves against any reduction in unemployment benefit. The bankers, however, said that the Labour government's inaction 'would not do', and Neville Chamberlain – an influential go-between for the City and the government – agreed. A stalemate ensued, and the cabinet increasingly felt it would have to resign.

When MacDonald explained the situation to King George, the monarch decided to consult the other party leaders. He and Herbert Samuel (standing in as Liberal leader for the sick Lloyd George) reached the conclusion that, since MacDonald had failed to secure support for the required cuts, the best alternative would be a 'National Government' composed of the three parties. MacDonald should remain as prime minister, because swingeing cuts would seem more palatable to the people if made by a Labour prime minister, and also to elicit Labour's support for the coalition. The king persuaded Baldwin of the efficacy of the idea, before asking his old friend MacDonald to lead a coalition in order to resolve the national emergency. After some deliberation, MacDonald assented, before calling a meeting of his cabinet. Rather than announcing the government's resignation, the policy which had been agreed upon, MacDonald informed them he would instead be forming a new emergency coalition to which only three of them were invited.

The motives of the protagonists in this episode have been scrutinized over the years. The king undoubtedly exercised extraordinary power by effectively nominating a prime minister and a government without consulting either parliament or the country, but there is no evidence to suggest that he did so in order to end Labour's tenure in office. MacDonald has been accused of putting himself before a party that he no longer loved, and it is true that he had become increasingly alienated from the revolutionary and trade unionist elements in his party. Even so, the Labour leader appears to have convinced himself that he was making a genuine renunciation by sacrificing his government, and perhaps his own political career. It should also be remembered that everyone involved saw the National Government as temporary and established for the single purpose of averting a national emergency. 'When that purpose is achieved,' the king explained, after 'about five weeks, the political parties will resume their respective positions', and an election would follow. This assurance enabled Baldwin to persuade Tory MPs to participate in the National Government for which they felt little enthusiasm.

But how could MacDonald bring his outraged party with him? Apart from three Labour ministers who would enter the new ten-man coalition cabinet, and eight backbenchers, all of the Labour MPs vehemently opposed the National Government. 'They choose the easy path of irresponsibility,' remarked MacDonald, 'and leave the burdens to others.' Within the wider Labour movement, he and Snowden were vilified as 'traitors' – they had betrayed their colleagues, their party and democracy itself by making an unconstitutional deal behind closed doors with an unelected monarch. The pair were also derided as the dupes of the bankers, who had, it was said, exaggerated the financial crisis in order to pass anti-working-class legislation and bring down the Labour government. Long-standing suspicions about MacDonald were now openly expressed. The man who had wanted Labour to replace the Liberals had become a Liberal himself; 'Gentleman Mac' had sold his comrades for praise in the right-wing press and access to high society.

Baldwin and MacDonald were both men of moderation who had shifted their parties towards the centre ground of politics. They shared a loathing of Lloyd George and a determination to keep him out of Downing Street. They now formed a solid, centrist coalition, which aimed to insulate the country from political extremism at a time of economic and social turmoil. Yet they also insulated their government from innovative ideas on the left and the right, which might have improved the precarious economic situation. Labour proposed the nationalization of the banks, the transport system, the staple industries and land, while on the right the rising Tory Harold Macmillan advocated a planned economy. Lloyd George, meanwhile, continued to espouse a proto-Keynesian programme of public works. But Baldwin and MacDonald dismissed these radical suggestions.

Snowden's budget of September 1931 drastically reduced government spending, cutting unemployment payments and public sector wages. It was opposed by 90 per cent of Labour MPs and the vast majority of union members, who were now irrevocably cut off from their former leaders. It was also attacked by civil service employees, 20,000 of whom organized a rally to protest against the government. The chancellor's critics predicted his cuts would not restore confidence in either sterling or in the City, and they were right – foreign investors continued to sell the former and withdraw money from the latter. The Bank of England was now obliged to use large amounts of its gold to shore up sterling. To add to the sense of emergency, part of the navy went on strike in protest at the proposed 25 per cent cut to sailors' wages.

On 21 September 1931, events forced the National Government to announce that no public sector pay cuts would exceed 10 per cent and Britain would leave the gold standard. Sterling was allowed to float freely against other currencies, and its value ceased to be linked to the amount of money the country possessed. It also meant that a government formed for the purpose of maintaining the gold standard had now abandoned it. 'For me,' wrote the novelist Alec Waugh, 'as for most born before 1910, the announcement . . . was the biggest shock that we had known.'

But the sky did not fall, and nor did the economy. Sterling dropped by around 25 per cent in value, but then stabilized: it was weaker but steadier, and its steadiness revived investor confidence. Investors were also reassured by the presence of Baldwin and Chamberlain in the cabinet. Britain's devalued currency, meanwhile, held out the promise of lower export prices and low interest rates, providing further cause for optimism. Going off the gold standard thus ended the currency crisis, where cutting unemployment benefit had had little or no positive effect. The bankers and the Treasury had been wrong all along, but the unemployed and the Labour government had paid the price.

In leaving the gold standard, the National Government lost its raison d'être, but gained a new one – to stabilize the new floating sterling. The Conservatives believed the currency could best be steadied by the introduction of a tariff programme; they demanded a general election, in order to secure a popular mandate for the policy. But they were happy to go to the country as part of a MacDonald-led National Government, since the king favoured its continuance. Besides, the Labour party would be isolated and vulnerable in its opposition to a cross-party coalition. 'The insidious doctrines of class warfare cannot make headway against the general desire for national cooperation,' Baldwin commented. 'The great thing is to give socialism a really smashing defeat.' Here was the real Tory agenda.

Yet MacDonald and the free-trade Liberals in the coalition were uncomfortable with the idea of promoting protectionism. The prime minister was also reluctant to campaign against the party he had helped to build. Nevertheless, Chamberlain correctly predicted that MacDonald would find the lure of power too strong to resist. Not even the cautionary tale provided by Lloyd George's fall from the leadership of a national coalition in 1922 could dissuade MacDonald from agreeing. In any case, Labour left their former leader little choice but to join the National Government, as they expelled him from the party.

When a general election was called, the MacDonald splinter group, 'National Labour', broke away from the bulk of the Labour party. The Liberal party, meanwhile, was split three ways. The 'Liberals' were pro-coalition but anti-protection and the 'National Liberals' favoured both, while neither was palatable to Lloyd George's 'Independents'. Though the party-political situation was confusing, there was nothing unclear about the messages the Tories and Labour tried to communicate to the electorate. With the help of their friends in the press, the Conservatives blamed Labour for causing the economic crisis and claimed a new Labour government would give people's savings to idlers on the dole. Labour, meanwhile, blamed the bankers for the crisis and vilified MacDonald, whose portrait at the party's London offices was turned to face the wall. In response MacDonald and Snowden effectively bade farewell to Labour by describing its election programme as 'Bolshevism run mad'.

MacDonald received his mandate, as the National Government won over 60 per cent of the vote and returned 521 MPs to the new parliament. The real victory, however, belonged to the Conservatives, who claimed 473 of the government's seats. The vast majority of the middle classes, and over 50 per cent of the working class and the female electorate, had voted Tory. Baldwin had proved to his party that his dream of a property-owning democracy could be turned into a reality. He had also convinced many voters that a spendthrift 'socialist' government had caused the country's economic malaise. Labour lost 235 seats and were reduced to a mere fifty-two MPs, an abysmal result that was probably also a judgement by some sections of the working class on the party's poor record in office. On the other hand, their massive reduction in seats could also be attributed to the bias of the electoral system – the party's share of the popular vote only decreased by 6 per cent. It was the middle classes, more than the workers, who had turned away from Labour. They also turned away from the Liberals, which was hardly surprising since the bulk now supported a Tory-dominated coalition. The election of 1931 marked the extinction of the great party of Gladstone and Lloyd George. For the rest of the century, it would be a simple fight between the Tories and Labour. And for the foreseeable future, there was no doubt which party would win. England was a Tory country of the south as opposed to the north, of the classes rather than of the masses.

Within the National Government the Liberals were now dispensable, while Snowden could be ignored. MacDonald was no longer even a figurehead but merely a cipher. Once more, there were clear parallels with the 1918 election, which gave Lloyd George office and the Conservatives power. Yet there was also an obvious difference: even fettered and outnumbered, Lloyd George had been an irrepressible and imperious leader; MacDonald, in contrast, was a spent force. The absence of dynamism at the heart of government would have devastating consequences for England, as would the lack of a substantial parliamentary opposition for the Tories. For the next eight or nine years the Conservatives would have everything their own way.

The Tories soon demonstrated their dominance in the coalition. Chamberlain, who replaced Snowden as chancellor, introduced a number of protectionist measures, despite the disapproval of some Liberals in the cabinet. At first he implemented import tariffs with the excuse of balancing trade; but then he did so more openly and paid tribute to his father, who had first espoused the protectionist cause. A general tariff of 10 per cent was imposed, while empire goods were exempted. The Tory's grand design was a self-sufficient empire separated from the rest of the world by imperial preference, just as Chamberlain's father had envisaged. The colonies and dominions would provide the 'mother country' with food and raw materials, as well as a market for its manufactured goods.

Yet there were a number of problems with the policy. The countries that comprised the empire had industries of their own, which they naturally wished to protect. They had also suffered during the recent crash, and could hardly afford English exports. Moreover, after the successes of the Irish and Indian opposition to direct British rule, independence was in the air. In the end, the colonies and dominions agreed to increase tariffs on imports from other countries, but left tariffs on British imports at their former high level. The Tariff Reform scheme – which Tories had promoted over the previous three decades – turned out to have a minimal impact on the economy. With the price of its goods too high, English exports increased only slightly. Critics of protectionism suggested that the Tories were not so much attuned to economic reality as in thrall to ideology.

The damp squib of Tory protectionism did, however, have significant political consequences. It alienated the free-trade Liberals in the government, and MacDonald, who was himself unhappy about the policy, struggled to keep them on side. Desperate to maintain unity, he reminded the Tories that they had promised to participate in a coalition. His appeal was not heeded, and when the chancellor refused to dilute his protectionist policies, the free-trading Liberals left the administration, along with Snowden. MacDonald was now even more painfully aware of his position as leader of a de facto Tory government; he became increasingly anxious, ill and enfeebled. The pro-protectionist 'National Liberal' faction, meanwhile, remained in the government and would eventually merge with the Conservative party. The Tories absorbed the right wing of the Liberal party, just as Labour had absorbed the left.

The Conservatives now finally accepted protectionism as a permanent aspect of the modern economy. They proceeded to take London's public transport into public ownership, and would later nationalize coal royalties. Chamberlain also 'rationalized' aspects of the agricultural sector, establishing marketing boards that guaranteed high prices for farmers and supporting them with lavish subsidies. The chancellor's 'socialist' approach to the 'shires', which were after all the Tories' traditional heartland, is less surprising than it first appears. It was as natural for Chamberlain to please the landowners and farmers as it was for him to reduce assistance to those who had lost their jobs – which he now proceeded to do, using the old argument that cuts would restore 'confidence' in the pound. There would be no 'socialist' planning for the unemployed.

22

The rituals of suburbia

None of the chancellor's measures had any great impact on the economy; far more influential was the policy that the Tory party had fiercely opposed – that of abandoning the gold standard. The weaker pound meant that English exports were more competitively priced; as global trade slowly picked up, they started to sell again on the international market. The difficulty of devaluation was that, in normal circumstances, the price of imports was bound to increase; but these were not normal times. The collapse of commodity prices after 1929 ensured that England's international payments became balanced again, while production increased significantly. Unemployment started to fall – slightly at first but then steadily, decreasing to 10 per cent in 1937. Naturally, the Tory chancellor claimed all the credit.

Abandoning the gold standard also meant that the currency no longer needed to be supported by high interest rates. The base rate of interest was reduced to approximately 2 per cent – it had been set at around 5 per cent throughout the Twenties. This made borrowing cheap, while also encouraging investment and spending. Although the Tory-dominated National Government was averse to borrowing and spending on public works, private investors and businesses took up the role. There was a housebuilding boom, which saw 40 per cent more houses built in 1934 than in 1929; well over

2 million houses were constructed by the end of the decade. For the first time in its history, England contained more houses than families. Most of the new dwellings were constructed in the suburbs of towns and cities in the south and the Midlands, or in the 'rural' suburbs of existing suburbs. Others were erected along the roads between towns, in a so-called 'ribbon development'. Around London, Slough, Hayes, Kenton, Uxbridge, Hillingdon, Feltham and Kingsbury were all greatly enlarged; geographers compared the capital to a giant octopus stretching its tentacles into the countryside. Such was the rate of expansion that various movements for the preservation of open space and the countryside were established, while criticism of suburban 'sprawl' was widespread. Baldwin – one of the architects of the mess – lamented the destruction of the countryside, yet took no practical steps to stop it.

The housing boom was funded by private investment, since the National Government had terminated the housebuilding programme Labour had tried to revive with its 1930 Housing Act. With building regulations and restrictions minimal, and money cheap, construction companies borrowed to buy up land, which was then quickly covered with houses. Over the interwar period, private firms built over 600,000 houses in London, while local authorities subsidized the construction of only 150,000 of the capital's new homes.

With interest rates low, lower-middle- and upper-working-class people could afford new homes. 'Cheap' houses were made available to those on regular wages by building societies such as Halifax and Woolwich that had flourished after the Wall Street Crash. Eager to lend from their overflowing reserves, the building societies reduced the deposit they demanded from prospective buyers to as little as 2 per cent. A new London house that cost £800 could be acquired with a deposit of £25, with the remaining debt paid off at an interest rate of 3 per cent; the government also offered tax relief on interest payments. Since there was little council housing available, the lower middle and upper working classes were compelled to take on debt to purchase houses. By the late Thirties, clerks, shopkeepers, foremen, postal workers, transport workers and teachers owned property, as did a fifth of manual workers. By 1938, 4 million people possessed a house, compared to less than 1 million fifteen years before. Thus the Tories continued to create a vast constituency of indebted suburbanites.

The new homes were filled with furniture and appliances. Goods acquired on 'hire purchase' would be delivered by an anonymous van, to spare the blushes of those who did not wish their neighbours to know they had bought them 'on tick'. Yet many families possessed enough money to buy goods without having to borrow it, despite – or perhaps because of – the economic depression. The great paradox of the crisis, and the chief reason the English economy was able to recover from it, was that it left many people with more money in their pockets. For while wages had been falling since 1929, the purchasing power of those wages increased as a result of plummeting prices. Real wages were 10 per cent higher in the midst of the depression than they had been before it, and the margin of income left over after a family's basic needs had been met was consequently larger. In 1938 a British family had double the income of a family in 1914, in real terms, and, with the size of families decreasing, income per head was almost 70 per cent higher. Increased family income, at a time when money could be borrowed cheaply, funded a national spending spree on houses, household goods and services.

The sudden emergence of a domestic consumer market in England meant that manufacturing and tertiary industries flourished, and new mass production processes enabled manufacturers to meet the increased demand. The cost of raw materials was now lower, as was the cost of the unskilled labour force required to oversee the machines, which kept prices down. The chemical industry was one of the strongest performers in the period. It produced pharmaceutical goods, fertilizers, artificial fibres for synthetic clothes, and plastics such as Bakelite, which were used for countless household appliances. The car industry also expanded rapidly, with assembly-line mass production turning out over half a million cars annually by 1937. Prices decreased as the decade went on, and by 1939 over 2 million British people owned private cars. In Longbridge and Oxford, Austin and Morris motors provided employment for thousands of people, whose wages could be spent on more goods, thus further stimulating the economy.

The greatest boom industry of the Thirties, however, was the electrical industry in its widest sense – electrical appliances, electrical engineering, and the production and distribution of electricity itself. Industrial demand for electricity was high since the new factory machines were run on this relatively new form of energy. Domestic demand was also high, with three-quarters of houses wired up for electricity by the end of the Thirties (compared to only 6 per cent in 1920). The price of electricity had decreased significantly since the Twenties, too, as a result of technological advancement and a fall in coal prices.

Baldwin, an experienced industrialist, understood that a new industrial revolution was taking place, in which the staple export industries of the former industrial revolution were being superseded by new industries serving the home market (over 80 per cent of English cars, for example, were bought in England). The Tory leader hoped that the expansion of the new trades would absorb the displacement of labour from the depressed heavy industries – that jobless miners and shipbuilders would become wireless technicians and electrical engineers. However, Baldwin did not indicate how the government would facilitate this 'transition', which would involve retraining and the relocation of countless communities in the north of England.

Other observers were more sceptical about the new industrial utopia. Charlie Chaplin's film *Modern Times* (1936) was a satire 'about the way life is being standardized, and men turned into machines'. In the film, Chaplin's tramp persona is set to work on an ever-accelerating factory assembly line, suffering physical injury and a nervous breakdown as he struggles to keep pace with the vast and voracious machine. It was as though modern technology was using humans to manufacture a new race of demented robots.

Whether they were built for sale or rent, the suburban houses of the Twenties and Thirties tended to be of the uniform semi-detached variety. They were easily distinguishable from their Edwardian prototypes by their external features. They had roof tiles instead of slates and 'Tudorbethan' timbers, together with unadorned stucco or pebbledash walls. Along with their pastiche of older architectural styles, half-timber gables, leaded lights and inglenooks gave them a 'rustic' appearance.

To enhance the illusion that the suburbs were in the countryside, every house had a front and back garden. 'It is amazing,' commented a journalist, 'how soon families, many of whom had never had a garden before, turn the rough land surrounding their new houses into beautiful gardens. In summer they are ablaze with colour.' The front garden often had a privet hedge, to increase privacy and reduce noise. The back garden sometimes contained a shed or a greenhouse and was surrounded by a fence. This was the English family's hallowed plot of land, the city dressed up in country clothes. The names of the new houses and streets contributed to the masquerade: 'The Myrtles' was situated in Meadow Rise, while 'Acacia Villa' stood in Fir Tree Crescent. The countrified, nostalgic architecture of the suburbs set the tone of Baldwin's England.

For those who moved to the suburbs from the slums, the most novel feature of their new houses was an indoor bathroom, often upstairs. There would also typically be three bedrooms on the upper floor, with two reception rooms and a kitchen downstairs. Wired for electricity and supplied with hot water, the houses were well lit, with standard lamps throughout. There were sockets in every room for electrical appliances: wirelesses, gramophones, electric hairdryers, vacuum cleaners and electric sewing machines. The kitchen had the most sockets to accommodate toasters, ovens, electric irons, kettles, washing machines and refrigerators. These kitchen gadgets were 'labour-saving' – designed for families without domestic servants, where the woman of the house oversaw its management and maintenance.

The new 'semis' were referred to as 'containers' for the new mass-produced consumer goods. Stainless steel cutlery was stored in the kitchen drawers, while plastic ornaments were displayed on the mantelpiece in the lounge. That 'living room' was often crowded with mass-produced furniture: three-piece suites with a 'jazzy' striped design, 'pouffes', wooden bookcases, and dining tables with chairs of limed oak. Pastel shades were generally favoured for the walls of the downstairs rooms, while bolder and darker colours were not uncommon in the smaller upstairs rooms. Everything was practical, standardized, time-saving and efficient.

If the family possessed a car, it would be parked in the garage or outside in the street. Car owners, however, were a minority in the suburbs; most travelled by means of public services. There was the electric 'trolley bus', more comfortable and quieter than the 'proletarian' electric tram, which shrieked its way along the streets.

The motor buses of the General Omnibus Company were also indispensable to those who lived just beyond the ever-expanding spider's web of railways that spread out from England's cities.

The daily commute from the suburbs was often a near-silent process. Men in dark hats and suits would quietly and neatly arrange themselves along train or underground platforms, or in the queue at the bus stop. Most buried their heads in newspapers and gave no more than a slight nod of greeting to the familiar faces around them. Those who did talk tended to speak in low tones and to stick to uncontroversial subjects, such as the weather, sport or gardening. Carriages were often full, but standing passengers did their utmost to avoid physical contact. Journeys passed without incident, but also without interest.

Train stations and bus stops were located next to the suburban shopping parade, which invariably offered the six essential trades of the period: a grocer's, greengrocer's, butcher's, baker's, dairy and a newsagent, tobacconist or confectioner, along with a post office. In mock Tudor style and with flats above the shops, these parades were meant to be the focal point of the suburban 'community', though they lacked the vibrant atmosphere of older urban markets. The shops were grouped together in order to isolate them from the surrounding residential streets, since tradespeople were unwelcome in addresses that aspired to respectability. The appetite for shopping among suburbanites was so great that it could not always be satisfied by the local shops or door-to-door salesmen. When suburban consumers demanded more, they headed to the high streets of the town or city.

These high streets were rapidly being colonized by 'chains' that purveyed mass-produced goods. Sainsbury's, C&A, Littlewoods, Home & Colonial and Boots the Chemist were supplanting local, family-owned shops. In 1929, Marks & Spencer had a turnover of £2 million; a decade later it generated £23 million in its 250 countrywide stores. The 'chains' borrowed huge amounts of money and bought cheap, mass-produced, standardized goods from new English industries and from overseas. They had small profit margins but achieved sizeable returns because of their exceptionally large turnovers – a testimony to high domestic demand. The 'chains' seemed to be miracles of efficient business management, while customers marvelled at the novel shopping experience they offered. No assistants goaded them into buying a particular product; they were left to browse the well-stocked aisles themselves, comparing quality and prices for as long as they liked, before making up their own minds. Shoppers could now buy every item on their shopping list within a single store, a striking everyday example of the efficiency espoused by politicians in the period.

Yet not everyone was enthusiastic about the advent of the chain stores. As local shops closed across the country, to be replaced by yet another Woolworths, English towns began to look alike. Moreover, as locally sourced products were replaced in the new stores by mass-produced goods from abroad, local producers complained about the loss of business, while consumers noticed a significant reduction in quality.

The food sold by chain stores was of the mass-produced variety, too. Colourful and tasty comfort foods became available to the masses: custard, jelly, ice cream, blancmange, sponge cakes and chocolate eggs were all favourites of the period. A generation that had experienced wartime rationing at last had an opportunity to indulge its sweet tooth, while savoury tastes could also be satisfied with Marmite, Bovril and Smith's crisps. Breakfast cereals arrived on the shelves of the chain stores, with Grape-Nuts, porridge oats, Kellogg's Corn Flakes and Shredded Wheat among the most popular. Most of the food sold in the new stores, however, came in tins – sardines, salmon, peaches, peas, pears, pilchards and Spam. Tinned food might have been abhorrent to the higher classes, but it was a blessing to those lower down the social scale, and the tin opener became indispensable in most suburban kitchens. Many of the tins were imported from abroad, along with much of the fresh food, including eggs and tomatoes. While the food revolution of the period was a blow to native producers and generally involved a reduction in both quality and freshness, the increase in consumer choice was undeniable. An older generation which had grown up with an unvaried and often meagre diet was astonished to be now able to purchase frozen meat and exotic fruit in tins, and at reasonable prices.

Evenings in the suburbs came round quickly in the Thirties. Working hours had been reduced from sixty hours per week to around fifty, largely thanks to the pressure of the unions, and work on a Saturday generally finished at lunchtime. This meant more evening leisure time, but the remoteness of many suburbs from urban centres and their lack of public spaces and venues encouraged people to stay in. Among the two most popular suburban pastimes were gardening and 'having a read of the newspaper'.

National dailies and local 'rags' found their way onto most suburban doormats each morning. The working man of the house would skim these papers at breakfast and peruse them with care at night (when he would also do the crossword, now a daily feature of newspapers). The total circulation of national dailies exceeded 10 million in the Thirties. By the end of the decade the *Daily Express* sold two and a half million copies per day, and the *Daily Mail* and the *Daily Mirror* one and a half million each. These papers offered entertainment and accounts of the lives of sports and film celebrities, while older publications such as *The Times*, the *Manchester Guardian* and the *Morning Post* were the serious purveyors of news, commentary and enlightenment. The high circulation of the *Express*, *Mail* and *Mirror* brought vast cultural and political influence, as well as wealth, to press barons such as Lord Beaverbrook and Lord Rothermere. Despite their earlier misgivings about Baldwin, the barons helped him consolidate the support of the Conservative-voting suburban lower middle class, and to identify the views of this new class with public opinion and the national interest.

Newspapers brought an avalanche of advertisements into suburban homes; as a result, advertising played a crucial role in stimulating the demand-driven consumer boom of the period. Manufacturers and retailers now spent over £60 million on newspaper advertising annually, with the heaviest investors including department stores and producers of cosmetics, cigarettes, medicines and processed foods. Flourishing publicity firms came up with catchy slogans for their products, such as 'Player's Please' and 'Friday night is Amami night'.

This second advertisement for shampoo was aimed at young women, a new and burgeoning market for advertisers. A particular form of femininity was being promoted, perhaps to counter the effect of large-scale female employment in the new light industries. In the Thirties, women generally dressed more conservatively than their flapper predecessors, with longer, tighter dresses emphasizing the 'feminine' figure. Although Edwardian heaviness had been banished from women's wardrobes forever, shoulders were now broader and waists were coming back. Hair became longer, softer and curlier across the decade, while make-up became heavier and more widespread. By 1939, 90 per cent of women under thirty regularly used lipstick, powder, mascara and rouge.

Along with the more traditional look, traditional gender divisions returned. While women might work immediately after they left school, their ultimate destiny was to marry, have a family and settle down. Housewifery was regarded by many as the ideal career for women; for many it was the only option, since their professional progress was still hindered by the marriage bar. The housewife brought up the children and managed the house, with the help of the new electrical appliances. New 'women's magazines', such as *Woman* and *Woman's Own*, instructed women on how to run a household, while urging them to 'be the junior partner' within their marriages. As a result of propaganda and economic pressures, English women were forced back into the home in the Thirties. It is telling that it was not uncommon for the rooms in new suburban houses to be separated along gender lines, with the male head of the household having access to a private study, while the housewife might occupy the morning room. It is unsurprising that many housewives complained of boredom and fatigue and longed to return to work. Some were disappointed that, having won the right to vote, they lacked the political power to improve their lot.

Lonely suburban women spent a great deal of time reading books, as did the men after work. The bookshelves of the new 'semis' were often stocked with the latest publications. 'Penguin' fictions and the 'Pelican' educational series were launched in the late Thirties for only sixpence a book, while the 'Reader's Library' hardback classics could be bought cheaply from Woolworths. By the end of the decade, book sales increased to 7 million per year. Books could also be borrowed from libraries, with 247 million loaned in 1939. The representatives of 'circulating libraries' would visit the suburbs on their bikes. 'A romance or a detective story?' they would ask young mothers, since these were the most popular genres among that demographic. Where Mills & Boon ruled the romance genre, Agatha Christie and Dorothy L. Sayers dominated detective fiction, providing suburban readers with intriguing puzzles in exotic or aristocratic settings. Gangster novels, meanwhile, transported countless male readers to New York, while thrillers tapped into their unconscious fears about foreign invasion and war.

An alternative form of suburban home entertainment was provided by the radio. When the family came together after dinner, it was often around the wireless, to listen to a news broadcast or a light entertainment programme. By the end of the Thirties, compact sets could be purchased for as little as £5, which meant that every suburban family, and even some working-class households, could afford them. Where working-class families tended to leave the wireless on to provide background noise, the middle classes switched selected programmes on and off and listened intently. In the Thirties listeners had access to continental stations such as Radio Luxembourg, which were financed by advertising and broadcast popular music as well as comedy shows. This 'American-style' commercial fare was less restricted than the typical offerings of the BBC, where earnest, lengthy highbrow programmes and public-school accents dominated. While the BBC alienated many working-class listeners, the aspiring suburban classes tuned in faithfully. Suburban families also listened to music on the gramophone, which had become cheaper and smaller since the Twenties, while 6-inch records were now available from Woolworths for sixpence. Popular songs of the period included 'Mad Dogs and Englishmen' and 'Boomps-A-Daisy', while among the most successful classical composers were Ralph Vaughan Williams and Edward Elgar.

In the wealthier suburbs, 'entertaining' would take place in the evenings, but social gatherings elsewhere would usually be divided by gender. Small groups of women would get together to talk over a 'nice cup of tea' in the afternoon, while men might meet in the evenings for a game of cards or to listen to music. Talk did not flourish among the male population of the English suburbs, some of whom confessed to their 'difficulties with English' as well as a certain 'terror of social intercourse'.

Contact between people living in the same suburb or street was limited. Neighbours were more likely to be heard than seen, since their radios or gramophones were audible through badly insulated party walls. The asocial lifestyle of the suburbs came as a disappointment to recent arrivals from rural or inner-city areas; they disliked the way their new neighbours just nodded when they happened to meet them. Some complained that the old social intimacy of the city doorstep was broken by the gardens and the distance between houses. Suburban living made the English a more private people, who saw their home lives as separate from the public spheres of work and politics. The weakening of class and political consciousness was an inevitable consequence.

Novelists satirized the 'sterile' suburbs, whose inhabitants were 'shallow' and 'staid'. George Orwell was probably their most ardent critic. 'To turn into the typical bowler-hatted sneak . . . To settle down, to Make Good, to sell your soul for a villa and an aspidistra!' That, according to the hero of Orwell's *Keep the Aspidistra Flying* (1936), was the appalling fate of suburbanites. Other intellectuals saw England's spreading suburbia as a symbol of national decline – an outward-looking country that still possessed the largest empire the world had ever known had become private, provincial and insular. A nation of gardeners and housewives seemed ill-equipped to carry out the global role England had once assumed, or to take up the torch of activism from the suffragettes and the trade unionist radicals who had preceded them. But for many suburbanites, despite their lack of neighbourliness, the suburbs represented a definite improvement on the countryside or the crowded inner-city slums. Besides, most people had little choice in the matter of where to live, so they had to flourish in the outer cities. As one suburban housewife put it, 'this was their life now and they weren't going to let it go'.

23

Now we can have some fun

Public houses had provided meeting points in traditional urban and rural communities, but far fewer of them were built in the new suburbs. In Becontree there were only five pubs for over 110,000 inhabitants; on some estates they were prohibited altogether. The few that were built struck contemporaries as uninviting. In some establishments drinks had to be ordered from waiters in bow ties and consumed when seated. These were not the sort of places you could casually visit after work for a few pints and a chat while standing at the bar. Unsurprisingly, beer sales fell by a half and spirits by a third in the Thirties, compared to pre-war levels.

The cinema was more attractive to suburbanites as a place of entertainment, in part perhaps because it offered a kind of privacy. Films had been championed by the urban working class on their arrival in wartime England, and the small city nickelodeons and picture palaces of those years had been predominantly proletarian institutions. Yet as the Twenties progressed, the cinema had gradually become a respectable pastime: for the first time in history, a distinctly working-class entertainment conquered the middle classes. The disappearance of snobbery towards the silver screen coincided with the advent of synchronized soundtracks, colour and the 'talkies' towards the end of the Twenties.

The talkies were at first billed as 'All Talking, All Singing, All

Dancing' films, and some of the most popular early productions were spectacular musicals, such as those starring Ginger Rogers and Fred Astaire. Other stars of the early cinema included Clara Bow, Greta Garbo and Errol Flynn, while Disney's Mickey Mouse and Donald Duck became household names among English children. Among the most popular genres of the Thirties were romances in exotic settings and Westerns, which depicted the life of frontier towns. Were these newly established American settlements a mirror image of English suburbia, or a free-spirited reproach to it?

Virtually all the films came from the United States, despite the introduction of protectionist Tory legislation to encourage the domestic industry. In comparison with American films, English productions were seen as stagy, lacking in action, and overpopulated by the middle and upper classes. Two of the greatest geniuses of cinema were, however, English: Charlie Chaplin and the director Alfred Hitchcock. Both men were from London but worked in the United States by the end of the Thirties, creating masterpieces that manifested the energy and ingenuity as well as the range and exuberance of the new art form.

Alfred Hitchcock's *The 39 Steps* (1935) begins, and ends, in a shabby London music hall. It is a world that is about to be swept away, as people sensed at the time. Although it was based on a novel by John Buchan that had been published twenty years before, Hitchcock's film has a contemporary setting and touches the hidden anxieties of mid-Thirties England. Apprehension for the future seems to cast shadows over everything. Nothing in the film feels real or solid; every set seems to be a backdrop to an imminent catastrophe. Scene follows scene, and climax follows climax. The main character, Richard Hannay, becomes unintentionally involved in a murder, and a plot to steal British military secrets by a ring of foreign spies. Hitchcock's camera seems to chase Hannay as he rushes from London to Scotland and back again, then down to the Channel coast, in an attempt to clear his name and thwart the spies. Hitchcock included a number of scenes set in the lower-class London streets he had known as a boy. He remarked that English filmmakers often 'ignore the people who jump onto moving buses . . . queues outside cinemas, music hall girls, traffic cops . . . [but] it's in them that the spirit of England lies'.

A ticket to see *The 39 Steps* cost only sixpence. By the end of the Thirties around 15 million sixpenny cinema tickets were sold in England every week, and there were one hundred cinemas in Liverpool alone. Almost half of the entire adult population of major cities and their suburbs went to see a film weekly; a quarter of the population went twice a week, especially in the colder months. In the Thirties 'super-cinemas' were built that seated up to 4,000 people and had appropriately grand names, such as 'The Ritz', 'The Majestic' and 'The Rialto'. On entering the cinema, the public passed through red-carpeted foyers and up wide staircases to their seats. Baroque or rococo-style cinemas, replete with cherubs, were not uncommon; others favoured designs with Egyptian, Greek, Indian or Roman themes. These were suitably exotic settings in which to see romantic films set in distant times and places and featuring glamorous stars. Before the film commenced a musician would play popular tunes on a Mighty Wurlitzer organ that rose slowly from beneath the floor to the level of the stage. During the film, audiences were invariably absorbed, and often opinionated; working-class spectators in particular offered audible criticisms of the spectacle.

There is no doubt that films were responsible for profound cultural and social change. They were among the first forms of entertainment lower-class men and women could enjoy together, the pub remaining a predominantly male preserve. The cinema also offered young people a place to meet unaccompanied by their parents, and under cover of darkness: 'To the Odeon we have come,' ran the hymn of the Odeon Club for teenagers, 'Now we can have some fun.' The fun might include smoking, drinking and 'necking and petting'.

The phrase 'necking and petting' testifies to another great cultural change wrought by the cinema – the introduction of American slang to the English streets. Nouns such as 'bunk', 'dope' and 'baloney' could now be heard in inner-city Manchester, while young boys in Durham threatened to 'bump off' each other, or at the very least give each other 'the works'. Most youths now used the adjective 'OK' where they had previously said 'all right'; many now said 'yeah' or 'yep' instead of 'yes', and 'nope' for 'no'. To working-class English ears, slang from across the Atlantic seemed democratic and liberating, since their own idiom signalled their lowly place within England's rigidly hierarchical class system.

The cinema weakened the hold earlier forms of entertainment had on the population. Punch and Judy shows and barrel organs now lost their charm for children, as music halls did for adults, while provincial repertory theatres struggled to stay open. Other traditional leisure activities, however, retained their popularity. People danced just as much in the Thirties as they had during the 'jazz age' of the Twenties. City dance halls attracted suited and frocked customers on a Saturday night, while countless people 'dropped in' for a dance on their way home from work during the week. The working classes often preferred to hire venues such as mission or municipal halls, where they would only have to charge two shillings for a ticket. One eyewitness described men entering a dance hall together and lining 'up on one side, the women on the other. A male made his choice, crossed over, took a girl with the minimum of ceremony and slid into rhythm.' By the early Thirties, jazz had already given way to big band music, and that in turn would soon be supplanted by swing. New dances swept the entire nation for brief spells, among them the patriotic 'Lambeth Walk', the conga and the hokey-cokey. In the north of the England, 'pattern' or 'formation' dancing, which we know as 'ballroom', became the fashion.

Sport extended the wide appeal it had commanded since the late nineteenth century, despite the fact that women were still generally excluded. Few sports facilities were available for girls at state schools, and there was limited encouragement for women to attend working-class sporting events as spectators. The Twenties had been the first decade of mass sporting crowds, with the construction of Wembley Stadium, the rebuilding of Twickenham and the expansion of Wimbledon. During the Thirties, the crowds of men swelled even further.

Yet, predictably, the particular sport depended on one's class. The question 'Anyone for tennis?' was never directed at the working classes, and the cricket authorities also strove to preserve the sport's aura of elitism. On scorecards the initials of 'gentleman amateurs' were printed, while only surnames were given for professional 'players' such as Jack Hobbs, despite the fact that he was the greatest cricketer of the age. Players had to address gentlemen either as 'Mister' or by their titles, while 'amateurs' referred to everyone by their first names. The captains of country and county teams were always amateurs – the idea of a 'professional' captaining England was unthinkable. While some spectators complained that an aristocratic pedigree did not guarantee runs and wickets, nothing was done to reduce the snobbery.

The most popular working-class sports were rugby league in the north of England and football everywhere else. Both sports were exclusively male – the Football Association had banned women's football in the Twenties. The passion for football among working-class boys and men was universal. There were 35,000 junior football clubs in England by the end of the Thirties, while many businesses also organized teams. The great professional team of the decade was Arsenal, who won five league titles and two FA Cups. During the interwar period, sporting occasions such as the FA Cup and the Grand National were designated 'national events'. They were reported by the BBC and often attended by members of the royal family, who presented the trophy. It was a fairy tale in which England's aristocracy complimented its meritocracy.

Countless 'punters' bet on football matches. The most popular form of betting was the 'pools', where people predicted results and cash prizes were drawn from the entry money. 'The extent to which the lives of so many in Liverpool centre round the pools,' one sociologist commented, 'must be seen to be believed.' Many people also bet on horse racing, and you could also have a 'punt' on boxing, rugby league, or pigeon and greyhound racing. It is no coincidence that these sports were almost exclusively working-class, since gambling was believed to have replaced drink as the vice of the workers. Their preference for speculation over saving was interpreted as a sign of profligacy, but it more obviously suggested a lack of faith in the future.

Other popular leisure activities of the period included hiking and cycling. The predominantly middle-class hikers looked and acted like grown-up Boy Scouts and Girl Guides, with their distinctive green shorts, long socks, rucksacks, and preparedness for any eventuality. On his solitary country rambles, the author J. B. Priestley would encounter 'twenty or thirty people together and all dressed for their respective parts. They almost looked German, organized, semi-military, semi-athletic.' The same writer also regularly came across cyclists, and wondered 'exactly what pleasure they were getting from the surrounding country, as they never seemed to lift their heads from their handlebars'. According to the sociologist Richard Hoggart, 'A sign of arrival at real adolescence' for working-class youths was 'the agreement from one's parents to the buying of a bike on the hire-purchase system. Then one goes out on it at weekends, with one of those mixed clubs which sweep every Sunday through town and out past the quiet train terminus.'

Hikers and cyclists were emblems of the decade's contradictory relationship with the natural world. Suburbanites, whose new houses had encroached on the countryside, were eager to visit the country proper and experience the beauties and benefits of nature. But they reached it by means of transport which was harmful to its inhabitants and its landscape. An endless procession of cars, motorbikes and buses left London at the beginning of the weekend, filling the country air with petrol fumes. Having arrived at their rural destination, the suburban invaders proceeded to behave like town dwellers, in effect bringing suburbia with them. Into the early hours the tourists would sing and dance in the meadows and quiet villages.

The mania for hiking and cycling was part of a yearning for fitness and fresh air that was not unrelated to concerns about the nation's health and military preparedness. The Health and Strength League, which boasted over 100,000 members, promoted fitness among England's youth, in order to make it ready for another war. They successfully lobbied the parsimonious Tory-dominated government for £2 million in grants to local authorities for the construction of sports centres, playing fields, swimming pools, youth hostels and lidos.

The most characteristic leisure activity of the decade was probably the holiday. Over the course of the Thirties, the number of people entitled to paid holidays increased from 1 million to 11 million (around half of the entire working population) – the Holidays with Pay Act (1938) granted a week's paid holiday per year to most factory, shop and office workers. This was a significant victory for

1. Edward VII. He was the eldest son of Queen Victoria and was considered to be the most popular monarch since Charles II.

2. King George at the opening of the Festival of Empire at the Crystal Palace in 1911.

3. A tram in Yarmouth. It was the cheapest form of travel, even along the sea-shore.

4. The Boy Scouts in 1909. By the following year, there were over 100,000 of them.

5. Emmeline Pankhurst in 1914. One of the first suffragettes, who also established the Women's Social and Political Union.

6. Herbert Henry Asquith, prime minister from 1908 to 1916. He was also known as 'Squiffy' because of his habit of over-drinking.

7. David Lloyd George, prime minister from 1916 to 1922. His passion for social reform was matched only by his energy and ambition.

8. The British Empire Exhibition, 1924. A vast and expensive propaganda exercise to promote the unity of Britain and its dominions.

9. Flappers in 1925: young women determined to dance and drink away the memories of war-time Britain.

10. The General Strike of 1926. It heightened the sense of revolution hanging over the country.

11. A Butlin's poster from the 1930s. The first ever commercial holiday camp was established at Skegness in 1936.

12. Members of the Bloomsbury Group in 1928, a set of writers and artists who fostered radical innovation in the post-war world. *From left to right*: Frances Partridge, Quentin and Julian Bell, Duncan Grant, Clive Bell and Beatrice Mayor; *kneeling*: Roger Fry; *sitting*: Raymond Mortimer.

13. Charlie Chaplin in *The Great Dictator*, a 1940 film in which he parodied Adolf Hitler.

14. George VI on the day of his coronation, 12 May 1937. He was a reluctant king, who nevertheless fulfilled his duties as monarch in war and peace.

15. Winston Churchill in 1940. Implacable and strong-willed, he guided his country to victory in 1945.

16. The *Empire Windrush* in 1948. Passengers from the West Indies disembarking in Tilbury.

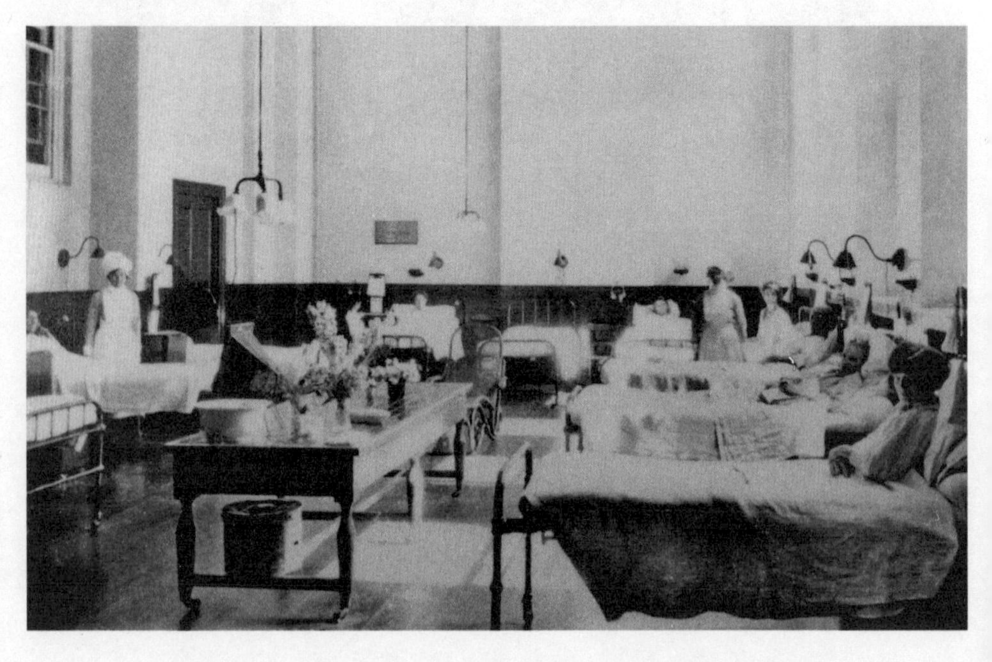

17. The birth of the National Health Service. Guided by Nye Bevan, it came into operation on Monday, 5 July 1948.

the unions, who had campaigned for paid holidays for over twenty years, and a great boon for the workers. The most popular holiday destinations were seaside resorts, with 70 per cent of the population of some northern industrial cities visiting the coast over the summer. Londoners also loved to visit the seaside, with Southend among the favoured destinations. Those with more time, and money, could travel down to the English Riviera in the south-west.

At the beach, children would build sandcastles or go on donkey rides, while adults would sunbathe, read or play football. Anyone who wished could swim in the sea, and sailing boats could usually be hired. Along the promenade there were pubs, cafes and restaurants. Funfairs, zoos, concert and music halls vied for custom, as did large venues for ballroom dancing. In this carnival atmosphere, people tended to drink more and wear less. One visitor to Margate described the fun: 'Singing, flirting, drinking, banjos and laughter; a distinct touch of sunburn; our lungs full of sea air, ourselves full of lobster and salmon.'

The passion for the seaside among the working classes prompted Billy Butlin to set up the first ever commercial holiday camp at Skegness in 1936. It proved so successful that he was encouraged to open other camps. By the end of the decade, there were more than one hundred commercial camps in England, which attracted over half a million holidaymakers each year. The camps offered three meals a day and entertainment for only 35 shillings per week in the low season. Entertainment typically included around-the-clock live music, dancing, sports, day trips, talent shows and beauty contests, including the selection of the 'glamorous grandmother'. After a day of frenetic fun, the presenter on the camp's Radio Butlin would say 'Good night, campers' at 11.45 p.m. Many holidaymakers ignored the announcement, however, and danced on long past midnight. At Butlin's, and at the seaside generally, the working classes were determined to prove their fun was as good as that of their so-called 'betters'.

24

The country of the dole

J. B. Priestley was one of millions of people who visited Blackpool in the Thirties, passing through the seaside resort in 1933 while compiling his survey of the nation, *English Journey*. Priestley liked the democratic atmosphere of the Lancashire resort: 'you are all as good as one another so long as you have the necessary sixpence', the town seemed to say to working-class holidaymakers. People had formerly lived in 'a network of relations up and down the social scale, despising or pitying their inferiors, admiring or hating their superiors'; but in the 'American' atmosphere of Blackpool, snobbery seemed to be losing its grip on the English psyche.

Yet some aspects of Blackpool manifested less welcome features of 'Americanization'. According to Priestley, the entertainment on offer at the resort was 'standardised', 'mechanised', 'calculating' and 'cheap'. In all these respects, the town was emblematic of the emerging England of mass production and mass consumption: the whole country, Priestley commented, was 'rapidly Blackpooling itself'. 'Everything and everybody', Priestley concluded, 'is being rushed down . . . one dusty arterial road of cheap mass production and standardised living.'

Priestley was depressed by the 'monotony' of this new mechanized country, but nevertheless thought it infinitely preferable to another England he encountered: the old 'industrial England of coal, iron, steel, cotton, wool, railways . . . square-faced chapels, back-to-back houses . . . slag heaps . . . doss houses . . . sooty dismal little towns [and] grim fortress-like cities'. England's urban centres had remained stationary in the nineteenth century, as if they were part of an industrial museum. Looking at the predominantly unemployed inhabitants of such places, Priestley thought there must still be a war on; this seemed doubly wretched to him since many of the unemployed he encountered had fought in France two decades previously.

This 'country of the dole' enjoyed none of the benefits of the decade's economic boom. Those who lived in the north of England, and much of the Midlands, did not regard the period as an age of plenty, but as 'the hungry thirties' or 'the devil's decade'. After the brief post-war boom, Britain's staple export industries were in terminal decline and reliant on shrinking international demand. By the late Twenties a quarter of British coal miners and steel and iron workers were unemployed, along with half of those who worked in cotton and a third of shipbuilders. The mining towns of Durham, the cotton towns of Lancashire and the metal and shipbuilding centres of Cumberland and the Tyne and Tees were officially designated 'depressed areas'.

And then came the crash. After 1929, international demand collapsed, cotton exports and steel production were reduced by half, coal production fell by a fifth and shipbuilding by 85 per cent. The consequences for workers were predictable and devastating. By 1932 over 40 per cent of miners, 50 per cent of iron and steel workers, and 60 per cent of shipbuilders were out of work. In many towns the unemployment rate was over 50 per cent and in some it rose to 80 per cent after the younger inhabitants left in search of work. Not only were more people out of work in these ghost towns, but they were unemployed for much longer – for years or even decades. Industrial action was no longer an option after the failure of the General Strike, while parliament offered little scope for protest, since Labour MPs now comprised a mere 8 per cent of the Commons. Yet many English people felt it was the government's duty to help the unemployed. Did the National Government have the vision to protect citizens who had lost jobs through no fault of their own?

* * *

The chancellor, Neville Chamberlain, insisted that mass unemployment was an inevitable consequence of market forces. All the government could do was wait until economic conditions improved, even if that was unlikely to happen for 'at least a decade'. The contrast with his attitude to the 1931 financial crisis was marked. The cabinet now believed that the currency and the banks could be saved by 'balancing the budget', which in practice meant making deep cuts to unemployment benefit. While the miners, metalworkers and shipbuilders could be left to face a maelstrom of market forces unaided, the banks could not. The government practised free market capitalism for manufacturing and manual workers, and socialism for the financial and monetary sector. Critics on the left reminded the coalition that England was one of the wealthiest countries in the world, and the centre of the largest empire in history.

By doing nothing for the unemployed, the National Government exacerbated the impoverishment of a large part of the population. They tried to reduce the existing unemployment benefit in the name of 'economy'; when the long-term unemployed exhausted the 'insurance pay' that was drawn from their own contributions or passed the six-month period of entitlement, the benefit they received was, in the words of one sociologist, 'limited to the smallest sum that will keep [them] from dying or becoming unduly troublesome'. This meagre relief was granted to the unemployed only after a 'means test' had been carried out to ascertain whether the applicant was truly 'destitute' and 'deserving'. If the unemployed man had alternative sources of income – either through savings, or because another member of their household was in work – then the benefit he received would be reduced or withdrawn.

The means test was popular among middle-class suburbanites. Money from the public coffers ought not to be 'wasted' on those who did not need it; besides, 'lavish' benefits would deter the unemployed from making an 'effort' to find work. It was believed to be perfectly reasonable that an unemployed man who refused to take up a job offer 250 miles from where he and his family had always lived should have his allowance cut off. The unemployed naturally took a different view – why should a man who was not responsible for the loss of his job be penalized for having saved?

Why should his family face a choice between starvation and leaving their community to resettle hundreds of miles away?

The unemployed loathed the way in which the means test was carried out. Officials from the local Public Assistance Committee (PAC) would drop into their homes unannounced to see if their children were working or if they had recently purchased clothes or furniture. If either was found to be the case, the benefit payments to the family were cut or stopped. Alternatively, the PAC men would insist that certain household items and clothes be pawned before benefit could be claimed. One woman tried to prove her poverty to a committee official by showing him the drawer in which her baby daughter slept. Unimpressed, the representative 'asked if the baby was being breast fed, and [when] I said yes he reduced the allowance for a child' on the grounds that it would not require other nourishment. The means test was psychologically as well as economically damaging. Workers who had been independent for their entire lives were forced to open their doors to the successors of the hated Poor Law Guardians before being humiliated by probing questions. There was an irony in the way an increasingly bureaucratic social service state functioned: it had the power to intrude into every aspect of people's private lives, yet it would offer them neither support nor security.

Between 1932 and 1933 over 180,000 benefit claimants had their relief cancelled, while it was reduced for half of those who continued to receive it, 'saving' the government £24 million. Chamberlain was forced to admit that the system required 'rationalisation', yet his attempt to improve its 'efficiency', via the Unemployment Act of 1934, did little to ease the plight of those without work. Nor did the provision of grants to certain 'special' areas of the country make much difference.

Unemployment became the focus of extensive sociological research. 'From the London School of Economics and other places,' commented the journalist Malcolm Muggeridge, 'went annually many earnest persons, male and female, to plant their tents in depressed areas.' Here was a manifestation of the political conscience of the age and also of its 'scientific' spirit. In 1936, the Mass Observation organization was founded to collect data concerning the

British people; its monthly magazine offered statistics on economic and social trends to a public that was eager for facts.

As a result of these investigations, we know a great deal about life in the 'hungry thirties'. According to Seebohm Rowntree's 'human needs' standard, 30 per cent of proletarian families lived below the poverty line in northern cities such as Liverpool and York, at a time when the working classes comprised over 70 per cent of the population in such urban areas. To give readers an idea of what existence on the poverty line was like, Rowntree described everyday life for a family in which the wage earner was 'never absent from his work for a single day'. Such a family 'must never spend a penny on railway fares . . . never purchase a newspaper . . . never save . . . never join trade unions . . . must smoke no tobacco . . . drink no beer . . . have no money for marbles or sweets . . . nothing must be bought but that which is absolutely necessary for the maintenance of physical health.' This meant a weekday dinner of boiled potatoes and white bread with 'a lick of marge', accompanied by 'a pinch of tay' with 'a screw of sugar' in it.

Those who lived below the poverty line lacked the income for the basic requirements of rent and the minimum diet. Parents in such households 'literally starved themselves in order to feed and clothe their children'. A Liverpool family whose male head was unemployed 'had nothing but bread, margarine and tea, with condensed milk, for breakfast and dinner' and went 'to bed early so as not to feel hungry'. They lived four or five people to a filthy room, in the squalid Victorian slums that remained standing after the National Government discontinued Labour's clearance programme. There were an estimated 70,000 such dwellings in Manchester and 60,000 in Sheffield. No other European country had such extensive or insalubrious slums. Dampness, leaking roofs, peeling plaster and infestation of bugs were commonplace in these back-to-back terraces. None of the houses had hot water and many lacked clean cold water; several people would sleep in each single bed.

Living in these conditions took its inevitable toll on slum dwellers' health. They were malnourished, with nearly 70 per cent of all working-class children in the period having rickets; many were also afflicted with tuberculosis and anaemia. Often it was the mothers who suffered most. 'Mam' sacrificed her portion of the meagre household diet for her children, yet she became weak in consequence. A third of all women living below the poverty line were classified as suffering from ill health, while maternal mortality was identified as one of the most serious consequences of unemployment. Yet such findings were dismissed by the National Government, which attributed ill health to irresponsible household management. When doctors who worked in impoverished areas publicly challenged this view, their livelihoods were threatened by the government.

Along with sociologists, numerous novelists and journalists flocked to the underworld. 'Dole literature' of both the documentary and fictional variety became a popular subgenre in the Thirties. Affluent southerners enjoyed reading detailed accounts of the plight of those who lived 'up north'. 'Misery,' as one novelist commented, is a 'marketable commodity', as was naturalism. The 'Condition of England question', which had been asked in the 1840s by authors such as Dickens, was now asked again with even more fervour. Autobiographies by manual labourers who had lost their livelihoods became popular, as did the volumes of essayists such as Orwell, who followed in Priestley's footsteps and recorded his impressions in *The Road to Wigan Pier* (1937). Popular dole novels of the period included Walter Brierley's *Means-Test Man* and Walter Greenwood's *Love on the Dole*, in which an archetypal image of the genre appears. 'Motionless as a statue', an unemployed man hangs around a street corner, 'gaze fixed on pavement, hands in pockets, shoulders hunched, the bitter wind blowing.'

Many of these books vividly evoke the psychological impact of unemployment. Orwell was horrified to find that many men in the north of England were ashamed of being unemployed. 'The middle classes were talking about "lazy idle loafers on the dole", and naturally these opinions percolated to the working class themselves.' Their feeling of personal degradation was accompanied by a sense of impotence, and by depression, cynicism, mental instability, defeatism and fatalism. It was through work that the older working classes had defined themselves and their place in the world; without it, they felt hopeless. Youths, on the other hand, were less affected: Priestley described them as 'undisciplined and carefree, the dingy butterflies of the back streets'.

The unemployed of all ages had a tendency to turn violent. Sometimes their violence was directed against officials at the labour exchange, and on other occasions it was directed against themselves. Home Office statistics show that two unemployed men committed suicide every day in England in the early Thirties. Yet the violence was generally sporadic, being smothered by an overwhelming sense of apathy and boredom. It was this, along with sheer exhaustion, that stifled the anger of the unemployed towards a system that had failed them. While some Tory MPs feared that a revolutionary situation had developed, the jobless displayed little appetite for revolution. 'It cannot be reiterated too often,' one sociologist commented, 'that unemployment is not an active state . . . The overwhelming majority have no political convictions.' Orwell was shocked by the lack of politically conscious misery he encountered in Wigan. He attributed it to the longevity of people's suffering – after years without work, many had simply settled down to the dole as a way of life. He also reckoned that cheap luxuries, such as 'fish and chips . . . chocolate . . . the radio, the movies' had 'between them averted a revolution'.

The unemployed may not have been revolutionary, but they did not suffer in silence. Thousands of unemployed people, organized by the communist-led National Unemployed Workers' Movement (NUWM), participated in protests against the means test and the benefit cuts. The press portrayed the demonstrators as violent Bolshevik troublemakers who used bricks and stones in skirmishes with police. The police's official policy was to 'disperse' any protesters who were 'disorderly or about to become disorderly' with baton charges on horseback. Some policemen even turned rifles on the protesters; many were wounded, and a few were killed. The police were granted greater powers by the National Government in 1934, when a Sedition Bill enabled them to stop and search anyone 'suspected' of 'sedition'. Countless arrests followed the protests, but the NUWM was undeterred. It organized a number of 'hunger marches' from northern cities to London's Hyde Park, the protesters sleeping in workhouses and hostels on the way. These marches attracted coverage in the press and were frequently mentioned in parliament by Labour MPs.

Yet Labour's official attitude to the protests and hunger marches was ambivalent. Under the new leadership of Clement Attlee, the party refused to organize demonstrations with the communist NUWM, and condemned the violence that erupted during some of the protests. It was a classic Labour compromise: the party members expressed solidarity with a popular left-wing movement, while distancing themselves from its revolutionary programme. The communists accused Labour of lacking the boldness to make the most of the revolutionary moment, but the truth was that the Labour leadership wanted to postpone that moment indefinitely. Although Attlee and other leading Labour figures attempted to distance themselves from the conservatism of the MacDonald era with radical economic proposals, they were as committed as their former leader to gradualist socialism, achieved through parliamentary reform.

The march that inspired most sympathy among Labour MPs was the 'Jarrow Crusade' of 1936. During the late nineteenth century, Jarrow's shipyard had flourished and its population had increased tenfold between 1850 and 1920. By 1932, however, there was no work for 80 per cent of its adult population, many of whom suffered from ill health, with deaths from tuberculosis higher than in the nineteenth century. The following year, the Labour candidate for Jarrow, 'Red' Ellen Wilkinson, implored MacDonald to help the town. The erstwhile Labour leader and current coalition prime minister promised he would keep Jarrow in mind, yet MacDonald was now politically irrelevant; Walter Runciman, president of the Board of Trade, told the inhabitants of Jarrow to 'work out their own salvation'.

In early 1936, Wilkinson, by now the town's MP, set about organizing the Jarrow Crusade. Funded by a popular appeal, the hunger march was intended to protest against Runciman's disregard and to publicize the plight of a 'town that was murdered'. The organizers had no affiliation with the NUWM or with communism; it was a Labour initiative. In the autumn, 200 unemployed male inhabitants of the town marched over 250 miles to London, taking just over a month to complete the journey. When they eventually arrived in the capital, the marchers declined to join a Communist party rally and instead organized a meeting attended by as many as 15,000 sympathizers at which speeches were given, songs sung and banners waved.

The marchers wanted to carry a petition to the government asking for assistance, but coalition representatives refused to receive their deputation. In parliament Labour MPs condemned this decision, describing the government's 'complacency' as 'an affront to the national conscience'; Runciman, however, defended the coalition's record and pointed out that unemployment in Jarrow had improved in recent months. No central government assistance would be offered to the town. As for Jarrow's local government, its Unemployment Assistance Board stopped the marchers' benefits while they were away, on the grounds that the men would not have been able to work had employment become available.

Many of the marchers believed their efforts had been a waste of time, yet other protesters took a more positive view. They argued that their demonstrations had 'highlighted the situation that people were in' and had 'shown the authorities we are not prepared to take things lying down'. Besides, even though the campaign may not have produced immediate results, the memory of the protests remained with those who had grown up in 'the devil's decade' and who would come of voting age in the Forties. That 'depression generation' would use its vote to demand the nationalization of Britain's ailing industries and the creation of a welfare state in which hunger marches would no longer be necessary.

25

The Fasci

The course of Britain's continental foreign policy had been set by Lloyd George at the peace conference in 1919. Its central aim was the reintegration of a peaceful Germany into the international community. A contented and economically flourishing Germany was, Britain believed, necessary for European stability; it was also vital to the balance of continental power, especially now that the 'threat' of communism had emerged in Russia. British and French suspicion of Soviet Russia deprived them of their former ally on Germany's eastern border. No one in Britain believed a successful war could be fought against Germany without Russian aid; therefore Germany had to be mollified.

Britain remained at a remove from European affairs throughout the Twenties. Some observers detected the revival of an age-old isolationist instinct, typical of an island people. We do not have to look very far back in history for the main cause of English aloofness: a terror of becoming embroiled in another European conflict, after the horrors of the Great War. Another factor was the country's perception of itself as an imperial, rather than as a European, power. Pre-eminent politicians of the age, including Baldwin and Chamberlain, regarded continental affairs as a sideshow to the empire and the ailing domestic economy. The main object of foreign policy was not central Europe but the Mediterranean and the East, where Japan was perceived as a growing menace. In the Twenties, government officials even regarded American ambitions as a bigger concern than the prospect of a resurgent Germany. These worries were partially allayed when a naval treaty was signed in 1922 between Britain, the United States and Japan, but they did not disappear entirely.

In any case, Britain believed it was unnecessary to intervene extensively in continental affairs, since the prospect of European war was remote. In the view of British politicians, previous European conflicts had been caused by the aggression of an overambitious continental power, such as Napoleon's France or Kaiser Wilhelm's Germany. In the Twenties, no power was capable of conducting a war beyond its frontiers. Following the Versailles Treaty, Germany had no army and no armaments, and Russia had been economically and militarily enfeebled by revolution; France, meanwhile, had neither the desire nor the military capacity to embark on a campaign of conquest. Successive British governments of the Twenties confidently told their military commanders that no major European war was likely for 'at least ten years'.

From 1918 to 1931, every British government pursued the country's key goals – reintegrating Germany within the international order, while promoting the League of Nations and disarmament. In 1923 France had been in dangerous confrontation with Germany when the latter had defaulted on reparation payments. In response French troops had occupied the Ruhr area of Germany. MacDonald, who assumed the role of foreign secretary as well as prime minister in the Labour government of 1923, helped to resolve the situation by facilitating the first negotiated post-war agreement, the Dawes Plan. The accord ended the French occupation and attempted to set reparation payments at a level that was both fair and feasible for Germany, which was then in the middle of an unprecedented economic crisis. MacDonald energetically promoted the League of Nations, and attempted to draw the 'selfish and unscrupulous' French further into its orbit, in order to moderate their hostility towards Germany.

In contrast to MacDonald, Baldwin was, in the words of his private secretary, 'reluctant to study Europe'. Nevertheless, his foreign secretary, Austen Chamberlain, built on MacDonald's work and helped engineer the Locarno Treaty of 1925. Through these accords

Germany and France guaranteed each other's frontiers and agreed to settle any future disputes by arbitration, with Britain and Italy promising to assist any party whose territory was threatened. On the armament question, while Labour and Tory governments both advocated arms reductions, their motives differed. MacDonald, a staunch internationalist and former pacifist, favoured disarmament for idealistic reasons; the Conservatives regarded it as an excellent way to save the Treasury money. Throughout the Twenties, defence expenditure was lowered by successive chancellors, including Churchill, until by 1933 it accounted for only 2.5 per cent of gross domestic product. The nascent Royal Air Force received limited funding, and the number of its squadrons was reduced from 187 in 1919 to 18 in 1923, while the army lacked the necessary equipment to fight a large-scale war. Plans were drawn up for a new British naval base in Singapore to counter a potential Japanese threat, but the idea came to nothing. Although a reduction in defence spending was usual in peacetime, some people saw it as a symptom of Britain's economic decline, while others were concerned about the country's capacity to protect its empire.

In the years following Locarno all was quiet on the European front, to the delight of British politicians eager to direct their attention elsewhere. Germany consistently paid its reparations, which were gradually scaled down; it also attended meetings of the League of Nations. Germany's Foreign Minister, Gustav Stresemann, was determined to place 'a peaceful Germany at the centre of a peaceful Europe'; this aim seemed realistic, since the country had recovered after the slump of the early Twenties. The improvement in German living standards, after the appalling poverty of the hyperinflationary years following the war, encouraged political stability in its democratic Weimar Republic.

In 1928 Germany signed the Kellogg–Briand Pact, along with Britain, France, the United States, Japan, Italy and several other countries. The signatories repudiated war as a means of resolving disputes; a multilateral armament reduction agreement, or even a multilateral disarmament treaty, at last seemed a possibility. The disarmament cause found a passionate and articulate advocate in MacDonald in the late Twenties and early Thirties.

During these years, many English intellectuals were in favour of disarmament. Historians espoused the view that the arms race, rather than German aggression, had been the main cause of the Great War. It was therefore imperative that all nations reduced their armaments and allowed the League to arbitrate international disputes. A variety of vivid war memoirs were also published at the end of the Twenties, reminding readers of the horrors of conflict. Partly as a result of these publications, pacifism gained great currency among the general population; the Oxford Union passed the motion that 'in the next war this House would not fight for King and Country', not that many English people believed war was imminent. In its commentary on 1929, *The Times* wrote, 'Except for sundry disturbances confined to imperial localities . . . the year passed everywhere in tranquillity.'

And yet closer observation of the continental scene would have revealed a disquieting development. Most of the independent democratic states created at Versailles from the ruins of the defeated Austro-Hungarian empire, such as Hungary, Poland and Bulgaria, had abandoned democratic government and turned to authoritarian rule. Nor had the ethnic minorities within these new countries been successfully integrated; much of the large German population living inside Czechoslovakia, for instance, regarded Germany as its true home. Meanwhile, Portugal and Spain also jettisoned democracy for military government. The shift towards authoritarian rule across Europe was seen as potentially detrimental to peace, since the new rulers criticized the League and espoused aggressive nationalism. The movement to which they belonged was as yet nameless and shapeless. Soon it would have a title of its own.

The miasma then spread to Italy. The country had arrived at Versailles determined to carry off some of the prizes of victory. During the war, the British and the French had promised the Italians extensive territorial gains in return for military support, including most of the Dalmatian coast and a number of colonies. Yet Italy's claims were rejected, with the British and French reneging on their 'gentleman's agreement'. In consequence the Italian representatives angrily withdrew from the conference, and the peace settlement was reviled in Italy. It was in this context that ultranationalistic and paramilitary organizations, or 'Fasci', emerged throughout Italy in the early Twenties. These disparate and violent groups were also summoned into existence by the rise of Italian communism during Italy's severe post-war economic depression. The communists organized massive strikes and demonstrations, inspiring fear among the industrialists and the property-owning classes, who no longer believed that the liberal political elite of Italy's nascent democracy was capable of dealing with them.

One of these 'Fasci' was led by the war veteran and former socialist newspaper editor Benito Mussolini. With rousing rhetoric and considerable charisma, Mussolini held out the vague promise of a 'national rebirth'. He would impose 'authority' and 'order' on a society that appeared to be descending into chaos, and take control of the failing economy with the help of the industrialists. He would also redress the terms of the 'mutilated war victory' by extending Italy's territories. His vision, at once atavistic and modern, appealed to many among the middle and landowning classes who saw no fundamental incompatibility between 'Fascism' and their staunch Catholicism. The movement flourished in the country at a local level, and by the autumn of 1922 possessed 300,000 members. Encouraged by the groundswell of support, Mussolini decided to try to seize power by marching on Rome with his paramilitary 'blackshirts'. The march instilled fear in an anxious establishment and the Italian king invited Mussolini to become prime minister. Despairing of Liberal politicians and democracy, the elite had simply surrendered.

The new prime minister made short work of his political opposition, altering the electoral law to his party's advantage and arranging the assassination of his rival, the socialist leader Giacomo Matteotti. He then proceeded to suppress all other political parties and non-Fascist newspapers, and locked up political dissenters. By these means, and with the connivance of the Italian elite, Mussolini established a totalitarian Fascist state that assumed control of the economy and the judiciary, while encouraging militarism and discipline in the population through the creation of youth organizations. It also restricted personal freedom, with the threat of arrest to any intellectual who opposed Mussolini in word or deed. Finally, the government created a cult around Mussolini, as Italy's godlike leader, or '*duce*'.

MacDonald soon established cordial relations with the murderer of Matteotti. Churchill praised the 'gentle' Duce in the press, as the saviour of 'civilised society' in Italy and 'the necessary antidote to the Russian poison'. The fear of communism invariably overcame concerns about the threat Fascism posed to democracy. Few British politicians were worried about Mussolini's expansionist ambitions, none of which were likely to upset the balance of power in Europe.

In other words, an ultranationalist, outwardly aggressive totalitarian state was tolerable in Italy because it was not Germany. Not only was Germany a powerful economic force, but the country was situated at the heart of the continent. Any attempt to extend its borders westwards would provoke another war, and, while eastern expansion was much less of a concern now that Russia was no longer a British ally, an enlarged Germany might still be a threat to continental peace and to British interests.

Another ultranationalist right-wing party had emerged in Bavaria during Germany's economic depression in the early Twenties. The National Socialist German Workers' Party offered an antidote to burgeoning German communism. According to the party leaders, Germany had been denied her 'rightful' position as the greatest European power by the 'Marxist' politicians who had 'stabbed' the country 'in the back' by surrendering in 1918, and by the 'vindictive' Allies at Versailles. The National Socialists were led by Adolf Hitler, a war veteran who earned a reputation as 'Germany's Mussolini' for his mesmerizing rhetoric and eagerness to use paramilitary violence against his opponents. Yet while Hitler's party attracted strong support among the Bavarian middle class and the landholding peasantry, it failed to secure the blessing of the Bavarian army. When it attempted a coup in 1923, it was easily quashed and its leaders were imprisoned. In jail Hitler composed his rambling semi-literate autobiography, *Mein Kampf*, in which he vilified the Jewish race as a 'poison' that had adulterated the 'pure' Germanic race. He also identified 'Russia and her vassal border states' as the territory into which Germany must expand in order to gain essential 'living space'. After his release from prison, Hitler renamed his party the 'Nazis', but they made little electoral headway, claiming only twelve seats and a mere 2.6 per cent of the vote in 1928.

When the financial crash came in 1929, everything changed. In severe economic depression, the appeal of the Nazis increased exponentially. It was stimulated by the widespread support for the Communist party, which organized strikes and protests throughout the country. The German economy appeared to be on the point of collapsing – production fell by 40 per cent, while unemployment rose to 30 per cent. Hitler blamed the crisis on the usual suspects – the Jews who 'controlled world finance' and the politicians who had drafted the 'punitive' Versailles Treaty. At the 1930 election the Nazis and the communists gained around a third of the popular vote between them; two years later they claimed over half, with the Nazis emerging as the largest single party.

It was difficult to see how the country could be governed without the consent of either the Nazis or the communists, and it was clear which party Germany's leaders would favour. President Hindenburg appointed Hitler as chancellor of the German Reich, in the belief that his presidential power could control the inexperienced and 'vulgar' Bavarian demagogue. The industrialists and the wealthier classes saw Hitler as a puppet, and preferred any alternative to communism. Yet once in power, Hitler proved to be as ruthless as Mussolini, arresting and killing political opponents, abolishing the unions and the free press, and establishing a one-party totalitarian state. His corporatist approach to economics echoed the Duce's, as did his emphasis on internal 'order' and 'discipline'. His obsession with German racial purity and persecution of Jews went beyond Italian Fascist anti-Semitism. Hitler was also more emphatic than Mussolini in his criticisms of the Versailles Treaty, demanding that its clauses should be revoked immediately and that Germany should be permitted to rearm.

Hitler's rise to power did not arouse great concern within the Tory party or England's right-wing press. Most Conservatives saw the Nazis as preferable to the communists, and many sympathized with Hitler's grievances. Newspapers such as the *Daily Mail* praised the new German leader as the 'saviour' of his nation and even applauded his anti-Semitism. Hitler's features soon became as familiar to the British public as those of a native politician. Churchill was virtually alone on the government benches, in the months after January 1933, in describing Nazism as a threat to the British Empire.

26

The bigger picture

The rise of Nazism caused the first significant division between the Tories and Labour over foreign policy since the war. In contrast to the Conservatives, Labour MPs vociferously opposed the Nazis from the outset, on ideological grounds. The party did not advocate rearmament as a means of preparing for a struggle with Fascism, but continued to promote multilateral disarmament. Labour had no faith in the failed diplomatic and military strategies of the pre-1914 era; instead they believed that the collective resolution of disputes through the League of Nations, coupled with disarmament, was the only way of confronting the Fascist dictators and guaranteeing a lasting peace.

Conservative MPs were equally enthusiastic about the League, though for more pragmatic reasons. They hoped the organization might maintain continental peace so that Britain could avoid an expensive and unpopular rearmament programme, and concentrate instead upon her pressing domestic and imperial concerns. The League inspired zeal among the population in the early Thirties. To a generation which believed that the senseless carnage of the recent war had been caused, in large part, by a lack of foresight and judgement among the major powers, the attraction of a supranational organization was obvious. It would, they believed, resolve all disputes, at minimal risk to its members.

The English saw the League as the answer to potential diplomatic problems, yet its existence begged many questions. How could the organization's authority be backed up by force, in the absence of an army or of rearmament of its most powerful members? The League's supporters appeared to believe that its moral authority made rearmament unnecessary: the mere threat of economic sanctions would, they thought, force an aggressor to back down. But while this may have sounded convincing in theory, it had yet to be proven in practice. Another potential flaw was the question of how the League could settle disputes impartially in cases where the interests of larger and smaller members clashed. In principle all members of the League were equal, but in reality states such as Luxembourg and Lithuania yielded far less influence with the organization than France, Italy, Japan or Britain. It augured ill that powerful nations such as Britain simply ignored the League whenever it was convenient for them to do so; they never, for example, referred disputes within the empire to the League for arbitration.

In 1931 Japan invaded Manchuria, officially a Chinese territory but in practice an autonomous province. In the months before the invasion, Manchuria had descended into a state of social and economic anarchy, and the Japanese took control in order to protect the numerous commercial interests they possessed there. Sympathetic to Japan's point of view, the Tory-dominated National Government ensured the League did not condemn the country as an aggressor or invoke sanctions against her. Instead the British conducted an inquiry into the conquest and found that many Japanese grievances were justified, though they had acted unlawfully. It was a classic diplomatic fudge designed to reconcile China to the loss of territory and justify a reprimand to Japan on the international stage, yet it satisfied neither party. China felt let down by the League, while Japan withdrew from it in protest.

The Manchurian incident demonstrated the limitations of collective security. The League failed to arrive at a satisfactory settlement because Britain and France were unwilling to confront Japan, a powerful League member like themselves, with sanctions or the threat of force. At the same time, the episode reinforced fears among Conservatives concerning Britain's commitment to collective security; might its membership of the League embroil the country in a disastrous war over an affair that was of little significance to its people or its imperial interests?

While the Manchurian invasion was still being investigated, the members of the League met in Geneva at the World Disarmament Conference. The meeting inspired optimism in England, partly because of the presence of representatives of the United States, now the world's pre-eminent power. However, it soon became clear that several of the participants, including Japan and Italy, had no real appetite for disarmament, while Russia was also reluctant to reduce its military capacity, since it believed itself to be surrounded by hostile neighbours. In any case, the conference soon ran into the difficulties that had bedevilled continental diplomacy since Versailles: Germany wanted parity of armaments with the other great powers, but France would not allow this in the absence of military guarantees from Britain and the United States to defend her borders. Eventually Germany was offered armament parity following a four-year trial period, but the proposal arrived too late: once Hitler was installed as German chancellor at the start of 1933, the time for compromise was over. Eager to consolidate his power and popularity, he rejected the offer as a 'personal and national insult', before withdrawing from the conference and the League.

Hitler's audacious move was greeted with approval in Germany, and dismay everywhere else. The gloom outside Germany intensified when he openly embarked on an extensive rearmament programme. The reaction of the National Government to these events was revealing. Without consulting the League or its old ally France, it decided to secure its own interests by striking a naval agreement with the Nazis, in contravention of the Versailles Treaty. The French, who regarded the Anglo–German naval pact as illegal and treacherous, drew the lesson that Britain would place its own concerns above those of collective security. Hitler, meanwhile, concluded that the Allies were divided, and that the League was weak; he could proceed to revise the Versailles Treaty with impunity.

The British chiefs of staff were disturbed by the League's inability to deal with events in Manchuria and Germany and urged the National Government to rearm. An additional £40 million should be spent on the army, £90 million on the navy and

£15 million on the air force. The civil service, overseen by Sir Warren Fisher, also recommended a review of Britain's defences, and advised the National Government to bear in mind that Hitler was the author of the expansionist manifesto *Mein Kampf*. Churchill, who believed he was 'preparing for war', also begged the government to rearm, and to immediately form a ministry of defence.

Yet the National Government was reluctant to increase military spending – neither Baldwin nor Chamberlain regarded Hitler as a serious threat. The idea that he was a deranged ideologue who would stop at nothing to extend Germany's borders was too absurd and appalling to contemplate. The government wanted to believe him when he declared that he merely wished to redress Germany's complaints concerning the Versailles Treaty, and that he desired 'good relations between England and Germany'. In Britain's view, Germany's grievances were legitimate, and nor would their remedy conflict with Britain's essential interests – the security of its empire and its supremacy of the seas. And if revoking the Versailles Treaty involved the acquisition of some 'living space' for Germany in the east, then perhaps that would be acceptable, since Russian rather than British interests would be threatened. 'If there is any fighting in Europe to be done,' remarked Baldwin, 'I should like to see the Nazis and the Bolsheviks doing it.'

Rearmament was, in any case, neither an economically nor electorally attractive policy. In 1932–3 Chamberlain reduced defence spending to its lowest level in eight years. An increase in expenditure on armaments would entail raising taxes or increasing the public debt, and Chamberlain had vowed not to do either. Meanwhile, the public clung to its belief in collective security and disarmament. The fact that Labour was gaining ground in local and by-elections on an overtly pacifistic platform encouraged the National Government to believe, as the civil service put it, that the 'public is not yet sufficiently apprised of the reality of our dangers to swallow the financial consequences of the official recommendations'.

Inertia and exhaustion also played their part in the government's feeble response to the Nazi threat. Baldwin and MacDonald were now beset with the afflictions of illness and age: increasingly deaf and suffering from lumbago, the Tory leader was, as Churchill spitefully put it, 'amazingly lazy and sterile', while MacDonald would be 'far better off in a home'. Even in their prime, MacDonald and Baldwin would have been unable to deal with the mad gangster who now ruled Germany; by the mid-Thirties they lacked the requisite lucidity, energy and decisiveness even to attempt that demanding task. Yet it was above all the prospect of another horrific war that determined MacDonald and Baldwin's cautious response. Both men were loath to rearm since they believed, as Baldwin put it, that 'great armaments lead inevitably to war', and both were convinced that a second world conflict would destroy Western civilization.

Even so, the government eventually acknowledged that the international situation had grown more ominous. Baldwin, who took over as prime minister from MacDonald in 1935, signalled a shift in the administration's attitude. He committed to maintaining Britain's naval strength and achieving parity with Germany's burgeoning air force, yet the civil service was not satisfied by these assurances. It took the unprecedented step of publishing a White Paper, in which it warned the government that given Hitler's decision to rearm, it could no longer rely on collective security to guarantee peace. Britain had to urgently address its military deficiencies. Baldwin finally admitted the truth of such arguments, and defended the White Paper in the Commons against criticisms from pro-disarmament Labour MPs. Meanwhile, Hitler used its publication as an excuse to reintroduce conscription in Germany, and to announce his plans to expand a German air force that he claimed had already achieved parity with the RAF.

The National Government responded by signing an agreement with France and Italy in April 1935. The 'Stresa' declaration committed the three countries to opposing 'by all practicable means' any 'repudiation of treaties which may endanger the peace of Europe'. While the agreement reaffirmed each country's commitment to the League, it also suggested that the National Government now accepted that collective security could no longer be maintained. In effect, the declaration represented a return to the diplomacy of pre-League and pre-war days, when alliances had aimed to create a balance of power. Britain and France had recruited Mussolini as an ally because they feared he might side with his fellow Fascist Hitler, and thus tip the balance in Germany's favour.

Despite Baldwin's conversion to the cause of rearmament and old-style diplomacy, his government still prevaricated when it came to implementing the recommendations of the White Paper. Rearmament was still unpopular among voters, and an election would have to be called soon. Since the beginning of the Thirties, countless pacifist movements had emerged in Britain, while organizations such as the League of Nations and the National Peace Council circulated millions of pamphlets and leaflets every year, promoting the cause of peace. Between 1934 and 1935 the League conducted a survey into British attitudes to collective security that became known as the 'Peace Ballot', because it revealed overwhelming support for multilateral disarmament.

In October 1935, Italy invaded Abyssinia, ostensibly to redress the Versailles Treaty, which had denied the Italians a share of the Allies' colonial spoils. Britain saw Abyssinia as a legitimate sphere of Italian economic and colonial influence; it also wished to maintain cordial relations with its recently acquired Mediterranean ally. Yet Abyssinia was a member of the League, and now appealed for assistance; its fellow members condemned Italian aggression and demanded decisive collective action. Britain, however, refused to criticize Italy openly; instead the National Government tried to tempt Mussolini to call off his invasion with the promise of land in British Somalia.

Yet Mussolini declined to be bought off, and his troops pushed forward. The League decided to impose limited economic sanctions against Italy, a proposal the National Government reluctantly agreed with, to the annoyance of some Tory backbenchers and the delight of a group of Labour MPs. The pacifist section of the party disagreed, however, and Labour split into two factions. Baldwin's unerring political instinct prompted him to call an election. During the campaign he successfully exploited Labour's divisions, while boasting of the National Government's success in hauling Britain out of its economic malaise. A Conservative-dominated National Government would, he promised, do everything in its 'power to uphold the Covenant and maintain and increase the efficacy of the League . . . collective security can alone save us'. Baldwin had not attended a single meeting of the organization, yet now posed as its defender.

Baldwin struck a winning formula on rearmament that confirmed his genius for equivocal language. He asked for a mandate from the electorate to 'remedy the deficiencies which have occurred in our defences' in order to further the aims of the League, while at the same time giving his word 'that there will be no . . . materially increased forces'. Since voters were themselves ambivalent about rearmament, they were perhaps inclined to give Baldwin the benefit of the doubt. In any case, he was Britain's most experienced politician following Lloyd George's retirement. Labour, meanwhile, was growing in confidence and cohesion under the leadership of Clement Attlee. Yet although Attlee was a unifying force within a divided party, he lacked Baldwin's public appeal.

At the election of November 1935 the Conservatives lost some seats, as was usual for an incumbent government, but still claimed almost 50 per cent of the popular vote. They also increased their dominance within the coalition, since both the National Liberal and National Labour parties suffered heavy losses. Attlee's Labour performed well, gaining 38 per cent of the popular vote, yet Labour's 154 MPs posed no serious threat to the government. With hindsight, the most significant consequence of the result was that it left in power the 'old gang', as they were derisively known at the time. Baldwin assembled a cabinet of the 'second-class intellects' he favoured, who could be trusted to react cautiously to events rather than to try and influence them. The sharpest and most dynamic member of the government was Chamberlain, the chancellor, but he had no flair for foreign affairs, which now dominated parliament.

Churchill, meanwhile, was alienated from the party leadership. This was partly because of his opposition to its cautious rearmament, but mostly because of his views on India. A few months prior to the election, Baldwin had passed the Government of India Act, which granted the country virtual self-government. Churchill had bitterly opposed the bill, on the grounds that it would lose British manufacturers a key market and cause unemployment at home. The introduction of democratic elections, he argued, was also of no real advantage to India, since the country was not ready for them. Besides, it would only increase the power of Gandhi, whom Churchill described as 'a seditious Middle Temple lawyer, posing as a fakir'.

Churchill had openly challenged Baldwin over the Government of India Act, yet only fifty or so Conservative MPs had joined him. Most Tory backbenchers had seen no reason to fight their popular leader over a lost cause, while many older Conservatives regarded Churchill as a shameless careerist. Meanwhile, younger politicians in the party, such as Harold Macmillan, saw him as a reactionary anachronism. Another prominent young Tory, Anthony Eden, was equally hostile to Churchill and stood by Baldwin, who rewarded him with the offer of a seat in the cabinet. Henceforth Churchill was isolated in the Commons; he made speeches in which he warned of impending disaster, but they invariably went unheeded.

Once in office, Baldwin reneged on his key campaign promises and rearmament now began in earnest. Over the next two years, the chiefs of staff looked to match Germany in every military department, having identified her as the potential enemy. The government's official aim was still to convince Germany to return to the League, yet a contingency diplomatic plan was necessary should that fail. Part of the strategy was the courting of Italy, a potential ally of Germany. As a result, Baldwin's electoral commitment to 'increase the efficacy of the League' was severely tested by events in Abyssinia, where the Italian invasion continued.

Representatives of the League now demanded full sanctions against Italy, including an embargo on oil. They also urged the deployment of a naval fleet in the Mediterranean, to halt the flow of supplies and men between Italy and Africa and to suggest the threat of war. Yet the government was unenthusiastic about both the embargo and the naval manoeuvres, which might involve losses and leave Britain exposed to Japanese ships in the Pacific. It did not believe the French would join the British fleet, and it was also intimidated by Italian air power. Behind these various excuses, historians have sensed the British government's overwhelming desire to avoid alienating a key ally, as well as the fear of provoking another war. Baldwin viewed that prospect with terror, as did the pacifist king: 'I will go to Trafalgar Square and wave a red flag myself,' commented George, 'sooner than allow this country to be brought in . . . to a horrible and unnecessary war.' Instead of taking action against Italy, the foreign secretary Samuel Hoare tried to buy off

Mussolini with an improved offer that involved Abyssinia ceding extensive territories.

Somehow Hoare's secret plan was leaked, to public outcry. The National Government had sworn to defend the League, but was now bypassing it in favour of an ally guilty of unprovoked aggression. Protest marches were organized throughout England, and countless petitions were drawn up, while Labour MPs spoke out against the government's perfidy. The government dropped the plan, while Hoare was forced to resign as foreign secretary. He was replaced by Anthony Eden.

In the absence of an alternative policy, Baldwin reluctantly contemplated imposing oil sanctions on Italy. But as the prime minister procrastinated, Mussolini urged his armies to press on. To break the staunch Abyssinian resistance, the Italians used poisonous mustard gas, in contravention of the 1925 Geneva Protocol; they also indiscriminately attacked civilians, Red Cross units and medical facilities. Eventually, in May 1936, the emperor of Abyssinia surrendered and left his country.

The exiled emperor demanded that the League condemn Italy's 'violations of international agreements' and criticized Britain and France for condoning the Italian conquest. 'It is us today,' he prophesied; 'it will be you tomorrow.' His efforts were in vain. Under pressure from the British and the French, the League recognized Italian Abyssinia and ended sanctions against Mussolini's regime. Once again the public was outraged, while Churchill accused Baldwin of 'discrediting' the League. The National Government believed that undermining the organization was justified if the goodwill of Italy was secured, yet its handling of the affair was an abject failure. By imposing limited sanctions, Britain had angered Mussolini, who now announced that the Stresa declaration was void. The news was welcomed by Hitler, who embarked on diplomatic discussions with his fellow Fascist dictator in Italy. European Fascism was uniting.

With Italy now friendly towards him, and the British and French preoccupied with the Abyssinian question, in March 1936 Hitler decided to remilitarize the Rhineland, in contravention of the Versailles Treaty and the Locarno Pact. He was relying on the British to reject calls from the French for united military action against Germany. If the National Government would not stand up to Mussolini when he had invaded the territory of a fellow League member, Hitler calculated that it would not oppose a peaceful movement of the German army into German territory, and his gamble paid off. The government declined to support French calls for military action, a tearful Baldwin admitting to the French government that Britain's limited military resources rendered such action impossible. He added that public opinion was also against military intervention – most English people had no objection to German soldiers going into their 'own backyard'.

Labour wholeheartedly approved of Baldwin's decision. The only voice of dissent was from Churchill, who warned of an impending catastrophe and urged the government to join the French in opposing Hitler with force. With the enormous benefit of hindsight, many historians have taken Churchill's view that March 1936 was the last time a military challenge to Hitler might have been mounted by the Allies without precipitating a devastating war.

The government justified its feeble response to Hitler by emphasizing the bigger diplomatic picture. 'It is the appeasement of Europe as a whole,' the foreign secretary assured parliament, 'that we have constantly before us'. His attempt to direct attention to the 'bigger picture' did not inspire much confidence, since the picture was not only bigger but bleaker. The treaties of Versailles and Locarno had been ripped up by Hitler, who was unwilling to agree to any new accord that might stabilize international relations. As for the League, it had been emasculated during the Abyssinian affair and was now moribund.

Hitler's remilitarization of the Rhineland was applauded by the German people, and by the country's elite. The German chancellor had proved to his country, and to the world, that he could dictate to the other European powers. He soon crowned his success by establishing an alliance with Italy, which was formalized as the Rome–Berlin 'axis' in October 1936 (and later confirmed when both powers signed the Anti-Comintern Pact with Japan). While publicly Hitler claimed to have no further territorial ambitions in Europe, he secretly extended his rearmament programme in order to prepare Germany for a 'worldwide conflict'. The first stage of his plan, announced in *Mein Kampf* over a decade previously, was to embark on a war against the Soviets, in order to secure land in the east. It is hardly surprising, then, that experienced observers of the diplomatic scene looked to the future with foreboding. Austen Chamberlain, the former foreign secretary, remarked that he had never 'seen blacker clouds on the horizon'.

27

The Spanish tragedy

Recent diplomatic events had been watched with fascination and horror by the English people. For the first time since the Versailles conference, foreign policy captured the popular imagination and dominated parliamentary debate. Hitler and Mussolini featured in countless British cartoons and advertisements, while their regimes were discussed endlessly in the papers and the pubs. Support for the League of Nations had been a decisive issue at the 1935 election, and the government's 'betrayal' of that organization during the Abyssinian invasion had brought thousands onto the streets in protest. While 'Leagueomania' was stronger on the left than on the right, it nevertheless cut across the parties and the classes. Yet the next act of the unfolding European tragedy would divide English opinion clearly along political and ideological lines.

In July 1936, the Spanish military hierarchy tried to seize political power, under the leadership of the ultraconservative General Franco, who admired the Fascist governments of Italy and Germany. Franco's aim was to re-establish 'Catholic Spain', and to crush the modern 'diseases' of democracy, socialism and secularism. To achieve this, the Second Spanish Republic would have to be defeated and a military dictatorship established. Spain was deeply divided between a Catholic, authoritarian and monarchical right and a secular, socialist left. The Left flourished in the urban, proletarian centres of Catalonia and the Basque Country, while the Right was dominant in most rural areas, where landowners and the Church held power. These deep social divisions ensured that Franco's attempted coup provoked a lengthy and bloody civil war.

The conflict soon expanded beyond Spain's borders. Italy and Germany declared their support for Franco, while the Soviet Union sided with the Republic. It became an international and ideological battle in microcosm, as well as a rehearsal for a full-scale continental war. It also posed a diplomatic and ideological challenge to the governments of Britain and France. A fellow European democracy was crying out for support, but what would be the diplomatic price of assisting her? And what would be the price of refusing aid to the Spanish Republic and standing aside?

France's left-wing government at first offered military aid to Spain's republican forces, yet fears that its assistance might provoke its own civil war convinced it to withdraw its offer. Since Britain's military and civil service favoured Franco, and its establishment feared Communism more than Fascism, the Conservative-led National Government encouraged caution. Baldwin's principal aim was to try to prevent the Spanish Civil War from turning into a continental conflict, even though there was a risk that maintaining European peace might result in the destruction of European democracy. Bypassing the League, the National Government brokered a non-intervention deal between the European powers and established a committee to enforce it.

The Italians and the Germans soon began to provide Franco with military support on a lavish scale; in response, the Soviet Union offered aid to the republican forces. Both sides wanted to secure an alliance with the future Spanish government; they also regarded Spain as a convenient training ground for their armies and armaments. The non-intervention committee lived up to its name by declining to intervene, even though evidence of Fascist and Communist meddling was conspicuous. The obsolete League, meanwhile, played no significant role. The failure of collective security, as well as British and French inaction, gave considerable advantage to Franco. Democratic British and French governments looked on as the democratic Spanish government was eventually defeated, and the influence of Fascism spread further across the continent.

Labour MPs criticized the National Government's policy of non-intervention, yet they had no appetite for the war that might follow the pursuit of an alternative strategy. Nor were they unequivocal in their advocacy of the republican cause, since it was supported by Communist Russia. The party's qualified response disappointed intellectuals on the English left, who took up the cries of 'Arms for Spain' and 'Fight against Fascism'. Some of these radicals left Labour and joined the British Communist party, whose membership swelled from 1,300 in 1930 to 15,000 by the autumn of 1936. Many on the left saw the civil war as a straightforward struggle between Fascism and democratic socialism, the only moral and political basis upon which a civilized future might be built. The English left wanted to hasten and share in this glorious victory. Opposing them were pro-Fascist intellectuals and the vehemently anti-Communist journalists in the right-wing press – the *Daily Mail* dubbed Franco's men 'Crusaders of Righteousness'. Some Conservative MPs also espoused pro-Franco views, while more pragmatic Tories, such as Baldwin, were happy to see Fascists and Communists killing each other.

The Spanish Civil War undoubtedly spread ideology among English youth in the Thirties, but there are deeper reasons for that generation's engagement in politics. It had, in the words of the poet Edmund Blunden, been in 'the nursery in 1914', and was now confronted with the increasingly real possibility of 'a world roaring with bigger bombs'. It is hardly surprising that the Thirties generation were, in many respects, the opposite of the bright young people. The Twenties cult of the hedonistic rich had been replaced by what Evelyn Waugh called the 'solemn cult of the proletariat'. A sober style of dress – corduroy trousers, woollen jumpers, plain white shirts – was favoured in the Thirties, together with thick moustaches and beards. Even the flamboyant Brian Howard was forced to tone down his appearance, lest the left-wing opinions he now espoused lack persuasiveness.

Earnestness and ideology also permeated English literature and art throughout the decade. In the Twenties, many authors and artists had tried to escape from history and contemporary politics by focusing on stylistic experimentation. In the Thirties, history and politics returned as the central theme of art and literature. According to a cliché of the decade, a work of art was 'first of all a social and political event' and its relation to the world and to history was more important than its place within an artistic tradition. In this climate many authors became topical and didactic, while others, like the plain-speaking Orwell, aimed at stylistic transparency. A parallel development can be seen in the proliferation of clubs formed in the decade to 'save', 'fight', 'defend', 'declare' or 'overthrow' various political causes.

One such organization was Victor Gollancz's Left Book Club. This socialist society sent its 60,000 members the magazine *Left News* and its 'Book of the Month', along with various educational titles. By the end of the decade it had circulated over half a million publications; many of them espoused the republican cause in Spain or anti-fascism, while others focused on poverty at home, the most famous example being Orwell's *The Road to Wigan Pier* (1937). A number of LBC publications championed the Communist cause, both in and outside Russia. In 1937 the club published an augmented edition of Sidney and Beatrice Webb's 1935 book *Soviet Communism: A New Civilization?*, dropping the question mark from the title in deference to Stalin. The fact that the Soviet dictator had recently conducted show trials as part of his 'Great Purge' of 600,000 officials and peasants did not tarnish his reputation in the eyes of the authors or the publisher. Such naivety was common on the left, where many saw Stalin as a champion of democratic socialism.

Throughout England, Left Book Club centres were established, providing venues for discussion groups and lectures. According to Orwell, who gave a number of LBC lectures, the meetings were typically attended by 'old blokes from the local Labour Party [in] overcoats'; argumentative youths from the local Communist party; and young women who sat with their 'mouths a little open, drinking it all in'. Many members of the audience wore orange LBC badges, which bore the organization's watchwords: KNOWLEDGE, UNITY, RESPONSIBILITY.

Some middle-class intellectuals did much more than write books, pledging to defend the Spanish Republic with their lives in the

International Brigades. Of the 30,000 European male and female idealists who fought on the republican side in Spain, around 2,400 came from Britain. Among them were undergraduates, artists and poets, such as Julian Bell and W. H. Auden, who wrote memorably about their experiences. For some of the middle-class soldiers, stretcher bearers, ambulance drivers and nurses, the war was the defining experience of their lives. It provided a mirror image to the defining middle-class political experience of the previous decade – the General Strike, when many volunteers had defended the status quo against the working-class strikers. Other volunteers in Spain, however, were disillusioned by their experience. Orwell's *Homage to Catalonia* (1938) tells the depressing tale of infighting on the republican side, which the author witnessed during his spell of active service. Communism in action proved a disheartening spectacle, with the Russian soldiers behaving brutally towards their allies as well as their enemies. Orwell's seven months in Spain turned him into a vehement anti-Stalinist; yet some on the left were not interested in his criticisms – the Left Book Club refused to publish *Homage*.

Partly because of the famous war literature produced by intellectuals, the English contribution to the republican effort is sometimes regarded as a middle-class affair, yet the largest numbers of English recruits were drawn from the working classes. The first English memorial to one of the fallen volunteers was erected to Percy Williams, a twenty-three-year-old apprentice railway engineer from Swindon, who died two months after joining the International Brigades.

Five hundred and twenty-six British volunteers died in Spain, and around 1,200 were wounded. These casualties, and the death of a quarter of a million combatants on all sides, curbed the idealistic optimism of the English left. The horrors of war, which included 80,000 executions on both sides and the Francoist bombing of militarily insignificant targets such as the town of Guernica, increased their disillusion. As Franco and the Fascist forces advanced, few on the left retained their hopes of victory in Spain and even fewer their optimism concerning the ultimate defeat of Fascism. Socialism no longer seemed to be inevitable, or even desirable, in its Stalinist form. Yet at the same time, the civil war strengthened the Left's conviction that the Fascists had to be opposed, and that a war between democracy and Fascist dictatorship was likely. 'To be anti-war,' wrote Julian Bell, 'means to submit to fascism, to be anti-fascist means to be prepared for war. War will come.' Pacifism steadily lost its appeal on the left. Socialists now urged the National Government to press ahead with rearmament and to stand up to Hitler and Mussolini.

The Spanish Civil War offered members of the English left their first real encounter with fascism, a political ideology that had failed to flourish in England, despite the best efforts of Sir Oswald Mosley. After Mosley was expelled from Labour in 1931, he had created a 'New Party' to promote his corporatist economic policy. Under the influence of Mussolini's ideas, and in the growing conviction that liberal capitalism and parliamentary democracy were unlikely to survive following the depression, Mosley transformed the party into the British Union of Fascists.

The BUF united various Fascist splinter groups under Mosley's leadership. Authoritarian, nationalist, anti-Semitic and rabidly anti-communist, the party offered itself as the only viable alternative to an eventual communist success. Like its policies, the BUF's ethos was Italian – a group of violent and uniformed paramilitary stewards called 'blackshirts' would 'protect' 'The Leader' from anti-fascist protesters during public meetings and marches. Their most notorious march took place in October 1936, through an area with a large Jewish population in London's East End. Around 6,000 police attempted to ensure the safe passage of the 2,500 marchers but they were repulsed by approximately 100,000 anti-fascist protesters, with many women and children among them. After a series of running battles with the police, the anti-fascist protesters forced the BUF to divert their march.

Mosley possessed charisma, and an aristocratic hauteur admired by his working-class followers. With impassioned and eloquent speeches, he bewitched the crowds and certain sections of the press. His populistic diatribes against the 'old gang' of the establishment impressed the young and the poor, who felt ignored and despised by mainstream politicians. During its first two years, the BUF attracted 50,000 members and also received the vociferous backing of the *Daily Mail*, which ran the headline 'Hurrah for the Blackshirts!' Yet the BUF's popularity never translated into parliamentary gains, and no more than a handful of Conservative MPs offered Mosley their support. Moreover, unlike the Communist party, the BUF lacked middle-class intellectual champions.

After 1934, Mosley's blackshirts became increasingly violent, and their activities were disowned by sympathizers who aspired to represent respectable opinion. The National Government attempted to eradicate political violence by introducing the 1936 Public Order Act, which banned all quasi-military organizations and demonstrations. After the bill passed into law the BUF's membership dwindled to a few thousand, and in the end it was no more successful than the British Communist party. After 1937 mutual vilification was the raison d'être of both parties, with communist protesters the largest presence at Fascist meetings.

Why did fascism and communism fail to sway England, despite widespread poverty and the ineffectiveness of the political elite? It has been argued that Mosley's movement was doomed because its mass meetings, uniforms and leadership cult had no antecedents in English politics, yet this explanation is unsatisfactory. Political violence was often seen on England's streets in the Thirties, while the English taste for military pageantry and for organizations such as the Boy Scout movement suggests that the Fascist ethos was not entirely alien to its culture.

Even so, a belief in parliamentary democracy and the rule of law was deeply embedded in English life, however undemocratic and fallible the political and legal systems were in practice. Through successive reform acts, the entire adult population of the country had been enfranchised, which had given the political system some legitimacy. The English governing class was allowed to govern by the people, ultimately because it offered them protection, whether actual or perceived, in return for their obedience, according to the traditional social contract.

28

This is absolutely terrible

At the beginning of 1936 it became obvious that the health of George V was declining rapidly. Regular BBC radio bulletins kept people informed about his deteriorating condition. On 20 January, the announcer read out the words of George's physician, Lord Dawson – 'the King's life is moving peacefully towards its close'. Dawson then administered two lethal injections of morphine to the monarch. A swift denouement guaranteed a relatively painless end for the king, and also ensured that his death could be announced in the morning edition of *The Times* rather than in the evening newspapers. George remained a model of decorum to the end.

Lord Dawson also accelerated the king's death in order to 'preserve dignity'. As he lay dying, his mind wandered and his speech was irritable. On being informed that he might soon be well enough to revisit the town of Bognor, he exclaimed 'Bugger Bognor!' The official version of George's final words was 'How is the Empire?' – he was the last British monarch who might have plausibly mentioned imperial matters on his deathbed. By the time of the next royal passing, the empire would be diminished beyond recognition.

George V had been a relatively popular king, to judge by the public grief that followed his death. Yet this may also have been evidence of anxiety concerning the future, as well as nostalgia for the supposedly stable nineteenth-century world in which his character had been formed. As George's coffin was drawn through London, it received a jolt when it crossed a set of tramlines and the sapphire cross and ball of diamonds on top of the imperial crown fell down into the street. Some regarded this as an ill omen.

George V was succeeded by his son Edward, who commanded as much popular affection as his father, though for different reasons. Nicknamed 'Prince Charming', Edward VIII was a dashing twentieth-century dandy with a distinguished war career and countless love affairs behind him. As Prince of Wales, the carefree Edward had shown as little interest in marriage as he had in preparing himself for his future public role. His current inamorata was Wallis Simpson, a striking American who had married a British-American businessman following a divorce from her first husband. George V had disapproved of the affair, as well as of his son's behaviour. 'After I am dead,' he prophesied, 'the boy will ruin himself in twelve months.' Edward VIII set the tone of his reign in his first weeks as king by repeatedly breaking with protocol. He was also unorthodox in his outspokenness on political matters, expressing sympathy for the unemployed as well as for the Indians who demanded full autonomy for their country. None of this went down well at court or in Downing Street. Neville Chamberlain resolved to tell the new king to 'settle down', but was dissuaded by Baldwin from doing so.

A few months into his reign it was rumoured that the king intended to marry Mrs Simpson, who had filed for her second divorce. The problem was that the government, along with the dominions, the Church of England, the wider royal family and the royal household, objected strongly to the proposed marriage. Edward was the titular head of all of these institutions, and bound, by precedent and protocol, to heed their views. Society, still dominated by the aristocracy, was equally disapproving, while the public's view was summed up by MacDonald – 'they do not mind fornication, but they don't like adultery'.

Edward underrated the strength of conservative opinion within the establishment, and overrated his ability to influence it. He espoused the view that his marriage was a private matter; yet most of the governing elite begged to differ. Adopting a firm yet tactful manner, Baldwin told Edward he would resign if the marriage proceeded; this was effectively an ultimatum, since it might provoke a 'king versus government' constitutional crisis. Edward's champions, who included Rothermere and Beaverbrook as well as Churchill, suggested a marriage by which Simpson could become Edward's wife but not queen. But Baldwin, along with the empire and the royal family, refused to compromise.

As the crisis dragged on, many people became tired of it, and blamed Wallis Simpson for threatening the survival of one of the oldest institutions in the world. Meanwhile, Edward was increasingly seen as brazen, dictatorial and unbalanced. In the end he was forced to make a choice between Wallis or the crown: 'I am going to marry Mrs Simpson,' he told Baldwin, 'and I am prepared to go.' He then made a farewell radio broadcast to the nation and became the Duke of Windsor once more, retiring from public life on a vast salary. He was succeeded as king in 1937 by his younger brother, George.

'This is absolutely terrible,' George VI told a cousin. 'I never wanted this to happen. I'm quite unprepared.' Diffident and volatile, George sometimes spoke with a pronounced stammer, and he responded to the news of his brother's abdication by sobbing like a child. Generally regarded as a 'good sort' with unexceptionable qualities, he emerged bewildered from a cloistered family into the limelight. As a young man he had been taught that routine, discipline and manliness were paramount, just as duty and loyalty were imperative. He learned that he must sacrifice his private interests for his public role. This upbringing moulded a 'sound' character, quite different from that of Edward. In one of his first public utterances as king, George said that he would respect 'the duties of sovereignty' and declared his 'adherence to the strict principles of constitutional government'.

Yet George's sheltered youth had hardly prepared him to rule over a country living through a difficult period of its history, with division inside its borders and menaces without. So far as foreign affairs were concerned, he supported the government's policy of appeasement. No one could deny that George had pluck – he had demonstrated this at Jutland, where he had seen active service in 1916, and he would draw on that experience in the years to come. The stolidity of his character reminded people of his father; some observers came to see his reign as contiguous with that of George V, with no intervening abdication. The flashy Edward was soon forgotten.

Baldwin had emerged triumphant from the abdication episode. To the surprise of many, 'Master Stanley' had seen off a series of apparently insurmountable challenges – a constitutional crisis, an economic depression and confrontations with Lloyd George and Churchill, the greatest politicians of the age. People now hoped that he would succeed in calming the confrontation brewing on the Continent. Yet the prime minister decided, at the beginning of 1937, that it was time to bow out. While his decision to retire was prompted by exhaustion and increasing deafness, it ought to have alarmed political observers: the supreme political survivor may have sensed that he would be unable to steer the nation through what Churchill called 'the gathering storm' of continental diplomacy.

'No man has ever left in such a blaze of affection,' commented Harold Nicolson in his diary. Baldwin had presented himself as a Victorian paterfamilias to the nation – earnest, benevolent and stern. Unfortunately, however, he was forced to deal with post-Victorian problems – including economic depression and Hitler – that were beyond his capabilities. Because he viewed England as an imperial power, he had taken little interest in the continental affairs that would determine the destiny of his country. On retiring, Baldwin was made an earl for 'services to the country', another emblem of the marriage of convenience between the English plutocracy and the aristocracy.

The man to whom Baldwin passed the chalice of the premiership received it eagerly, showing no concern that it might contain poison. Neville Chamberlain had been in Baldwin's shadow since the Twenties; his family had been waiting for Britain's highest office for almost forty years. Neville's father, Joseph, had been the most influential politician of his day, yet had never managed to climb to the summit in an age when aristocrats still dominated politics. Neville's stepbrother Austen had led the Conservative party but not the country – an anomaly in an era of Tory hegemony.

Neville Chamberlain had a fair domestic record. He had been a diligent health minister and a conscientious, if unimaginative, chancellor. He would enhance his reputation during his time as prime minister by passing the Factories Act, the Coal Act, the Holidays with Pay Act and a Housing Act, all of which improved working-class conditions without costing the Exchequer, or offending Tory sensibilities, too much. Only a skilful and determined politician, with a vast capacity for work and for mastering microscopic technical detail, could have formulated and passed such legislation. Chamberlain was also a consummate manager of all departments of government, who knew in detail what each of his ministers was doing. The contrast with his indolent predecessor could not have been more marked. Where Baldwin looked like John Bull in slippers, Chamberlain, as one contemporary put it, 'was corvine, with piercing eyes and a curving beak of a nose'.

Yet along with his efficiency, earnestness and single-mindedness, Chamberlain had several character flaws that would come to impede him. He was shy and oversensitive; his introversion and self-reliance made him obstinate, arrogant and tactless. This charmless man was as rigid as the black umbrella he seemed to carry with him everywhere. Entirely deficient in imagination, emotion and intuition, he put his faith in common sense, rational self-interest and fair play. Since he was guided by these values and motivations, he assumed the same of everyone else. His personality represented the narrow, puritanical and thrifty side of the English mercantile, Nonconformist character. It had been revealed during the abdication crisis, when he had urged the king to make his mind up over the marriage before the end of 1936, lest his shilly-shallying 'hurt the Christmas trade'.

Chamberlain wanted to deal with continental matters quickly, so that he could concentrate on more important domestic and imperial issues. Like his father and his mentor Baldwin, he saw his country within the global context of an empire of 'white dominions' rather than as a European power. Unlike Baldwin, however, Chamberlain had a hubristic belief in his capacity to settle all difficulties and disputes through personal negotiation. One consequence of this attitude was that he adopted a far more active approach to European diplomacy; another was that he ignored the Foreign Office and Churchill when they warned him about Hitler's untrustworthiness and territorial ambitions. Chamberlain preferred to rely instead on his own judgement and on the advice of an inner circle – all of them members of the so-called 'old gang' of experienced but unimaginative politicians. Churchill was disturbed by the 'marked dearth of men of ability' surrounding Chamberlain. Perhaps only an ageing, insular empire, and an archaic political system, could have produced such leaders. 'These men', Mussolini remarked, 'are the tired sons of a long line of rich forefathers and they will lose their empire.'

As Lloyd George had once said, 'Neville has a retail mind in a wholesale business', and it was this meticulous 'retail mind' that now attempted to deal with the gangster and gambler in charge of Germany. Chamberlain's strategy was the apparently reasonable and in some respects well-intentioned policy of appeasement, first invoked by Eden after Hitler's remilitarization of the Rhineland. Appeasement involved addressing Hitler's grievances regarding the 'flawed' Versailles Treaty, and permitting the extension of Germany's influence in Eastern Europe. Germany might be permitted to absorb the German populations who lived in Czechoslovakia, Poland and Austria, all of whom 'merited' self-determination. If any of these developments sparked a regrettable war, it need not involve Britain. In terms of military policy, Britain would continue to rearm, while its diplomatic strategy would be to court Mussolini, in a bid to weaken the Rome–Berlin axis.

Chamberlain and his inner circle believed that the restoration of Germany's power and status would satisfy Hitler and encourage him to 'settle down'. Appeasement would be promoted through direct negotiation with the German dictator; conferences were suitable in some circumstances, but there was nothing better than face-to-face discussion for resolving difficult issues. In November 1937, Chamberlain sent his trusted cabinet colleague Viscount Halifax to inform Hitler that Britain was sympathetic to German territorial claims to Austria, Danzig and Czechoslovakia. At the same time the prime minister opened up a private line of communication with Mussolini: 'an hour or two tête-à-tête with Musso,' he mused, 'might be extraordinarily valuable'.

The motivations of the appeasers, and the relative merits of their policy, have been endlessly debated. Appeasement was above all else inspired by the desire to avoid another bloody and costly conflict, and the English press amplified the message. In the late

Thirties, the appalling consequences of a second world conflict were endlessly discussed, with visions of the coming apocalypse vividly depicted by the wireless and the newspapers. England's cities would be reduced to rubble; its future generations would live amidst ruins. Since the English population was overwhelmingly anti-war, appeasement was an eloquent expression of its mood.

Yet appeasement also revealed a reluctance on Britain's part to attend to its European responsibilities, as well as an unwillingness to condemn the Nazis, either on ideological or moral grounds. Continental issues often appeared as a distraction to Britain. With its colonies and dominions averse to participating in another conflict, the country sought continental peace at any cost. Hitler's persecution of the Jews, as well as his assassination of political opponents, had become common knowledge, yet reports of Nazi brutality did not concern the men who formulated Britain's foreign policy. Some Conservatives admired the way Hitler had 'restored' his country's economy, while the English upper classes flocked to the extravagant parties laid on at the German embassy. George VI spoke for the ruling class when he described Nazi Germany as preferable to the 'Bolshevik' alternative.

Some historians see appeasement as part of Chamberlain's subtle plan to play for time and to address the deficiencies in Britain's defences. Rearmament was intensified between 1937 and 1939, while all departments of government were prepared for another war. Yet Chamberlain's rearmament effort was too little and too late. The £1,500 million he earmarked for defence expenditure in 1937 fell short of the £1,884 million the various defence departments saw as essential. In any case, Chamberlain had supervised the economy since 1931 and could have spent more on defence before 1937.

Other historians follow Churchill in regarding appeasement as both hapless and hopeless. Chamberlain and his colleagues, the argument runs, turned out to be the victims of Hitler's hypocrisy and mendacity, and vainly clung on to the hope of peace because they could not face the prospect of another war. The government should have embarked on a more extensive rearmament programme, while Chamberlain ought to have constructed a grand anti-fascist alliance with France and Russia. With powerful allies and weapons behind him, the prime minister might have called Hitler's bluff. In the end, it is hard not to see the period 1937 to 1939 as a series of wasted opportunities and, in Churchill's memorable phrase, as a 'line of milestones to the disaster'.

Between 1937 and 1938, Britain tried to persuade Mussolini to withdraw his troops from Spain and to recognize the Mediterranean status quo, in return for an acknowledgement of his Abyssinian conquest; the Duce was not tempted. Neither would he help Chamberlain with his attempts to persuade Hitler to resolve the 'Austrian question' through negotiation. In March 1938, without warning the other European powers, Hitler sent troops into Austria to incorporate the country into a Greater Germany. There was no opposition from the Austrian army or government.

Chamberlain was not averse to Germany absorbing Austria, despite the fact that the country was a democratic republic and a member of the League. But he was 'deeply shocked' by Hitler's unilateral show of force and sent an official protest to Berlin. When German diplomats told him that Austria was none of Britain's business, Chamberlain became angry. But what was he going to do about it? This was the question Churchill asked in the Commons, warning that Europe was 'confronted with a programme of aggression, nicely calculated and timed, unfolding stage by stage'.

It is doubtful that Hitler ever engaged in precision planning, yet Churchill's argument was soon justified by events. After Austria, Hitler turned his attention to Czechoslovakia, where a majority of Germans lived in the north-west area known as the Sudetenland. He declared that he would 'defend' the 'liberties' of these Germans and ensure their right to join a Greater Germany. His intention was to incorporate the Sudetenland, perhaps as a prelude to the annexation of other parts of Czechoslovakia.

Following Hitler's absorption of Austria, Chamberlain had been asked in the Commons to pledge support for Czechoslovakia's independence. Created by the Versailles Treaty, the country had been exceptional among the new Eastern European states in maintaining its democratic institutions since 1919. Rich in industrial and military resources and occupying an important geopolitical position, its borders had already been guaranteed by France and Russia. Yet Chamberlain declined to follow – ensuring the Czech frontiers would be militarily impossible and diplomatically risky, carrying with it the possibility of provoking another European war. Army chiefs, meanwhile, had warned the prime minister that British intervention would be like 'a man attacking a tiger before his gun is loaded'. Chamberlain believed that neither the public, nor the armies of the empire, would 'follow us . . . into war to prevent a minority from obtaining autonomy; it must be on larger issues than that'.

The Russians, eager to halt any possible German territorial advance in the east, proposed a conference whose aim would be to stop continental aggression. The Labour party and Churchill saw this as an opportunity to establish an alliance that would deter Hitler and encourage opposition to him within Germany. Yet Chamberlain declined to participate – he loathed Communism and thought the Soviets wanted to embroil Britain in a war with Germany. He informed the 'idealistic cranks' and 'warmongers' in the Commons who criticized his decision that conferences were, any case, ineffective. It was far better to take the direct, personal route.

Over the spring and summer of 1938, Chamberlain talked things over with Hitler and Mussolini on various occasions. These private discussions took place in a public climate of fear and panic, created by the threat of German invasion of the Sudetenland. During these talks, Chamberlain came to believe that Hitler was prepared to use force to facilitate the 'self-determination' of the Sudetenland Germans. Nevertheless, his confidence in Hitler's trustworthiness, and in his own ability to orchestrate a peaceful solution, remained undimmed. For his part, Hitler came away from the discussions confident that Britain would not oppose him with force should he annex the Sudetenland.

But Chamberlain was determined to do far more – or rather far less – than simply back down. The prime minister now privately persuaded France to renege on its commitments to upholding Czech borders. This was not difficult, since the French had no appetite for another war and nor could they guarantee Czech borders in the absence of British assistance. Chamberlain urged France to accept the absorption into Germany of all Czech areas containing a majority of German people, in return for the promise that Britain would guarantee the new Czech borders. Reluctantly France agreed. The prime minister then pressured the democratic Czech government to accept these terms, making it clear that the alternative would be a German invasion during which France and England would stand aside. With both the French and the Czechs in tepid agreement, Chamberlain returned triumphantly to Hitler on 22 September 1938, to announce that he had come up with a settlement that satisfied everyone.

Yet instead of thanking Chamberlain, the German chancellor now insisted on the immediate occupation of German-speaking areas by German troops. Chamberlain demurred on the usual grounds that 'the use of force' should be avoided. The French and the Czechs agreed, and a diplomatic stand-off ensued. France now declared she would stand by Czechoslovakia's frontiers and Britain reluctantly pledged to assist France. In the Commons, Churchill urged the government to hold its nerve, since the partition of Czechoslovakia would represent 'a complete surrender by the Western democracies to the threat of force'. The choice, he told a friend, is between 'War and Shame. My feeling is that we shall choose Shame, and then have War a little later.'

In the last week of September, however, it seemed likely that war would come first. London schools and hospitals were evacuated, sandbags were piled around public buildings and millions of gas masks were distributed. In anticipation of air raids, numerous trenches were hastily dug in city parks across the country and the navy was mobilized. The mood among the people was fearful: 'We were expecting 30,000 casualties a night in London,' the historian Arnold Toynbee wrote, 'and we believed ourselves . . . to be within three hours of the zero hour. It was just like facing the end of the world.'

On 27 September, a weary Chamberlain addressed the nation on the radio: 'How horrible, fantastic, incredible, it is,' he said, in his stiff, thin voice, 'that we should be digging trenches and trying on gas-masks because of a quarrel in a far-away country between people of whom we know nothing.' It was an extraordinary description of Germany and Czechoslovakia from a man who spoke of the intimate ties within the far-flung empire. Yet it is precisely because Britain was a vast global power that its governing class saw European 'quarrels' in these distant terms.

Despite his weary tone of resignation, Chamberlain still hoped to find an escape route. When Hitler asked Chamberlain to intervene with the Czechs, the prime minister grew optimistic once more, assuring the German chancellor he would secure his 'essential' demands 'without war, and without delay'. With the help of Mussolini, a four-power conference was hastily organized at Munich. There, on 30 September, an agreement was struck that gave Hitler almost everything the British and French had denied him a few days previously. It dismembered Czechoslovakia, ceding to Germany the industrially rich Sudetenland, which effectively destroyed the country's infrastructure and military capability. Britain and France guaranteed Czechoslovakia's new borders with the threat of force, but since Germany and Italy did likewise, the agreement was worthless. How would the Fascists oppose their own acts of aggression? Representatives of the Czech government were forced to wait outside the room in which the deal was struck; Chamberlain yawned as he informed them of its details afterwards.

After the conference, Chamberlain had another of his tête-à-têtes with Hitler, during which he asked the chancellor to sign a declaration committing Germany to 'the method of consultation . . . to deal with any other questions that may concern our two countries' and describing the Munich Agreement as a symbol 'of the desire of our two peoples never to go to war again'. Hitler was delighted to sign the declaration and, when Chamberlain stepped off the plane on his return to England, he waved the accord in the air. 'The settlement of the Czechoslovakian problem,' he announced, 'is only the prelude to a larger settlement in which all Europe may find peace.' Later that evening he was even more jubilant: 'There has come back from Germany to Downing Street peace with honour,' he declared. 'I believe it is peace for our time.'

Many newspapers echoed Chamberlain's triumphalism, while most English people felt overwhelming relief. 'The general opinion,' commented a clergyman, 'is that the P.M. has saved civilisation . . . No one seems to care which side has got the better of the other. The one thing they care for is that there will be no war . . . Thank God.' Sugar umbrellas were sold in the shops, confirming that the prime minister who carried a brolly with him everywhere had become a national hero.

Yet voices of dissension soon rose in the Commons. Attlee

complained that a democratic European country had been 'betrayed and handed over to a ruthless despotism', while Churchill called the affair 'a total and unmitigated defeat'. He predicted that Hitler would now advance triumphantly 'down the Danube Valley to the Black Sea' without 'firing a single shot', and that Britain would, in the near future, be forced to accept 'subservience to Germany'. After returning home from one parliamentary debate, the diarist Harold Nicolson went to bed 'pondering the Decline and Fall of the British Empire'.

Yet perhaps Chamberlain was not taken in by the rhetoric he had used on his return from Munich. In the winter of 1938 he claimed to have signed the Munich Agreement only in order to buy necessary time to rearm. He now made plans to create an army capable of fighting a continental war and bolstered the RAF. On the home front, meanwhile, detailed evacuation plans were drawn up for the major cities, and an increasing number of gas masks were distributed. Sandbags accumulated at the end of residential streets, and 'blackout' tests were carried out across England, in preparation for air strikes. The population watched these developments with a mixture of anxiety and disbelief. How could it have come to this, only two decades after the carnage of the Western Front?

The descent from Munich to war was rapid. A few days after the conference, Hitler, with his eye on the Free City of Danzig, declared his determination to settle the fate of 'other German populations' not yet incorporated into the Fatherland. He then demonstrated his belief that he could act with impunity by carrying out a pogrom against Jews, foreshadowing the genocide to come. In Austria, the Sudetenland and in Germany, Nazi thugs murdered hundreds of Jewish German citizens and destroyed their houses, shops, schools and synagogues. The widely reported massacre provoked outrage in Britain, but did not immediately alter its government's foreign policy.

In January 1939, with the help of Germany and Italy, Franco finally defeated the Spanish Republic. Fascist forces had again prevailed over a democratic continental government, and Britain had been unwilling, or unable, to prevent it. In an attempt to improve relations with the Italians, Chamberlain recognized Franco's Spanish government a few weeks later, and embarked on further talks with Mussolini's government in Rome. The prime minister left these talks convinced of the 'good intentions' and 'good faith' of the Fascists, while the Italians were convinced only of Britain's weakness. A decidedly unimpressed Mussolini rebuffed Chamberlain's advances and moved closer to Hitler, transforming Italy's political axis with Germany into the military 'Pact of Steel'.

Meanwhile, Hitler encouraged internal division inside what remained of the Czech state. In the early months of 1939 the mutilated country disintegrated, and the western half fell into his hands, with the eastern portion becoming the independent state of Slovakia. By annexing 'Czechia', Hitler not only ripped up the agreements he had signed at Munich, but he also contradicted almost every official statement he had ever made on foreign policy, by absorbing non-German peoples into the Reich. There seemed to be no limit to his expansionist ambitions, and no rationale to his policy.

Over the spring of 1939 there was a sea change in English opinion. The papers now advocated standing up to Hitler, even if this made war probable. 'Who can hope to appease a boa constrictor?' asked one journalist. At long last, the threat of Fascism was widely recognized. 'We'll have to stop him next time,' people commented in pubs across the country. 'We'll have to cry Halt. We'll have to go to war.'

Even Chamberlain now changed his tune. In a public speech made after Germany's annexation of Czechia, he asked: 'Is this the last attack upon a small State, or is it to be followed by another?' Even the prime minister could see that appeasement had failed. He also warned Hitler that Britain would 'take part to the uttermost of its power in resisting' any attempt to 'dominate the world by force'. The prime minister backed up his words with action, by announcing the conscription of 200,000 men for six months' military training.

Chamberlain also made a momentous diplomatic commitment when reports of German troops' movements on Poland's border prompted the prime minister to pledge Britain's support for Polish independence, a promise that was seconded by the French. It was an uncharacteristically bold gesture from Chamberlain, and unprecedented from a British prime minister in peacetime. It was also extremely rash, since there was no access to Poland for either British or French troops. Moreover, with only France supporting Britain, the country was in a much weaker position than she had been a year previously when Czechoslovakia and Russia would also have stood up to Hitler. 'I cannot understand,' the seventy-six-year-old Lloyd George complained in parliament, 'why before committing ourselves we did not secure the adhesion of Russia . . . If we are going in without the help of Russia we are walking into a trap.' Churchill and Labour agreed, and once more demanded a 'Grand Alliance against aggression' including Russia. Yet Chamberlain did not rate Russia highly as a military power and had a profound loathing of communists: 'I distrust Russia's motives,' he said, 'which seem to me to have little connection with our ideas of Liberty.' The contrast with his attitude towards Hitler and Mussolini could not have been more marked.

Nevertheless, discussions did take place between Britain and Soviet Russia in the first six months of 1939. The British wanted a pledge of military assistance from the Russians, should that be desired by both Britain and Poland; the Russians, meanwhile, sought a more general and mutual guarantee against German aggression. The talks did nothing to diminish suspicion on either side, and were conducted half-heartedly by Chamberlain's government, who may have seen them as a means of prompting Hitler to return to the negotiating table. Once there, Chamberlain was prepared to offer the German chancellor the control of Danzig, and economic influence in Africa and in the east of Europe – exactly what the Russians most feared.

Once again, Chamberlain's hopes were not realized. Instead of opening fresh discussions with Britain, Germany embarked on its own talks with Russia, which would pave the way for the Nazi–Soviet Pact of August 1939. Russia agreed to remain neutral should Germany become embroiled in a war, and Germany agreed to limit its territorial ambitions in Poland. Germany was no longer 'encircled', and Russia was no longer isolated. News of the pact was greeted with consternation in Britain. Conservative MPs, who had seen Nazi Germany as an infinitely lesser evil than Soviet Russia, felt betrayed by Hitler, while the Left felt betrayed by Stalin.

Chamberlain spoke publicly of his determination to honour Britain's agreement with Poland, while privately trying to lure Hitler away from Poland with the promise of economic rewards. Pressure was also placed on Poland to accede to German demands over Danzig, but the Poles stood firm. Hitler, unconvinced that Britain and France would go to war over Poland, thought he could once more deceive the enemy with a successful yet limited war in Poland, followed by negotiations in which Britain and France would cede to his demands.

On 1 September 1939, German troops entered Poland, and its planes attacked Warsaw. Britain's response was to urge Hitler to withdraw his troops, as the prelude to a negotiated solution to the 'Polish question'. When Chamberlain mentioned this plan in the Commons the next day, he was greeted with silence. Arthur Greenwood, acting as leader of the Labour party for the convalescing Attlee, demanded that Chamberlain send an immediate ultimatum – 'Every minute's delay now means the loss of life, imperilling our national interests, imperilling the very foundations of national honour.' Chamberlain agreed and an ultimatum was sent the following morning at 9 a.m. When it expired two hours later, Britain was officially at war with Germany. She was soon joined by France, India, the colonies and the dominions. Ireland, which had declared itself a sovereign state in 1937, exercised its right to remain neutral.

On 3 September 1939, air-raid warnings could be heard across London, sandbags were filled and thousands of children were evacuated to the countryside. They filled the platforms of the capital's railway stations, gas mask boxes in hand, just as a violent thunderstorm burst in the skies above them. The contrast to the mood in 1914 could not have been more marked. There was no rejoicing, no enthusiasm. Instead, as the writer Vera Brittain put it, 'the expected had happened, and was accepted with philosophic pessimism'.

29

The alteration

If war had indeed fallen on England, then it appeared to have done so with remarkable diffidence. Preparations for the predicted casualties of bombing had been intensive, with two million beds set aside in Greater London alone, and yet the terrible bombardment from the air remained unseen, unfelt and unheard for eight months. Rumours of war lay far off. The blackout had been put in place, the children prepared, and rationing had begun, but where was the enemy?

In fact, the enemy had other concerns. Until 1938, the possibility of war with Britain had not been seriously entertained by the Nazis. There had been no attempt, for example, to identify the most vulnerable or valuable targets. German intelligence had been uncharacteristically amateurish. In any case, Poland had to be secured before any further ventures could begin. Defended by an army that combined great gallantry with pitiful weaponry, Poland swiftly fell and burned. The Poles had rejoiced at Britain's declaration of war, but as the bombs fell on Poland's cities, the French and the British divisions in France did nothing. They outnumbered their German counterparts by more than two to one and yet a brief French incursion into the Saar region of Germany was all they achieved. Indeed this 'invasion' served only to convince the Germans, if further persuasion was needed, of Allied timidity. The Polish commander-in-chief was informed that the Siegfried Line had been broken and then that the operation 'must be postponed'. The first was a simple lie and the second one of those painful euphemisms that were to characterize so much of the conflict. Why then did France and Britain stand by when they were committed by treaty to intervene 'within two weeks' with a ground attack on Germany? The French, led by a commander who trusted to the strategy of the previous war, felt unprepared, and the British were still divided.

Meanwhile, a German official wrote, 'it is the Führer's and Goering's intention to destroy and exterminate the Polish nation. More than that cannot even be hinted in writing.' But the clandestine madness, and the vindictive cruelty, should soon have become obvious. From the outset, a policy obtained of bewildering the conquered peoples; savage violence alternated with hypocritical gestures of conciliation, particularly where the Jews were concerned. Even the forced moves to artificial ghettoes were presented as a means of protecting the Jewish minorities from their gentile neighbours. Nazi policy towards other Poles, however, was forthright from the first. They were plucked from their homes and shifted in vast numbers to the east, frequently before being casually murdered. It was considered vital to destroy the nation's cultural leaders, so the intelligentsia went the way of industrialists and nobles. Priests were singled out for particularly savage treatment.

In time, the use of buses, theatres, concert halls and even churches was prohibited to all but those of German stock. The intent was to kill or drive out all but a rump population, kept alive solely to furnish the Greater Germany with slave labour, leaving the land 'free' for German settlement. Polish children were given a bare minimum of education, the most important task of such 'education' being to engender in them a sense of inferiority to their conquerors. This was to prove a template for later conquests. A policy of removing elements considered 'unfit', 'undesirable', 'degenerate' or 'useless' commenced. In suburban Brandenburg a euthanasia centre was established, where the insane and mentally impaired were destroyed.

Anxiety and terror were the responses of those in England who listened to the wireless and accurately heeded the signs: horror at the rapid German advance and fear that the 'Blitzkrieg', or 'lightning war' would soon be visited upon their own country. The term well evoked the successive shock, terror and destruction that characterized the German military approach. Soon enough Britain would feel the force of its first wave. Hitler teased his next victim cruelly. At a rally he proclaimed, 'They are asking themselves in England, "When will he come? Will he come?" I tell you: He is coming.'

Norway had done its best to remain neutral, but the Reich had invaded anyway. The Allies had sent forces against the great battleships that heaved their way up the fjords, but were soon obliged to withdraw. Britain's first active engagement with the enemy had ended in humiliation at Narvik. On 7 May, the mood in the House of Commons was incandescent. Lloyd George openly called for Chamberlain to 'sacrifice the seals of office'. Before proposing a division, Herbert Morrison of Labour reminded the House that defeat would be 'a fatal and terrible thing for this country and, indeed, for the future of the human race'. Most celebrated is the appeal of Leo Amery, who, invoking Cromwell, urged: 'In the name of God, go.' The stern, succinct reproaches of Sir Roger Keyes, a war hero who had bedecked himself in full uniform for the occasion, carried perhaps more weight than anything. His refusal to blame any individual or party, and simple protest that it 'was not the Navy's fault' was eloquent enough. As for Churchill, he had been reinstated as First Lord of the Admiralty on the day that war was declared, and thus felt bound to support the government he had so relentlessly attacked, whatever his private misgivings. When the results of the division were announced, the government found that its majority had been reduced to double figures. It was a defeat in all but name.

On 10 May, Chamberlain asked Clement Attlee and the Liberals whether they would be prepared to join a coalition government. Attlee's polite but firm response was that the party's National Executive Committee must be consulted before any decision was made; they confirmed that Labour would not serve with Chamberlain as prime minister. The jibe 'If at first you don't concede, fly, fly, fly again' had been thrown at him for months, but now he could concede with honour. That evening he resigned. Lord Halifax was regarded as more reliable than Churchill, but he knew that he was not the man to lead the nation at such a time; Churchill immediately assembled a war cabinet of all parties and persuasions.

On the day of Chamberlain's resignation, German forces invaded Belgium and France. Churchill promised the House 'only blood, toil, tears and sweat'. These all soon poured out as the British Expeditionary Force – sent to France in September 1939 – fled to the coast. Britain was isolated and seemed likely to be crushed, but Halifax believed peace could be salvaged from the wreckage of honour. On 25 May, he proposed to the war cabinet that Italy be approached as mediator between Britain and Germany. Many in the cabinet had expressed admiration for Mussolini, Churchill among them; surely the Duce could be persuaded to soften the demands of the German enemy? In the following days, Churchill left the Italian option open, but at the last, seeing his war cabinet inclined to a dishonourable peace, he suddenly recalled both duty and panache. On 28 May, he appealed to the twenty-five members of the outer cabinet: 'If this long island story of ours is to end,' he declared, 'let it end when each of us lies choking in his own blood on the ground.'

On 10 July 1940 came the first attacks from the air; the Germans had come at last. Bombers like the feared Junkers Ju 88 pounded the cities and ports of Britain, while the nimble Messerschmitt Bf 109 engaged the Hawker Hurricanes and Spitfires. Many commentators wondered how Britain could survive such an assault. Hundreds of thousands of civilians would die, the radar would prove useless, and the Royal Air Force was surely no match for the invincible Luftwaffe. Yet by the end of the summer of 1940, the Luftwaffe, overstretched, outgunned and outfought, was forced to abandon its attacks on the country beyond the metropolis. Now it was the turn of London.

'The spirit of the Blitz' was at the time seen by foreigners as a miracle of the communal soul. From 7 September 1940 to 11 May 1941, by night and day, the German air force sought to destroy London. Aside from the obvious target of the East End Docks, St Paul's Cathedral, Buckingham Palace, Lambeth Palace and the House of Commons were hit. Pubs also seemed to attract their due share of attention from the Luftwaffe. After one such attack, an observer remembered alcohol pouring into the street and 'an old man with a cup, scooping it up out of the gutter'. In such straitened times, the sight must have evoked less disgust than rueful admiration.

The populace as a whole was not always responsive to government appeals. It is characteristic of Londoners to shrug off a summons to vigilance; in spite of the deaths and the burnt-out homes, the misery and the fear, they showed themselves unbowed. Dance halls still opened, pubs were busy and the children who were left still played. Since no one knew when bombs might strike, after a while there seemed little point in worrying about them. In time the city came to regard 'blitzing' as only another instance of bad weather. Nevertheless, while the Nazis made typically malevolent provision for the weak and helpless, Britain made a very different kind of provision for its own. Tales of what might happen under aerial attack had been circulating for years; at all costs, the defenceless must be moved to safety. 'Operation Pied Piper' was the fanciful name given to the mass evacuation of the young from Britain's cities.

Plans for the evacuation of children had been drawn up long before the declaration of war; Baldwin himself had warned the nation about the horrors of aerial bombardment. The Spanish Civil War had shown how much destruction could be wreaked on cities from the air. The bombing could also break hearts – nothing destroys morale like the death of children. This was made plain in a public information leaflet thrust through every letter box in the country in July 1939:

> We must see to it that the enemy does not secure his chief objectives – the creation of anything like panic, or the crippling dislocation of our civil life. One of the first measures we can take to prevent this is the removal of the children from the more dangerous areas. The scheme is entirely a voluntary one, but clearly the children will be much safer and happier away from the big cities where the dangers will be greatest.

For the purposes of evacuation, the country was divided into three regions: 'danger zones', 'neutral areas' and 'reception areas'. Danger zones were areas of obvious importance to the nation and therefore to the enemy, including big cities, docks, factories and industrial complexes. Neutral areas comprised the smaller towns, larger villages and the suburbs, while reception areas were exclusively rural. Parents and children were enjoined to keep gas masks at the ready in small boxes hung about the children's necks. In the event, no gas attacks came, but that they were expected at all is telling.

On 31 August 1939, the order came from the ministry of health: 'Evacuate Forthwith'. War had not even been declared, but one evacuee, Irene Weller, remembered mothers standing on their doorsteps 'crying as we walked to the station . . . I said to my brothers as we walked past our house, "Don't look round whatever you do," because I knew my mum would be there waving.' They all looked straight ahead, weeping. It had been anticipated that 3.5 million children would need to be withdrawn in the three days scheduled for the evacuation; in the event the number was nearer to 1.9 million.

Many children turned up where they were not expected. Anglesey had been expecting 625 children and found itself host to 2,468. Cultural clashes were frequent – an English child billeted in rural Wales, for example, could find herself having to learn an alien tongue. As the social scientist Richard L. Titmuss observed: 'Town and country met each other in critical mood.'

Yet practical inconveniences were inconsiderable beside the uneasy awareness that you were yourself considered an inconvenience. That this might be overlooked if you were personable cannot have proved very much of a solace. Susan Waters, a twenty-one-year-old teacher, arriving in Bedford from Walthamstow, remembered a scene 'more akin to a cattle or slave market than anything else'. Some women would specify 'two fair-haired, blue-eyed little girls', while farmers might size up boys to see if they were strong enough to work. John Wills from Battersea noted that 'if you were similar to Shirley Temple you were grabbed right away'. A woman appeared to be checking the evacuees' hair and inspecting their mouths. A helper suddenly intervened to save the children from further indignity. 'They might come from the East End,' she said, 'but they're human beings. They're children, not animals.' And the evacuees could scarcely be expected to have the necessary clothing. Few had serviceable boots, for example. Indeed, Liverpool quickly became known as 'plimsoll city' – the children's parents could afford nothing hardier, and plimsolls were worthless as protection against countryside mud.

'Verminous heads' were reported in Weymouth, and the response of some foster parents and 'aunties' was to shave them bald. A Lancashire chemist mentioned one particularly resourceful, or cash-strapped, woman who used sheep dip on her charges. Impetigo, a particularly virulent skin disease, was rampant among almost a quarter of the evacuees sent to Wrexham. There had been no time to medically examine them prior to departure. Yet in the universal cliché applied to every precarious situation, no one was to blame.

There were also happier tales. Between the frets and the joy, a middle note may be heard in the recollection of one reluctant evacuee. She was met by an equally reluctant 'grey-haired lady', who welcomed her new charge with the remark: 'Well, come in. I didn't want you, but come in anyway.' A large dog was the first to greet this child, its paws on her shoulders. 'The people of Littlehampton are the kindest in the world,' reported one relieved headmistress. Experiences varied according to area, cultural and social expectation, and human nature. Mothers who had waved off ten-year-olds were to find themselves, six years later, hugging teenagers. Sharp-eyed scrappers came back chastened, wild ones were tamed and soft ones hardened.

In September 1939, the government was and was not prepared. Officially, it had been firm in its commitment to peace, but, as is so often the case in British affairs, Whitehall proved more prescient than Westminster. Civil servants had been turning the cogs of war while Chamberlain hoped for peace. The devastating power of aerial bombardment was not underestimated, though it happily proved to be exaggerated. The penultimate roar of the Nazi dragon came in the shape of the V1, a pilotless plane better known in Britain as the 'doodlebug', whose rise led to a third wave of evacuees. Then came the V2, hitting the earth at more than 3,500 miles per hour. Milton may have named Pandaemonium, but Hitler created it.

30

The march of the ants

On 10 May 1940, the Germans carved their bloody trail into Belgium and towards Holland. The more factional among Labour MPs still found it hard to accept that Hitler was the true enemy; for Aneurin Bevan, hostility to Germany was a distraction contrived to divert the workers' energies from the real business of destroying capitalism. Small wonder, perhaps, that Churchill was later to say of him that he would prove 'as great a curse to his country in peace as he was a squalid nuisance in time of war'.

But a new government must be formed, and with Chamberlain gone and Churchill as prime minister and minister for defence, Labour could join it in good conscience. Meanwhile, the German forces continued to advance, crossing the French border and threatening Holland. The British and French failed to hold their positions and the British Expeditionary Force, outflanked and outgunned, retreated to the coast. The Germans reached Brussels, their fifth conquered capital, and captured Antwerp and Cambrai. 'This,' said Churchill, 'is one of the most awe-striking periods in the long history of France and Britain.'

There was a ray of hope in May, when the experts of Bletchley Park disarmed the most formidable of Germany's secret weapons. Under the guidance of the mathematician Alan Turing, a machine was devised which could crack the feared Luftwaffe's Enigma code.

Generated by a device adapted by the Germans from a Polish model, the code's settings were changed every twenty-four hours. It was necessary to use the prophetic powers of Turing's machine only in desperate need, and the authorities were forced to let many ships sink rather than reveal their ability to decipher the German code. It was perhaps the greatest breakthrough of the war, but tragically compromised by the realities.

On the evening of 26 May 1940, 'Operation Dynamo' was launched by the English to rescue the men of the Expeditionary Force stranded on the beaches of Dunkirk. Every available water vessel was commandeered in pursuit of this miracle, but official ineptitude and the exigencies of the moment ensured that some of the troops were left behind.

On the following day, the King of the Belgians abdicated; he had had enough, as had other continental rulers overtaken by Fascism. 'We must possess the continent,' Churchill declared, 'to make our way with every stop through "disaster and grief".' One major disaster was the capture and occupation of Paris. Was there worse to follow? On 2 July, Hitler ordered his forces to make detailed plans for the invasion of Britain. The plan gives an early glimpse of the erratic and deluded mind later evinced by the Führer. Even Göring did not believe that the preconditions for invasion could be met.

But if the nation was not aware of the possibility of invasion, it was scarcely the fault of government. All the talk about turning pots and pans and kettles into Spitfires and Blenheims kept the home fires burning. In 1943, 110,000 tonnes of scrap metal were being collected weekly. Iron railings, many of them ripped up from stately homes, fed the furnaces. 'The Great Saucepan Offensive', during which the women of Britain were exhorted to 'give us your aluminium', proved alarmingly successful once Lady Reading gave it her support. Only minutes after a speech in which she had urged her sisters to act, she walked home to see women converging on the nearest depots, saucepans in hand.

Nor did the fever to give stop with armies of women. The famous Children's Salvage Group were enjoined to gather whatever they could – and they responded, their nimble hands collecting when the national need demanded it. 'There'll always be a dustbin,' they sang, to the tune of 'There'll Always Be an England'. Tales of

First World War veterans offering their artificial limbs abound, although they were courteously refused. By 1943, government statistics claimed that each of the country's homes had provided about half a ton of salvage.

In the drive to save paper, even libraries were not spared. Private owners denuded themselves of all but those books that were of national importance. All paper had to be salvaged, and wrapping paper was prohibited. By 1945, the National Book Drive had brought in more than 100 million books. Rationing, meanwhile, was extended to all foodstuffs apart from bread, vegetables, offal, game and fish. The result was a great upsurge in general health, but also in flatulence. The spirits of the people were still robust. While the army fought, the civilians, amidst making, mending, rummaging and whistling, did their best to laugh both at circumstance and at the enemy. A spoof pub sign portrayed Hitler's distinctive hairstyle and moustache, and underneath 'The Bore's Head'. Comedy, whether in the music halls, on the wireless, or in homes, rose to happy heights.

It was as well that it did. The Battle of Britain, as it was known, beginning in July 1940, was Hitler's experiment on British preparedness; German High Command recognized that unless German force could dominate the island's air defences, there could be no security for the Nazi project in Europe, let alone an invasion of Britain. More attacks followed: the docks of London were particular targets, together with those of Liverpool, Manchester and Bristol. Göring directed operations; he opposed the wanton bombing of civilians because he saw no strategic advantage to it. By the end of September 1940, 1,500 civilians had been killed, but by the beginning of November, the Germans no longer dived over London. Their pilots and their planes had reached the limit of their usefulness. But within the areas of Europe 'under German influence', terror and violence mounted ever higher. Thousands of infants, boys, girls, crippled men and women were flung on burning piles and shot in ditches before being obscenely violated.

But Hitler's will was undeniable, and by 14 November 1940, the city of Coventry was in ruins. A photograph of the time shows a priest standing quiet beside the lines of bodies. By contrast, the city of Oxford was spared – Hitler had intended it to be the capital of an occupied Britain in the event of a successful invasion. In similar fashion, he decided not to destroy Paris.

Russia, however, as the ancestral leader of the 'degenerate' Slavic nations, was to receive less considerate treatment. The Ribbentrop–Molotov Pact had been signed the previous year, but Hitler had no intention of honouring it. The failures of the USSR in the Winter War against Finland, coupled with Stalin's timely cull of his own officers, gave him his opportunity. Hitler had issued a decree that 'The struggle against Russia was one of ideologies and racial differences and will have to be carried out with merciless harshness.' This was not a war, he said, that could be waged 'in a knightly fashion'. The language of spite, violence and murder sprang to his lips as if from some secret recess of Hell. Hitler told his officials that his great invasion of Russia was to occur on 20 May.

Slaughter by conventional means carried on. During the bombing of Belgrade, 17,000 civilians were killed in a single day. The Yugoslavs signed an act of surrender, and national dissolution followed. Serbia, now under occupation, was succeeded as leader of the former union by a newly forged Fascist state of Croatia, with results that would be felt decades after the war had ended. Elsewhere in the Balkans, the Greek dictator Metaxas refused the Italian demand that he surrender his country's ports. The Italian invasion of Greece, undertaken largely to impress Germany, was considered 'easy to accomplish', but it quickly sank into a vortex of lives lost in the cause of national self-respect. An overconfident Italian army found itself driven back into the mountains of Albania by dogged Greek opponents, but this hope for a free Europe quickly died when the Germans moved in to aid their ally, and Greece was divided between the two Axis powers.

Another large annexation was taking place. In the early morning of 22 June 1941, the Germans initiated their attack on Russia. Sixty-seven aerodromes were attacked and five cities subjected to bombardment, before the Germans began their march across the frontier. Three thousand Ukrainians were killed by the NKVD, the Communist secret police, followed by the massacre of Jews in Romania. This was not war as it had ever been envisaged. As the Germans advanced closer to Moscow, barbed wire and deep ditches were laid along their route. Seven thousand Jews at Borisov were shot 'in the manner of tinned sardines'. The killers confirmed their slaughter by consuming bottles of alcohol. Such a recourse was not unusual: German doctors engaged to separate the healthy from the sick in the death camps could stomach such work only when drunk.

Everything changed on 11 December 1941, four days after the attack on Pearl Harbor and the subsequent American response, when Germany declared war on the United States. The Allies, immensely heartened, counselled time and patience – victory was by no means a foregone conclusion. Hong Kong surrendered to the Axis powers on 25 December, and 11,000 Allied prisoners were taken. The death camps multiplied in almost unimaginable ways. In Sobibor, in the Lubin district of Poland, the Axis troops killed 250,000 Jews in a year. Auschwitz was one of the most notorious of the camps, but the procedure was to be one of 'concealment'. Whether this suggests guilt or fear of punishment is difficult to determine, though the euphemisms employed are telling: 'special treatment' referred to the mass murder of Jews; a 'special action' was an individual massacre. The latter often served as popular entertainment for visiting officials.

31

Would you like an onion?

In Britain, as rationing became even more severe, the most unlikely foodstuffs became luxury items. Jokes about onions wrapped up and offered as house-warming presents or wedding gifts quickly proved prophetic, but beer was still very much available. Despite severe rationing of grain, the government accepted that it would be foolish to deny the nation its follies. An unintended consequence was the new acceptance of women in pubs, or, rather, the new willingness of women to enter them. And grain could go to still more salutary uses. As a sign outside one bomb-wrecked pub proudly proclaimed: 'Our windows are gone but our spirits are excellent. Come in and try them.'

Nevertheless, life for civilians was harsh and uncertain; it was increasingly felt that the nation's soldiers had it easy by comparison. Aerial bombardment had ensured that the ordinary citizen was placed in the front line, while the soldier was frequently kicking his heels, waiting to leave. One observer, speaking for many, noted: 'Although I can readily believe that most serving men want to play their part in winning the war, I can't resist the taunt that joining the Army is about the quickest way to forget all about it.'

Such sentiments were generally felt, if rarely uttered, and instead found their way into the nation's disgruntlement as a joke. Caustic jeers about soldiers 'practising for when they meet Rommel' (in other words, running away) abounded in a nation whose sense of deference to the military had worn thin. Others jibed at 'the chair-borne troops', the vast sub-army of auxiliary staff, who seemed to many to be little more than clerks. And in a time of austerity, some could not fail to notice that soldiers had certain material advantages over their compatriots. Much of this resentment was groundless, of course, and nor did it preclude gratitude. Yet the perceived discrepancies in life between soldier and civilian engendered an attitude quite different from that of twenty years before.

When the soldiers did encounter Rommel, the jokes about flight withered in the speakers' mouths. The first battle of El Alamein had checked the German Eighth Army in its advance against Alexandria, but it had not been as successful as the second battle, under Bernard Montgomery. Like Wellington, 'Monty' was a martinet who cared deeply for his troops and received from them a respect leavened by wry affection. Sir John Cowley, recalling his first meeting with Montgomery, was to say that it took only the sight of that slight, wiry figure unhitching his jacket and rolling up his sleeves to know that all would be well. Lord Dowding, who commanded the air force, was of similar constitution; stern in most other ways, he would call his men his 'lambs'.

The first battle, in the summer of 1942, had stopped the Axis advance. The second went much further, resulting in the retreat of the Afrika Corps and the German surrender in North Africa in 1943. It was the turning point of the war, the culmination of the Allied desert campaign that changed the whole conflict. If the invincible Rommel could be stopped, what else might be achieved? That turning of the tide was matched with the Russian defence of Stalingrad and the ability of British and Commonwealth troops to expel the Germans from Egyptian territory. This may have been the moment when Hitler and his officers were revealed as superior only in the art of killing. The campaign was related to 'Operation Torch', devised to expel the Germans from North Africa with 300 warships, a large force of merchant ships and over 100,000 men. The church bells rang through England.

In the same month as the invasion began, November 1942, the Red Army launched an opposing force against the Germans north of Stalingrad, before moving south of the enemy forces and encircling them. The siege of Malta was also broken. Roosevelt and Churchill met at Casablanca, with Churchill insisting that the Allies 'cannot let Russia down'. It was also agreed that 'Hitler's extinction' must take priority over the defeat of Japan. The Stalingrad trap had caught the Germans, and the Axis surrendered the city. It was a great victory and must have suggested to Hitler and his cohorts that the writing of destiny was on the wall, not that Hitler had succumbed internally. The air raids against Germany continued day and night. Preparations were now being made for a cross-Channel invasion, with an elaborate deception arranged to convince the Nazis that the Americans and English were to aim for Pas de Calais rather than their true destination of Normandy. The monthly loss of German aircraft rose to 1,581.

Both Western and Eastern Fronts were now being attacked by the Allied forces, with mutual distrust set aside. The nightmare of Hitler's Aryan empire was being torn apart piece by piece. The Red Army had advanced almost 1,000 miles in a year, while the breaking of the Enigma codes gave the Allies an accurate and invaluable insight into German military preparations. The situation in Berlin became disordered, yet still the Germans threw more and more innocents upon the fire. Several thousand Jews were sent each day to Auschwitz, including more and more from newly annexed Hungary. The most obscure islands in the Aegean were raided to find the handful of Jews who had escaped the Greek mainland, and all this while the Allies marched further north and approached the gates of Rome. The Reich had reached the last limits of self-delusion.

By 6 June, the Allies had landed on the strand in Normandy, and in less than twenty-four hours 155,000 were assembled there. Hitler, not knowing the enemy's true destination, was for once unsure of himself. At the same time Churchill was informed that the Axis was running out of aircraft fuel. Its empire had been sustained by resources plundered from other nations, which were slowly being detached from their conqueror. A more private note of revenge was struck when a group of conspirators attempted to destroy Hitler; after its failure, the would-be assassins were hanged or shot, with Hitler invited to watch their bodies swinging.

In the spring of 1944, Churchill announced the number of casualties so far: 120,958. A report from the Reich noted, 'in this uneasy period of invasion and retribution . . . The people of Germany are beginning to long for peace.' British intelligence had now, by virtue of Ultra, discovered the position and size of all German military formations. It is one of the great mysteries of the war that the Germans did not suspect some secret military intelligence. The Allies were on the verge of a cross-Channel invasion of northern Europe, and Goebbels felt obliged to write that 'Germany must be made more desolate than the Sahara.' It came from the depths of despair, but it also evoked Hitler's belief that if Germany was defeated, it did not deserve to survive.

The ending had come. On the evening of 5 June, the Allied flotilla approached the beaches of Normandy. Hitler had ordered that the aim should be to repulse the enemy and send them 'back into the sea', but it was as futile as Canute's order to the waves. By midnight, more than 50,000 Allied combatants were on French soil. By 25 August, the general commander of Paris, General von Choltitz, had surrendered, to be triumphantly replaced by General Koenig. Yet it was not members of his group who liberated Paris, but the legions of the free Spanish. A German general who visited Hitler reported that 'it was a tired, broken man who greeted me, who shuffled onto a chair, his shoulders drooping, and asked me to sit down . . . He spoke so softly and so hesitantly, it was hard to understand him. His hands trembled so much he had to grip them between his knees.'

By February 1945, Berlin was deemed to be a fortress city in the charge of the Germans, but a further gesture was needed. This was the American and British attack upon Dresden from the air. The rocket scientists nurtured by Hitler fled for haven. As the Russian soldiers closed in on Berlin, the Nazi leaders made their final preparations. Their fates are well known. Hitler shot himself in the mouth, while his wife swallowed poison. Their bodies were soaked in petrol and enveloped in fire. Goebbels and his wife, loyal to the last, died with him, making sure to kill their children first. The justification for this was given by Goebbels's wife in her last letter to the world: 'everything beautiful', she wrote, 'is about to be destroyed.'

Their allies in militant nationalism fled such a fate, only to be outrun by justice. Mussolini and his mistress were shot and suspended by their legs in a market square. Vidkun Quisling, 'minister president' of Norway, whose name would become a byword for collaboration, was shot in October 1945, still proclaiming that he had had his nation's best interests at heart. In Slovakia, Jozef Tiso, the priest turned Fascist dictator, was caught and hanged in 1947. Ion Antonescu, the Romanian '*conducatore*', was executed in 1946. Hungary's Ferenc Szálasi, the brutal mummy's boy of 'Hungarism', was executed in the same year. Only Ante Pavelić, the head of the infamous 'Ustashe', the Croatian separatist movement whose cruelty had shocked even the Nazis, managed to evade justice. He found a sympathetic host in Juan Perón of Argentina, who also welcomed a remarkable number of fugitive Germans. Regarding the war in Europe, the last word belongs to its victims. One of the inmates of Buchenwald, snatched from death at the last hour, wrote that 'you were our liberators, but we, the diseased, the emaciated, barely human survivors, were your teachers. We taught you to understand the Kingdom of the Night.'

In Britain, the celebrations that had greeted the end of the First World War were muted, even sombre, when compared with the geyser of joy that burst forth on VE day. In no previous war had the English civilian been made to feel the force of the conflict so intimately or relentlessly. The notion of the 'home front' would have been almost inexplicable to a previous generation. Londoners had faced obliteration once every thirty-six hours for over five years, threatened at their work, having their meals, putting their children to bed, and going about the ordinary business of their lives. It had been a time when the 'moral economy' of war had been complicated, at times even reversed. If the soldier had suffered and died as a combatant, so too had the civilian.

But there was to be a moral inventory for the Allies to complete. The names of Hiroshima and Nagasaki would not be forgotten, and nor would that of Dresden. Closer to home, the Channel Islands had been liberated from the Germans, but the tale there is not wholly comforting. A photograph from that occupation shows a German officer and a British 'bobby' chatting amicably by a roadside. It may be that this image was taken for propaganda purposes, but it seems unlikely. Either way, it serves as a sobering corrective:

Britain could afford a sense of triumph and relief, but not of complacency or self-indulgence.

When VE day was announced, a ration-ridden nation felt able to loosen its halter for a moment. For the children, there was a special treat of free ice cream. One mother, speaking of the day when the surrender of the German armed forces was announced on the wireless, remembered offering this earnest injunction to her four-year-old: '"Marian," I said. "You must remember this all your life. It's history." But the reception was poor; and I could see that she would forget at once any word she happened to hear.'

32

The pangs of austerity

The nation that gathered at the polling booths in June 1945 was weary and ripe for a gust of optimism. But where the Labour party threw up the sash and flung open the window, the Conservatives seemed huddled in a corner, growling out their maledictions with little regard for the national mood. As Churchill warned, 'Socialism is, in its essence, an attack not only upon British enterprise but upon the right of an ordinary man and woman to breathe freely, without having a harsh, clumsy, tyrannical hand clapped across their mouths and nostrils.' Many might have agreed, but he went further: 'No Socialist Government conducting the entire life and industry of the country could afford to allow free, sharp or violently worded expressions of public discontent. They will have to fall back on some form of Gestapo.' If his reference to wartime conditions was merely unfortunate, this proved disastrous. Its manifest hyperbole at once disgusted and alienated many supporters.

By contrast, the Labour party attacked the profiteer and promised that most elusive of grails: economic equality. While Churchill invoked his wartime record, Labour looked further back, citing the hardship that had wasted the Thirties. In the *Daily Mirror*, a cartoon showed a veteran holding out the promise of peace to the people of Britain, with the plea that they should not squander it 'this time'. More subtly, Labour slipped a lever under the very cornerstone of

Conservatism. 'Freedom is not an abstract thing . . . there are certain so-called freedoms that Labour will not tolerate: freedom to exploit other people, freedom to pay poor wages and to push up prices for selfish profit, freedom to deprive the people of the means of living full, happy, healthy lives.' There was, of course, an element of 'shadow-boxing' in all this: the claims of the two parties were not irreconcilable. Nevertheless, the majority of the people, stirred by the appeals to solidarity and equality, made their choice. The success of the Labour party in 1945 was as unexpected by some as it was desired by others.

There were those who drew up elaborate plans for a better, safer world. Although Sir William Beveridge has great claim to be the founder of what became known as 'the welfare state', the Tories were also part of the group of experts that fashioned the report entitled *Social Insurance and Allied Services* in 1942. This, in turn, built upon the work of Lloyd George and the Liberals in the 1900s. In any sense that matters, the new welfare state was the lucky progeny of natural enemies. In 1944, one commentator declared that 'the time and energy and thought, which we are all giving to the Brave New World is wildly disproportionate to what is being given to the Cruel Real World'. Every second thought was now directed towards the goal of reconciling the claims of employer and employee. It was believed that the unions would lie down with employers as lambs with lions.

The Labour party had no desire to continue in coalition with Churchill and the Conservatives. Many aspired to some 'good old days' after the years of hardship, and a few were foolish enough to trust them. But the vision expounded by the Labour party was to be a new dawn for a new epoch, and with a new breed of man in mind.

This was reflected in the rival campaigns. Labour fought with the vigour and vitality derived from a new horizon, while Churchill could not help but dwell upon his victories. Few relish being reminded of a period of pain, even by their deliverer, and so it proved. In the general election of July 1945, Labour won 393 seats and the Conservatives won 219, an exceptional result. Even the most stubborn Tory might have felt the force of a rising wind.

Despite his reputation for diffidence, the new prime minister,

Clement Attlee, had a strong and independent mind. He formed a group of men who had that much in common with him, though little else, and neither did they have a great deal in common with each other. Aneurin Bevan, the minister of health and housing, was a Welsh bull with the face of a cherub, gravel in his belly and helium in his heart; the minister for fuel and power was Hugh Gaitskell, his stare one of almost lunatic intensity, as fierce in his centrism as Bevan was in his socialism; there was Hugh Dalton, the new chancellor, of vampiric appearance, loyal soul, brilliant mind and disastrous naivety; Stafford Cripps, his successor, lean and prematurely withered, an austere tribune always licking his upper lip as if to moisten his punishingly ascetic vision. And then there was Attlee himself, small and tight-featured, with a grin that could disarm the most obdurate adversary. Their very dissonance was to prove their glory.

The world was still much as it once was, with Lyons' Corner Houses and steam trains. Most goods were still rationed, paid for with warm heavy coins. The slump had left its mark, and 7 million houses were without hot water. It was the same old pre-war world, steadily more constricted and diminished. The effect was all the more unusual since the public sector of the country was slowly being populated by ministries, departments, red-brick boxes of officials packed together in computations for the future. In the spring of 1948, 42 per cent of people wanted to emigrate, compared with 19 per cent in 1945. Everyone was locked to the future, except those who were deluged in the dizzying present of jazz and bands. Others were preoccupied with planning to better their families, and even their nation – there was real hope that a more serious-minded consciousness would outweigh frivolity. But as Orwell wrote: 'Everyone wants, above all, a rest.'

But who had the time to rest? And what was there to sweeten it? 'Clothing? Not here, mate. Food? Try next door. Fuel? There may be a can nearby. Beer and baccy? No chance.' The *Express* announced 'Meat and Eggs going to be Off next week', a term widely used deep into the Fifties. One group, however, promised 'On', come what may. This was the 'spiv', the ringmaster of the wartime underworld. He was a profiteer, of course, but though despised, he was still needed. He was instantly recognizable: a trilby, a pencil moustache and a sloping stride. He could not proclaim his wares in the time-cankered fashion of the street hawker, as his antecedents might, but murmured them in a downward glissade of confidentiality. Behind him would stand his straight man, lending him a patina of respectability, with the available wares in a little box. He was a creature of the twilight, amoral rather than immoral.

In Cecil Day-Lewis's children's novel of the post-war years, *The Otterbury Incident* (1948), the chief villain, Johnny Sharp, is a spiv. Against two plucky bands of boys, themselves rather prone to scavenging, he and his accomplice wage a quietly implacable war. Sharp is softly spoken, slinky in movement and prone to Americanisms. He addresses people as 'buddy', another affectation typical of the spiv; but the American influence on the national voice was to outlast the spiv by generations.

After the war, over a quarter of the working population had to be brought back into the fold and retaught the ways of the civilian. Overseas service had trained men and women for combat, but not for the demands of a nation in a state of material haemorrhage. The rigours of austerity, the demands of regular work and the expectations of wives, husbands and sweethearts could prove both bewildering and dismaying. Where was the opulent, cheerful nation they had left? Why were there so many ruins? And what had happened to the courtesy they remembered?

The contraction 'demob' has the sting of dismissiveness, and its connotations were ambivalent. On the one hand, such men and women were conquering heroes; on the other, they had escaped much that the civilian had been obliged to endure, and were often reminded of it. More than one returning soldier overheard, 'There's one who had a good war!' Some among them, prisoners of war in particular, could be certain of sympathy and respect. But however they were greeted, there can be little doubt that 'demobs' were regarded as a burden. One child of the time remembered her father digging hungrily into the cheese on the dining table and asking her mother whether there was any more. 'No dear,' she replied, 'you've just eaten the family's ration for the week.' Afterwards 'he was very quiet'.

From the viewpoint of the returning soldier, it was often a question of having one's expectations upended. 'It had made my blood boil,' recalled one, 'while we were sweating in a jungle on a few shillings a day. Now I'm beginning to see how impossible it is to live on present-day civilian wages – let alone pre-war pay. The value of money is topsy-turvy.' Another said, 'I have to take the laundry, and calculate so that I have enough to wear before I can collect it again . . . I'm more harassed by small worries than I have been for five years.' Such 'small worries', coalescing often into implacable panic, were the staple of the world in which the demob was forced to acclimatize.

But the population wanted social change; for what else had the war been fought? Were the impoverished days of the 1930s to return? The celebration of the royal wedding in November 1947 might have been considered a positive jubilee, but the reports sound muted. Ursula Wood, later married to Ralph Vaughan Williams, considered it 'as quiet as a Sunday'. Orderly crowds gathered in restrained groups with the occasional bonfire to enlighten the proceedings. Some travellers waited to join the last 68 bus, illuminated with pale-blue lighting. Nor were civilians always impressed by the demob's efforts in the workplace. He was supposed to be complacent and work-shy – a host of satirical terms were soon coined. 'Stripes disease', 'pippitis', 'air crew's chest', 'storeman's clutch', 'ranker's dodge' and 'scrimshanking' were all expressions flung at the demob's back, and sometimes at his face. A veteran, writing in the *Picture Post*, felt minded to offer a counterblast: 'As one who has had five years' holiday in foreign lands at public expense, I feel that it is high time I turned my hand to honest work and civilian life, while some over-burdened civilians are given the chance of rest and recuperation in the Forces. Why should the delights of a camping holiday in sunny Burma or a cruise to Japan be denied these jaded people?' It is clearly unwise to speak of demobs in general. Their narratives touch every point: from ease to starvation, from 'cushy' staff posts to incarceration under unrelenting hosts.

33

The cruel real world

This was a time for even more privation. Bread rationing was re-introduced in the summer of 1946, and the cloud of a new terror occluded the sun with the threat of atomic war. It may seem odd that people can prevail under such circumstances, but patience and resignation had become customary. After constant attacks in the press, the prime minister, Attlee, felt obliged to reassure the nation that 'many of these restrictions fall heavily on the housewife. You can be assured that the Government will ease them as soon as it is possible to do so . . . On the question of bread rationing, your knowledge and good sense was an important factor in steadying and educating public opinion in the face of the press campaign last summer.'

The late 1940s inaugurated what may be termed the 'housewives' war', which was in part a war against the political classes. That the burden of increasingly restrictive rationing fell heaviest upon housewives was a fact denied by none, but while Conservative women aimed their darts at the government, women loyal to Labour reserved their wrath for the opposition. It was an unglamorous affair, and there were no clear or certain victors beyond the pale of Westminster and Whitehall.

The measures were provoked by a dollar economy, and by huge food import cuts. There was a further reduction in the clothes ration, and the use of foreign currency for pleasure travel was suspended.

Hugh Dalton was forced to resign after he inadvertently supplied a journalist with details of the 1947 budget. He was perhaps the first victim of what became known as the press 'leak'. Stafford Cripps was now chancellor, and seemed quietly intent on spreading his own brand of punitively abstract philanthropy. But, like Churchill himself, he led by example. A proud Spartan, he demanded nothing of others that he was not prepared to do himself.

As the 1940s progressed and a new election came closer, political rhetoric rose both in heat and in shrillness. 'We're up against it', 'We work or want', 'A challenge to British grit' – such appeals were characteristic of the Labour approach. They would have had a certain resonance only a few years before, but many were now beginning to wonder why wartime appeals were being made in a time of peace. As ever, the press was divided. Where the Labour-supporting papers emphasized that the cuts were inevitable, their Conservative counterparts scoffed at what they saw as excuses for simple mismanagement.

While it was generally agreed that wartime rationing had introduced a diet that was far healthier than before, by the late 1940s the case was not so clear. The suggestion that rationing had begun to badly affect the nation's basic health was first raised in May 1947 by Dr Franklin Bicknell in his paper 'Dying England'. Speaking for the government, Michael Foot proclaimed that on average children were 'stronger . . . than any breed . . . we have ever bred in this country before'. It is true that not even the Conservatives went so far as to say that the nation was starving. On the other hand, the medical world was increasingly troubled by the effects of the low fat ration. The fatigue and irritability so characteristic of the age might have been provoked less by the existential agonies of a war-weary nation, and more by a lack of carbohydrates.

The opposition's case was put most forcefully by Lord Woolton, former minister for food during the war. He is now remembered best for the Woolton Pie, composed of whatever was left in the larder, but at the time he was still revered as the quiet saviour of the nation's health and heart. He had refused to allow the fat ration to dip below 8 oz 'if we were to maintain the nation's health and productive capacity'. Now it had fallen to 7 oz. 'That is a dangerous position,' he maintained.

Labour countered such concerns with an appeal to community spirit. What was needed was the attitude of 'co-operative effort', 'courage' and 'common sense' – in short, something like the spirit of the Blitz. But to many, that spirit had come to require not so much sturdiness and solidarity as an almost angelic forbearance. The word 'propaganda' was now used without embarrassment by all sides in the austerity debate – the cuts of 1947 worked both ways. Horns sounding in the cause of export production and solidarity were answered by trumpets for free enterprise and individual effort. The local elections of that year heard the first answering murmur to the trumpet. The 'food and basic petrol election', as it was termed by Morgan Philips, resulted in large local election gains for the Conservatives, but did not sway the nation as a whole.

By 1948 the rationing had eased somewhat, the shop lights were on and the electric lights flashed occasionally. But prices were rising. 'Dreariness is everywhere,' one school teacher lamented. 'Streets are deserted, lighting is dim, people's clothes are shabby and their troubles [laid] bare.' 'Oh, for a little extra butter!' one social worker complained. From the late 1940s onwards, a tilt towards consumerism may be discerned.

It is often maintained that there was little to choose between the competing parties' aims, but that claim was made in hindsight – the differences were clear enough at the time. The Labour demand for a socialist democracy with full employment and a state that provided for its citizens 'from cradle to grave' sat uneasily with the Conservative promise of individual affluence and freedom from state interference. A tacit acquiescence in the post-war settlement grew to be the hallmark of all parties, but that was to come later.

Rationing had tightened under Stafford Cripps. The public's initial reaction was understandably resentful, but the mood swiftly softened when it was discovered that ordinary households could cope with the new austerities, however uncomfortably. Some resentment remained, yet in spite of continued shortages, the English could at last share in a luxury that had been rationed for centuries: a sense of gratitude. The new government was no sooner in power than it began to make good its promises; foremost among them was that none in these islands should ever again fear illness or want. In 1942, the Liberal William Beveridge had drawn up a paper in which he identified 'Five Giants': want, disease, ignorance, squalor and idleness. By 'ignorance' Beveridge meant lack of education, by 'squalor' poor housing and by 'idleness' unemployment. These could, and should, be amended by the state. Thus, in 1946, the National Insurance Act was passed, ensuring benefits against unemployment and sickness and provision for mothers and widows. No one, in principle, needed to starve. The Industrial Injuries Act provided for those stricken at work, and the Butler Act offered free schooling for all. There remained only the matter of the nation's health, and that would take longer to resolve. On 5 July 1948, three years after Britain went to the polls, the labourer, the clerk, the miner, the midwife and the seamstress, together with their children, could go to the doctor without fear of paying a penny. For Labour, it was the great new promise for the great new era. 'It's real Socialism,' proclaimed Aneurin Bevan, adding, 'and it's real Christianity too, you know.'

Here was a revolution with no clear precedent in England. Whatever G. K. Chesterton may have believed, the monasteries and friaries of pre-Reformation England were not 'the inns of God where no man paid'. Similarly, those who drew up the Tudor poor laws and established the parish system of relief had no conception of universal healthcare. Victorian refinements to those laws taught the lesson that sickness should be understood as the consequence of feckless living. Even the comparatively enlightened provisions of the 1911 National Insurance Act were confined to working men.

Rationing might have slimmed the nation down, but it had done nothing to avert disease. Tuberculosis, 'the white plague' of the Victorians, was still abroad, with few X-rays available to detect it. Diphtheria could cause a child to choke. Rickets and polio crippled the young as surely as they had a century before. Measles could be fatal. Scarlet fever, smallpox and influenza were as widespread as ever. Furthermore, the nation was simply run-down. The faces of the poor showed concave cheeks, chap-fallen jaws, grey, stubby teeth, and a nutcracker profile. As if poor sanitation, overcrowding and unsympathetic elements were not enough, children were still subject to Victorian notions of nutrition, being fed on starchy breast milk substitutes. Indeed, artificial feeding could be as dangerous for children as lack of hygiene. At a time when diarrhoea alone could kill a small child within days, it was common for a hospital administrator to spend half her day filling out death certificates. The imbalance of provision between rich and poor was dark and ugly. There was one GP for 18,000 people in the East End, while in the suburbs 'it was one for every two hundred and fifty'. Money had to be put on the shelf for the doctor in case anyone fell ill; if there was no money, people would pay in kind, with eggs perhaps, or vegetables.

Medicine was, in every sense, a private affair. Even funding for hospitals was secured by charity parades or private benefactors. The doctor himself was a breed apart. You did not visit him – he came to you. Pre-eminent in that world was the consultant, tailed by his subordinates in the hospital as a king by his courtiers. Any love he or the general practitioner had for the sick might have been considered incidental. Yet the reason for what seems like a rather mercenary approach is simple enough. Before the NHS existed, a GP bought his practice. Like any other professional, he sought to enlarge his business, improve it, and perhaps sell it on at a profit. He had a capital investment in his work and sought to preserve it.

Nye Bevan, for one, did not see why matters should remain so. His own father had 'died from dust', in miners' parlance. Bevan himself had started working in the pits of Tredegar at the age of twelve. He spoke of how food on the plate became a family's calendar: you knew it was the weekend when there was almost nothing. 'My heart is full of bitterness,' he wrote, 'when I see . . . the ill and haggard faces of my own people . . . There must be another way of organising things.' There was, and it lay nearby. The Tredegar Medical Aid Society had been founded at the end of the previous century as a means of providing the local workers with healthcare they could not otherwise have afforded. Workers put in 'thruppence a week' of their earnings and received free medical, dental and optical care. It was, as one resident recalled, a 'mini-National Health Service'. Bevan took it as his template.

The National Health Service Act had been passed along with the rest of the welfare legislation, but the other bills would not need quite such lavish preparation. The Conservative party under Churchill was opposed to Bevan's proposals on the basis of cost. Bevan wanted a truly *national* health service, invested in by the employee but sustained by taxation. But this, its opponents argued, would be costly, unwieldy, ineffective and, given the high levels of taxation required, would necessitate a threat to English liberties. Surely such matters could be devolved to the regions. But the population wanted social change; for what else had the war been fought?

On 3 January 1948, Bevan offered his pledge: free healthcare for all, to be delivered on 5 July of that year. In a speech he reflected that 'there is a school of thought, you know, that believes that if a thing is scarce, it ought to be dear . . . But this is not an orthodox government, and I am not an orthodox Minister of Health.' It was an assessment shared by his most implacable opponents, the nation's doctors, represented by the British Medical Association.

Members of the BMA had already become known as the 'shock troops' of the middle class. For the BMA, the proposed reforms were tantamount to an invasion of medicine by the state. The objection was not as disingenuous or self-interested as it appears: teachers would later display similar concerns about national curricula. And how would lawyers react if they were told to become servants of the state? Medical science had become a true science by the early Forties, and doctors were rightly proud of what had been achieved.

Dr Charles Hill, the leader of the opposition to Bevan, had been the 'Radio Doctor' during the war, dispensing homely advice to 14 million people in a voice as warm as a freshly baked loaf. Now, speaking on television against the reforms, his voice was grim and dour as he raised the old Tory shibboleth of freedom. 'We all want better healthcare, better treatment . . . But in organising them, let's make sure that your doctor doesn't become the state's doctor, your servant, the government's servant.' For all that Hill came from Islington, he acquired a slight West Country accent for this occasion, reassuringly bluff and English.

On 13 January 1948, the BMA called a plebiscite of its 35,000 members. 'Our independence,' it insisted, 'will have been sacrificed to a soulless machine.' An openly vituperative press campaign was launched, with Bevan satirized as 'fuhrer' in letters to the nation's newspapers. The whole project was denounced as a 'socialist plot'. On 9 February, Bevan presented his bill for an unprecedented fourth time; while in Newcastle, London and Liverpool, the BMA's efforts bore fruit and the NHS was rejected outright by doctors. In Brighton, the ratio of rejection was 350 to 1.

Amidst all this, a subgroup emerged: the Socialist Medical Association, composed overwhelmingly of students, led what support there was for the NHS, in the face of hostility and ridicule. It was not uncommon for members of this group to be pointed out as 'communists' in the middle of a lecture. It was of a piece with the BMA's language. They were convinced that with assimilation would come regimentation. Doctors would be forced to 'march up and down'. The word 'totalitarian' was ubiquitous.

On 18 February 1948, the results of the BMA's plebiscite came in. Thirty thousand had voted against, 86 per cent of the membership. Outwardly Bevan contrived to appear at once unbendable and good-humoured, but in private he confessed to a growing desperation. He consoled himself by trying to recall what first provoked his mission. 'When I hear the cacophony of harsh voices trying to intimidate me, I close my eyes and listen to the silent voices of the poor.' The man who it was said could make others believe that 'their dreams were realisable' was beginning to doubt. The bill had been passed but could not proceed. With victory in sight, the BMA felt it could begin to patronize its foe. Bevan was compared to 'a very difficult patient', self-willed but powerless.

Now at last the nation spoke. On 1 March 1948, a Gallup poll showed 87 per cent of the people in favour of the NHS, yet even this endorsement could not end the impasse. The National Health Service had a head but as yet no body, and if doctors chose not to work within his system Bevan had no means of compelling them. And so, unable to persuade the middle men of medicine, Bevan determined to woo its aristocracy. On 10 March he paid a visit to Lord Moran, president of the Royal College of Physicians and former doctor to Churchill. Moran headed the nation's consultants and they in turn controlled the great charity hospitals: Barts, St Thomas's, the London Hospital. These mighty institutions had reached financial extremis; in their vulnerability lay Bevan's advantage.

The two men took an instant liking to one another. Moran, known as 'Corkscrew Charlie' for his supposed deviousness, saw in Bevan not the orator in his parliamentary pulpit, but a charming and persuasive man with whom one could reach an accommodation.

Everything now rested on Moran, but he faced a challenge from Lord Horder, physician to kings and queens and a man whose views tallied with those of the BMA. On 26 March 1948, the Royal College of Physicians held its election. One by one its members dropped their silver coins into the bucket. Moran won, by only five votes.

Moran wrote to Bevan, explaining the deeper causes of the BMA's intransigence. 'My dear Nye,' he began. 'The irrational fears of GPs [are] that one day you *will* turn them into salaried servants of the state.' This, Bevan felt, could be addressed. He therefore presented an amendment on 7 April which ensured that GPs would never be civil servants or wage slaves without a new Act of Parliament. What was more, he promised that the GPs could join the new health service while maintaining their private practices, something he had learned from the Tredegar Association. The cynicism was as striking as the magnanimity. 'I stuffed their mouths with gold,' Bevan boasted. But the BMA, still confident of final victory, remained unbiddable.

In spite of growing scepticism in the press, on 12 April Bevan insisted that his health service would be launched on time. The government appealed again to the nation, this time via a press campaign. 'Every forty minutes, a child dies of diphtheria', it was emphasized. Twenty million people now signed up for the service. Within five weeks, 75 per cent of the adult population had put themselves down for the free healthcare promised.

On 4 May 1948, the BMA turned again to its members for support. Now, however, almost 40 per cent had changed their minds. The swing was by no means complete, but it was enough. And so, on 28 May, the BMA advised all its members to join the NHS. What seemed a remarkable capitulation carried a caveat: they called for a delay. This would have meant final defeat for Bevan, whose riposte was to point out that there would always be more demands and more delays. The reply worked admirably.

But the NHS was still far from ready. Moreover, in two years costs had almost doubled, to £180 million. Most of the 3,000 hospitals were crumbling; age and the Blitz had seen to that. In London, not one hospital was unscathed. Most worrying of all, with five weeks to go, 30,000 new nurses were needed. Another campaign was launched, revealing once again the Labour government's readiness to adapt to new media, but the press resumed its attacks: 'Free for All' and 'Stop this Bad Bill' were among the milder headlines.

It was Sunday 4 July 1948 and the NHS was to be open for business on the following day. Yet Bevan chose this day to launch an attack on his political opponents so intemperate as to be self-defeating. All the resentments of the past few years inspired this otherwise generous man to describe the Tory party as 'lower than vermin . . . They condemned millions of first-class people to semi-starvation.' Why did Bevan launch his spectacular assault the day before the birth of the NHS? There was little in the way of calculation at work. In truth, while he spoke like a poet he thought like a child, with an immovable sense of right and wrong.

On the next day, the NHS was inaugurated. The event was signalled by the opening of the Trafford Park Hospital in Manchester. 'It was like a wedding,' remembered Mary Bane, a nurse. True to form, Bevan greeted everyone. He proclaimed that 'we have been the dreamers, we have been the sufferers. Now we are the builders.' Attlee himself, in a period of illness, refused a side ward, insisting that he should be treated like anyone else. Nurses would find him chatting happily with his fellow patients. A spirit of gratitude, so long dammed up, now gushed forth. Even administrators would be given little presents, as if they had wrought this miracle themselves. There was, of course, a huge backlog of diseases, phlegmatically borne for want of any alternative. Women came to their GPs with their uteruses turned inside out. Men had gone about their affairs with hernias 'the size of balloons'.

All this came at a cost: 240 million prescriptions were filled out, a fourfold increase in two years. The budgetary caps were soon broken, and an upper limit of £170 million swelled to £352 million in the space of two years. A citizen would soon have to wait half a year to see an optician. Thirty-three million sets of false teeth were made in the first nine months, many of them for children. Bevan and others had imagined a decrease in the numbers of people using the NHS as the nation became healthier, but a different law applied: gas expands to fill the space available. As medicine developed and demand increased, so costs rose. But the effects of the new service could not be denied. Deaths from infectious diseases fell by over 80 per cent. For a while, the opposition remained unconvinced and unrepentant. Lord Horder spoke of 'this temporary minister' and predicted that the good old days of private practice would soon return. But the NHS remained, and its GPs remained its motor. The role of the doctor had come full circle: he was again the helper and healer.

Bevan himself resigned in 1951 over Hugh Gaitskell's introduction of prescription charges for dental care and spectacles. The funds were needed for a project particularly loathsome to a man of Bevan's sympathies, the Korean War. Attlee felt obliged to speak of Britain's 'very serious financial position'; the Americans withdrew their 'Lend-Lease' provision, which had provided supplies without Britain having to pay for them, resulting in a disproportionate excess of imports over exports. In eighteen months, a committee was set up on the 'Socialisation of Industries' to concentrate on the Bank of England, civil aviation, the coal industry and cable and wireless, but the fatal continuation of union opposition, mismanagement and general incompetence did not respond to optimism. The era that had offered so many sweeping commitments was finding it harder to sustain them. In the Labour manifesto of 1950, the party in government still felt able to recall its New Testament roots:

> Socialism is not bread alone. Economic security and freedom from the enslaving material bonds of capitalism are not its final goals. They are means to the greater end – the evolution of a people more kindly, intelligent, free, co-operative, enterprising and rich in culture. They are means to the greater end of the full and free development of every individual person. We . . . have set out to create a community that relies for its driving power on the release of all the finer constructive powers in man.

Never again was any party able to speak in such utopian terms. Once again the country seemed to be stumbling towards crisis. If it could happen in war, it could happen in peace. The scheme of nationalization had been put in place but many questioned whether it was of any actual benefit. They might have agreed with Churchill, who said it was 'proving itself every day to be a dangerous and costly fallacy'. Nothing was going as well as it appeared.

An almost hung parliament in 1950 led Attlee to call a second election. Perhaps he had grown complacent, or perhaps he desired vindication. In 1951, after only six years, the Conservatives were returned to office, promising an end to austerity and the beginning of wealth. But austerity, in one form or another, was to last until 1955.

34

An old world

On 6 February 1952, the king died, and, quite by accident, an Elizabethan age was established. Another herald was the establishment of the Conservative government in 1951. Domestic duties were no longer considered as inevitable as they had been, and the status of nursing and teaching rose proportionately. Women were no longer merely duchesses, mistresses, housewives or labourers, but teachers of mathematics and gymnastics. It had taken the carnage of the world wars to illuminate that. There were complaints, as at all times of social change. Surely it was not proper to train women as doctors in a world where cuts in services were continually threatened?

The coronation of the young queen was, if anything, more panoplied and pearled than that of her father. For those with ears to hear it, however, a new and sombre note had been struck. The new monarch of Great Britain was not the Empress of India; she was proclaimed simply as 'of the United Kingdom of Great Britain and Northern Ireland and of Her other Realms and Territories, Queen, Head of the Commonwealth, Defender of the Faith'. Her declared devotion to 'our great Imperial family' was celebrated, but she understood her new place.

The preceding year had been marked by the Festival of Britain. If it could not match the opulence of its Victorian model, then that was its glory. The times were quieter, pockets shallower and the people less inclined to triumphalism, but the bunting fluttered and the beer flowed. The Festival inaugurated, too, the establishment of the 'South Bank' as one of London's cultural centres. There were jarring moments, of course. One of the exhibits was a collection of printed rayon cloths, and the king was invited to inspect them but had no notion of their purpose. When enlightened, he was heard to mutter: 'Thank God we don't have to wear those.' Despite all outward gestures to popular sentiment, the royal family could not fully share the shared experience. Their role during the war years was revealed as an anomaly.

The empire was in fact on the brink, though few cared to recognize the fact. India had gone in 1947, lost, according to political legend, by the condescension of the middle-class English rulers. In truth, the efforts of Gandhi, Congress and the Muslim League had done much to convince the British that they had outstayed their day. The government was presented with a choice: the nation could afford an empire or a welfare state, but not both. The princes of the subcontinent were warned by Lord Mountbatten that if they resisted integration into the successor states of India and Pakistan they would be cut adrift, with neither dominion status nor a place in the Commonwealth. Independence came at midnight on 15 August 1947, and with it partition. Although none had foreseen this, some 14 million people were displaced as a consequence and countless lives lost. The line dividing India from Pakistan was drawn by the British, with scant regard for local realities or feelings.

Without India, what value the empire? To be sure, people admired the blaze of imperial pink on the map, but the empire had been a faint glimmer of gaslight in the minds of most. The paradox of an imperial and industrial superpower that allowed so much poverty in its midst was precisely what had inspired Marx and Engels. Cyril Radcliffe, on many occasions a defender of the empire, and the man who was tasked with dividing India from Pakistan, found himself agonizing over the question for the rest of his life: 'The gifts we brought . . . were Roman: peace, order, justice and the fruits that those things bring . . . Such benefits were admirable.' But he also felt obliged to issue a caveat: 'It may be that the government of one people by another can never be the best government in the long run, since benevolence and fairness are no substitute for national inspiration.' Though he was speaking of India, his remarks may serve for the empire as a whole, which was to undergo osmosis on a vast and humbling scale.

It began quietly enough. When the *Empire Windrush* docked in the summer of 1948, it brought less than a thousand people from the Caribbean. Some had paid their way and some had hitched a lift, while others were soldiers. They had heard of the 'mother country', as it was still known, but few had visited it. At first, they and other groups were met with placards bearing the legend, 'Welcome to Britain'. But what welcome lay behind the placards and the smiles? As the settlers settled, the legends changed and 'No Coloureds' became a common sight on boarding-house windows. In its own hideous way, it was inclusive. Any skin pigmentation darker than pink was refused. Who knew what might happen to the sheets?

The experience for the immigrants was dislocating in many senses. You arrived, and then you moved and, more often than not, moved again. The migration did not stop at Southampton. A soldier recalled:

> When we arrived at Tilbury, a few people, political people, mostly Communists, you know, tried to befriend us . . . But all it needed at the time was who hadn't got any place to go to, wants somewhere to go, and that was uppermost in our minds . . . you've got to go around and look, because in those days, it's either two or three of you in a room, in those days, as a black man, it's very hard to get a room, you wouldn't get one. They always put on the board, 'Black – niggers not wanted here', on the board you know, these boards out there, 'No Niggers' or 'No Colour', things like that.

Vince Reid, the only teenager on the boat, highlighted a fact that many in England had chosen to forget: the Windrush generation represented only the latest chapter in the long tale of a Black England. 'I was a boy. And I wasn't expecting anything. But how I was received was when I went to school, first of all, I was a subject of curiosity, which is quite surprising when you think that you had black soldiers in England. And, you know, people would come up and rub your skin and see if it would rub off the black, and rub your hair and, you know, it's really insulting.'

War films of the time, and later, show little of black men and women contributing to the country in any way. But for the immigrants, visibility could prove a curse. Tryphena Anderson recalled: 'You're not thinking of your skin, but you feel other people are thinking of it. And every little thing you do reflects on your reaction . . . if you get on the bus, and there's an empty seat, you sit down . . . But when the bus fills up and you find you're the last one to have somebody beside you, then you know something is wrong.'

Then there was the cold, which could steal through the thickest clothing, let alone the light but formal dress favoured by the new arrivals. Theirs was not solely, however, a tale of dislocation and prejudice. Warmth and friendliness could be found, often in the most surprising places. One immigrant recalls a visit to a butcher: 'I got a mixture of genuine affection and a lot of curiosity. I always remember going into my first Dewhurst butcher's shop, when I was about seven, and this big, large lady looked at me. She kept looking at me and then she turned to the butcher, and said, 'Ooh, I could eat him.' I'll always remember Dewhurst butcher's shops.'

The England to which they had come was hag-ridden and worn. The proud imperial nation of rumour or propaganda could be discerned with difficulty in a small, cramped island, still gasping from the blows of a war it had nearly lost. The promise of 'diamond streets' was belied by ones that seemed paved with lead, gashed by bomb sites, beside grey houses interchangeable in size and shape and a population which seemed so old. Along with anxiety, fear and relief, the immigrants sometimes felt a certain pity for the nation that had adopted them:

> But what was most striking, I think, was the age of the people. At that time there were old men working on the stations, and on the buses there were old men or old women. There weren't very many young people. And then we began to realise that the war had taken its toll of the young people between eighteen and probably thirty-five . . . and people were living in prefabs, and that was quite strange. You couldn't understand why they were living in what we saw as huts.

Other customs also attracted bewilderment. There was a vast and varied network of child support, but many Caribbeans found it at once invasive and remote – the deeper support of family appeared to be lacking. Another novelty for many of the Windrush generation was being addressed as 'sir', which seemed bizarre rather than respectful. Some of the customs they encountered provoked fear and dislike among the immigrants, and for many it was difficult to determine which was harsher, the coldness of the climate or the coldness of the people.

It is easy to forget that while England might have wanted cheap labour, the early immigrants had other concerns, with education not the least of them. Among other blandishments, England had been touted as the land of educational opportunity, yet not all found it so. Russell Profitt found many sympathetic teachers but also a wayward and confusing secondary system. He had come from a culture where education was taken seriously as a tool for self-betterment; where study, not leisure, was the point of schooling. He encountered the new welfare-state approach to education, and racism was not quite the issue:

> Most people in senior positions wanted to be helpful, but I don't think they really understood the emotions I was experiencing, having to come to terms with the racial issue, having to come to terms with an education system that was quite different from the one I'd experienced in the Caribbean, where we were a lot more formal and a lot more structured and set in relation to work that we had to do by certain times. A number of black kids just got lost in the system.

Twenty years later, many mothers of Caribbean origin would be expressing concerns similar to those of Profitt's mother: 'My mother hadn't gone through education in Britain, and so I don't think she fully appreciated the way the system worked . . . The pressure was not on in the way I think Caribbean families expected pressure to be on teenagers.' Baroness Amos recalls being relegated to the bottom of the class as a matter of course:

> When I went to school, that was a bit of a shock, because I wasn't tested before I was put into a class, and I was put into the bottom class, and I found everybody was kind of way behind what I'd been used to. But my parents were very

> assertive about that and went up to school and ensured that I was given a test, and I was moved. I think the other thing that I found difficulty dealing with was the environment, and the fact that it felt like a much less disciplined society.

She recalls reactions that derived from simple ignorance, an ignorance that was not unkind but inadvertently intrusive. 'I was in the school choir, we would go and sing in what were then called old people's homes, at Christmas. And they would all touch my skin and touch my hair, and I was the first black person they had ever seen.' The empire had been an abstraction to most; now it was made flesh. Englishmen and women had new neighbours, new shoots in their garden, new influences to accommodate. The best in all major parties acknowledged a duty of care to the immigrants, whether because one should pay a debt of reparation to those colonized or because one does not let down old retainers. But no leader could afford to shout out the benefits of a multiracial community.

Just as the controversy concerning race rose higher and sharper in the Houses of Parliament, in clubs and in private homes, the very notion of racial supremacy was given its quietus. On 25 April 1953, Watson and Crick revealed the existence of DNA. With this discovery, our inheritance was shown to respect neither persons nor ideologies. 'Racial' origins might exist, but they determined nothing that might lead one group to consider itself superior to another. The lesson was to take many decades to filter down, and such affirmation would certainly be needed.

35

The washing machine

On 5 April 1955, Churchill retired as prime minister. He had had enough of his post, of parliament and even of power. For some years, anecdotes had circulated about his decline. He had known, and adapted to, more worlds than any of his generation, yet he could never reconcile himself to the loss of empire. His younger years had been spent fighting for it, and his later years maintaining it. Even his belief in a united Europe was born in the conviction that the Continent should take care of itself; Britain had an empire to govern. His successor would have agreed.

Anthony Eden had been the heir apparent for some time and could not always hide his frustration. Chafing at Churchill's intransigence, he once dropped a hint about retirement. Churchill was heard to growl: 'Don't worry; it'll be yours soon.' There was little in Eden's character to suggest that he would be anything less than a credit to his party. He had won laurels on every field: academic, military and diplomatic. And it doubtless helped that he was handsome and with a gentle charm. But there were worrying signs. Eden showed himself to be a foot-stamper, raging when he could not get his way. And it was unkindly suggested that he 'bored for England'. Nor was the impression Eden gave of unassuming sincerity always borne out by events.

Eden distrusted his predecessor's Atlanticism, but equally

disapproved of any involvement in the nascent European Communities. His position was perhaps that of a latter-day Salisbury: unemphatically imperialist, but emphatically Tory. He was often accused of a lack of conviction but maintained that the preservation of peace was his lodestar. In any case, his conviction and resolve were soon to be tried. As the decade progressed, it was as if the submerging empire sought to whirl him down in its wake. The British state left its possessions with many backward glances of longing and not a little brutality, though the British people themselves had other concerns. And while it has been suggested that India had become unmanageable and even uneconomical by 1947, that Gandhi and Congress were 'pushing at an open door', many other colonies were restive.

Kenya was one such. If India was the jewel in the diadem of empire, East Africa was the string of pearls binding it. But British rule in Africa had left many communities at odds with each other. The Kikuyu had been the dominant tribe in the Kenyan highlands before the arrival of Europeans. During the Thirties they were expropriated, the final insult. The largely abandoned houses of 'Happy Valley', the supreme symbol of decadent Britishness in the colony, fell to the torches of the Mau Mau in the Fifties. Blood-letting became familiar on all sides, with colonial authorities resorting to the methods that might brand them as 'imperialists', and the Mau Mau to those techniques that would confirm them as 'savages'. The death toll was vast. The Mau Mau outlasted the death of their leader in 1959, and four years later came independence. In the case of Kenya, the grievances were at least clear. Far less clear was the case of Cyprus.

On 1 April 1955, Britain's most peaceable colony received a violent calling card from a new guerrilla group, EOKA. It seemed inexplicable to the mandarins of Nicosia, let alone to those of Whitehall – Cyprus had no obvious economic problems and its people were renowned for their lack of political ardour. When EOKA attacked a police station in Limassol, the initial reaction was one of bafflement, but the complaint of the assailants was simple. Why would the British not surrender their claims on Cyprus and let it join with Greece? In his memoir *Bitter Lemons*, Lawrence Durrell found that his sympathies lay with the authorities: 'as a

Conservative, I saw their point. If you have an empire, you do not simply give it away.' It was the presiding spirit, and at the time it still seemed an obvious and immutable law.

But such tempests rolled over distant seas; at home, all was calm. Eden, only weeks after Churchill's resignation, felt ready to call an election. His confidence was vindicated. On 26 May 1955, the Conservatives again won the general election, with 345 seats to Labour's 277. Among other considerations, the result represented something like a kiss blown to the new prime minister. The mandate was as much personal as political. Eden's popularity sprang from his modest manner, his lack of overt jingoism and from the fact that he did not appear to be of the old guard. The age of ardent rhetoric and mighty personalities had passed, to be succeeded by that of ardent goodwill and good intentions. People were now ready for relaxed and unstated glamour.

That Eden was very much of the old guard, having been trained and educated under their systems, was overlooked. But surely the ancient conflicts had been dissolved in the post-war solution? For while the decade was Conservative in flesh, it remained Labour in soul. That a Labour epoch should result in a Conservative era was an irony that few statesmen, thinkers, housewives or labourers had the time or will to ponder. Once again, they had other concerns. The perennial needs were how to secure food, water and a roof. Beyond that, how to give them life and grace? The washing machine was a start.

36

Plays and players

Household appliances, or 'white goods' as they were termed, made slow and hesitant headway through British households. The glories of the 'labour-saving device' were not always apparent, but the washing machine undoubtedly aided the harassed housewife. It revolved and churned, slowly but assiduously, before the results were passed through a hand-operated or automatic mangle. It was the age of modern conveniences, or 'mod cons'.

Some older traditions could still be found, although they often came in a modern guise. Families were encouraged to adopt a fashion known as 'DIY'. The ancient art of pickling, too, was practised in households long after formal austerity had ended. It was to be expected: fridges were both expensive and cumbersome. Nor, in a climate that was scarcely subtropical, was the usefulness of these new appliances immediately clear. Still, they advanced on the swell of prosperity.

But there was a catch: these utensils were not always built with durability in mind. This was an unsettling development but perhaps an inevitable one, given that Britain had moved from being an exporting to a consuming society. A survey conducted in 1953 found housewives' chief concern was that these new gadgets should last, but it was increasingly recognized that they did not. The market was skewed in favour of the supplier, and the interests of supplier and consumer were inherently at odds.

One of the more distinctive developments of the Fifties was the emergence first of the milk bar and then of the coffee bar. England had been a nation of tea-drinkers from time immemorial: tea, after all, had rescued England from the gin craze of the early eighteenth century and was the settling beverage of what has been called an instinctively phlegmatic nation. Coffee had been the drink of intellectuals, of the restless and the politicized, and had never gained wide popularity.

As is often the case, it was immigrants who changed this – Italian immigrants in this instance. The coffee bar, fuelled by the sprightly and galvanizing espresso machine, began to appear first in Soho, then all over London, and then throughout the land. At first glance, it bore little relation to the coffee houses of the eighteenth century, yet a family relationship can be discerned even in the variations: pipe smoke had been replaced by cigarette smoke, the stench of bodies by that of cooking grease, and the politics by music.

There were other signs of emerging affluence. In 1954 the meat ration ended, and wartime austerity fell away. Another shoot sprouted on 14 September in that very eventful year, when the first comprehensive in London, Kidbrooke School, opened its gates. Less than a decade after its inception, the grammar school system was already under assault. Children were selected, at the age of eleven, for grammar schools, secondary moderns or technical colleges. It is perhaps best understood as a mentality that saw privilege as something that must be earned. Paradoxically or not, we may see in it the impulse that led William of Wykeham, in the fourteenth century, to establish a college for boys disadvantaged by circumstance but avid for learning. It is noteworthy that neither Attlee nor his successors in the Fifties attempted to dismantle the public schools. Perhaps they had more nostalgia than some of their successors. By these lights, the grammar school meritocracy set up under Labour in the Forties was unimprovable. If universal education was to be imposed, then a basic fact had to be acknowledged: different pupils had different aptitudes. Let the academic become academics, and the handy become handymen. If you failed the eleven-plus you were simply meant for other tasks, often more socially useful.

The first objection lay in the title of the exam. Was it wise, just or even sensible to determine the future prospects of a child at eleven? The second objection, of course, was that rejected pupils could not help but feel that failure, and express it. Secondary moderns became bear pits for the unwary. The third was that the role of technical colleges was ill-defined, for all the benefits they brought to many, and as a result they were underfunded. They soon disappeared, and even now they represent an unmarked grave in the history of education.

It was a year of advances. On 2 February 1954, the government announced £212 million for road development, including the first motorways. In the same month, it announced that 347,000 new houses had been built in the previous year. They were sturdy and serviceable, if oddly designed; they tended to the triangular, particularly in the suburbs of London.

While England's physical highways thickened and deepened, the country's moral certainties seemed increasingly fragile and vulnerable. On 13 July, Ruth Ellis was executed for the murder of her lover, becoming the last woman to be hanged in Britain. The calm courage in her decision to admit her guilt impressed many. When the prosecuting counsel asked whether she had truly intended to kill her lover, she replied: 'It's obvious when I shot him I intended to kill him.' In true eighteenth-century fashion, she dressed herself immaculately for her trial, and even dyed her hair. A campaign for her reprieve was launched, but she wanted no part of it. Her executioner, Albert Pierrepoint, wrote later that hers was the one execution for which he felt not a jot of remorse. Her record was against her, certainly, but then so was that of many men.

Ellis's execution pricked awake a sleeping giant: the justice of capital punishment itself. The cabinet was divided on the question. The Commons were to vote for abolition in 1956, but the Lords voted against. When Pierrepoint sought the position of official executioner, it had to be explained to him that no such office existed: it was not quite English. Rab Butler, home secretary in 1957, was not at first an abolitionist, but his agonies over the choice of life or death were palpable. 'Each decision,' he wrote, 'meant shutting myself up for two days or more . . . By the end of my time at the Home

Office I began to see that the system could not go on, and present day Secretaries of State are well relieved of the terrible power to decide between life and death.'

The Homicide Act of 1957 was a compromise that satisfied no one, least of all the humane Butler. It was predicated on the notion that punishment should be exemplary rather than condign. The legal and moral incoherence of this approach would soon be apparent, and only a few years had to pass before government was obliged to choose between unravelling the tangled noose and cutting it.

It was a decade in which many supposedly inviolable traditions would be questioned. In 1957 a report on sex and sexuality was assembled. It is ironic, perhaps, that the Wolfenden Report echoed many of the concerns raised by the law it sought to overturn: the Labouchere Amendment. The issue, as before, involved prostitution. The 'blackmailer's charter', as the 1885 amendment was known, was motivated in part by its author's drive to extirpate underage prostitution. The Wolfenden Report sought to protect prostitutes from being exploited any more than they were already. Two years earlier, the Church of England had assembled a memorial on the question of sexuality, urging the government to 'separate sin from statute'. It is hardly coincidental that the Church's reputation for gentle compromise arose just as its political influence began to falter.

Meanwhile, the Cold War crept across minds and cabinet tables in a new Ice Age of anxiety. In its progress, it encouraged a curious doublethink. On the one hand, Stalin's purges, the Ukrainian famine and even the Gulag itself were scarcely known; Stalin was still invoked as 'Uncle Joe'. On the other, the Red Menace hung like a crow over a peaceful meadow. Its hour would come soon, it was whispered, and in that hour all freedoms, and perhaps all life, would be extinguished. For it, too, had the Bomb.

The Labour party under Attlee disavowed any connection with communism and even expelled members suspected of being fellow travellers. Communists were held to have powers of concealment almost preternatural in scope, and on 11 February this superstition seemed vindicated when Guy Burgess and Donald MacLean, who had disappeared in 1951, now took shape again in Moscow five years later. Of the two, it was Burgess who caught the public imagination. He was charming, erudite, handsome and clever, qualities that made his apostasy all the more puzzling. 'Surely only the aggrieved could become socialists?' ran the reasoning. But Burgess had no genuine grievance, beyond a conviction that his peers had failed to appreciate his gifts. Like many English radicals, Burgess quickly found that he had little taste for Russia or the Russians. Apart from anything else, he missed cricket. Again, like many radicals, his nursery was Eton College. This school has often been seen as the forcing ground of the English establishment, but any paradox dissolves under scrutiny: Eton taught self-reliance within an atmosphere of uneasy equality.

Anger howled in many alleys during this supposedly settled period. The English theatre, dominated for four hundred years by bourgeois or aristocratic concerns, was to celebrate the kitchen and the bedroom along with the fury they might nurture. On 8 May 1956, *Look Back in Anger* was first staged.

English theatre was previously notable for three professional playwrights and two poets. J. B. Priestley, Noël Coward and Terence Rattigan had very different styles and political opinions, but their subjects were broadly the same: middle- or upper-middle-class people whose ingenious attempts to fend off reality led to comic or tragic failures. They were schooled in the tradition that the business of art was to entertain rather than preach. While these three wrote in a style that owed at least something to the cadences of ordinary speech, T. S. Eliot and Christopher Fry wrote in verse, on explicitly or subtly religious themes. During the post-war years, overt religious affiliation was gradually being diminished. How could it draw audiences when it could scarcely keep congregations?

John Osborne's *Look Back in Anger* embodied other spirits. And when Jimmy Porter, a young man fulminating against the world, savages the women in the play for their supposed distance from reality, he sets the tone for later generations. The play could only have belonged to the newly affluent, newly educated Fifties. The Royal Court used the expression 'angry young man' to describe Osborne, shrewdly hinting that they had coined it. But it was a term already current in 1951. And its most distinctive avatars appeared in fiction, not on the stage.

To call the movement 'leftist' would be reductive and inaccurate, and 'working-class' will not quite serve. The opening salvo of the movement is an instance in point. John Wain's *Hurry On Down*, published in 1953, tells the story of Charles Lumley, an irritant abroad, and his search for freedom and authenticity. Such a quest is ideally bourgeois, but the time was not ripe for that irony to be apparent: the middle classes were not yet rich enough. Lumley becomes a window cleaner, a chauffeur and a drug dealer. True love proves his salvation in an ending that is at best uneasily hymeneal: he and his love simply look at each other, their expressions 'baffled and enquiring'.

In an introduction to the 1985 edition, Wain took up the gauntlet of critics who had accused him of being peripheral to the angry young men. As he pointed out, his novel predated those of others in the movement. 'If anything,' he wrote, 'I started it.' This claim can be justified on other grounds. In many ways, Charles Lumley is far more typical of the movement than either Osborne's Jimmy Porter or Kingsley Amis's Jim Dixon. Though in no sense a son of the tenements, Charles contrives to reinvent himself as one. Once a social fetter, a working-class origin had become a rosette.

One of the book's characters, an old soldier, speaks of how the working classes had 'got above themselves since the war'. C. S. Lewis, too, felt that the working classes had been 'flattered' under the post-war settlement. If so, it was a flattery that many were eager to accept. A superstitious dread grew around what had once been known as 'middle-class values', even as the middle classes spread inward from the suburbs and so deep into the heart of national life that they seemed close to comprising the majority.

Like the post-war consensus itself, the phenomenon of the angry young men was in part the creature of public perception. In any case, it would have defeated the object of those authors to be placed in a group; it was a confused and fissiparous trend. And what provoked the anger? Partly the perceived failures of the political class, but primarily the continuing existence of class in the first place. The culture of aristocracy had gone up in steam, and a mist of gentility fell. 'True' democracy lay as far off as ever. The promises of the Left had addled, and those of the Right were so much chaff. England seemed a drab, chiffon-choked, tea-and-cake-smothered boutique, all too often with a 'CLOSED' sign. So what remained for a reflective soul but indiscriminate anger? As Kingsley Amis suggested in later years, 'annoyance' might be the better term. Amis himself made a literary career of it, and his protagonists evince this quality to a high degree. In *Lucky Jim*, Jim Dixon ends his lecture on 'Merrie England' with a comically drunken diatribe directed at 'The Esperanto crowd', but the rage expressed is curiously apolitical. In this, Amis was as much of his nation as of his class. The English rarely maintain intensity in political matters – sooner or later, their instinct is to wipe the sweat from the demagogue's collar and propose a soothing cup of tea.

The post-war years had brought fables of spiritual or material collapse, from *That Hideous Strength* to *Brave New World* to *Nineteen Eighty-Four*. During the Fifties, the novel seemed to be settling back to its journalistic roots – quotidian in subject, unpretentious in style – but the zeitgeist is a wayward wind. Among writers of fiction, another response was offered to the bewilderments of the post-war world, which was to fly above it. In 1955, *The Return of the King*, the last instalment of J. R. R. Tolkien's *The Lord of the Rings*, was published. It was the resurrection of heroic romance, tempered by its author's memories of war.

It tells of a small, unregarded race of Middle-earth, the 'hobbits', who 'arise to shake the counsels of the great'. The freedom of the world hinges upon the destruction of something tiny, beautiful and evil, a ring forged by a fallen angel. While elves, men and dwarves fight, two hobbits are tasked with the destruction of the great destroyer. A whole world, formed of its author's experiments in language, came into being, to the extent that if anyone were to point out that 'Middle-earth' is only a translation of the Norse 'Mittlegard', the hearer would respond with a shrug. It was there, whatever its origins.

For the English journalist Bernard Levin, it offered a beautiful and salutary reminder that the 'meek will inherit the earth'; for the American critic Edmund Wilson, it was 'juvenile trash', a story of good boys being rewarded. In spite of the naysayers, the popularity and influence of *The Lord of the Rings* grew to unprecedented heights. Tolkien himself, a scholar and devout Catholic, was later to find his work taken up as a banner by most unlikely allies, a group that came to be known as the 'hippies'.

In 1958, T. H. White offered a quite different vision of the past and of how it should be interpreted. Like Tolkien, he was an academic, and unappeasable loathing for the cant of politicians and the horrors of imperialism also bind the two. But there the comparisons cease. Where *The Lord of the Rings* progressed from being a story for children to a novel for adults to a romance for our ancestors, *The Once and Future King* was postmodernist, which so soon after modernism was a remarkable feat. A picaresque version of the story of King Arthur, it subverts everything possible in the revered legend. Here, Arthur is 'Wart', an idealistic but callow boy who is to be sent to Oxford in the Dark Ages. Merlyn is an eccentric tutor with birds in his hair, whose wisdom comes from having lived backwards.

Beneath the aphorisms and persiflage, White's book hews its way into the rotten heart of statecraft and of power. Anachronisms abound, and the last is the most terrible. Mordred's troops use shells on London, at which juncture Arthur knows that the age of chivalry is truly dead. In time, 'fantasy' would be the lazy catch-all term for this genre. It is one that both authors would have rejected – they were addressing reality.

37

Riots of passage

In an age renowned for its dourness, foliage seemed to sprout from the furniture. Roses were stitched on bedspreads, lilies on sofas and orchids on 'pouffes'. Images of the countryside enriched an increasingly suburban England. That the countryside was in retreat lent the fashion an added poignancy. But if interiors had become cosier, public spaces had grown unforgiving. The ersatz opulence of rose-scattered sofas was met by a countertrend in public spaces, owing much to the new severity of American and continental fashions. Clean, sharp lines were favoured in cafes, clubs and office blocks, as if the world of science fiction had already landed.

Another group of angry young men began to appear; they may have been rebels without causes, but they possessed flags and war cries in abundance. In 1953, vague references to the 'New Edwardian style' sharpened to a name: the Teddy boys had arrived. They bore little relation to the clean, pretty boys of the Eighties who would wear bright colours and winsome smiles – the 'Teds' of the Fifties did not set out to please. It had begun as an upper-class trend. After the war, tailors had attempted to encourage trade by resurrecting the fashions of the Edwardian era. Their market was the wealthy, but working-class teenagers developed a taste for the new style. How could they afford it? Either by paying in instalments or by sticking to the cheapest but most distinctive items of the look. Its prodigality spoke of a new phenomenon in an affluent working class. The Teds did not merely copy the clothing of the 1900s – they parodied it, adding elements such as the 'zoot suit' favoured by black gangs in the United States. A mirage of respectability would become the conduit for rebellion. Quickly, and cheerfully, they established a reputation for violence. The Garston 'blood baths' of Liverpool, where Teddy boy gangs regularly clashed, were infamous.

But not all teenage boys were Teds, and not all Teds were members of gangs. The stigma was largely unearned; it was, above all, a style. More significant was the role of the press in creating that stigma. English youth had been cynosures of disapproval since the glory days of the apprentices in the seventeenth century. The Teds were heirs to the apprentices, in spirit if not in diligence, and thus a fear of supposedly feral youth was again coaxed from its cave. No one who stood out in those days could be trusted, particularly when they wore a costume which was considered to be 'as outlandish as it was sinister'.

Here, Edwardian elegance was twisted. In place of fob watches, the Teds sported bicycle chains, their purpose unsettlingly clear. The tight 'drainpipe' trousers stopped just below the ankle. Broad, crêpe-covered 'beetle-crushers' stood in place of brogues. And then there was the famous hairstyle, on which two birds made their mark: a cockatoo's comb in front and a 'duck's arse' behind. Just as the last strands of aristocratic influence were falling between the shears, the dandy had been resurrected, though now he was working-class.

And in this perhaps lay the true offence. For though it was only ever hinted at, many must have felt that it was simply not 'proper' for the working classes to ape the dress of their betters. Swinging their chains, combing their hair, locking and unlocking their razors, the Teds paced the streets. Their uniform was their own rather than the garb of a trade, for they had no trade. Thus we may truly speak of the first teenage 'style', not that they were in the slightest measure revolutionary. If anything, they could show a vein of fascism. Events later in the decade were to bear this out.

Whether the Teddy boy was as great a source of societal pollution as many believed is doubtful; it was more significant that pollution as a whole had become an urgent matter of public health. When the mist of the Thames met the murk of the chimneys in a fog of eerie green, silence and blindness fell. For years, Londoners had told visitors not to trouble themselves about it, but any such insouciance lost its charm in 1952. In that year, the 'London Smog' claimed 4,000 lives. The gay, gaudy city that Monet had painted less than a century before was obliged to clear its lungs. On 5 July 1955, the Clean Air Act was passed, a somewhat delayed response to the smog that had struck in the coronation year.

A simple trade agreement between France and Germany in the late Forties was now taking root as the European Communities began to cohere. The cabinet's Economic Policy Committee remained unconvinced on Europe. It was 'against the interests of the United Kingdom to join the Common Market', it asserted in November 1955. This was understandable. There was a confidence that England, supported by the Commonwealth and with her mighty transatlantic ally beside her, could retain her former stance.

In 1956, the island received a double irruption from East and West. Khrushchev and Bulganin arrived from the Soviet Union to begin an official visit to the UK. Little came of it in practical terms, but its symbolic significance was enough. Bullish, brash but shrewd, Khrushchev had nothing in common with Eden, who on this occasion offered little but a blustering assurance that Britain would go to war to guard her oil reserves. The visit was further marred by the mysterious loss of a British soldier around the wreck of a Russian submarine. The other irruption was the showing of *Rock Around the Clock*, a short American film about nothing in particular. Its significance was to be far more than symbolic, since it was the first rock-and-roll musical extravaganza.

The first signs could be felt of a fraying in the post-war consensus. On 1 June 1956, Macmillan warned Eden of financial collapse. Inflation would continue if Britain continued to live beyond its means. The promise of full employment had been central to the Attlee settlement, but, coupled with defence spending and overseas commitments, it was proving hard to sustain. From the disenchanted and disenfranchised Left came a new approach. In that year, Anthony Crosland's *The Future of Socialism* was published. Crosland remains an ambiguous figure in the annals of the Labour movement, and this in part reflects the ambiguity of his thought. His book was well regarded at the time, but it is little remembered now. The oversight is easily explained: his ideas were taken up, almost forty years later, by a politician far more ambitious and considerably more accommodating.

Crosland argued that the post-war consensus was in danger of failing its own goals. Nationalization had become an empty shibboleth. Socialists were in danger of mistaking means for ends. They must remember that their primary mission was to abolish poverty, not inequality. He wrote: 'We need not only higher exports and old-age pensions, but more open-air cafes, brighter and gayer streets at night, later closing hours for public houses, more local repertory theatres, better and more hospitable hoteliers and restaurateurs, brighter and cleaner eating houses, more riverside cafes, more pleasure gardens on the Battersea model, more murals and pictures in public places.' There had been too much flattening in the socialist vision; it was time for humanity to be lifted. In one respect, Crosland's insights were tacitly acknowledged to be unanswerable. Nationalization needed nourishment, after all. The trope 'while stocks last' increasingly applied not just to necessities in the home, but to those that fed and fired the household. How long could coal, gas or electricity last?

Perhaps Calder Hall, now known as Sellafield, was named by someone with a sense of historical irony. No hall of the fading nobility needed to be demolished for this nuclear power station to replace it. Thus, on 17 October 1956, it became Britain's first nuclear power station. The young queen opened it 'with pride'. England was ready, in principle, to have her firesides warmed and her streets made safe by what Oppenheimer, the inventor of the Bomb, called 'the destroyer of worlds'.

In 1956, England was to be weighed and found wanting. Far away, in a protectorate that had grown tired of being protected, a man had seized power – with cunning, bullets and a brilliant smile as his weapons. Gamal Abdel Nasser had plans for Egypt, and indeed for the whole Arab world. In what was proclaimed as a simple assertion of sovereignty, on 26 July 1956 he nationalized the Suez Canal. This was taken badly in Westminster.

Anthony Eden was in many respects an instinctive diplomat, with an almost preternatural gift for languages and for compromise.

He had no obvious reason to clash with Nasser. They were both patriots, after their fashion; both knew well the limits and dangers of militarism. But Nasser was a consummate opportunist. In quietly shifting from Egyptian nationalism to pan-Arabism, he had amassed far greater moral resources than his British counterpart could boast.

When Nasser took the Canal, for many countries the chief artery of oil into Europe, Eden was moved to respond. And his response was unequivocally warlike and strangely personal. What moved him to compare his former ally to Mussolini and Hitler remains a puzzle. He was to claim in his wilderness years that he could not stand by and see the lessons of the Thirties forgotten. Whatever his motives, on 5 November 1956, Britain and France invaded Egypt.

The dishonesty in the plan was palpable even then. Israel was to launch an attack on Egypt, and then France and Britain would 'intervene' before leaving an armed force for the maintenance of peace, the cooling of tempers and the reopening of Suez. Israel had some reason for her actions; the other aggressors had only an excuse. Besides, too much in the plan had been predicated on the support of the United States. Churchill might have been able to coax them, but he would have had a deep well of respect to draw from. Eden did not, and his hunger to bring down Nasser led him to disregard the most glaring tokens of American unease. The United States had in any case made clear its opposition to any act that might so much as smell of European colonialism, and Eisenhower denied any American support for the Suez adventure. With that, a barren cause became a lost one. As they were advancing down the Canal, British and French troops were given the order: cease fire.

Reactions to the debacle were mixed. People who had never cared about the empire were moved to wonder why Britannia invicta had been worsted. Eden attempted to brazen it out but heart trouble struck, a misfortune seen by some as less an act of God than of expediency. Perhaps they were right, and his life was not in fact as deeply in peril as his doctor suggested. He never disavowed his decision over Suez. Perhaps, having committed himself so far, he could not withdraw. Eden was not stupid, but his judgement was bewildered by the fear of being considered a weakling. Churchill foresaw it all and feared for his successor: 'Poor Anthony' was his verdict. In any event, on 9 January 1957, Eden resigned.

It was as well that he did. The empire he had known and loved had begun to haemorrhage. The Mau Mau in Kenya were unbroken, despite the capture and execution of their leader. The EOKA fighters in Cyprus still raged. And on 6 March 1957, Ghana won independence, precipitating the end of British colonial rule in West Africa. Suez is often seen as the moment when the British Empire collapsed. It was not: the Second World War had rendered the empire unsustainable. But it represented the moment when the absence of something never before valued began to be felt.

Having lost its empire, Britain had to find its strength, or 'credibility', in other arenas. Britain might have established Calder Hall for innocent, or at least neutral purposes, but the nuclear arms race must still be run. On 15 May 1957, Britain tested its first hydrogen bomb. The battle to achieve this was painful for everyone, whatever their political stripe. Churchill, who had seen more wars than any of his peers, was horrified at this new development.

Aside from building houses and dismantling empires, caring for the old and for the young, and receiving guests that it had once known only as servants or slaves, England had to address the perennial problem of how to direct and mobilize its citizens. Inspired as much by the German as by the American example, the first motorway was laid. On 5 December 1958, the M6, the Preston Bypass, was opened and the 'motorway age' was thus tacitly inaugurated. And in 1959, the M1 was opened. The motorway was to acquire almost mythic connotations. In later years, it became, like the Thames, a cynosure of wonder.

To call national service a 'rite of passage' would be simplistic or misleading. For many it had the character of a pointless hiatus, robbing the participants of precious years that could have been spent working or playing. For others it was an exhilarating introduction to manhood and responsibility. In either case, it was almost impossible to avoid. A nation that had only recently emerged from war needed to keep its spine stiff and its sinews supple. National service was a typical example of how a temporary emergency can prompt a major alteration. Britain still had the peace to keep in Europe, allies to support and an empire to protect. It was promoted as a kind of trade-off for all the benefits of the welfare state. But the allies proved unstable and the empire untenable.

The training itself was if anything harsher than that imposed in wartime – there was an illusion to protect, along with the remains of empire. Dangers there were, whether roaring or skulking, and the still renowned British military was needed to face them. But in any case Britain needed its youth to be healthy, if they were not to end up like Teddy boys, shiftless and disobedient. In the event, the Teds flourished under national service. The hair was a problem, of course, but it could be hidden. In fact, the style was the only real objection of the training officers. One observed: 'We're a proud lot in the Airborne and feel that these modern fashions that a few of the chaps like rather lets (*sic*) the mob down.'

Other contemporaries were less predictable. Among the few who mourned Eden's departure deeply were four young men whose brand of humour created at a stroke the modern alternative tradition. Eden's consonants, snipped off by his protruding front teeth, had been succeeded by the languorous vowels of Harold Macmillan, which were far less susceptible to imitation. The Goons, the lords of Fifties radio comedy, must have sighed in disappointment at the gently genial new PM. They came together above a fruiterer's shop in Shepherd's Bush, and their backgrounds were as difficult to represent as the new age itself. Michael Bentine was an Old Etonian, Peter Sellers a Jewish boy from Muswell Hill, Harry Secombe was a Welshman, and Spike Milligan had been born in India, his father an army captain.

Unlike many later comedians, the Goons had no interest in innuendo, or indeed in sexual matters of any sort. It was comedy in the tradition of Ben Jonson or the Restoration playwrights, with the difference that the types shown by the Goons were all not merely eccentric but palpably insane. The nation had excitement and opportunity, but too little in the way of salutary madness, which now the Goons unveiled. To get life insurance, all one had to do was to 'get deceased', for example. And the names were a feast. Denis Bloodnok, always blaming his wind on 'curried eggs', tells us nothing and suggests everything. And it was comedy for radio, for airwaves that could carry at last something more bracing than cheerful propaganda and interminable organ music. The voices, whether shrieking or whining, bellowing or wheedling, filled the home with brisk and contrary winds of every sort.

A forgotten irony lies in the notion of the post-war consensus, since in truth it had been developed under both Labour and Tory auspices. By the mid-Fifties, however, notions of a grand ideological confrontation existed only as fodder for journalists. The belief that the state must support its citizens if it is to demand anything of them had been tacitly absorbed by all parties. The post-war consensus was at last in place. The only question was whether it could hold its own.

Nationalization of services was almost complete by the mid-Fifties. To return the means, and the fruits, of production to the producers had been the grand mission. But how much had really changed? The children's book series *Thomas the Tank Engine* by Wilbert and Christopher Awdry spanned three decades but began in 1945. The anthropomorphic engines have a fond mentor in the rotund shape of the Fat Director, Sir Topham Hatt, Bt. In the tale of *James the Red Engine*, the Fat Director becomes the Fat Controller. Clearly, nationalization has struck. It had been a project advanced as much by Conservatives as by socialists, and it was not always easy to see how the central cast had altered. The Fifties saw a gradual acceptance of the post-war settlement. Government cooperation with the union movement continued, and even accelerated, under the Conservatives. At this point, all appeared to be in agreement.

With widening education, however, came a certain unease. Was to be educated to accept the thirty pieces of silver? Such a notion would have seemed strange a hundred years earlier, when an education was a source of pride for many of the working class. But the working class was itself in transition, culturally and racially. The word 'minority' also changed its meaning in the Fifties. Before, it had usually referred to the Welsh or to women; now it turned outwards, to signify the immigrant. The notion of a 'white' England was most often a chimera; there had been black communities in England long before the Windrush generation, just as there had been black servicemen in the war. And as for the empire, the English knew it as something in the papers – now they learned of it through their neighbours.

But the riots that broke in Notting Hill in the summer of 1958 had nothing to do with neighbours. It was a hot, hate-filled summer. One black resident recalled the riots thus: 'We could feel the pressure was there . . . You were constantly being threatened on the streets.' 'Kill the niggers!' rose the cry on Portobello Road and Colville Road. It was a grisly echo of the Thirties, when 'We've got to get rid of the Yids' cawed from the throats of blackshirts. Caribbeans were targeted, and their property attacked. But then, after years of battening down the hatches, they turned. 'We were getting the worst of it, until a few of us decided to fight back . . . And when they came, we attacked before they did and they ran away.' The police did their best, but the tide had turned. As well as bruisable skin, 'minorities' had heart, muscle and spirit. It was not the Teddy boys' finest hour. They participated gleefully in the baiting of Caribbeans, but were then repelled.

Racism was not the only neurosis to afflict the country. As Hugh Gaitskell saw it, there was a creeping undercurrent of anti-Americanism too. 'It is easy to see,' he said, 'how powerful anti-American sentiment can be when to this already difficult relationship is added the genuine fear felt by many people that America will land us all in war.' It was prophetic in many respects, but he need not have worried. Beyond the environs of Westminster, the people were largely untroubled by the concerns Gaitskell ascribed to them. By the Fifties, any residual resentment towards American culture was balanced by a hunger for its boons. And the music sent over the airwaves was a boon indeed. Whatever was resented in the fiscal debt to the United States, the youth of England appreciated this inrush of hope.

First from the jukeboxes of the milk bars and then from the cafes, in the music that cooed over the airwaves there was an influence both old and new. It was the brash, generous, overbearing confluent of the United States. During the Second World War, willing girls and reluctant boys had begun to notice that Americans seemed to have it all, and the Fifties did everything to encourage that impression. In 1956 Bill Haley & His Comets released 'Rock Around the Clock', an example of the new trend known as rock 'n' roll. The genre had numerous parents, all of them black, but political considerations required that its ambassadors be white. Haley himself was a plump little man with a kiss-curl on his forehead, fronting what was, in essence, a jazz band. Yet his energy and panache submerged all objections.

He was followed by Elvis Presley, or 'the King', as he became known. Songs like 'Blue Suede Shoes' and 'Hound Dog' would not have passed muster later, when musicianship and wordcraft were prized, but when sung in the Elvis purr and accompanied by gyrations so suggestive as to give the singer the sobriquet 'Elvis the Pelvis', they achieved mass hysteria and Olympian sales. It also helped that he was not merely handsome but beautiful, exciting but unthreatening. This was not, of course, the rock 'n' roll that purists recognized; for them, Chuck Berry was the king. In lifting the old blues from the piano to the guitar, he had become the founder of a genre. This would be remembered in the slumbering years.

The blaze of excitement soon settled in England. Sooner or later, the instinct of a young audience is to scramble onto the stage and join in, but despite its working-class origins, rock 'n' roll needed instruments that were far beyond the means of English youth. Pianos, double basses, drums and even guitars lay at an impossible distance. It seemed as if an old law would reassert itself: the passion dies that cannot be performed.

The name 'skiffle' was a dialect word from the West Country, meaning 'a mess'. In the United States, the term came to be applied to a kind of music in which only the most rudimentary instruments were employed. Appropriately enough for such a ramshackle genre, skiffle came to England by accident. Chris Barber had formed a jazz band, and its new banjoist was Lonnie Donegan. They were recording a disc but had run out of songs to play. Donegan had a suggestion: 'What about some skiffle?'

In the United States, its homeland, skiffle had already been forgotten. Unlike jazz or the blues, it was barely a genre. This was interlude music at best, a distraction proposed when there was nothing worthwhile to be played, no real musicians to play it and few instruments to play it with. Nonetheless, the other two unpacked their instruments. And then, in what has been called his 'pseudo-blues wail', Donegan broke into 'Rock Island Line'. No one knows when the song was written, but all agree that the songwriter was a convict, and the song is one of yearning for escape.

The song tells of an engine driver who successfully smuggles a stash of pig iron past a railway toll gate. A more American theme could scarcely be imagined, but that was the point. Not Bill Haley & His Comets, nor Elvis, nor even Buddy Holly so galvanized the British young. They were haloed at an almost unbridgeable remove from British realities. In any case, white rock 'n' roll, or 'rockabilly', the music offered by Haley and Elvis, could be a curiously sedate affair; it was music for joyful or even elegant dancers. Perhaps, when the Teddy boys tore up the cinema seats, they were not so much fired by rock 'n' roll as impatient with it. Skiffle might have been rudimentary, but it was never sedate.

Moreover, Donegan, short, thin, ostentatiously working-class and British, was 'one of us' – if he could do it, so could everyone. And then there was the simple rush of the tune, and the wild, whooping triumph in its chorus. The skiffle craze was sparked. As has been many times remarked, 'We owe it all to Lonnie Donegan.' The principle was simple. If you wanted rhythm, you scraped a washboard; if a double bass, then you strung a washing line to a sweeping brush and rammed it into a tea chest. If you couldn't afford a guitar, you could surely get a banjo. A comb-and-paper kazoo could serve for a harmonica, and puffing into a jug created a sound not unlike a tuba. In short, you could create such music on your own.

Skiffle itself might have died without issue. The sound was thin and scratchy, and the ease with which it could be played made it restrictive for serious talents. That it did not die is in some part due to a man nicknamed 'Dr Death', whose real name was Paul Lincoln. On 22 April 1956, he and Ray Hunter refounded a club in Old Compton Street as a coffee bar, 'The 2i', with a music venue downstairs. There was little or no seating. The tiny stage for the musicians was built from milk crates and planks. Even the microphone had been a relic of the Boer War. Performers were paid, so the legend ran, in coffee and Coca-Cola, and alcohol was not served. Skiffle could not have wished for a warmer cradle. It did not last long into the succeeding decade, and in this it was typical of the coffee bar boom. Espresso bars still flourished, but no longer as conduits of musical talent. They would never die, but they would have to adapt.

38

North and south

On 8 October 1959, the Conservatives under Macmillan won the election by 365 seats to Labour's 258. The unofficial campaign slogan was 'We've Never Had It So Good'. Macmillan had proved himself worthy – now he had only to make 'it' even better, whatever 'it' was. He had beguiled and persuaded the nation by virtue of his Edwardian charm, but he remained in certain respects a little-known figure.

'A born rebel' was how Lloyd George described the young Macmillan. The young of Sixties England might have found it hard to spot a rebel in their prime minister, but those living further afield would not have been surprised. By 1960, decolonization was already underway, but the process had been halting. Macmillan had always believed in the nascent strength of the smaller Commonwealth nations, and on 6 January he reaffirmed this in a speech in Ghana. The choice of location was deliberate: Ghana had won its freedom by peaceful means, its new leader following the example of Gandhi. This, coupled with the sobering examples of chaos and bloodshed in former French and Portuguese possessions, led the shrewd and compassionate Macmillan to conclude that empire could not coexist with African nationalism.

This speech passed largely unnoticed, but when he repeated its central points in the parliament of apartheid South Africa, the world took note. After thanking the relevant dignitaries, Macmillan proceeded:

'At such a time it is natural and right that you should pause to take stock of your position – to look back at what you have achieved, and to look forward to what lies ahead.' The tone was that of a kindly headmaster sending his boys off into the wider world, and was received as such. However, his next observation garnered him a good-natured laugh. 'This afternoon I hope to see something of your wine-growing industry, which so far I have only admired as a consumer.'

The following section could have been received as a polite nothing, but for the more attentive there was a bite beneath: 'We in Britain are proud of the contribution we have made to this remarkable achievement. Much of it has been financed by British capital.' He praised the South African contribution to the two world wars, saying, 'As a soldier, I know personally the value of the contribution your forces made to victory in the cause of freedom. I know something too of the inspiration which General Smuts brought to us in Britain in our darkest hours.' The reference to Smuts, a hero of Anglo-South African relations but no friend of apartheid, would not have been missed. Then came the sweetener: 'Today, your readiness to provide technical assistance to the less well-developed parts of Africa is of immense help to the countries that receive it.' At last, he moved to the image for which the speech would be remembered. South Africa, he said, was ready 'to play your part in the *new* Africa of today . . . Ever since the break-up of the Roman Empire, one of the constant facts of political life in Europe has been the emergence of independent nations . . . Today the same thing is happening in Africa, and the most striking of all the impressions that I have formed since I left London a month ago is of the strength of this African national consciousness.' Macmillan's voice rose in declamation as he rapped the lectern. 'The wind of change is blowing through this continent. And whether we like it or not, this growth of national consciousness is a political fact. And we must all accept it as a fact, and our national policies must take account of it.'

There was silence in the hall at this blasphemy. But Macmillan, the consummate performer, was prepared. His message, if not his tone, became unctuous. 'Of course you understand this better than anyone; you are sprung from Europe, the home of nationalism. And here in Africa you have yourselves created a new nation. Indeed in the history of our times you will be recorded as the first of the African nationalists.' It was a masterly performance – this was logic not so much employed as deployed. And with his most resonant image behind him, Macmillan came to the true point. 'We may sometimes be tempted to say "Mind your own business". But in these days I would expand the old saying, so that it runs, "Mind your own business, but mind how it affects my business, too."'

For of course, if South Africa continued along its present course, mayhem would be the result. Macmillan concluded with what may best be described as a sermon.

> Our aim has been . . . not only to raise the material standards of life, but to create a society which respects the rights of individuals – a society in which men are given the opportunity to grow to their full stature. And that must in our view include the opportunity of an increasing share in political power and responsibility; a society in which individual merit, and individual merit alone, is the criterion for a man's advancement, whether political or economic . . . Those of us who by the grace of the electorate are temporarily in charge of affairs in my country and yours, we fleeting transient phantoms of history, we have no right to sweep aside on this account the friendship that exists between our countries.

Rarely has one speech had such an influence. In its aftermath, South Africa fulfilled the ugliest expectations of the world first by committing the Sharpeville Massacre and next by withdrawing from the Commonwealth altogether. By the end of Macmillan's tenure, the fourteen colonies of Africa had been granted independence and reduced to four. Macmillan had won many friends for Britain abroad – in the United States, the UN and in Africa itself.

And Macmillan needed all his friends, for the ranks of his critics were swelling. Recalling a broadcast by the prime minister, Malcolm Muggeridge observed unkindly:

> He seemed, in his very person, to embody the national decline he supposed himself to be confuting. He exuded a flavour of mothballs. His decaying visage and somehow seedy attire conveyed the impression of an ageing and eccentric clergyman

> who had been induced to play the prime minister in the dramatized version of a Snow novel put on by a village amateur dramatic society.

Nevertheless, Macmillan could boast of many admirers. While his cabinet was composed overwhelmingly of public schoolboys and while his family connections stretched from Westminster to Chatsworth House, he had a fan in a tall, saturnine young student with a fondness for sweaters by the name of Peter Cook. With Jonathan Miller, Dudley Moore and Alan Bennett, Cook formed the 'Beyond the Fringe' group. Unlike the Goons before them, they derived their humour not from caricature but from observation. They performed with almost no set beyond a piano. The target appeared to be what was becoming known as 'the establishment', and yet their humour had always a samizdat quality in its ironical deference. In one sketch of 1961, Peter Cook played the prime minister in a spoof party-political broadcast. His meandering, deadpan delivery was uncanny. Such satire was addressed at a persona, of course, but this persona was itself a role that Macmillan assumed. It was a success. Intransigent foe and improbable allies were to be swayed by it.

Macmillan, who was dubbed 'the most radical politician' in Britain by Attlee, was in fact a 'soft' socialist, and the economic policies he urged upon his chancellors reflected this. In times of dearth, demand must be stimulated. Thus was inaugurated a period of 'stop-go' economics; government spending was increased to ensure growth, and then curtailed in order to stanch inflation. The result was 'stagflation', a monster sired by spending and bred upon austerity.

By the spring of 1962, Selwyn Lloyd, the upright, talented, but unimaginative chancellor of the time, was the target of ever more hostile feeling. The Orpington by-election of March, where the Conservatives were heavily defeated by the Liberals, was only one sign of a wider disaffection. Leicester was also lost, to Labour. Called to the cameras, Lloyd was unrepentant. The important thing, he maintained, was that the chancellor do 'the right thing', regardless of by-elections or popular feeling in general. Yet his sharp, fluent delivery was belied by his hands, which swayed and jerked like those of a puppeteer. Quintin Hogg, later Lord Hailsham, was not alone in feeling that the malaise sprang from the leader rather than from the chancellor. He wrote to Macmillan, claiming that 'the party had lost its sense of direction and its sense of conviction, and this was due to neglect from the centre'.

Macmillan was unmoved. While he felt respect, affection and even pity for his brilliant but troubled chancellor, he had grown dissatisfied. The country had turned against the Tories, and it would not be long before it turned against Macmillan himself. Lloyd, he wrote in his diaries, was 'finished'. There were fears that the government might tumble. Iain MacLeod, Conservative party chairman, privately urged the prime minister to remove Lloyd, and events moved swiftly. A leak to the *Daily Mail* suggested that Macmillan was intending a radical reshuffle. The source was never named, but all knew that Rab Butler was responsible. When Macmillan summoned Lloyd for a talk, the chancellor was at first perturbed and then astonished; Macmillan seemed 'flustered' and upset, staring at the floor. The affable, imperturbable grandee babbled about mysterious 'plots'. At last, Macmillan broke the news. A 'less tired' mind was needed in the Treasury. Outwardly, Lloyd remained cheerful, but Jonathan Aitken, the sole remaining member of his staff, recalled, 'He was broken by it, shattered . . . He walked up and down our croquet lawn for five hours.'

As Butler put it, 'A prime minister has to be a butcher, and know the joints.' Other 'joints' would now be severed, in what became known as 'the Night of the Long Knives'. On 13 July, Charles Hill, the housing minister, Lord Kilmuir, the Lord Chancellor and an early supporter of Macmillan against Butler, Percy Mills, Sir John McLeigh, Harold Watkinson and David Eccles were all informed that they must step aside. Macmillan later claimed indeed to have felt greater pain than the men he had removed, yet his reaction was not surprising. Macmillan's grandson observed that even before giving away prizes at a prep school, Macmillan would be 'sick and quivering'. There had been no plot, of course, and the only result of this professional butchery was a widespread loss of faith in Macmillan. 'Supermac' became 'Mac the Knife' and then 'Supermacbeth'.

But two more victories awaited him. Both were in his dealings with the United States, in the contested field of nuclear defence. Macmillan had long urged the need for Britain to possess an independent nuclear capacity. The Americans were sympathetic, but there was one difficulty: why should Britain feel the need for a deterrent of its own, the 'Europeanists' at the White House enquired, just when it was seeking admission to the protective pale of Europe? And what would the Europeans themselves feel about this? Macmillan believed that without a deterrent of its own, Britain would lose stature. Moreover, surely the strength of Britain's proposed marriage to the Community lay in its substantial military dowry? First, the Skybolt missile was proposed, but, after endless wranglings and misunderstandings, the scheme was dropped. With weeks to go before negotiations with the EEC were to begin, Polaris was substituted. Britain was now a true nuclear power. The arrangement had been smoothed by the warm personal relations between Macmillan and President Kennedy. While their subordinates bickered, the two war veterans quietly took matters in hand at Nassau. It seemed that the 'special relationship' had been triumphantly reaffirmed. One cloud crossed the bright, hopeful sun. When, in a telephone conversation, Macmillan recalled the glory days of Nassau, the president was oddly distracted and unresponsive. 'When was that?' asked a puzzled Kennedy. 'The Nassau meeting,' answered Macmillan. 'Oh yes – very good.'

But if relations with the United States had now warmed, those with the European nations were floundering. Among the six original nations of the Community, France, led by de Gaulle, was the paramount power. His hostility to his former benefactors had always rather slumbered than slept; the knowledge that Britain possessed an independent nuclear capability yet seemed unwilling to share it with its continental neighbours pricked it awake. But now, it seemed, mighty Albion wished to join the European Economic Community. Neither de Gaulle nor Adenauer, his German counterpart, was minded to make the process easy.

'I don't believe in abroad,' Quentin Crisp once wrote. 'I think that all foreigners speak English behind our backs.' Crisp's words would have had resonance for many in England. Now many felt that the United Kingdom was about to wander into the same crevasse as its predecessors, at unfathomable cost. Thus the Labour politician George Brown remarked on Britain entering the Common Market: 'It is not the price of butter which in the end really matters. It is the size, stability, strength and political attitude of Europe that matters. We have got to have a new kind of organisation in Europe

. . . if we don't succeed, I doubt whether there will be much of a Britain for our children's children.'

Yet even so ardent a Europhile as Brown believed that Britain could, and should, enter the fold as its shepherd. The new chancellor, Reginald Maudling, was forthright on the question when he confessed that 'the French do not want us in Europe at all. The Community of the Six has become a Paris/Bonn axis'. This complaint would echo down the decades, though with Berlin in place of Bonn. In opposition, Harold Wilson invoked a fear that entry into the Common Market would be a betrayal of the Commonwealth: 'If there has to be a choice, we are not entitled to sell our friends and kinsmen down the river for a problematical and marginal advantage in selling washing machines in Düsseldorf.' Gaitskell, though in many ways sympathetic, was also realistic. Many Labour members saw Britain being 'sucked up in a kind of giant capitalist Catholic conspiracy . . . unable to conduct any independent foreign policy at all'.

It is salutary to remember that at its inception, the European project was what we might call 'faith-based'. Purely practical considerations came later, when the aftermath of the Second World War made trade cooperation a matter of overwhelming urgency. But now negotiations for Britain's entry had begun, led by the chief whip, one Edward Heath. He spoke for many of his generation when he recalled what he had seen at the Nuremberg trials: 'We were surrounded by destruction, homelessness, hunger and despair. Only by working together had we any hope of creating a society which would uphold the true values of European civilisation. Reconciliation and reconstruction must be our task.'

Heath was a magnificent negotiator, whose talent for detail, doggedness and deep love of all things continental raised him above any previous British minister. However, he had to deal with the hostile de Gaulle and the suspicious Adenauer. On 29 January 1963, France announced that it would veto the British application. Familiar objections were advanced: Britain was an insular nation with maritime interests and had too close and dependent a relationship with the United States. But de Gaulle went further: 'In the end,' he said, 'there would appear a colossal Atlantic community under American dependence and leadership which would soon swallow up the European Community.'

It was hard for the British delegates to determine which was the more demoralizing, the veto itself or the hypocrisy with which it was sauced. De Gaulle, for all his swagger, was simply frightened at the thought of the British crashing into his pond. He acquired infamy as a man who could neither forget nor forgive a benefit. Macmillan himself, who had supported de Gaulle during the war in defiance of his superiors' doubts, felt less bitterness than grief. The mass of the people were either delighted or, more worryingly for their leaders, indifferent. The success of Macmillan's 'stop-go' economic policies was also under increasing question, as was his continuing fitness for rule. But it was neither incompetence nor senescence nor nemesis which brought down this wily innocent.

John Profumo, the minister for war, was respected in the Commons. He had a modicum of talent, an easy charm and a weakness shared by many men in power. At a party at Cliveden House, then owned by Lord Astor, Profumo had met a model named Christine Keeler, the protégée of one Stephen Ward, osteopath and socialite. Initially cool, Keeler was nonetheless an impressionable teenager and soon began an affair with Profumo that lasted just under a month, and there the matter might have rested. But Keeler had also made the acquaintance of 'Eugene', a Soviet attaché and spy. Periodicals picked up on the increasingly insistent hum of rumour, and Keeler herself began to blab.

Profumo denied any impropriety to the House and even sued the relevant newspapers. But when the case came to court and both Keeler and her friend Mandy Rice-Davies testified, he was left helpless. He resigned and vanished into the East End to do penance by helping the poor. Meanwhile, Keeler went to prison for perjury, the largely innocent Ward committed suicide, and Mandy Rice-Davies contrived an elegant skip from notoriety to fortune. The leader of the opposition, Hugh Gaitskell, knew better than to exploit the scandal for its sexual content. Instead he stuck to the question of national security, leaving Macmillan diminished and lame. At last the prime minister resigned, for reasons of ill health, protesting his innocence of the whole affair. He had presided over boom and bust, prosperity and uncertainty, had restored, or perhaps even created, the 'special relationship' with the United States, had rescued his party from the disaster of Suez and overseen the end of empire. Who then was to replace this splintered colossus?

The Establishment Club in particular, set up by Peter Cook to continue the tradition of *Beyond the Fringe*, mourned his loss: he had been prodigal meat for satire. But while the satire boom was only scotched by television, the Establishment Club was killed by it. The vein of alternative comedy was by no means exhausted, however. *Private Eye* was founded in 1961, produced by a very different crowd from that of *Beyond the Fringe*. They were more acerbic and less funny, but the venture flourished.

With the airing in November 1962 of *That Was the Week That Was*, the new comic movement moved to the television. After the show was cut to a watchable length, its fans were treated to the growing presence of household names on the screenwriting credits. Keith Waterhouse was one. Above all, there was David Frost, flat and uninspiring but a television 'natural'. But the show's appeal soon waned. It became, of all things, pompous: wit descended to invective, harmless joshing to self-important malice.

In *The Other England*, the journalist Geoffrey Moorhouse attempted a survey and analysis of England as a whole. It was published in 1964 as a kind of sequel to Priestley's *English Journey*, although 'corrective' might be the more fitting term. Moorhouse begins by referring to an article entitled 'The Condition of the North'. It was written by George Taylor, chief education officer for Leeds, who commented that

> it is fairly safe to assert that the Northern child will receive his education in an old, insanitary building planned on lines wholly inappropriate for contemporary teaching, his teachers will be too few in number, probably inexperienced, possibly unqualified, and constantly changing . . . If he attends a grammar school, its children will be, like him, drawn entirely from the local working-class community.

The assumption that grammar schools catered for the working class is one Moorhouse challenges. The grammar schools were intended primarily for the industrious working class, but they somehow abandoned an ethos of intellectual endeavour for one of material advantage. He went on to add, 'I would suggest that one of our

Englands today is a circle whose perimeter is approximately one hour's travel by fast peak-hour train from the main London termini; the other England is the whole of the country outside that circle.' In short, the Home Counties represented a hallowed pale of wealth and opportunity.

An anonymous article written in the early Sixties by a resolutely southern author for a national newspaper, and quoted by Moorhouse, sums up best what was wrong with the metropolitan mind: 'I was eating a moussaka in Bolton the other day which (though nice) was made of potato, and it suddenly made me realise how little you can take aubergines for granted out of town.' The inadvertent comedy is of course twofold: the sneer is ostensibly directed at the north, but it also reveals how little the author knows of what most Londoners ate. For Moorhouse, the real divide is between the Home Counties and everywhere else. Yet for all his affection for the regions he knew, Moorhouse was ready to cheer on the wrecking ball and the bulldozer; in this he was typical of the cognoscenti. 'I, too, should hate to see these [customs] go because they mark a people still in touch with their roots. But if they represent the price to be paid for making Lancashire cleaner, less dilapidated, and generally more wholesome, then I'm afraid I should be on the side of those who are prepared to pay it.' It may be suggested that this approach has fallen foul of history.

It was no longer true that 'Britain's bread hangs by Lancashire's thread', as the slogan put it in the Fifties. Most of the cotton mills still remained at the beginning of the Sixties, but they were scarcely the source of the nation's prosperity. Nonetheless, the looms rattled on; in the third quarter of 1963, they numbered 123,400. As a cultural or political force, however, Manchester was in hibernation. In 1963, the United States closed its consulate there, and the *Manchester Guardian* was the *Guardian* by the early Fifties.

Manchester Grammar remained the leading light in pre-university scholarship, however, putting the public schools to shame. The city even had its own answer to the 'London Peculiar' – the phenomenon known as 'Darkness at Noon', the great canopy of soot that occluded the city.

39

Elvis on a budget

Religious differences could still linger. In the early Sixties, the Scottish community, anxious to preserve Liverpool as a bastion of the Reformed faith and the Tory party, cried out in a pamphlet: 'Romanism is the greatest enemy of our civil and religious liberty and if we lose these inestimable privileges for a mess of Socialist pottage we shall indeed be unworthy of the heritage won for us by our grand Protestant sires.' However, such conflict began to ease when the slums were cleared and new houses built; the communities were no longer sequestered. Those of different confessions were obliged to cooperate.

Then there were the football fans who were, as Moorhouse observed, Liverpool's most controversial export. 'A strange, alien people they were, too,' he wrote, 'who swore more fluently and often than we did and who openly relieved themselves on the Bolton terraces, which didn't go down at all well in that continent town.' The Cavern Club on Mathew Street also had little to recommend it to the non-specialist. Yet it was to acquire a certain cachet and even piety of a kind.

> The bouncer on the door disapproves of unexpected visitors. 'This place,' he observes gently, 'is becoming a bloody shrine.' And so it is. There are CND symbols and other daubs of paint

> crudely applied around the entrance. Half-way down the steep wooden staircase you find yourself stumbling into an atmosphere which is thick, sweet, almost tasty. In the Cavern something like a couple of hundred youngsters are compressed together under three low barrel-vaulted ceilings separated by stubby, arched walls . . . The walls are running with condensation. No one seems to notice the acute discomfort of being there.

This 'foetid ill-ventilated hole', as Moorhouse puts it, was an unlikely 'shrine' to what was soon known as 'the Mersey Sound'.

The well-attested but elusive link between delinquency and a lack of education had long preoccupied all the major parties. In October 1963, the Robbins Report on higher education led to a flowering of new universities. These were not 'red-brick', in colour or in connotation. Rather they were of plate glass. They won many awards but few devotees. Yet they were quite as rigorous in their demands upon the students as any that preceded them. It was surely no accident that the iconic quiz show *University Challenge* was aired on TV just as the building of 'plate glass' reached its apogee in 1963, nor that the first university to win the challenge was the humble University of Leicester.

On 19 October 1963, Sir Alec Douglas-Home became prime minister, to the dismay of Rab Butler's supporters, who felt that the natural successor had been passed over in favour of a desiccated Scottish nobleman. For its own part, the opposition was delighted. Here was a prime minister whose very appearance ran counter to their vision of a nation gleaming and galvanized. But though cadaverous, aged and out of touch, Douglas-Home had a thorough mind and was helped in his role of physician to social grievances by a courtesy and warmth rare in politics and rarer still among the aristocracy.

The inevitable election fell, and was won by Labour – the only surprise lay in the narrowness of the victory. 'Be prepared' is the Boy Scout's watchword, and Harold Wilson – who had assumed the leadership of the Labour party after the death of Gaitskell – adhered to it throughout his political life. Even in the presence of the queen he could not restrain himself from harking back to his days as a Scout. Like Enoch Powell, he had spent his time at Oxford indulging in what was still considered a rather eccentric pursuit – learning. Those who had observed his intimidating capacity for work chose to recall him as a plodder, forgetting his formidable intelligence. Yet he was a member of that surprisingly common breed, the unreflective prodigy. Grand political creeds held scant appeal for him and even at university he had shown little interest in politics. He was also genuinely benign, wanting the best for everyone as long as not too much was required in the way of moral courage. In short, he was almost as kind as he was genial and almost as genial as he was clever.

Wilson was vastly aided in his work at Number Ten by his wife's indifference, which left him free to spend the necessary hours closeted with aides and ministers. Mary Wilson, reclusive, devout and devoted to her husband, took little part in parliamentary life. Instead of doing the rounds, she composed poetry. One of her volumes sold 75,000 copies on its first print run. Whether explicitly religious or simply expressive of a vague but poignant yearning, her poems are suggestively titled: 'The Virgin's Song', 'If I Can Write Before I Die', and a piece that might have been named by one of her husband's more ardent critics on the left: 'You Have Turned Your Back on Eden'.

Still, Harold Wilson needed a helpmeet. Though Marcia Williams was strictly only Wilson's political officer, she soon became his confidante, imposing her will in matters that lay far beyond her remit and openly challenging ministers of the crown. Predictably, hints of a dalliance sometimes surfaced, but for all Wilson's lapses into political infidelity, he was devoted to Mary. He was also a northerner, quick-witted, seemingly phlegmatic and reassuring. In this he had his luck to thank, for the north had already come to prominence with a speed that none could have predicted.

'Did you have a gramophone when you were a kid?' asked an American interviewer of George Harrison, lead guitarist of the Beatles. The answer came in the amused, undulating tones of Liverpool. 'A gramophone? We didn't have sugar.' It was a classic Liverpudlian tease, and of a piece with Harrison's character.

Liverpool was not quite in the doldrums suffered by Manchester, but it was scarcely a cultural hub, at least not so far as London was concerned. For all its racial and religious diversity, and its accomplishments in trade, it seemed, in the words of a contemporary, 'utterly unglamorous'. And yet in one vital respect, Liverpool was blessed. It had access to the sea, which meant access to records and American music.

Boredom can awaken the sleepiest creative urge. The banality, as much as the poverty, of post-war Britain inspired the musical bloom of the Sixties. For there was little or nothing to do when John Lennon, Paul McCartney, Keith Richards, Pete Townshend and the Davies brothers grew up, little at least in the way of leisure. The family could provide music, fun and a hearth, but this triad is itself suggestive that England had not only declined but contracted. Beyond the home, the world of pleasure was thin. The music halls were in retreat and the cinema was a minnow beside the whale it had been in previous years. Rationing was still in force. Children still played in bomb craters, often finding toys sturdier than any to be glimpsed in shop windows.

For those in their teens, the world was scarcely brighter. Simple pleasures, furtive transgressions, sporadic and apolitical violence were the recreational prospects to hand. The young men brought up amidst the ruins of the Blitz had nothing but a promise of freedom offered from abroad. And one could always *improvise*: having nothing, the young had to make. As we have seen, however much rock 'n' roll might be worshipped, loved and danced to in England, it could not easily be emulated in its most glamorous form. Even guitars were almost a luxury item. As for drum kits or amplifiers – these items might as well have been the golden fleece. How could anyone follow Elvis on a budget of shillings?

Liverpool had a proud, if murky, past but no observable future until, as if by magic, there appeared four saviours. The Beatles arrived at the Cavern Club via a long and winding road. In the late Fifties, John Lennon, an artistic maverick of working-class stock and middle-class upbringing, had established a skiffle group called the Quarrymen. When the polite Paul McCartney offered to play, Lennon was confronted with a choice. The younger man's obvious talent was clearly a threat, yet it would enrich the band immeasurably. Later, George Harrison, a friend of McCartney's, joined, with nothing but a slow, wise wit and 'the dogged will to learn' to recommend him. The future Beatles lacked only a drummer. Indeed, the search for a permanent drummer, one who moreover would be a true 'Beatle', was to exercise them for almost three years. During those years, the Beatles had served in Hamburg. Their career had been undistinguished to date. One rival even complained of the impresario Alan Williams' decision to recruit 'a bum group like the Beatles'. But it was in Hamburg that they became the Beatles. Forced to contend with nightly bar fights, they learned that playing music was about pleasing others, or else. When they returned to Liverpool in 1961, they were hardened and fast. The songwriting partnership forged between Lennon and McCartney seemed to later commentators a gift from the gods: a minor lyrical genius (Lennon's) was smelted with a major musical talent (McCartney's). Now they needed only a manager far-sighted enough to see this.

He appeared in the shape of Brian Epstein, a charming, gifted salesman, who owned a record shop in Liverpool, and was, moreover, homosexual. Invited to the Cavern, he found himself entranced by the group and offered his services as their manager. 'All right then, Brian,' said the typically gracious Lennon. 'Manage us.' 'Guitar groups, Brian,' said one unimpressed producer. 'They're on their way out.' And so it seemed. The record labels were unimpressed by the Beatles' music, and still more by their caustic humour. Decca, the biggest corporation of all, turned them down. But there was still Parlophone, which had George Martin, a classically trained musician who was used to orchestras and the occasional novelty act. He recognized their talent and, having recently worked with the Goons, was amused by their irreverence. When, at the end of one session, he asked if there was anything they didn't like, Harrison observed, 'Well I don't like your tie, for a start.'

They had to do the rounds of cover versions, of course, but then they presented Martin with a song of their own, 'Love Me Do'. It was pronounced an 'odd little dirge-like thing' by Martin. When Keith Richards of the Rolling Stones first heard it, he felt 'physical pain', and he cannot have been alone. It was not much of a song by later standards, but it reached number seventeen in the charts and was a respectable achievement.

'How Do You Do It?' would, in George Martin's words, 'make the Beatles a household name'. But they were unimpressed – they had grown bored of performing others' work. They had a song of their own, they said. This was 'Please Please Me'. When they had finished, George Martin spoke over the tannoy. 'Congratulations, gentlemen,' he pronounced, 'you have just made your first Number One.' And so it proved. From its opening notes, the song is a cascade of ebullience, with the inimitable harmonies that would soon emerge as the Beatles' trademark. Written largely by Lennon, it was sung in the 'mid-Atlantic' accent used by all British performers at the time. The chords, too, were American-inspired, and yet it was clearly English. The harmonica 'riff' which opens this rock song almost precisely replicates that most English of sounds, the peal of church bells.

The oyster had been prised open at last. 'From Me to You', 'She Loves You', and 'I Want to Hold Your Hand' all went to number one. And the sound at their concerts was 'one of incessant screaming' from delirious fans. Having seduced the United Kingdom, they conquered the United States, and the phenomenon known as 'Beatlemania' was born. It has been said that the British bands of the Sixties were simply offering the Americans American music, stripped of any ugly political associations. But they were also offering the United States a version that was distinctively English, with rhythms, tunes, traditions and frustrations peculiar to England. By now any musician from Liverpool was hunted, then feted. The Mersey Sound was succeeded by Brumbeat, and the Tottenham Sound. There was hope for everyone. The Beatles were followed by the Kinks, the Rolling Stones, the Yardbirds, the Troggs, the Dave Clark Five, the Animals – all both singing and composing.

For those of a certain age, the history of this English music is well known. Where once it was surprising it is now familiar, but the music and lyrics seem fresh. That was their contribution, to the Sixties and beyond.

The Stones and the Beatles were friends, uneasily sometimes, but the Kinks were not friends with either. Prickly and intense, they did not make friends easily. Gerry and the Pacemakers had known

18. Rationing in 1949. The long lines proclaim that, even four years after the war, tea, sugar and eggs were still in short supply.

19. The coronation of Elizabeth II in 1953. She was to become the longest reigning monarch in English history.

EXTRA

Mirror News

YOUR INDEPENDENT NEWSPAPER

COMPLETE STOCKS

WEDNESDAY, OCTOBER 31, 1956

BRITISH BOMB 5 EGYPT CITIES

Incendiaries Dropped in Combined Sea-Air Action

LONDON, Oct. 31 (UP)—British and French air and sea forces today assaulted Egypt. Cairo radio said British jet bombers dropped incendiaries and high-explosive bombs on five key Egyptian centers including Cairo where seven persons were reported killed.

Britain's Foreign Secretary Selwyn Lloyd told the House of Commons tonight that "it is quite untrue that Cairo has been bombed." He said the attacks were restricted to airfields.

British officials in London insisted that Cairo, a city of 3,000,000, was not considered a military target. They said the bombers were operating against military targets only.

However, Cairo radio said:

"At 8:30 p.m. local time British bombers carried out attacks on Cairo, Alexandria, Port Said, Ismailia and Suez.

"Seven persons were killed in Cairo and minor material losses occurred."

The broadcast said Cairo was bombed twice with casualties resulting in the second attack.

There was no mention of ground-force operations.

LATE BULLETINS

Ike to Meet With Leading Military Men

Russ in Full Retreat Out of Budapest

A MISSING LINK

Where Does It All Leave U.S.?

TODAY'S POLITICS

WEATHER

Stocks Take Sharp Drop in Reaction to Hostilities

Jet Crashes; Pilot Bails Out

Poulson Gets Hospital Exam

MIRROR-NEWS INDEX

20. The Suez Canal in October 1956. The newspaper headlines emphasize the significance of what turned out to be a British disaster.

21. Harold Wilson, in October 1964, entering Downing Street after his election victory. The defeated Conservatives had been in power for thirteen years.

22. A scene outside the Royal Court in June 1956. It marked the premiere of John Osborne's *Look Back in Anger*.

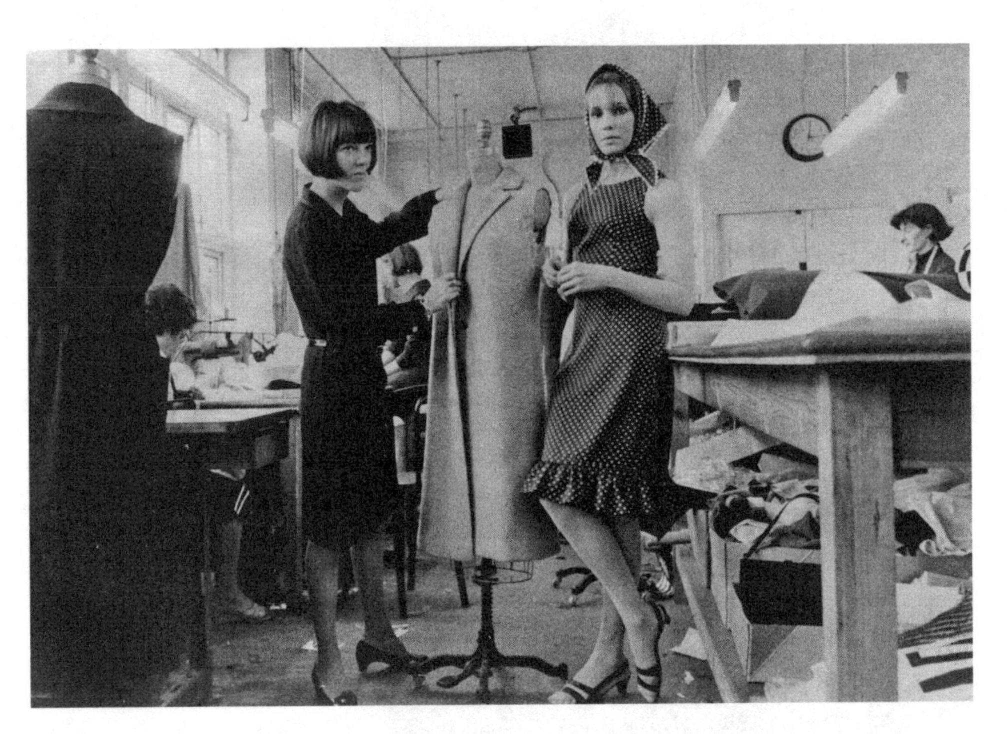

23. Mary Quant in April 1964. She became known as 'the queen of fashion' in a fashion-conscious era.

24. The 1966 World Cup final. The victory of England in the final was perhaps the summit of the country's sporting achievement.

25. The Beatles in August 1966. The four members of the group were at the pinnacle of their success, but the tour of 1966 was their last.

26. The queen watching television in 1969. A relaxed family scene, suggesting that the royal family was becoming more 'open' to the public.

27. A British family watching television in the 1970s. The 'box' was now essential and ubiquitous.

28. The three-day week, 1973, imposed by Edward Heath at the end of that year to minimize the use of electricity.

29. The miners' strike of 1984. Arthur Scargill, president of the National Union of Mineworkers, confronts the police.

30. Margaret Thatcher, prime minister, in 1986.
She had already gained recognition as the Iron Lady.

31. Princess Diana being interviewed in November 1995 about her life apart from the royal family, which led to her divorce from the Prince of Wales.

32. Tony Blair, on the day after the election of 1 May 1997, when he defeated John Major and the Conservatives.

33. The Millennium Dome, now known as the O2 Arena for music and entertainment.

the Beatles since the beginning. The Who didn't know anyone. But the point was not friendship so much as fruitful competition.

Where the Beatles were influenced primarily by rock 'n' roll, the Stones were a blues band, and never strayed very far from those roots. And between the Beatles and the Stones lay a tiny but crucial age gap. Lennon and McCartney had both been 'Teds', while Jagger and Richards were part of a new breed peculiar to the Sixties, the 'Mods'.

The term itself derives from 'modernist'; unlike the Teds, the Mods saw themselves as the heirs to the American 'beatniks'. They were, in short, of the middle class. Not that they advertised the fact. Rather, they followed the trend established in the previous decade for aping the manners and mannerisms of the street. They wore their hair long, in imitation of bygone Chelsea artists. The accent, however, was all their own, comprising a nasal drawl – in this respect, Mick Jagger was the exemplar. In the words of one radio journalist, his cadences were imitated 'by almost every middle-class public schoolboy in the land'.

In respect of violence, however, the Mods stood proudly in the Teddy boy tradition. Sentencing a Mod, George Simpson JP offered a denunciation worthy of Cromwell: 'These long-haired, mentally unstable, petty little hoodlums . . . came to Margate with the avowed intent of interfering with the life and property of its inhabitants.'

The Stones had been in no real sense 'rivals' to the Beatles. Under the leadership of Brian Jones, they were undoubtedly talented and distinctive, but they were also derivative, and seemed content to rework the forgotten classics of the Mississippi Delta. Their new manager Andrew Loog Oldham had other plans for them. They must become the 'anti-Beatles'. 'The Beatles want to hold your hand; the Stones want to burn your town!' and 'Would you let your daughter marry a Rolling Stone?' were among the slogans he coined. Above all, he had plans for Mick Jagger. It was the frontman, not the leader, who caught his attention. Brian Jones would or could not write songs in the new style, which he despised as chintzy and commercial. Loog Oldham saw that his protégés would disappear if they didn't follow the Beatles in songwriting. By the mid-Sixties, most of the major bands were writing their own material – there was simply no choice. The Beatles had not only opened the gate for others, but inadvertently chivvied them through. Neither Jagger nor Richards was an instinctive or natural songwriter. But with 'Satisfaction' this was to change. It had its origins, so legend has it, in a dream. The opening guitar instrumental, or 'lick', is ominous, funereal, even threatening. In its harsh rise and fall it seems to growl that 'I'll be waiting for you!'

40

This sporting life

It is most unlikely that Harold Wilson sympathized with this new musical aesthetic, for all his extolling of youth. But he felt some allegiance to his fellow northerners. This led him to propose that the Beatles be awarded MBEs for services to export. The queen approved, and in 1965 John, Paul, George and Ringo received their small gold crosses. Of Her Majesty herself, they said: 'She was great, just like a mum to us.' One disgruntled old soldier sent back his own MBE, protesting that the honour had been awarded to 'vulgar nincompoops'. And even those who were more sympathetic must have agreed with Geoffrey Moorhouse: 'One day it will all be over,' he wrote. 'We shall have worn out our records of "She Loves You"'.

In politics, as in music, nothing is ever certain. Given his five-seat majority, Wilson could not embark on the restructuring of Britain to the extent that he desired. His wishes, however, were Olympian. The rush of provision between 1964 and 1965 for the most vulnerable now seems uncanny in its beneficence. In 1965, redundancy payments were introduced. Council homes increased from 119,000 in 1964 to 142,000 in 1966. The Protection from Eviction Act ensured that tenants need never fear a rap on the door in the early hours. The Industrial Training Board provided for generations of workers to come. The Trade Disputes Act of 1965 restored the legal immunity of union officials. And the Race

Relations Act made it an offence to discriminate against any on the basis of race. Most revealingly, widows' pensions trebled in 1966. It was as if a sacred well had overflowed into a river of gold. The government's majority needed all the support it could muster, yet the goodwill of Wilson and his colleagues was beyond question; it was their deep intent to unfurl the canopy of the welfare state far wider than Beveridge and even Bevan could have conceived. By 1965, the sociologist T. H. Marshall could speak of a new consensus in the belief that it was the business of the state to look after the people.

It was education that had brought Wilson from Huddersfield to Downing Street, and he wished that advantage for all. Under his aegis, the percentage of GNP spent on education outstripped that on defence. Thirty new polytechnics were built. There were free school meals for children. The number of teachers in training vastly increased and the student population grew by 10 per cent each year. Every citizen, Wilson hoped, would soon be assured of some form of tertiary education. In 1969 the Open University was inaugurated; if you still could not go on to higher education, it would come to you. The dream of universal education was not as radical as it appeared, yet it was not to be. Instead, Wilson was to be credited for a step over which educators, politicians and parents have been at war ever since.

On 12 July 1965, Anthony Crosland assembled plans for a fully comprehensive system of secondary education, one that would do away with the divisive eleven-plus. Many had received a grammar-school education superior to that of the best public schools; but for those who failed the eleven-plus, the experience of a secondary modern had only served to dig a deeper sense of inferiority. Wilson's own attitude was hard to gauge. Outwardly, he gave Crosland his familiar support, while privately he felt corralled by the Labour Left. He had even been heard to declare that grammar schools would go 'over my dead body'. The problem grew more urgent as Labour's tiny majority fell to one. The balance of payments, moreover, was revealed to be the worst since the war. The government had to go to the country.

The prevailing mood in the government and party was sleepy, unhurried and even bored. It was another sign of Wilson's infectious self-belief, which the obvious unpopularity of the opposition's new leader, Edward Heath, buffed to brilliance. Where Wilson came across as easy-going and confident, Heath seemed awkward, intense and uninspiring. And who, after all, could have expected an election less than two years after the previous one? Richard Crossman recalled the mood on the day of his own re-election, a day of 'steady, perfect electioneering weather . . . Now it is we who are on the top of the world.' The public agreed, and the Labour party resumed government with over a hundred more seats in the Commons.

It had been a beautiful morning, but there were ominous signs. Jim Callaghan, the chancellor, now faced a storm-tossed pound, and for the first time a forbidden word began to be whispered – devaluation. Just as this new threat emerged, an old one, union militancy, rose up from a long slumber. The NUS, the seamen's union, walked out over weekend shifts. A shipping strike could do nothing but damage British maritime trade, perhaps catastrophically, and it would also make a nonsense of George Brown's voluntary incomes policy. He had set the rate of wage increases at 3.5 per cent, while the workers were asking for 17 per cent. In a furious bid to break the impasse, Wilson spoke of 'politically motivated men who . . . are now determined to exercise backstage pressures, forcing great hardship on the members of the union and their families, and endangering the security of the industry and the economic welfare of the nation'.

Blaming communist agitators worked and the strike was called off, but the victory came at an almost prohibitive price. It did nothing to help the pound and it sapped Wilson's popularity among the backbench left and even within his own cabinet. This, in turn, led to a stillborn coup against Wilson, known as the 'July plot'. The nation would never have accepted the erratic George Brown as a replacement for Wilson, but nonetheless it had been an enervating few weeks, and Wilson was ready to accept any distraction.

Since the Edwardian period, organized sport had acquired increasing prominence in national life. But it was cricket that dominated the early half of the century. Football was a local affair and inspired fierce loyalties, but the success or failure of the national team usually evoked little more than well-disposed apathy. With the growth of television, however, popular sympathies began to shift. Football was exciting to watch, but gentle on people's attention span. A ninety-minute game was perhaps preferable to a five-day test match. Nonetheless, the news that the 1966 World Cup would be hosted by England caught the nation unprepared. It was hard for his aides even to make Wilson understand that football might stretch further than his native Huddersfield Town. As ever, he quickly adapted. But after a dispiriting series of failures, few imagined that England could win the tournament.

Alf Ramsey could imagine it, however, and he set out to ensure it. Ramsey was a scion of the respectable working classes; football was not a game to him, and his players were encouraged to understand that. While it would be unfair to suggest that England sleepwalked through the first three matches, theirs was not a game to inspire the faithful. But with the match against Argentina, all was changed. The England players might have been less skilful than their opponents, but they were dogged and relentless. Towards the end of the game, a header by Geoff Hurst won the game for England.

The Argentines took the defeat badly, despite having bent the rules to breaking point, and Ramsey's inflammatory words after the game did not help matters. He used the term 'animals' to describe the defeated South Americans, and much of the world sympathized openly with them. The formidable Portugal side then lost to the English in the semi-final, in another result that confounded expectation. England was now in the final, and on home turf. At last the public was stirred and 'football fever' born.

The opponents in the final were West Germany. Joshing in the press about two other recent conflicts could not conceal the lack of real anti-German animus in the population – if anything, the German economic miracle of the post-war years had attracted admiration. The two sides were similar in many respects, tending to persistence rather than flair. The Germans scored first, a setback that served only to prick the torpor of the England side. England first equalized, then drew ahead. In the last frenetic ten minutes, the game became a true contest. The Germans drew level with one minute to go, and then the whistle blew. The English players were almost despairing, but Ramsey recalled them to their duty during extra time. 'You've won the World Cup once,' he told them. 'Now go out and win it again.' What followed proved one of the most controversial goals in history. The ball ricocheted between the German goalposts and at last the goal was given, to huge German protests. There was no debate about the next one, however: with seconds to go, Geoff Hurst lashed the ball into the German net. 4-2. England had won the World Cup.

The players collapsed, wept and embraced. The sun blazed brighter, the fans roared, and Bobby Moore, having wiped his hands before greeting the queen, held aloft the World Cup. The austere Ramsey, delighting in his players' happiness, doffed his usual reserve and kissed the trophy.

With its new mandate, and despite a deeply unpopular austerity programme, Wilson's government could at last begin its social programme in earnest. And so, after a long and often bitter battle, the efforts of Wolfenden, Lord Acton and their colleagues were at last vindicated. In 1967, the Sexual Offences Act legalized homosexual relations conducted in private between consenting adults over the age of twenty-one. Amidst the relief, joy and outrage, the act also provided some light comedy. In later years, a cartoon appeared, showing two middle-aged men in a bed, in the open air. Beside them, a police officer remarks: 'Over 21 you are, consenting you may well be, but I question the privacy of Berkeley Square.'

41

Old lace and arsenic

It is in a sense ironic that 1967 should be remembered as the 'Summer of Love'; the previous year had produced rather more of that commodity, for it was in 1966 that London had come to flower. The realms of drama, film, art and music glittered with palaces and blazed with gardens. It was the year of Lesley Hornby, a tiny, huge-eyed ghost of a girl better known by her family's affectionate nickname, 'Twiggy'. Led, or misled, by her example, young girls strove for a shape that later generations would regard as emaciated.

Twiggy herself was only the newest petal on an unprecedented bloom of English fashion. Indeed, by 1966, even Italy was prepared to offer an only slightly ironic bow to English efforts. Mary Quant was hailed as 'the queen of the miniskirt' by *Epoca*, while boutiques such as 'Lady Ellen' and 'Lord Kingsay' were to be found in Milan itself. Like many of a Welsh background, Mary Quant had recast herself as English almost at the moment she arrived in London. Her mission was simply 'to open a bouillabaisse of clothes and accessories . . . sweaters, scarves, shifts, hats, jewellery, and peculiar odds and ends'. This was hardly enough to distinguish her from many other designers, but she went further. She wanted, as she put it, 'clothes that were much more for life, much more for real people, much more for being young and alive in . . . clothes to move and run and dance in'. It was to have huge repercussions, not so much for the country itself as for others' perception of it. The young were the new market, and youth was all. From the King's Road in Chelsea to the United States, her clothes – bright in colour, sharp in outline, endlessly adaptive – spread over continents. Rightly was Quant named the 'Queen of Fashion'.

She had imagination and could tease out the silken quality in gingham, tartan, flannel and even PVC, the delight of fetishists. For her, there were no marriages of convenience between material and shape, only love matches. By 1966, she had been awarded the OBE, her companies bringing in more than £6 million a year, and five hundred designs soaring from her sewing machines annually. The boutique style also took off elsewhere, with Carnaby Street as the leader. The new clothes swirled around a new type, and indeed created it: this was the 'dolly bird', skinny, girlish, sexually assured and affluent. For despite the gushing of Quant and others, the new trends in fashion lay far beyond the reach of 'dockers' wives'. Twiggy herself was unimpressed. 'Bazaar in the King's Road,' she said, 'was for rich girls.'

It was likely, too, that the theatre was for rich patrons. The dominant item on the early-Sixties stage was still the kitchen sink. The dark, the 'gritty', the consciously inelegant, were paramount, just as affluent audiences expected and required. When a shift occurred, it did so teasingly.

Joe Orton was born plain 'John', of immaculately working-class stock. After training as an actor, he met Kenneth Halliwell, an aspiring novelist. When Orton and Halliwell appeared in her office to discuss their joint novel, their prospective agent, Peggy Ramsay, was left with one clear impression. 'Kenneth was the writer, John was basically his pretty and vivacious boyfriend.' Yet it was the consort who was ultimately to wear the crown. Unlike his lover, Orton had never particularly wanted to be a writer, and this lack of vocation counted in his favour. It was writing rather than being a writer that appealed to him.

His first play, *Entertaining Mr Sloane*, appeared to owe much to the kitchen sink drama of the Fifties. It was set in a dank suburban household, with little in the way of glamour and a large rubbish tip outside. Kath and Ed, siblings in middle age, live with their father,

Kemp. Enter Mr Sloane, a young working-class man to whom both brother and sister find themselves irresistibly attracted. Kemp is suspicious and hostile, with some justification, for the callow ingénu of the first act soon reveals himself to be a cool, manipulative sociopath. Having impregnated Kath, he goes on to beat Kemp to death when the latter identifies him as the murderer of his former employer. Although the death is strictly manslaughter, Kath and Ed succeed in blackmailing Sloane, and he is forced to let them 'share' him. The unforgiving austerity of the plot is, however, belied by the play's idiom. The flat cadences of the early scenes recede and a puckish, Wildean note intrudes. When Sloane asks whether he can be present at the baby's birth, Ed assures him: 'I think to be present at the conception is all any reasonable man need ask.'

Buoyed by the generosity of Terence Rattigan, the play performed well and profitably. Only a few days after the opening night, however, the papers received a letter from one 'Edna Welthorpe (Miss)'. Indignant at the 'filth' displayed, she concluded that 'today's young playwrights take it upon themselves to insult the ordinary, decent public . . . the ordinary, decent public will shortly strike back – now!' The solecism at the end was the master touch, for of course Miss Welthorpe was none other than Joe Orton himself. The forename was offered in tribute to Rattigan, who always maintained that 'Aunt Edna' was his ideal audience member.

Loot, Orton's next performed work, was a black farce in which Inspector Truscott, a cheerfully corrupt policeman, investigates a burglary, only to pocket much of the titular loot before sending an entirely innocent widower to jail. The kitchen sink had yielded centre stage to the coffin, where the casket holds the stash. When faced with the proposition that it is the business of the police to protect the honest and decent, Truscott remarks, 'I don't know where you get these slogans, sir. You must read them on hoardings.' This Wildean strain dances with still greater abandon in Orton's later plays. *What the Butler Saw* was performed posthumously. Orton's finest work, depicting the gradual unravelling of sanity and justice in a psychiatric ward, it ends with the cast, traduced, abused, ravished and raving, ascending a stair into the light, carrying the 'missing parts' of a statue of Winston Churchill. Every kind of 'perversion' is gleefully displayed for the audience's disgust and delectation.

The play was jeered and heckled at its opening. Sir Ralph Richardson, who played the charming, sinister and palpably insane Dr Rance, was advised from the stalls to 'give up your knighthood!' Orton's penchant for 'black farce' had its counterpart in what has been called the 'comedy of menace'. Where theatre was concerned, black was a tone that leaked into the brightest palettes of the time. Harold Pinter gave tacit approval to the expression 'comedy of menace', but the comedic quality was not always easy to discern. He had begun to write in the late Fifties, but it was in the Sixties that his reputation began its true ascent. *The Caretaker* was performed in 1960, and *The Homecoming* six years later. In *The Homecoming*, the tale springs from the common motif of two strangers coming to town. In the course of the plot a husband returns from America to his working-class family, all male, with a woman he announces as his wife. She behaves in a remarkably unwifely manner, proceeding to seduce two of his brothers in front of him. It soon becomes clear that the brothers and paterfamilias want to keep her, as sister, as mother, and as something else – a something hinted at in the word 'business'. The husband departs for America, leaving his willing wife in the hands of his father and brothers, who comprise a brood as clinging as it is predatory. Pinter's gift to the theatre of the Sixties was his willingness to carve in negative space, to saturate the pause and the silence with generally malevolent intent. Asked what his plays were concerned with, even what they were about, he replied, 'The weasel under the cocktail cabinet.'

As if in harmony, the dystopian strain in English fiction returned. Anthony Burgess composed *A Clockwork Orange*, 'being the adventures of a young man whose principal hobbies are rape, ultra-violence and Beethoven'. Set in a not-too-distant future, it lays out a society at once authoritarian and feckless, in which the untrammelled young have adopted an argot called 'nadsat'. The intent behind the devising of this patois, a kind of thieves' cant of the future, was to render the book ageless. It incorporates English, Romany, and cockney rhyming slang, but above all, Russian. In a West that had heard Khrushchev's grandiose threat 'We will bury you!', it was all too plausible that Russian should become the language of power.

The young man, Alex, has nothing to complain of. He is clearly of the middle class, and as clearly a sociopath. There is no reason behind his savage quest for unending self-gratification – indeed, it is his lack of obvious criminal motivation that makes him so unsettling, particularly to those who look for some 'trauma' to explain the existence of evil. He leads a gang of three 'droogs' on night-time escapades which reliably end in careless and sickening violence. When not with his pals, he is given to the casual rape of underage girls, and to Beethoven. When the gang turns against him, he finds himself in prison. There he is subjected to the Ludovico Technique, a kind of extreme aversion therapy which renders the patient incapable of violence or lust. When he is released into the world, his former victims, finding that he is helpless, beat, humiliate, abuse and incarcerate him. At last Alex is given the opportunity to reverse the treatment, an opportunity of which he happily avails himself. In the last chapter (omitted from the American version), a sedate and subdued Alex realizes that the lust for destruction has ebbed from him. Rather than remaining a 'clockwork orange', he may find the will to rejoin the human race.

Of the many people anxious to let wholesome light into this dark world, Mary Whitehouse, a Warwickshire housewife, was the most vociferous. Spurred on by what she considered the moral cowardice, even treachery, of the BBC, she founded the National Viewers' and Listeners' Association in the early Sixties. From the pens of the bespectacled, redoubtable Whitehouse and her followers poured a steadily swelling torrent of complaint. Once, asked whether she had actually seen a programme that had so offended her, she replied with mocking disdain: 'I have too much respect for my mind!' When it was insinuated, in an interview with Johnny Speight, that her views were fascist, Whitehouse successfully sued the BBC. It was one of several private prosecutions she mounted – few had the same success, though many proved influential.

Those who disagreed with her were apt to do so in satirical fashion. Soon after the Speight affair, *Till Death Us Do Part*, a television series written by Johnny Speight which depicted the comically hapless struggle of Alf Garnett against the forces of progress, had Garnett reading one of her works and cheering every line. Whitehouse had objected to the repeated use of the word 'bloody' on that programme; in that episode, the 'bloody's flowed without cease.

To her supporters, Whitehouse was a brave, decent Christian, attempting to reverse a contagion that had spread from the world of entertainment and into the English household. To her detractors she was a bigot intent on halting and even reversing any increase in freedom of expression and social progress. The truth is perhaps more subtle: she seemed convinced that to be a Christian entailed being a theocrat. Yet her influence proved greater than her supporters dared hope. Her campaign 'The right of a child to be a child' led many years later to the passing of the Protection of Children Act.

In her conviction that wild flowers are never more than weeds, she often aimed at the most seemingly innocuous TV programmes. Violence, as much as sex, disturbed her deeply, and when a show she wrongly understood to be for small children depicted a humanoid plant throttling one of the characters, she felt bound to lodge a protest. This was a pity since she and the protagonist of *Doctor Who* had much in common. Both were outsiders, rebels who saw themselves as healers, and both sought to interfere as much as they could in matters they felt to be of moral consequence.

A man finds himself trapped in an alien and primitive environment. His craft, which had once traversed many lands swiftly and fluently, now creaks and shudders. So far, the traditional motifs need no introduction. Here, however, a curious anomaly is introduced. The man's ship alters its shape to suit its environment, but something has gone wrong, and the ship is stuck in the shape of a Sixties police box. His story begins in inconvenience, and what else is a story but a succession of inconveniences? *Doctor Who* had a difficult birth. First broadcast in 1963, it struggled to crawl from script to screen, but by the late Sixties it amounted to a national addiction, with production values best described as homely and a central figure who was old, eccentric and unglamorous. England's answer to Superman looked, and thought, rather like Bertrand Russell.

It was part of a wider trend, discernible even in *A Clockwork Orange*, in which 'white heat' forged only monsters of metal. This is most apparent in the figures of the Daleks. With their pepperpot armour, spindly weapons, lavatory plunger eyes and, above all, their voice – like the bark of a cockney sergeant – the Daleks should have been comic. Instead they were terrifying, for under the metal exterior lurked the loathsome result of an experiment in eugenics.

In this dreadful parody of humankind lay, it was hinted, our common fate if science were ever given the power to rule. Time and again, the Doctor must confront the prejudices of frightened races whose leaders have told them that the gods will punish them if they do not obey. Miracles are then revealed as scientific trickery, with gods shown to be mere computers. The Doctor thus acted as a kind of corrective to the missionaries of the Victorian period, urging the primacy of facts over faith.

His other great enemy was imperialism. The mass will to conquer and devour was outmanoeuvred again and again by the Doctor's courage and wisdom, but never finally defeated. On the screen, as in the world, evil recuperates as if by reflex. But the Doctor was no superhero. Aside from his longevity, his only weapons were his intellect, his trench humour, his pluck and his sometimes quixotic compassion. The Doctor, in short, was a profoundly English creation, in manners, accent and wit. It is tempting to hear in his tones an echo of what one journalist referred to as 'benevolent post-war paternalism': Britain no longer ran the world, but it could perhaps heal it. This was an unarguable manifestation of the Sixties spirit.

The visual art of the Sixties was the result of schooling in the Fifties. Its roots had been planted in 1957, and from then on the plant grew as swiftly as willow. In the decade of the consumer, art had become public. As the critic Robert Hughes observed, in any clash between pop culture and art, art could not possibly win. Very well, then art would become pop; buildings, album covers, advertising logos and theatre sets all evinced the new spirit.

The world of colour, so long occluded, found its greatest exponent in David Hockney. A true child of the grey moorland, he caught the rising sun and like a sunflower bent towards it. Coming to prominence in 1963, he went on to dominate the Sixties with paintings of swimming pools, beautiful men, sun and sea. In his paintings, colour and light, exuberant splashes and clean, crisp lines are composed in a manner that lifts the most cynical heart. In many ways, modern art had begun as an act of retreat rather than of advance. With the fashionable efflorescence of photography, it was widely predicted that figurative art would wither and perish. Yet the remarkable flourishing of art in the Sixties is best known for being shamelessly figurative in character, largely in its subverting of images familiar from popular consciousness. The 'Situation' exhibition in 1960 established a paradox: the primacy of all things American and the distinctiveness of all things British. The contributing artists were keen to identify with all things American, from 'action paintings' to Dacron suits.

But the American influence can be exaggerated. English artists did not follow the American lead in art any more than in politics. In fact, the relentless succession of stars and soup tins across the ocean found little favour in Britain. Even when they used such images, the instinct of the artists was to subvert rather than merely replicate. Peter Blake's *Self-Portrait with Badges* (1961) embodied the paradox with charm and delicacy. A short and unprepossessing Englishman in middle age, standing in a suburban garden, looks flatly at the viewer, his clothes adorned with badges from America. His eyes seem to say: 'I'm trying to look American. It isn't working, is it?'

As much of this art reveals, the decade was increasingly exercised by the rapidly growing influence of psychotropic substances. Cannabis had been available for years, if you knew where to look. The houses and tenements of the West Indian community were widely supposed to be thick with resinous smoke, but like all such racial totems this was largely a myth. What cannot be denied is that by the mid-Sixties, a few hours of 'ease' was cheaper and more accessible than ever it had been before. However, cocaine was the toy only of the rich, heroin was scarcely heard of, and 'magic mushroom' could be found only in the less salubrious markets of the capital. To be sure, the pills known as 'uppers' and 'downers' were widely used, but they had been in circulation for years.

The peculiarly Sixties offering was lysergic acid diethylamide, or LSD. Its origins were innocent enough. When LSD was developed in the late Fifties, it was hailed in some quarters as balm for hurt minds. This reaction derived from LSD's unique property among hallucinogens: it provoked what was called 'synaesthesia'. While under the influence of 'acid', the subject found that his senses swapped their functions: sounds could be seen, smells heard. This was followed by a state in which the senses simply elided, leaving the subject in a state of whimsical ecstasy.

No less an authority than Aldous Huxley had praised its curative powers. More significantly still, Bill Wilson, co-founder of Alcoholics Anonymous, had tried acid and declared it beneficial, a remarkable endorsement from one understandably suspicious of altered states. The problem, as so often, was that the recreational user could never be sure that the acid he had bought was quite what it appeared. It was not long before acid was 'cut' with strychnine, producing a state of agitation and fury. Sometimes substitute hallucinogens were sold and these offered only horrible visions, lasting sometimes for days. LSD had sunk into the mire by the end of the decade, leaving little trace.

Like so many trends of the Sixties, this largely metropolitan habit scarcely grazed the consciousness of most people, yet the wider effect, as filtered through the arts, was incalculable. Michael English and Nigel Waymouth composed posters and album covers that at first recalled art nouveau, but which belonged in temper and in subject only to the Sixties. Wild images, extravagant lines, colours that refused to cooperate, swirled about and about within a fantastical vision that came to be known as 'psychedelic'.

42

The new brutalism

Brandy apart, the prime minister himself did not indulge in mind-altering substances, though few could have blamed him. For three years, the government had been attempting to fulfil its social and strategic commitments while placating its creditors. It had even resorted to borrowing from the IMF, a humiliating position for a supposedly great power. Now there was nothing for it, it seemed, but to devalue the pound.

While Wilson's government had hugely increased welfare provision, the difference in economic outlook between Labour and Conservative was still one of degree rather than of kind. Wilson had largely followed his Conservative predecessors, who in turn had largely followed Attlee. The post-war consensus had yet to be challenged on any scale. It is hard to see how any one party, let alone any individual, was to blame. This thought cannot have greatly consoled the prime minister as he faced the cameras on 27 April 1967. With a smile that seemed almost a plea for mitigation and in a voice that sought rather than offered reassurance, he told the nation that 'From now the pound abroad is worth 14 per cent or so less in terms of other currencies. It does not mean, of course, that the pound here in Britain, in your pocket or your purse or in your bank, has been devalued. What it does mean is that we shall now be able to sell more goods abroad on a competitive basis.'

It was a gift to the opposition, and Edward Heath was scathing: 'Having denied twenty times in thirty-seven months that they would ever devalue the pound, they have devalued against all their own arguments.' The image of Wilson as a political eel was now fixed in the minds of parliamentarians, while his reputation among the public for amiable bluntness suffered accordingly.

Once again, however, it is hard to see how things could have been better managed. The clue lies in Wilson's preamble to the announcement. He had said that the 'decision to devalue attacks our problem at the root'. Later economists might have observed that the 'problem' lay not in the root but in the branches – overladen, overextended and caught in a mass of tangles. The Labour government of the late Sixties, like the Macmillan government before it, had committed itself to a programme in which a hundred irreconcilable aims jostled for priority. Nor could the effects of the six-day war on oil prices have been predicted. The current account for the balance of payments did recover, however, and its recovery lasted until 1970. It would be left to another generation to address the problem of money supply, the 'root' problem.

The spring had been dour indeed; what hope then for the summer? The Beatles had conquered America, but the joys of live performance had started to pall. 'One more hotel, one more stadium, one more run for your life,' was their summing up of the experience. The disillusion had begun after a carelessly provocative remark by John Lennon that 'Christianity will die, it will vanish and shrink. We're more popular than Jesus now.' Lennon's startled apology in the wake of public protest did nothing to mollify the deeply religious states of the American South and Midwest. And when crowds began burning Beatles paraphernalia, the Beatles began to sense that their popularity was not after all unassailable. The coup de grâce, however, came with their visit to the Philippines. The dictator Ferdinand Marcos had arranged a meeting with them, but due to an administrative glitch they failed to appear. It is never prudent to snub a despot, and when they were assaulted by the very guards assigned to protect them, the Beatles fled. Touring, they decided, had lost its charm. Instead they closeted themselves in their studio, writing, composing, editing and, above all, experimenting. When asked what magnum opus they were assembling, they were uncharacteristically coy.

In the world of fashion, a dual trend of nostalgia and mysticism became apparent. The seeds had been laid in 1964, when Barbara Hulanicki set up Biba, a fashion boutique whose ethos was quite different from that of Mary Quant or Carnaby Street. In 1965 she remarked, 'I love old things. Modern things are so cold. I need things that are lived.' It soon became obvious that her taste was widely shared. The clothes marketed were voluminous, richly coloured, and just decadent enough to excite without offending. The 'Belle Époque' of the early twentieth century was everywhere evoked but at affordable prices. In this, as in every other respect, Biba broke with its predecessors. By 1967, its store on Kensington High Street, with its Egyptian columns and stained-glass windows, was drawing as many as 100,000 customers a week.

Biba set the pattern for the era, and its influence was to last deep into the Seventies. It was more prophetic than countercultural, but those who came to be associated with its bedizened, opulent style stood defiantly against the prevailing culture. From 1967, the more troubled current of youth found a tributary that ran into tree-tangled Middle-earth. Their proclaimed values were those of peace, brotherhood (and sisterhood), universal (and free) love, and recreational use of the softer drugs. The hippy trend was without obvious precedent. The Mods and the Teds could boast of an inheritance of bloodiness, but the hippies turned away from it. The cult had many limitations and absurdities, but its devotees forswore the fist or the broken bottle; the object was peace.

At first, they were instantly recognizable. The body was swathed in scarves, beads, kaftans, voluminous trousers. The word 'hippy' is of uncertain provenance, but it seems to have had its origins in black American 'jive' in the early twentieth century. It signified 'with it', or 'cool'. Neatly inverting the circumstances of the pop invasion, here was a largely American stem grafted onto English roots. The 400,000 who gathered for the Isle of Wight Festival in 1967 were imitating American models, yet they were at one with their sisters and brothers in the United States in invoking English masters: Gerrard Winstanley, the English interregnum anarchist, Aleister

Crowley, the early-twentieth-century mage and visionary, William Blake and J. R. R. Tolkien were held to be the prophets of the movement. Later, the hippies began to assimilate the influences of the East, and the 'hippy trail' from Istanbul to India became a fixture of their lifestyle. In this practical orientalism, they took their lead from the Beatles.

On 1 June 1967, the Beatles' long-awaited album, *Sgt. Pepper's Lonely Hearts Club Band*, was released. The cover alone was a feast. The Beatles, dressed as Edwardian bandsmen, stood against a vast collage of famous or esoteric figures, while to their right stood the effigies made in their honour by Madame Tussauds. The album was arranged as to give the impression of a concert in the grand old style of the village pavilion. In some of the songs, like 'Being for the Benefit of Mr Kite!' or 'When I'm Sixty-Four', this impression was reinforced. Over others, like 'Lucy in the Sky with Diamonds', a silken, starry cape of psychedelia spread. Paul McCartney sang of working-class parting in 'She's Leaving Home', and of the unsuccessful wooing of a meter maid in 'Lovely Rita'. No one song resembled another. *Sgt. Pepper* was not perhaps the Beatles' best album, but like the Beatles themselves it was greater than the sum of its parts. Its example inspired musicians of the later Sixties both to further heights of creativity and to further depths of pretension.

The expression 'British architecture' had become almost oxymoronic by the mid-Sixties. The eager acolytes of Le Corbusier dominated the Royal Institute of British Architects, and were austere in their attitude to anything that smacked of native sentimentality. Le Corbusier himself had declared that cities were 'far too important to be left to their citizens'; to the English, this was not so much heresy as blasphemy. The lawn, the flower bed, the garage and the tumbledown house stood for the spirit of homely self-reliance that the English have always imagined to be their birthright.

There could be no denying the impact of brutalism, on individual lives and on the English skyline. The Sixties marked the apogee of the 'high-rise' building. Its benefits seemed obvious. Unlike the new towns, which ate into the countryside at a rate that appalled many in the countryside and suburbs, tower blocks trespassed only on the territory of birds. Considerations of safety and even practicality counted for little. Ian Nairn, one of the most far-sighted of architectural writers, made the point baldly: 'The outstanding and appalling fact about modern British architecture is that it is just not good enough. It is not standing up to use or climate, either in single buildings or the whole environment.' British brutalists were trying to ape continental models while ignoring continental standards.

The poet John Betjeman showed himself the true heir of Chesterton in his fulminations against soulless modernity. He was to save St Pancras station and countless other examples of Victorian architecture from demolition. But it was the proposed abolition of nature that angered him most. We will never know the extent to which Betjeman and others saved the English landscape from being 'improved' beyond recognition, but it is unlikely that the mass supplanting of families from their homes could have long continued. The tower block and the new town were both going the way of all fashions by the end of the Sixties, although the latter was to have a brief and undistinguished revival in the Eighties. The compound failures of the brutalist experiment had led by the late Sixties to a resurgence in softer, older traditions. After a long enchanted sleep, art nouveau had begun to stir, in housing as much as in fashion. Wallpaper in the William Morris style was pasted on walls; the beams on Tudor houses were uncovered.

In October 1967, a private member's bill by the Liberal MP David Steel became law. Although it concerned the contentious matter of abortion, it was proposed in the same spirit as the Sexual Offences Act as a compassionate means of ending distress. The bill enjoyed broad cross-party support, allowing trained doctors to perform what had hitherto been the preserve of unscrupulous and often unqualified backstreet practitioners. In the Sixties film *Alfie*, the eponymous working-class lothario, played by Michael Caine, gives a girl he has seduced some 'help', as it was termed, in the form of a shifty doctor. When Alfie later goes into the room where the abortion has taken place, his face contorts in a daze of horror. Many such films dealt with the question, few so powerfully; the image must have swayed many to the belief that no woman should have to suffer such conditions or such shame.

* * *

On 20 April 1968, Enoch Powell, the honourable member for Wolverhampton, gave a speech in the Midland Hotel in Birmingham. His audience was the West Midlands Conservative Political Centre and his subject was immigration. The audience was expecting edification and even entertainment; what they witnessed was an eruption of lava from a suburban lawn. With his jaw clenched, his voice caught between a bark and a snarl, and eyes which, in the words of Kingsley Amis, suggested someone 'about to go for your throat', Enoch Powell was never biddable and seldom diplomatic. Ever willing to hector, to argue, he could not steel himself to woo or placate. This quality brought him to high office but rendered negligible any chance of his retaining it.

Powell had been a brilliant classicist at university, a superb organizer during the war, a fiercely meticulous minister, and a conscientious MP, his ear ever open to the concerns of his constituents – whatever their origins. He had a command of fourteen languages and was able to canvass in six of them. If he had shown concern over the rate of Commonwealth immigration in the early Sixties, he was scarcely alone. And it should be noted that when the more extreme elements of the anti-immigration lobby asked for his support in the late Fifties, they were met by cold reproof or icy silence. He was thus a plausible demagogue, but an improbable racist. As the speech gathered in pace and hyperbole, the moustachioed, methodical public servant became a bearded John Knox. 'Those whom the gods wish to destroy, they first make mad. We must be mad, literally mad, as a nation to be permitting the annual inflow of some 50,000 dependants, who are for the most part the material of the future growth of the immigrant-descended population. It is like watching a nation busily heaping up its own funeral pyre . . . Like the Roman, I seem to see "the River Tiber foaming with much blood".'

The so-called 'Rivers of Blood' speech earned Powell immediate dismissal from Heath, lasting opprobrium in the House of Commons and the warm endorsement of 74 per cent of the electorate. He was to be remembered as the man who had deliberately stirred a sleeping dragon, but Powell had only himself to thank for this. His speech was not just inflammatory, but mendacious. He had cited unnamed constituents feeling afraid in their own homes. He had spoken of 'excreta' being shoved through the letter box of an elderly white woman. A man was quoted saying that 'the black man will have the whip hand over the white man'. It is probable that these mysterious constituents never existed. All the tokens of a mind warped by passion were in place. His friend Michael Foot, as far from Powell in political outlook as he was close to him in patriotism and intellect, reflected that 'It was a tragedy for Enoch . . . a tragedy for all of us.'

Powell scorned the notion that one race could be 'superior to another', but logic compelled him to follow his reasoning wherever it led. His premises, however, were not universally shared. For him the object of politics was the coherence of the state and society, and many might have agreed. Many, too, would have accepted his notion of a realm united under a queen, with parliament as sovereign. But he considered this coherence or unity to be as necessary in town and village as it was in Westminster and believed that if it should be threatened, bloodshed would follow. As he never tired of asserting, it was not for him a question of colour. However that may be, his speech destroyed his chances of ever again attaining high office. It did not, however, curtail his influence on politics. Although his more apocalyptic predictions came to nothing, in the field of economics he was to prove the prophet of the movement that would become known as monetarism.

43

The soothing dark

For members of the 'commentariat', the early Sixties had been heavy with pessimism, even of fatalism. *The Economist* had noted that 'All the political parties are going into their annual conferences with plans . . . to put Britain right by bringing it up to date; each promises that, like a detergent, it will wash whiter. The British have become, suddenly, the most introspective people on earth.' It was not alone. Non-fiction presses ran almost dry with laments for the 'state of the nation'. One of the most influential was *Suicide of a Nation* (1963), edited by Arthur Koestler. In this book, Malcolm Muggeridge articulated an ominous thought. 'Each time I return to England from abroad the country seems a little more run down than when I went away; its streets a little shabbier; its railway carriages and restaurants a little dingier . . . and the vainglorious rhetoric of its politicians a little more fatuous.' This mood had lifted in the second half of the decade, but it was to reassert itself. It cannot have helped that, in 1967, de Gaulle had for the second time vetoed Britain's joining the Common Market. The Wilson administration seemed dazed and bewildered in the face of continental obduracy.

But, as ever in the Sixties, the people had their diversions. Watching the television had become something of a national sport in itself, and by the end of the decade, all but the poorest homes had their own set. And the small screen accommodated every taste – one could be stirred by *The Avengers*, comforted by *The Forsyte Saga* or amused by *Till Death Us Do Part*, *Steptoe and Son* and a gentle but brilliantly observed comedy about the Home Guard called *Dad's Army*. Certainly, there was little to draw people to the larger screens. British cinema comprised scarcely more than Bond, pop art pretension and camp comedy. It could hardly be otherwise: by the late Sixties, funding for British films came almost exclusively from the United States, and when the quality of British film began to wane, the flow of money stopped.

One fine Sixties innovation, however, was the so-called 'caper movie'. The greatest, and silliest, example of this genre was *The Italian Job*, released in 1969. Here, a plausible crook named Charlie Croker steals 4 million pounds' worth of bullion from under the noses of the Mafia, aided by a team of very English criminals. They manage to get their stash up into the Alps when disaster strikes. The film ends with their bus leaning over a vast gulf, and Croker (played by Michael Caine) assuring the gang that he has 'a great idea', with somewhat frayed confidence.

For all the film's virtues, it might have vanished had it not so winningly caught a particular brand of Englishness: amateurish, sunny and yet quietly implacable. And it represented, too, a reversion to the spirit of the early Sixties. This was not the slick, self-assured world captured in the Bond films. The times were less certain and so was the culture reflecting them; perhaps, in spite of the empty promises of statesmen, the dulled diamonds of flower power and the disappointments of technology, there existed the conviction that ordinary, traditional pluck might see the nation through. In any case, the end of American funding was not the disaster it might have been. For one thing, it led to the success of the Hammer studios. Towards the end of the Sixties and deep into the Seventies, films about Dracula and Frankenstein, witches and werewolves were devoured avidly by audiences and excoriated eagerly by critics.

Then there were the *Carry On* films, which in the Sixties took a turn for the bawdy. Sid James, Kenneth Williams, Barbara Windsor and, on occasion, Frankie Howerd, starred in films where no sacred cow was left unmolested. From the hospital to the camping field, from ancient Rome to imperial India, the *Carry On* team titillated and tickled the audience. In a very English eschewing of the erotic, they brought back a spirit of holiday fun, with brassieres popping and zips jamming.

For those with money or taste, the theatre could still offer distraction and even intellectual challenge. Tom Stoppard, the Czech-born 'university wit' who had never gone to university, began to bewitch audiences with plays of punishing erudition, unabashed persiflage and broad comedy. Less ostentatious in his erudition but no less lyrical was the young Peter Shaffer, whose *The Royal Hunt of the Sun* reimagined the Spanish conquest of the Americas from the perspective of the compromised Incas. Such interpretations were to become his unchallenged demesne.

The great pop bands of the early Sixties were scarcely in retreat, but the hysteria surrounding them was spent and a long-delayed scepticism could at last be felt. Fleet Street, once the Beatles' most ardent well-wisher, was beginning to roll its eyes at what seemed their growing perversity. Why couldn't they just stick to playable tunes? Why all this cleverness? Satirists, too, were again sharpening their knives.

The musical invasion of the Sixties had been an invasion of groups. Just as the United States was the arena of individual endeavour, so it tended to be the cradle of the solo artist. Britain, comparatively more communal in its approach, represented the land of the band. Thus there were the Who, the Animals, the Yardbirds, the Dave Clark Five, and in the latter half of the decade, the Moody Blues, Led Zeppelin and Pink Floyd. Certain patterns emerged: the upper- or upper-middle-class manager, full of enthusiasm but short on experience, the predominantly working-class origin of the band members, the American influence and its subsequent jettisoning.

Of all the bands, the Kinks were the most distinctively English. Towards the end of the Sixties, they began to compose wistful elegies and biting eulogies for the country, its vistas and its customs. Like many of their contemporaries, they had begun as a rhythm and blues band, but by the end of the decade they celebrated and satirized contemporary life in the cadences of the music hall and the folk song.

The 'beautiful people' did their best to quiet the warring world through 'flower power', yet the hippies and musicians of England were less strident in their anti-militarist stance than those of the United States. It was not, after all, the sons of the English who were fighting in Indochina. For all the mockery he suffered, Wilson was by no means the poodle of Washington. He refused, for example, to allow British troops to serve in Vietnam. The pop songs of the time often seemed to celebrate or advocate a certain kind of liberty, but the singers themselves were rarely revolutionaries by conviction. A sometimes forgotten bond between the various groups was art school. Nowadays considered a middle-class institution, it was, for those coming of age in the Sixties, a wardrobe through which the aspirational working class could enter the Narnia of the arts.

The role of a British group had been to learn from the American masters and then offer them the ultimate homage of a cover version. But to write your own songs? Could it be done? Was it not a hubristic betrayal of the masters to try to improve upon them? While classical music is, of all the forms, the most rooted in individual genius, pop music had been authorless. In that it resembled, of all things, the music of the sacred. With the advent of the Beatles and their followers, this had changed. In previous eras, the music and dance of the working class had either been adapted for polite society or dismissed; now it stood alone, unadorned and unapologetic. This had wider consequences. During the Sixties, the aspirational impulse that drove many to speak 'posh' began to recede. In interviews, a young musician whose stage name was Cat Stevens spoke in the languid tones of bohemian Chelsea. Middle-, let alone upper-class, tones were to be flattened or expunged.

This new grit flew everywhere, changing accents and idioms. Laurence Olivier and John Gielgud had been known to rehearse in evening dress, but this was not the Sixties way. The working class had always exerted a deep influence on film and the theatre, but in this decade the influence was actively celebrated. Michael Caine, Richard Burton, Terence Stamp and a flock of others gave the working class not respectability, but glamour.

By the late Sixties, recreational drugs, previously a minority interest even among the wealthy, were impinging upon popular consciousness. Rates of cocaine and heroin addiction had tripled by

1970. The embedding of a drug habit was in some ways easier then, and the reason seems clear: government had forbidden without informing, and no one knew exactly why these delightful diversions should be proscribed. As Mick Jagger put it: 'We didn't know about addiction then; we thought cocaine was good for you!'

44

In place of peace

Industrial relations had been cordial for much of the Sixties, at least by comparison with many of Britain's neighbours. But by the end of the decade, 'strife' was again apparent, and Wilson and Barbara Castle, the new employment secretary, could feel in the nation a growing unease. Castle took to the task of taming the unions with something akin to despair; as a member of the party's left, she knew better than most what the harvest would be. Nonetheless, her northern persistence and native ardour drove her on. After a lengthy period of consultation, on 16 January 1969 the White Paper 'In Place of Strife' was published. The tenor of the document was simple. The unions must restrain their brood or government would declare them unfit parents and act accordingly. In detail, this included the right of the employment secretary to demand a strike ballot if she felt that the national interest was imperilled, a twenty-eight-day period of mandatory work in the event of a stalemate in negotiations, and, crucially, the establishment of an Industrial Board which would have the power to bind and to loose in any confrontation between unions. Its decision would be legally enforceable. This was of particular importance since the most intractable union 'troubles' tended to arise not between employers and employed but between unions competing for the highest wages. Much of this would have seemed unexceptionable, but for the contingencies the White Paper envisaged. A threat crouched over all; financial penalties awaited if the unions refused to comply, and, if these too were flouted, prison.

It is perhaps surprising that even then most Labour voters and MPs were generally supportive of these radical proposals. But neither MPs nor voters counted beside the unions who funded the Labour party. Moreover, a new breed of union leader had come to power; he was a militant, as often as not a Marxist, whose only care was to fence his members' rights in a girdle of barbed wire. And he had an ally in cabinet: the home secretary, James Callaghan. Callaghan had been an undistinguished, if tenacious, member of the cabinet. At once instinctively loyal and quietly ambitious, of the Left but never a Marxist, he was above all a union man. Callaghan disliked Barbara Castle, partly on the dubious grounds that she was somehow less working-class than himself and partly because she was university educated. His time would soon come.

The bill announced by 'In Place of Strife' was swiftly put to the test. In February 1969, a strike broke out at the Ford Motor Company. It was in some ways a textbook case of irreconcilable interests. Management had drawn up a plan whereby, in exchange for forswearing any unofficial action, members would be awarded a generous pay rise and larger holiday benefits. Having initially approved the plan, union leaders swiftly altered course when their members, unmollified, walked out. The impotence of adjudicators was further emphasized when a court injunction in favour of the offer fell on deaf ears.

Those on the parliamentary back bench would have none of the White Paper's provisions, the press was divided, the unions scornful, and many formerly amenable MPs increasingly disillusioned. Still worse was to come. On 26 March, the NEC (the National Executive Committee of the Labour party) gathered to discuss Castle's proposals. Fifteen colleagues had already proclaimed their opposition to the paper when Callaghan joined their number, with arm uplifted. 'In Place of Strife' limped on for a few weeks, but Callaghan's blow had struck it to the heart and soon it collapsed. In its place the unions accepted a 'solemn and binding' commitment to keep its members within the bounds set by government. That stirring, utterly vacuous expression was to rumble through the next decade.

The increasing malaise of 1969 was only slightly offset by the news of a glorious collaboration between French and English designers: the supersonic aeroplane, Concorde. If there were any notably high spirits, however, these were occasioned chiefly by the spectacle of Tony Benn at the airport in Toulouse quite literally worshipping the great sleek vulture of steel beside him. Technology was, he explained, his religion.

When the last election of the decade was announced, in 1970, Labour's mood could not have been more buoyant. The balance of payments seemed healthy, and the disappointments of the past few years were matters on which the government chose not to dwell. After all, much good had been done. Labour could point to its care for the disadvantaged, for the young, even for the elderly – though for many in the Sixties, England was no country for the old. It could boast of its international standing, and it could claim that the young had never been so fully or richly educated, the poorest never so well provided for. Yet there seemed no need to dwell on the past when the future too would surely be Labour.

There were moments of farce to enliven what otherwise promised to be a cosily predictable result. George Brown went so far as to punch a student who had heckled him. He was to lose his seat, alas, to the surprise of none. Crossman was uneasy, however. 'We have given [the electorate] three years of hell and high taxes. They've seen the failure of devaluation and felt the soaring cost of living.' Yet all the auguries suggested not only that Labour would win but win comfortably. The superstitious Wilson was convinced that, as in 1966, the World Cup would prove his biggest asset. It was perhaps unwise, however, to indulge too close an association between Labour's success and that of the national team; on Sunday, 14 June, England was kicked out of the tournament by West Germany. Some felt that the tide had turned.

Ted Heath, dour and unpersonable though he might be, was pulling his considerable weight in his party's cause, to great effect. When he spoke on television, many were struck by his urgency and clarity. By contrast, Wilson came across as complacent and superior. Then arose the worry that Labour voters might not turn out in the numbers needed. It took all too little to tip the scales – a shift of no more than 5 per cent. The Conservatives won 46 per cent of the vote and 330 seats; Labour 43 per cent and 288 seats; while the Liberals had to make do with six.

Wilson contrived to remain phlegmatic; perhaps he knew that his era had not quite ended. He bequeathed to his successor a balance of payments rather less than projected, and a nation rather less optimistic than it had been some six years before. Indeed, among the many swansongs for the Sixties, a gentle ballad by the Stones perhaps best captures this mood: 'No Expectations'.

45

Bugger them all

When Edward Heath received applause, it was with an open-mouthed beam. It was as if, beneath his carapace of surly self-reliance, he could not quite believe his good fortune. But this smile was seen after concerts he had conducted, not after his electoral win. The expression he wore when he walked into Downing Street was more sombre – there was work to be done. It has been said that the choicest prey for nemesis is the man with too many talents, and this was certainly true of Heath. A skilled yachtsman, conductor and musician, he was also a far abler politician and prime minister than many allowed at the time or have conceded since. His failure, if such it was, was a table of misfortunes ready-laid for him. Then he had his own nature with which to contend. More than any prime minister before him, he was convinced of his self-sufficiency.

Douglas Hurd recalled the moment when he realized that the election had swung to the Conservatives: 'The car radio persisted in telling us extraordinary good news . . . Extraordinary to me, but not to Mr Heath. To him it was simply the logical result of the long years of preparation, and of the fact that the people of Britain, like the people of Bexley, were at bottom a sensible lot.' Heath had planned for power, and his appointments reflected this. Many of the old guard were to remain, and others to be promoted. It was a 'young' cabinet, with forty-seven the average age. His 'power base' was to be formed of those who owed everything to Heath himself. His mood may be inferred from an uncharacteristic instance of vulgarity: 'Bugger them all,' he is said to have exclaimed. 'I won.' 'They' were the naysayers, the sneerers and jeerers of the Tory right and of the press. However, they were not yet routed, whatever Heath may have hoped.

It was unfortunate that Heath's premiership should have coincided with a miners' strike in January 1972 followed by a dockers' strike in July of the same year, both of them ominous auguries. Nor did matters improve when the government, having so loudly proclaimed its compassion and commitment to 'fairness', announced that it would be renewing sales of arms to South Africa. This, and the Rhodesia question, would sour relations with the Commonwealth for years to come. But, as Heath never wearied of explaining to the nation, there was work to be done. The dockers' strike led to the proclamation of the first state of emergency. Four more were to follow.

Of all the relations that concerned the people, particularly after the compromises and failures of the previous government, those with the unions loomed largest. On television, Heath was challenged on the question. 'Would you face a general strike?' 'Yes. I have always made it plain. I have said we are going to carry out a thorough reform of industrial relations.' He promised, too, a 'quiet revolution'. Such revolutions rarely set the public aflame, and this was to be no exception.

In any case, there was no real revolution. Heath's chief object was to contain the forces of organized labour, rather than to undermine them. Indeed, he always proclaimed a steadfast admiration for the TUC in particular and the unions in general, however opaque this regard often seemed to the public. Union leaders usually found him both responsive and affable. Jack Jones was to recall Heath's willingness to give his opponents a sensitive and respectful hearing, a judgement that would have surprised those who saw only the unsmiling face or unbending rhetoric. He was not to be the last prime minister betrayed by his affection for organized labour.

Heath had long been convinced that politics was a matter for specialists, and so he began to invite businessmen into the business of government. Like so many of his ventures, it was well-intentioned, but he had Whitehall to reckon with. His Programme Analysis and Review was an attempt to bring a degree of specialist knowledge to questions of policy and reduce the need for bureaucracy. Whitehall's response was polite and inexorable. It was noted by a Whitehall observer, Peter Hennessy, that 'their first step was to remove it from the grasp of Heath's businessmen . . . and to draw it into their own citadel in Great George Street from which it never emerged alive'. It was to become a familiar story: Heath's attempts to reduce bureaucracy more often than not added to it. In this instance, the number of civil servants increased by 400,000.

It was Heath who coined the expression 'think tank', to describe a body chosen to advise the cabinet on policy. A scion of the Rothschild clan headed the first of these bodies, but its warnings of an oil crisis went unheeded. Most importantly perhaps, Lord Rothschild had identified the enemy: 'that neo-Hitler, that arch-enemy, inflation'. Inflation, long recognized as a hindrance, was now the foe-in-chief.

A further strike by miners in February 1974 led to a second state of emergency. The willingness of Heath to resort to such a measure under conditions that rarely justified the title 'emergency' revealed much about his attitude to opposition. Beneath the granite self-confidence could often be heard the slam of a childish foot on a floorboard. And yet it was a time for which the expression 'U-turn' might have been coined. Rolls-Royce, in trouble over engines to be supplied to American 'Lockheeds', had to be rescued, in clear defiance of Heath's election promises. But what could he do? It would not be true to suggest, as some have, that Heath despised or underrated America's contribution to world prosperity or world peace. There can be little doubt, however, that he viewed the 'special relationship' as a hindrance to his European ideal. That the United States had consistently supported Britain's attempts to join the bloc was a circumstance that Heath contrived to ignore. Henry Kissinger put it thus: 'His relations with us were always correct, but they rarely rose above a basic reserve that prevented – in the name of Europe – the close co-operation with us that was his for the taking.' As ever, it was not that Heath had no ear for advice or public opinion, merely a poor nose for changes in the wind.

On the question of the swelling war between India and Pakistan, Heath's rejoinder to Kissinger could not have been clearer:

> What they wanted from the special relationship was to land Britain in it [the war between India and Pakistan] as well . . . and I was determined not to be landed . . . Did we lose anything by it? No, of course not. We gained an enormous amount. I can quite see that it's rather difficult for some Americans, including Henry, to adjust themselves to this, but it's necessary for them to do it. Now, there are some people who always want to nestle on the shoulder of an American president. That's no future for Britain.

In this, as in so many respects, Heath wished to place himself in opposition to Wilson. As Kissinger put it, 'There was a nearly impenetrable opacity about Heath's formulations which, given his intelligence, had to be deliberate . . . [He] could not have been more helpful on diagnosis or more evasive on prescription . . . He wanted Europe to formulate answers to our queries: he was determined to avoid any whiff of Anglo-American collusion.'

Heath went further: the nine countries of the EEC should henceforth act as one in their dealings with the United States. The irony, of course, was that his relentless cold-shouldering of the United States compromised the very advantage that Britain was supposed to be bringing to the EEC. But Heath supported Nixon over Vietnam, and it is one of the more curious ironies of the age that Wilson was accused of sycophancy in his dealings with America, while Heath, who actively supported her when times were propitious, was accused of obduracy. In any case, it was clear to all by now that Heath's priority was to gain Britain entry into the Common Market. His love of the EEC did not lie in the tradition of pragmatism characteristic of most British Europhiles, and it owed little even to the earnest talk of 'supranationalism' characteristic of Thirties and Forties intellectuals. His Europhilia was patriotic in origin – he believed that Britain must shrink to become great again.

Heath had been the chief negotiator during the failed application of 1963. For all his vigour, intelligence, attention to detail and Europhilia, the French had vetoed Britain. But Heath would never give up, and the experience gave him the clue to a solution; he saw that it was France, not the smaller nations, which must be wooed.

He turned what powers of charm he possessed to the seduction of Georges Pompidou, the new president. One difficulty presented itself even before negotiations began. This was the Common Agricultural Policy, clearly designed to advance French agriculture. If Heath recognized that France was the chief beneficiary of European largesse, with Germany as the patient provider, he determined to overlook the fact. A greater difficulty was the demand that sterling, as the world's paramount currency, be removed as a precondition for European monetary union.

The public was to prove itself ambivalent, as was the opposition, with opinion polls suggesting resistance to entry was as high as 70 per cent. As for the opposition, it was deeply divided. On the one hand, Labour under Wilson had also attempted to join the Common Market. On the other, ordinary members and MPs were for the most part highly suspicious, on both socialist and patriotic grounds. The EEC was capitalism incarnate, and a threat to Britain's sovereignty. It did not help that even with the urbane and benevolent Pompidou at the French helm, negotiations remained halting and ponderous. Once again, Heath determined to deal with matters himself. In conversation with Willy Brandt, Heath pressed the British case with almost messianic urgency: 'The world will not stand still. If Europe fails to seize this opportunity, our friends will be dismayed and our enemies heartened. Soviet ambitions of domination would be pursued more ruthlessly. Our friends, disillusioned by our disunity, would more and more be tempted to leave Europe to its own devices.'

For the climactic meeting with Pompidou, Heath prepared himself by drinking tea in the park, and receiving the opinions of experts. It was all suitably English. Pompidou himself put the European case, politely but clearly, when interviewed by the BBC. 'The crux of the matter,' he said, 'is that there is a European conception or idea, and the question to be ascertained is whether the United Kingdom's conception is indeed European. That will be the aim of my meeting with Mr Heath.' However, the European idea represented, in practice, a French one. Perhaps recognizing this, Pompidou went on to disavow federalism, and thus was the issue of the 'European conception' left to slumber. Its reawakening in later years was a reversal that Heath would not live to see.

The meeting was almost uncannily successful. The two men liked each other, and, more significantly, understood one another. It took a mere two days to reach agreement. Nothing was yet official, but nothing needed to be. When Heath spoke before the Commons, a still, small voice raised an objection on the minor matter of sovereignty. Would the prime minister please clarify the nation's status as a member of the EEC? Heath's reply was brusque and dismissive. 'Joining the Community does not entail a loss of national identity or an erosion of essential national sovereignty.' The first stage had been passed, with the Commons advised merely to 'take note' of the terms.

Like it or not, Heath was meanwhile obliged to give his attention to some outstanding matters which the country considered to be of more pressing concern. The first was the continuing issue of industrial relations. For many who grew up in the Seventies, 'the union' was a creature of vague menace, endowed with preternatural abilities. By night, it hung 'closed' signs on shop doors. It gobbled food from supermarket shelves. It had only to lift its trident and traffic would stop. It was popularly supposed to have power even over the weather; when the union leaders shook their heads, snow would fall in endless, spirit-crushing showers. Nothing could be expected of the world while 'the union' was supreme. This dragon was neither red nor white, but grey, its polyester suit defying sword and lance alike.

1970 had been a punishing year for industrial relations, with more days devoured by this dragon than at any time since 1926. Heath's response was the Industrial Relations Bill. He said, 'I do not believe for one moment that the unions are likely to put themselves in breach of the law. They will not choose to act in such a way as to risk their funds . . . in ill-judged and unlawful actions.' However, he would be disappointed. The bill achieved the remarkable feat of being rejected by the TUC even before its provisions had been published. Barbara Castle, herself carrying the bruises from her attempts to reform the unions, was unimpressed and asserted that 'We shall destroy this bill!' In fact, it promised little more than had Castle's own paper 'In Place of Strife', but the unions could hardly treat a Conservative government with greater latitude than they had shown a Labour one. Jack Jones, the head of the

TGWU, foresaw difficulties ahead for all sides. The unions had little choice but to man their palisades against a government that refused to compromise.

The act was passed on 5 August 1971, but its weakness soon became apparent. As the unions swiftly realized, a way out of the provisions was to obey only one of them: that which gave them the right not to register. Most unions did just that, and those that did register – notably the electricity union – were suspended. The bill was not killed, but merely atrophied from disuse until it was given its quietus by the next, Labour, administration.

So if the unions themselves were as mettlesome as ever, what of the incomes policy by which the government had set so much store? In principle, inflation would still be kept at bay by non-statutory wage restraint. For a long time, it represented one of the government's quiet victories. But it was not to last. In a speech at Eastbourne, Heath trumpeted the achievements of the government by 1971. 'Our strength is not just figures on a balance sheet, although we have those too, our strength is not just courage in adversity, although we have shown that time and time again . . . We never know when we are beaten and that way we are never beaten. We know no other way than to win . . . For too long we have walked in the shadows. It is time for us now to walk out into the light to find a new place, a new Britain in this new world.' The platitudes rolled out, all the more dispiriting for their hollowness. The fact remained that the government could not honour its electoral promise to leave industry to its own devices.

The same was true of its attempt to sell council houses to their tenants. A mere 7 per cent of council housing was sold during the Heath years. Nor could Labour councils be blamed – Conservative-run councils were quite as unwilling to sell valuable stock. Other misadventures occurred. It is perhaps not surprising that the notion of a Channel Tunnel was first advanced under Heath, but this too proved elusive. It should be remembered that few of Heath's projects wilted entirely; rather, they needed different gardeners and better weather.

The appointment of Keith Joseph to the Department of Health and Social Security was perhaps paradigmatic both of Heath's strengths and of his weaknesses. At first glance, Joseph was the ideal choice. Insatiably compassionate and ferociously able, he was a man whose intentions could not be faulted, but the result of his efforts to reduce bureaucracy was a remarkable multiplication of officials. It was in many ways a tragedy, yet Heath was determined to follow his vision. He felt, as many Tories felt, that the time had come to prioritize. The elderly, and large families on low incomes, were consistently neglected and he felt bound to redress this. In a speech, he also made clear his conviction that the welfare state was acting as a crutch to healthy limbs. 'Unless we are prepared to take on more of the responsibilities for the things we can do for ourselves, then the State itself will never be able to do properly the jobs which genuinely demand community action.' Nye Bevan could never have accepted this, and nor could his successors.

Meanwhile, the comprehensive boom had acquired an unstoppable momentum, despite the efforts of the new education secretary, Margaret Thatcher, one of Heath's many promising protégés. She found herself presiding over the creation of more comprehensives than any such minister before or since, and she showed herself willing to adopt and even extend socialist programmes when she felt the need. Her saving of the Open University was a case in point, though her decision to abolish free milk for primary school children chilled many, and earned her the sobriquet 'Margaret Thatcher, milk snatcher'. Perhaps her gender counted against her, as it would do on future occasions. Other initiatives met with similar obloquy. When Heath decided that museums should charge visitors an entry fee, there was mass protest. The justification, that people appreciate more what they must pay for, seemed shallow beside the imperative to offer the poor opportunities for nourishment that they would otherwise be denied.

Strikes had been a feature of the Heath premiership from the beginning, but rarely had they imperilled the nation's basic needs. In 1972 they did. The mining industry was in the last stages of senescence, with 600 miners leaving every week. Pits which at the turn of the twentieth century had dominated skylines, villages and lives were progressively abandoned. But moribund or not, the industry still provided the one fuel upon which people could safely rely. So when the government was faced with a demand for a 47 per cent rise in wages, to be spread out over the different jobs at the pit, it was in a quandary. The amount asked was surely prohibitive. But there were two factors that countered this. The people were solidly behind the miners, and secondly, coal stocks were not as high as they might have been. The resources lay with the miners.

Even as they had seen the wages of their fellow labouring groups rise inexorably throughout the Sixties while their own remained static, even as the number of pits halved during that decade, they had uttered barely a murmur. Their working conditions were abominable. The heat was such that Kentish miners frequently worked naked. Flooding claimed many lives, and the dust was not merely a daily torment but a constant cause of early death. Visibility in the mines was extremely poor and the shifts long. Miners had been hailed as heroes of the home front, renowned for their loyalty to the twin Victorian virtues of self-reliance and solidarity. For these reasons alone, they could count on a deep reservoir of support and sympathy among the general public. Until 1972, however, the true extent of their grievances was little understood.

It was the Yorkshiremen, already known as the most politicized among the miners, who raised their heads above the parapet. In July 1971, their call for an overall pay rise of 47 per cent was approved by the NUM (National Union of Mineworkers). Given their patience over the previous decade, the claim was scarcely exorbitant, but it ran directly counter to government policy. The Heath administration had committed itself to a pay 'norm' of 8 per cent for all manual workers. Only thus, it was felt, could inflation be kept down.

Joe Gormley, the head of the NUM, did not approve of unions attempting to guide government, let alone subvert it, and he had no time for communists, who were increasingly unabashed in proclaiming their allegiance. But the days when a union leader could count on the unqualified support of his nearest subordinates were nearing an end. The generation below Gormley had grown weary of acquiescence, and in any case he still had his members' interests to protect. After fruitless bargaining with the Coal Board, a ban on overtime was declared, to be followed, on 8 January 1972, by a general strike.

The press, the public and the politicians were united in at least one conviction: the strike was doomed. Coal stocks were healthy and the industry was not the indispensable artery it once had been. Besides, it was argued, the nation surely had enough oil. But the optimists were taking far too much for granted. Initially, the miners had been lukewarm in their support for a strike, but once the ballots were filled the decision could not be rescinded. Although the press saw the strike as hopeless, it believed it to be just. Nor were coal stocks quite as full as many wished to believe, or the power stations as invulnerable. And as for oil, many seemed to have forgotten that it had quadrupled in price.

What is more, the miners had a new weapon. Both law and tradition had long accepted the right of strikers to surround the disputed workplace and dissuade any of their fellows from entering to resume work, but Arthur Scargill, a young Marxist from Barnsley, had developed a refinement in the 'flying picket'. If local numbers were insufficient to dissuade the potential 'scab', the answer was to bus in striking miners from elsewhere. Moreover, he knew that for the strike to be effective, it must not merely shut down the pits, but render the entire network of energy inoperable. He was quite frank in his aims. 'We were out to defeat Heath and Heath's policies . . . We had to declare war on them and the only way you could declare war was to attack the vulnerable points . . . we wished to paralyse the nation's economy.'

It was one of the many tragedies of Heath's tenure that he was obliged to combat a group that he greatly admired. He had been heard to proclaim that the trouble with the unions was that they were not 'too strong, but too weak', but such scruples gained him little sympathy in this struggle. So the coal pits lay idle, and the nation began to suffer. An unofficial three-day week began. Candles disappeared from shop shelves and the mood among the public grew darker. But the miners could count, for the time being, on its support. For its part, the government was bewildered and desperate. Robert Carr, employment secretary, confessed that 'there was no doubt about it, our intelligence about the strength of opinion within the miners' union generally was not as good as it should have been. We just didn't know the miners.'

There was one vast coke plant in Saltley, a suburb of Birmingham, which still held out. Here the lorries defied the strike, passing through the gates every day unhindered, and Arthur Scargill saw his opportunity. The police were there, of course, but it was not long before they were hopelessly outnumbered. Yet the so-called 'Battle of Saltley' on 10 February 1972 was in most respects a peaceable affair, with what violence there was emerging from scuffles between miners and lorry drivers.

Scargill still lacked the numbers he needed, however. He addressed the workers of Birmingham itself with the appeal that 'We don't want your pound notes . . . Will you go down in history as the working class in Birmingham who stood by while the miners were battered, or will you become immortal?' The call reached deep and far. What happened next began with a banner appearing on the top of a hill. Behind it was a mass of people. And then a 'roar' was heard from the other side of the hill. They had come in their thousands. In the crowd were last-minute reinforcements, the weak fired with the passion of warriors. As a result, the Battle of Saltley seemed a peasants' revolt bedecked with the colours of chivalry; indeed, it was as 'King Arthur' that Scargill was to be commemorated.

It is idle to observe that the victory was largely a symbolic one; as so often happens, the symbol had become a sacred ritual which struck those who did not observe it. 'We looked absolutely into the abyss,' said Willie Whitelaw. Thus a strike that most thought would die within days paralysed the nation. A council of state announced a third state of emergency. Victoria Graham caught the mood of many of her generation when she observed to a friend: 'When we were suffering for the nation's survival during the war the task was easy, but now we seem to be silently suffering, as we watch the country brought to its knees.' For her, as for many others, the miners' struggle evoked tyranny. Douglas Hurd expressed the prevailing mood in government from the standpoint of the defeated: 'The government was now wandering vainly over the battlefield looking for someone to surrender to – and being massacred all the time.'

A new blackout seemed to beckon. The sombre truth was that the nation needed fuel and could no longer afford oil. The stocks of coal could not be used, and power stations were running at 25 per cent capacity. Nurses were forced to care for their patients by candlelight. A nation without electricity was, it was said, only weeks away. It was time to lay down arms and sue for peace. The truce, for such it was, was ignominious. Lord Wilberforce, who presided over an inquiry into the strike, gave the miners almost everything they wanted; and, where he did not, Heath himself obliged, sullenly and desperately. On 19 February, he granted everything the NUM demanded, conceding more than even the Wilberforce Report had suggested.

Characteristically, Heath appealed to the country. Appearing on television, he conceded none of his adversaries' claims. No one had won, he stated. All had lost. Without naming the unions directly, he made clear his view that the world had changed, and for the worse, and that if the spirit of unity were abandoned, there would be further trouble. For his part, Arthur Scargill had learned that the 'unions united can never be defeated'. Perhaps he had not heard of the error of Stoicism: the fallacy that you have only to succeed once to succeed always.

46

The first shot

It was the fate of the Heath administration to know no respite. The strongest city will fall when attacked from all sides and 'Heathco' faced a ceaseless barrage. Principal among its vicissitudes was the unrest in Northern Ireland. For years, the Province had been held in fief by the Protestant majority. The Catholic minority was disadvantaged in most ways that free citizens might be expected to resent, in matters such as housing, employment and even the electoral register. Thus far Martin McGuinness was correct in calling the Province 'a unionist state for a unionist people' – its borders had been fixed to ensure that an otherwise narrow Protestant majority would be a decisive one.

The Unionists had their own resentments. When they looked south of the border, they saw not the benign nation recognized by the English, but a predatory theocracy determined to lash them to the mast of Rome. Their chief spokesman in the Seventies was the Reverend Ian Paisley MP. He was feared by many in the north as a fanatical and bigoted zealot, but in truth he was neither. Though he detested the papacy and feared the Republic, he won warm plaudits from his Catholic constituents as a fair-minded and considerate MP. Similarly, he never lent his name or support to the Protestant paramilitaries, and he was to oppose the policy of internment. Those who knew him best were wont to ascribe his public stance less to fanaticism than to irresponsibility. He was a show-off rather than a demagogue, and in this he resembled another staunch defender of the Province's integrity, Enoch Powell.

The 'Troubles' began in the late Sixties. Unionist wrath had been aroused by a series of incidents and, as a result, Catholics now stood in fear of their lives. Hundreds of families were driven from their burning homes until it seemed that little less than a pogrom was under way. In 1969, frantic appeals to the government both in Northern Ireland and on the mainland at last bore fruit when Callaghan agreed that troops must be sent in. The army was greeted with tea, cakes and chips in a carnival of relieved gratitude, but the honeymoon soon waned. Loyalists had drawn first blood, although this was soon forgotten. The Ulster Volunteer Force killed a barman, for no better reason than that they were drunk and he was Catholic. Although IRA atrocities were more frequent and larger in scale, Loyalists showed from the first a penchant for elaborate sadism. The IRA justified its deeds as acts of war, the Loyalists as demonstrations of 'loyalty'. Both sides proclaimed that they were protecting their own communities, and neither respected sex, age, or civilian status. The innocent were killed on the basis of supposed complicity with the foe, and dead civilians were passed off as combatants. Indeed the conflict in Northern Ireland was above all one in which the civilian was placed in the front line.

The IRA always maintained that the English were at fault; in a sense they were, for one Englishman can certainly be blamed for much of the havoc and misery that blighted the Province during the Heath years. Sean Macstiofain's life was a tragicomedy of self-reinvention. He was baptized John Stephenson; his father was an English solicitor and his mother was born in Bethnal Green, rendering their son rather less Irish than most of his enemies. Nonetheless, his mother early imbued him with a keen sense of his supposed Irishness, and in this certainty was incubated a fierce nationalism. Those who adopt a cause are often far more zealous than those born to it, and so it proved here.

Until 1969, there had been only the Official IRA. Its leadership, however, increasingly drew away from Irish nationalism and towards theoretical Marxism. Both bullet and ballot were considered bourgeois distractions. Its stated goal now was to 'educate' the workers of

Northern Ireland, Catholic and Protestant, to the point where they would, of their own volition, throw off their economic oppressors. However, Macstiofain and other romantic nationalists hungered for flesh. The result was a split from which arose the Provisional IRA, formed to protect and avenge Catholic communities, fight the army and subvert British rule. Its time soon came. The honeymoon of the British army and the Catholic population had long soured when, in the summer of 1970, a detachment of troops entered the Falls Road in search of a cache of weapons. When they re-emerged it was to a street filled with men and women in a mood of raging protest. After all that had been endured, this was too much. The troops came under attack and soon had to call for reinforcements. The best they could achieve was a stalemate. On 3 July 1970, a curfew was imposed on the Falls Road. The Troubles had taken wing.

The English were for the most part indifferent. Given that the Province was a problem that would not go away, would it not be sensible to *send* it away? Why not withdraw from Northern Ireland altogether? After all, the terrorists had struck only those people across the sea, and misery and violence were felt by many to be the birthright of the Irishman. Let him get on with what he knew best, as long as he didn't bring his baggage over here. But then in 1971, the IRA detonated a bomb at the military camp in Aldershot. Five people were killed, all of them civilians. Among the dead were two elderly cleaning ladies and a Catholic priest.

With Belfast soon subject to a bombing campaign, with almost daily reports of murder, and children dismembered by shrapnel, Brian Faulkner, the Northern Irish prime minister and a bastion of the Unionist establishment, begged Heath for powers of internment. On 5 August, Heath granted them, with the proviso that such internment must not target the Catholic community alone. On 9 August, the army burst into the homes of almost four hundred Catholic families, destroying sacred statues and tearing up family photographs all on the basis of useless intelligence. Many of those ensnared had little or no connection with militant republicanism and, of those that did, one had last been active during the Easter Rising. The IRA leadership was quite untouched, and now had a host of new volunteers.

As if all this were insufficient to crack the last foundations of trust, there was also the nature of internment itself. The notorious five techniques of interrogation were used, which included subjecting the internees to 'white noise' and sleep deprivation. Beatings and forced confessions were commonplace. Such techniques seemed only to vindicate the IRA's central premise that this was indeed a war against imperialism. Internment was a disaster, not least because, in defiance of stated government policy, the vast majority of suspects were Catholic. It scarcely helped that this debacle was presided over by Reginald Maudling, a minister temperamentally and morally unfit for the task in hand.

With internment exposed as a moral and political failure, social cohesion in a state of haemorrhage and the two communities terrified of one another, another option began to drift into political discourse. It needed only a crisis for it to take flesh. Derry (or Londonderry, as the British called it) was the Province's second city, and for months the army had attempted to ensure order there with the minimum of intervention. However, sniper attacks upon soldiers were a weekly occurrence, and the Protestants had begun calling for a curfew. By August 1972, civil rights marches had been banned. One group, peaceable in intent, decided to call one regardless. Paratroopers were sent in with orders to halt or at least redirect the march. Nervous, resentful and with a tradition of toughness to defend, they were not perhaps the ideal choice.

Even today, no one knows who fired the first shot or why. The paras later claimed that they had only opened fire when they were shot at. However that may be, a peaceful demonstration became a rout, as screaming people fled the soldiers' bullets. By the end of the day, thirteen Catholics lay dead. No direct IRA involvement was ever proven, and the houses from which the soldiers saw firing were later shown to have held neither snipers nor weapons of any kind. And yet it is scarcely conceivable that trained men would have opened fire with no provocation whatever. The truth may never be known. For the time being at least, 'Bloody Sunday' stripped the British government of any moral authority: for those in the Catholic community, the Republic and many in the wider world, it had the burning brand of imperialism. Only two years before, the army had been admired for the tolerance and good humour it had usually displayed. Now what was left of that reputation was gone.

It was the end of the Northern Ireland parliament, and Direct Rule at last took shape. The government proclaimed it was left with 'no alternative to assuming full and direct responsibility for the administration of Northern Ireland until a political solution for the problems of the Province can be worked out in consultation with all those concerned'. Whatever decision was to be made regarding the future of the Province, it was clear that the Republic must in some way be involved. Given that such a proposal would have been quite unacceptable to the Unionists, there was only one man who had a chance of presenting it: William 'Willie' Whitelaw. Genial, loyal and boundlessly benevolent, he could charm the claws from a tiger.

Whitelaw and others forged a national executive at Sunningdale, composed of all parties, including representatives from the South. In later years it would be seen as the precursor to the Anglo-Irish and Good Friday Agreements. Had goodwill prevailed it might perhaps have succeeded, but it was stillborn. Scarcely had the necessary antagonisms been aired when Whitelaw was summoned back to England to deal with the second miners' strike. If only he had stayed to chair the executive, if only the Unionists had been more tractable, if only the Nationalists had seen the other side's point of view: but it was not to be. In any case, the more zealous in the Protestant community saw the agreement as nothing more than an attempt to subvert the clear will of the majority. The Province fell victim to a general strike, and worse was to follow. Belfast was taken over by Loyalist paramilitaries, while the army stood by and the RUC colluded. The rule of law had been replaced by the rule of a faction. The options remaining to the government were martial law or capitulation, and they chose the latter. There was a further political price to be paid; the Unionists never forgave Heath for the Sunningdale Agreement, which they regarded as an attempt to subvert what they saw as their ancient rights, and their foes saw as their unjust privileges.

47

The fall of Heath

Amidst what can seem only a forest of white flags, some undoubted victories for Heath's government may be discerned. The Family Income Supplement was one. An early piece of legislation, it helped countless poor couples to raise families on very little. Other laws to help the disadvantaged were legion. That Heath had turned his political energies in that direction was a source of puzzlement to many of his foes.

But perhaps this humanitarian impulse showed itself most clearly in Heath's decision to allow the Asians of Uganda to enter Britain as refugees. Expelled by Idi Amin, these people still held British passports granted by Macmillan, and now looked to the mother country for succour. In retrospect, it seems remarkable that there should have been the slightest resistance to such a plea, but concerns about immigration were still alive. The meat porters of Smithfield came to parliament in a crowd of 500 to show their support for Enoch Powell. He had declared that the question of passports was 'a spoof', and maintained that ownership of one conferred no right of residence. In the circumstances, it was an ugly and specious argument, and the government crushed it. Heath himself never wavered; the refugees arrived, and the country showed itself at its best. Government help aside, Asian communities were quick to offer shelter, food and housing, as were other groups. It was perhaps Heath's noblest hour; his grandest was still to come.

Having wooed and won the French, Heath had now to persuade parliament; while it had approved the decision to enter the European Community, it had yet to examine the terms. Ominous growls of future dissent could already be heard. The first difficulty lay in the sheer bulk of the papers involved. The task of reducing the terms to a digestible length fell to, among others, the future chancellor, Geoffrey Howe. Howe had a thoroughly, even oppressively, academic mind, and the arranging or clarifying of minutiae was perhaps his greatest gift. The result was a triumph, with the rolling ribbons of barely comprehensible directives cut down to a simple set of clauses. At one level, this could not but backfire, for with all obfuscation now removed, the full extent of the EEC's new powers stood open to the naked eye. One clause in particular was prominent. Clause Eleven stated unambiguously that EEC law would prevail over British law and be 'enforced, allowed and followed accordingly'.

None could ignore this, and Michael Foot, for one, had no intention of doing so. He had been dissatisfied by the whole process of simplification, calling it no more than 'a lawyer's conjuring trick'. But Clause Eleven deeply dismayed him. He and Enoch Powell did their best to filibuster, but the Speaker would not budge. He apologized for the fact that the House had not had the opportunity to consider the protocols more fully, but such was the hour. The House was assured that 'a thousand years of English Parliamentary history [was] not about to be supplanted by the Napoleonic code'. Despite this, there was never any doubt as to the outcome. Although 'full-hearted consent' to the terms of entry was notable by its absence, a clear majority of MPs voted through the last of the legislation. And thus, on 17 October 1972, royal assent for entry was granted. On 1 January 1973, Britain entered the EEC.

The birth pangs of membership had only just begun – in little over two years' time the whole issue would be subjected to the first of two plebiscites – but for now, Heath, Howe, Whitelaw and Pompidou could congratulate themselves on a duty well performed. Besides, the angry and the ignorant would surely see sense once the benefits of membership had become apparent. It was as well that Heath had realized his deepest dream, for as the year unfolded he had once more to face a recurring nightmare.

Over a billion pounds had been poured into the mining industry since the last miners' strike, a clear reversal of previous policy. The miners, most assumed, were not spoiling for a second round. But their wages, though healthier than they had been, were not enough to draw more young men into the pits; an estimated 600 men were still leaving the industry every week. Then there was the renewed question of oil. Prices had been high enough two years previously, but now, after the Arab–Israeli war, they had quadrupled. In the miners' gradual progress towards a second strike, there was no element of malice or greed. Their case was simple and even innocent in its way. They were going to ask for a further 35 per cent because they knew they were likely to get it. And so, once again, the cogs of negotiation creaked into movement. Heath was determined that the miners should stay within the bounds of his celebrated 'stage three' (a wage bracket which included some 4 million manual workers), while the miners and their leaders were equally determined to move out of it.

It was oil that proved decisive. The nation now relied upon it for 50 per cent of its energy. This in turn led one 'little man', who had been hanging back during one of the negotiations, to offer an observation. 'Prime Minister,' he asked, 'why can't you pay us for coal what you are willing to pay the Arabs for oil?' It put Heath in a false position. Friends and colleagues noted a new lassitude in him, a weariness that cloyed his usually agile movements. What few of them realized was that Heath had physical as well as political handicaps with which to contend. An underactive thyroid gland had rendered him sluggish in thought and movement. The affliction could not have struck at a worse time.

Just when most, if not all, seemed lost, the General Council of the Trades Union Congress issued a remarkable minute. 'The General Council accept that there is a distinctive and exceptional situation in the mining industry. If the Government are prepared to give an assurance that they will make possible a settlement between the miners and the National Coal Board, other unions will not use this as an argument in negotiations in their own settlements.' Such a statement amounted to a hitherto unimaginable concession. The TUC seemed to be offering its sacred cow to the knife. Was it, many wondered, too good to be true?

Alas, it was. In a pattern that had become depressingly familiar, each side blamed the other for the failure of the agreement. As far as the unions were concerned, Heath rejected the offer, and as far as he was concerned, the fault lay with his subordinate, Tony Barber. But it is unlikely in any case that an agreement could have been reached: the government was too suspicious and the TUC was in no case to honour its resolution. In later years, some union leaders still insisted that 'we could have made it stick', but Gormley was always dubious. Len Murray, already a leading light in the union movement, even claimed that the government had the unions 'over a barrel': 'If [Heath] had taken the offer and it had failed to work, and other unions had broken through, he would have been home and dry with all his anti-union policies – Industrial Relations Act and incomes policy. If it had worked, it would have been his great political triumph, showing he could bring the unions to heel.'

But Heath was not the man for such politicking. He was weary, and his capacity for optimism was running low. For months negotiations limped along, but after two years of economic U-turns, and with a defeat still fresh in his memory, Heath could scarcely surrender now. On 13 December 1973, he announced the three-day week. Another such had been put in place less than two years earlier, with ruinous runs on candles, but this one was official. It came into force on 1 January 1974. Unsurprisingly, the measure was resented, but the resentment sprang not merely from the inconvenience; it was felt to be premature and therefore politically futile. Against the advice of Whitelaw, Heath decided that the impasse with the miners could be broken only by going to the country. William Rees-Mogg of *The Times* agreed, though for reasons Heath was unlikely to have welcomed. 'The Government's policies have changed so much since 1970,' observed Rees-Mogg, 'that there is ample constitutional justification for an immediate election.' But Heath had not called the election to defeat the miners; for him, the issue was broader and deeper. In a political broadcast, he summarized his stance. 'The issue before you is a simple one . . . Do you want a strong Government which has clear authority for the future to take the decisions which will be needed? Do you want Parliament and the elected Government to continue to fight strenuously against inflation? Or do you want them to abandon the struggle against rising prices under pressure from one particular group of workers?'

As we have seen, Heath was broadly sympathetic to the unions, having himself risen from a scarcely privileged background. Ever assiduous, he had made it his business to understand the struggles and complexities of working-class reality. But he could never bring himself to endorse the principle of collective bargaining, and without that he could make no headway with the unions. He stated his objection with customary frankness: 'We have all seen what happens in that situation. The strongest wins, as he always does, and the weakest goes to the wall.'

And so, weakened in body and morale, Heath called an election, and a minute but telling swing to Labour was noticeable from the first. Still he soldiered on – there was work to be done, if only he could be given just a little more time. Meanwhile, the irrepressible Wilson returned to the attack, cheery and confident, the friend of the unions and the tribune of the people. When the results of the February election came through, it was clear that Heath's attempts to balance the budget while satisfying the unions had left the country unmoved.

But Wilson's victory was not yet complete. His was a minority government, and it would take a further election in October to secure power. Heath fought for time and a coalition with Jeremy Thorpe's Liberals. To his sad and undignified fall, the *Spectator* played both raven and cockerel. 'The squatter in No. 10 Downing Street has at last departed . . . Mr Edward Heath's monomania was never more clearly seen than in the days after the general election when, a ludicrous and broken figure, he clung with grubby fingers to the crumbling precipice of power.' It was sadly suggestive of Heath's tenure that the most vitriolic of the attacks upon him should have come from a conservative periodical. And there was one more humiliation to come, from a quarter he could never have suspected; it was the work of one of his own protégés, and, more shocking yet, a woman.

When he took over government in June 1970 he had little idea of the tribulations which were to beset him. The faltering economy, the disintegration of Northern Ireland, two coal strikes and the exploding price of oil during the Arab–Israeli war were to leave him with the demeanour of a waxwork. His attempts at a corporate exercise in state affairs ended in failure, largely because the trade unions refused to participate, but this was only one of many disappointments that afflicted his premiership. The worst was the one which lingers in historians' memory. Before the gruesome climax of the second miners' strike he had reversed his policy of non-interference in industry, losing much authority in the process. He was in many respects a hapless figure, rendered more powerless by the first miners' strike. The miners were carefully arranged to make the maximum impact, and the 'flying pickets' increased the strike's efficiency. The miners won their case and climbed the ladder of industrial pay, while at the same time trumping other workers. The leaders of richer unions such as power workers and the dockers set their feet on the government's rickety incomes policy, snapping it. The CBI, the TUC and the government could go on no more. The parlous state of Northern Ireland only thickened the brew.

Even his greatest achievement, Britain's acceptance by the EEC, was not greeted with great celebration. Many felt indifferent, hostile or bored by any closer relationship to the adjoining land mass; it brought pizza parlours and wine bars, but it was not enough to change anyone's way of life. It was certainly not enough to persuade the Labour party to embrace the European Community. The party was in any case in such disarray that it was almost impossible to know what was happening.

Yet to close with such a sweeping catalogue of failure would be as unjust as it would be unfeeling. Heath began with a solid majority and the warm wishes of press and public behind him. He was highly able and formidably diligent; and there could be no denying his patriotism. Unlike the expansive Wilson, he was uneasy before camera and microphone. The English love an underdog, and he had his ardent sincerity and sense of mission to recommend him. However, a leader must inspire courage in others, and Heath had not the skill to do so.

Harold Wilson did not expect to reoccupy Number Ten so soon after his recent eviction, and nor, it seemed, did he greatly want to. On the steps of Downing Street, on 10 October 1974, he announced:

'Well, there's a job to be done, and I'm going to go in and start on it now.' As rhetoric, it was scarcely Churchillian. From that statement alone, it should have been clear that his white heat had cooled to grey ash.

The miners' strike was swiftly resolved, to the benefit of the miners; there seemed little choice. Other matters outstanding were to prove soluble, after the fashion of the time. The Labour party had promised a referendum on the United Kingdom's membership of the EEC, for the reason that the Tories had mishandled the negotiations, conceding too much too soon. Behind this palpable window dressing were sharper concerns. One was that the Labour movement as a whole remained unconvinced of the benefits of EEC membership. Most pressing of all, the new government needed a distraction from what Wilson himself admitted to be 'the same old solutions to the same old problems'.

The 'divine right' of kings in England had been replaced by the 'supremacy' of parliament, but the proponents of British membership of Europe knew well that this supremacy was now limited; there was the overriding authority of the EEC to be reckoned with. This presented a democratic anomaly: how could the laws of parliament be at once sovereign and contingent? The government had no answer to this, so the problem was handed over to the people. Of the two main parties, it was the Conservatives who were the more ardent in the cause of continued participation. As the opposition, they would not have to face any adverse consequences for some time yet; furthermore, most of them sincerely believed that the Common Market meant just that – a sisterhood of capitalist nations, with no governess to answer to.

Before the Seventies, there had been little native entertainment for children on the television, and none in colour. With the growing availability of colour televisions, parents might have expected a rainbow of wholesome family fun, but it proved otherwise. Instead, the children of the decade opened a doll's house and found that it was haunted. The Seventies were the heyday of what has been termed 'shoestring fright', when horror could be expressed from floodlights and cardboard. However, while the new programmes were not invariably dark – there was much in the way of comedy and whimsy – they had an eeriness that later decades could not emulate. *Doctor Who*, already perhaps the greatest single influence on this new demographic, entered what has been called its 'Gothic phase'.

And so in this period the pre-teens of Britain were cowering behind their sofas. The ghostly music of *Children of the Stones* left even adults reluctant to linger near the television. *The Feathered Serpent* had human sacrifice and unholy resurrection. In *Escape into Night*, a young girl's attempts to recreate reality beget only nightmares. Adults, sitting through the trials of *Crossroads*, must often have felt a wistful envy.

And the worlds to come could be quite as forbidding. In *Timeslip* and *The Tomorrow People*, the future imagined was at once authoritarian and apocalyptic. In *Blake's 7*, England's somewhat straitened offering to the science fiction genre, 'the Federation' is a vicious, dictatorial oligarchy that, like the Party in *Nineteen Eighty-Four*, seeks to replace memory and warp identity. And so, caught between these pincers, the childish imagination was offered a homely, if gritty, version of the real in *Grange Hill*, a series based upon the trials of a suburban comprehensive school. Here we were introduced to benignly anarchic 'Tucker' Jenkins, the vicious 'Gripper' Stebson, and the long-suffering Mrs McCluskey, high-minded and well-meaning but doomed to grapple with the intractable perversity of adolescence.

On the older medium of the radio, the English were offered a comedy series for adults that could have been sheltered only under the quietly crumbling cliff face of the time in *The Hitchhiker's Guide to the Galaxy*. Arthur Dent had imagined an ordinary day beckoning, before remembering that his house is to be demolished. His friend Ford Prefect, in reality an alien from Betelgeuse Seven, informs him that something rather greater than his house is soon to be destroyed; from far above mankind hears: 'People of earth, your attention please . . . As you are no doubt aware, the plans for the development of the outlying regions of the western spiral arm of the galaxy require the building of a hyperspatial express route through your star-system, and regrettably your planet is one of those scheduled for demolition.' Oh dear.

48

The slot machine

The aliens who have come to destroy the earth, the sadistically dutiful Vogons, happiest when disgruntled, could only have been conceived by an Englishman of the Seventies. Later in *The Hitchhiker's Guide to the Galaxy*, we are introduced to two philosophers who have gone on strike in protest at the creation of a computer designed to solve the ultimate question of 'life, the universe and everything'. The computer, for them, is trespassing on their territory. 'You'll have a national Philosophers' strike on your hands!' 'Who will that inconvenience?' asks the computer, Deep Thought. 'Never you mind who it'll inconvenience, you box of blacklegging binary bits! It'll hurt, buster! It'll *hurt*!'

That last assertion, of course, is somewhat improbable, hence the bite of this topical lampoon. For on the one hand, strikes hurt the people a good deal; on the other, the usefulness of the work withheld was not always clear. At any rate, it was between the two elections of 1974 that the Labour government made peace with the unions, but on the unions' terms – no other choice seemed available. For this was the era of the Social Contract, by which parliament guaranteed the rights of the working man and received, in theory, the goodwill of the unions. It was never a formal or legal arrangement, and no statute of that name was ever enacted. It was Michael Foot, the scion of Fabian idealism, who prepared the acts with which this high-minded but hazy concept will always be linked. 'The Parliamentary Labour party and the unions are linked as never before!' he asserted.

Michael Foot was born in Plymouth into an overtly political family of Liberals, who naturally held the ascendancy in the West Country. Since his father, Isaac Foot, was elected MP for Plymouth on two separate occasions and subsequently became the city's lord mayor, it would be fair to assume that the young Foot had inherited the mantle of influence. He was a clever child; his headmaster declared that 'he has been the leading boy in the school in every way', and he naturally took the familiar path to Oxford and then moved on to the presidency of the Oxford Union. This was a time of political transition, as the Liberal party slowly gave way to the burgeoning Labour party. Foot soon identified himself as a socialist, in part under the influence of Stafford Cripps, the father of a close friend, and in part propelled by the poverty of Merseyside and Liverpool, of which he had been previously unaware – there had been no such sights in Plymouth. He learned the reality as a shipping clerk in Birkenhead immediately after leaving Oxford. He also read voraciously to bolster his new-found beliefs: Bennett, Wells, Shaw, Russell and others were all on his new curriculum.

Foot began his political career in journalism, moving from the *New Statesman* to *Tribune* and then to the *Evening Standard*, of which at the age of twenty-eight he was appointed editor. He went on to the *Daily Herald*, a fully paid-up organ of the Labour party, and then reverted to *Tribune*, in January 1937. He had a thorough understanding of the left-wing press in England, and equally knew the spite and prejudices of right-wing proprietors like Northcliffe, who dominated the political debates of the day.

Along with two colleagues, he wrote a tract entitled *Guilty Men* attacking the appeasement of the Chamberlain government, before becoming the most celebrated of the anti-war journalists. He became an integral part of the English dissenting Left and a close ally of Aneurin Bevan, the greatest and most eloquent of working-class politicians. Foot's political rise reached its first summit in 1945 with his election as Labour MP for Devonport.

He lost the election of 1955 by just one hundred votes and renewed his editorship of *Tribune* at the time of Suez. On the issue of the enveloping nuclear fear of that decade, Foot and Bevan were at odds, with Bevan veering towards the nuclear option so as to avoid 'going naked into the conference chamber'. Nevertheless, Foot was strongly supported by committed unilateralists like Frank Cousins. After his return to parliament in 1960, representing Bevan's old constituency, he embarked on another phase of his life with his membership of the Campaign for Nuclear Disarmament. In its first years it was a national phenomenon but gradually it began to lose support. Gaitskell pledged to 'fight, fight and fight again to save the party we love' against unilateralism, and the ragtag procession of activists began to seem less relevant in the changing world. There were many in CND who hated the Labour party, and there were many in Labour who were indifferent to the issue of nuclear disarmament. So his return to the Labour party was fractious and troubled, but his abiding pleasure came in his representation of Ebbw Vale, which was equivalent to going home.

By 1974, when he was sixty-one, Foot had become a member of the cabinet in Harold Wilson's government. As secretary of state for employment, his primary purpose was to administer the Social Contract, with no fewer than six bills for the purpose of uniting the trade unions with the Labour party. Two of the major proposals were the establishment of ACAS (Advisory, Conciliation and Arbitration Service) and the Employment Protection Bill, to defend the rights of workers. He was the most prominent socialist in the cabinet and believed he had every right to stand as the leading left-wing leadership candidate, after the resignation of Harold Wilson. He did not succeed but did sufficiently well to become in effect deputy prime minister under James Callaghan. It was a time of pacts and alliances, and Foot led the way to a 'Lib–Lab' pact late in the spring of 1977, though it fell apart in the following year.

After Callaghan's defeat in 1979, Foot returned to the opposition. Then, with the political demise of Callaghan, a vacancy revealed itself. Three candidates stepped forward – Denis Healey, Peter Shore and Jon Silkin – but each exhibited an Achilles heel, and Foot emerged as leader in late 1980. It cannot be said that he was a natural leader, though he was not helped by the split between the Labour party and the SDP at the beginning of 1981.

But Foot remained the stalwart and self-confident exponent of the socialist creed. He was the living embodiment of left-wing values in the twentieth century, to be compared with Russell and Orwell. He was, according to his biographer Kenneth O. Morgan, 'an utterly committed symbol of permanent opposition, a rebel, a maverick, in eternal conflict with authority'. He was an orator and not a politician. Perhaps most importantly, he maintained the role of public culture and civic discourse at a time when they seemed to be fading away. He was, in many ways, the last of the great Labour intellectuals and deserves an honoured place in the history of the twentieth century.

The Social Contract was reached between the TUC and the Labour government from 1974 to 1977. The premise on which it was founded now seems quixotic; the unions would show restraint if the government worked with them – in other words, if the government was prepared to accept every union demand for the protection of its members. 'Please play nice,' was the government's hopeful exhortation. It was thus a corporatist experiment, and far more radical than the post-war consensual politics with which it is sometimes confused.

Beneath the Social Contract lay a basic ambiguity in the power relation between employee and employer, and, later, between employees and government. It was also predicated on the assumption that the unions would act as one, but they were effectively in competition with each other. The only certain effect was that, by 1976, it was as if the unions had discovered, according to Tom Jackson, leader of the postal workers, 'a gigantic Las Vegas slot machine that had suddenly got stuck in favour of the customer'.

The unions were led not merely by old-fashioned working-class socialists, but often by men who had fought against Fascism. When they had begun their crusade, the most basic workers' rights were still to be attained, but the new generation had gained a degree of prosperity. The union leaders, however, often applied their 'street-fighting' mentality to contemporary conditions; capital was still the enemy and the union member was still the underdog. But by the late Seventies even the most ardent union leaders had begun to fear that their members' demands had become unsustainable. Jack Jones spoke of 'fair for all, not free-for-all', and Hugh Scanlon openly expressed doubts about the country's ability to cope. By this stage, however, a shift, so slow as to be almost imperceptible, had begun; the old guard was losing control over an increasingly 'individualist' membership. And so the late Seventies were marked by a discontent that was more petty capitalist than socialist.

But this still lay some way off. By 1976, there were few instances of industrial action. The unions had, after all, got almost all they wanted. But with prices rising and the pound falling, Wilson felt it was time to honour his promise to give the people a referendum on Europe. Previous polls suggested that only a minority supported Britain's membership. The advocates of a 'yes' vote in the referendum set for 1975 should have had no grounds for complacency, yet their mood on the campaign trail was buoyant. Unexpected alliances coalesced: Conservatives offered their canvassing skills to Labour; Labour members lent Conservatives their buses. A festival atmosphere prevailed.

The mood in the 'no' camp was quite different. Although the government of the day had given equal funding to both sides, the 'yes' campaign could count on the support of big business – the 'no' campaign was a humble pile of pea-shooters beside the cannon of their rivals. Like their opponents, they came from seemingly incompatible positions; unlike them, these positions appeared to be those of the radical fringe. The National Front and the British Communist party, for example, were Eurosceptic. And so, as Enoch Powell and Tony Benn hectored the people from the same platform, many wavering voters saw only division and demagoguery. How could a nation that so obviously looked askance at Europe listen so warmly to the Europhiles? Across the Channel lay the Continent, where an ordinary family could now take its holidays; there was the Common Market, which made those holidays possible; and then the EEC, which surely had nothing to do with either holidays or the Common Market, was not regarded as having designs on English liberty.

The prime minister's attitude to the EEC was informed by cheerful ignorance. Wilson knew little of Europe and cared even less. The Scilly Isles were his preferred holiday destination and he considered champagne a poor substitute for beer. For Wilson, the referendum represented little more than an opportunity to steer the nation's attention away from more proximate concerns. For his part, Callaghan was unconvinced. His apathy was apparent in a television interview where he refused to say whether the people should vote for or against remaining in the Common Market, even though his own government theoretically supported it. Yet even the government's indifference counted in favour of the vote for 'yes'. When the votes were counted, the referendum showed a majority of over 60 per cent in favour of remaining. The matter, for the moment, was closed. Now remained the question of failing exports, and other commitments which extended beyond the power of any single government to address, let alone resolve.

Harold Wilson had planned to resign at sixty, yet there was little to suggest that he would give up what power he had. However, there were no policies that were likely to come to fruition, and no garlands left to win. One civil servant recalled that Wilson seemed to be 'living through one day to the next', and there were more disturbing tokens of decline. His paranoia grew more acute as the Seventies progressed, and he saw spies everywhere. So fearful was he of the supposed influence of BOSS, South Africa's infamous Bureau of State Security, that when rumours were brought to him about a dark conspiracy to murder Jeremy Thorpe, his friend and rival, he contrived to assure even parliament that BOSS was behind it. He was convinced that Number Ten was being bugged.

In the course of one remarkable interview he went further yet, to the brink of sanity itself. 'I see myself as the big fat spider in the corner of the room,' he informed two journalists. 'Sometimes I speak when I'm asleep. You should both listen. Occasionally when we meet, I might tell you to go to the Charing Cross Road and kick a blind man standing in the corner. That blind man might tell you something, lead you somewhere.' He began to delegate, and to drink, more and more. His once unassailable memory had begun to totter. The cabinet had not known of his plans to resign and, when the announcement came, it took everyone, even Callaghan, by surprise, and shock overwhelmed feelings of relief or regret. In March 1976, at a farewell party at Chequers, a photograph of the outgoing prime minister showed a little old man with wandering eyes and a vacant smile.

49

Let us bring harmony

After the surprise of his departure, Wilson was largely forgotten. But he had deserved better. In terms of his electoral record, he was the most successful prime minister in history. He had united a party whose constituent elements were never at ease with each other; he had presided over the golden age of the welfare state; and he had shown himself an unsurpassed political tactician. But he had outstayed his day.

In previous years, Roy Jenkins had been the favourite to succeed him, at least among members of the press. But as a passionate Europhile with tastes to match, he could never command the allegiance of the Left, while Michael Foot would never woo the Right. And Denis Healey, for all his brilliance, was simply too rebarbative. In any case, Wilson had picked his successor. In the event, 'Big Jim' Callaghan won the leadership by 176 votes to Michael Foot's 137. The result was a clear endorsement, yet, for those on the right, an unsettling augury; Foot's hour would come. Callaghan had long dreamed of the moment when he would kiss the sovereign's hand. 'Prime Minister,' he was heard to murmur, 'and never even went to university.' The queen herself had been puzzled and disturbed by Wilson's decision, but she acquiesced with her habitual grace.

During the Sixties, the Labour government had tried desperately to ensure full employment while keeping down inflation. Wilson had attempted a six-month price and pay freeze, but it had not answered. Between 1964 and 1979 there had been no fewer than eight incomes policies, and all had run aground. The centre could not hold when the periphery was under assault. Healey's attempted rescue of the economy was testament to his remarkable agility and persistence. Thanks to his efforts to curb public spending, deeply unpopular though they were, inflation fell from 29 per cent to 13 per cent in under nine months. The fragility of sterling, however, was a matter that none could ignore. The government employed every resource to prevent its collapse, but the world was unconvinced. Appearances were still against the pound. The Bank of England spent almost all its reserves in propping it up, but it seemed set to equal the dollar. What could be done? There was the eccentric proposal offered by Tony Benn that Britain become a 'siege economy', placing tariffs on imports yet somehow still able to export freely. Other members of the cabinet knew that there was no recourse left but an appeal to the highest financial authority in the world, the International Monetary Fund. The crisis came when Denis Healey, arriving at Heathrow to fly to the United States, was told of the pound's collapse. His place, he saw, was at home. He drove back to Westminster. And so the United Kingdom, once the world's banker, had to doff its pride and beg money of its allies.

For that is what it amounted to. The IMF was funded largely by the United States and Germany, which made absurd the suggestion of Anthony Crosland that it could be blackmailed by threats of Britain withdrawing its foreign military commitments. Britain was in no place to make demands. The IMF team, when it arrived on 1 November 1976, was composed of several nationalities, but there could be no disguising the fact that the spirit informing their mission was American. It was clear to the IMF that Britain would not only need a thorough spring clean; it would have to throw out many objects of sentimental value. It had been usual for such loans to be renewed indefinitely, but no such latitude was extended to the feckless British. A December date was fixed and a rigorous programme of spending cuts demanded. For a loan of almost £4 billion, it seemed to the IMF scarcely unreasonable. And yet the British proved to have some fire in their bellies still. At a moment of seeming impasse, Callaghan picked up the telephone in front of the chief negotiator, and threatened to call the president if no leeway was offered. Was it pure bravado? Perhaps, but it had the desired effect and the loan was agreed.

Despite the fact that matters turned out remarkably well, it was a sombre prime minister who addressed the Labour party conference in 1976. He had begun to undergo a change of heart, one too subtle and incremental to be called a conversion, but it must have seemed a shift of tectonic proportions to the delegates in Blackpool. After paying tribute to Harold Wilson, who perked up from a somnolent doze when he heard his name, Callaghan began to dismantle the post-war consensus. 'Mr Chairman and comrades,' he said. 'No one owes Britain a living, and . . . we are still not earning the standard of living we are enjoying. We are only keeping up our standards by borrowing and this cannot go on indefinitely.'

Amidst all the agonizing about inflation, deflation and disinflation, Callaghan had found the wound. Those to the left of the party, like the young Dennis Skinner, were aghast that questions of 'productivity' could be mooted at all, but Callaghan was unmoved: Britain had been singing for its supper rather than earning its keep. Here was an old socialist speaking, and he was impatient of fecklessness. The world the people of Britain had known could no longer be justified: 'That cosy world is gone.' His tone was dull and gravelly; he relished the words no more than did his listeners.

It is hard to appreciate the extent to which inflation exercised the finest minds. In Seventies Britain, 'push' and 'pull' on supply and demand worked simultaneously; with increased wages, spending power grew, and prices rose. A largely unionized nation responded by asking for higher wages, and employers had to raise prices to cover their costs, which in turn led to higher wage demands. If you were affiliated to a union, the spiral need not inconvenience you, but if you were not so affiliated, or were not a wage earner at all, you could find yourself unable to afford anything beyond the absolute necessities. There were other factors too. For example, the problem was exacerbated by the unions' fondness for 'free collective bargaining' for wages, but that can only work where they have similar traditions, where their interests do not intersect, where the nation has no other commitments, and where there is money in the collective pot. These conditions could not be met. Small wonder that Roy

Jenkins likened the role of government in this period to that of the mountaineer on a wild and unpredictable upland. 'The bigger [beasts] were known as union leaders and the smaller ones as constituency parties, and . . . when they did come down, they must on no account be enraged.'

Certainly Bill Bryson, an American observer, found this to be so. While working for a UK newspaper, he found himself having to deal with the print checker. This man looked through the proofs at his leisure, if at all, and was not averse to using force to prevent anyone, however important, from crossing the line into his office; for this of course represented a breach of 'demarcation'. When Bryson himself attempted to proffer the proofs, the man retorted, 'I don't know if you've noticed, but I'm eating pizza!' The print unions were run on lines that recalled medieval guilds or Masonic lodges: each union had its 'chapel', and each chapel had its 'chapel father'. If miners had their 'pit villages', so the printers had what we might call 'print families': it was not so much a cartel as a family concern. Other unions could boast similar traditions.

It was all a far cry from the world envisaged by Barbara Castle, who in February 1975 had reflected in her diary: 'To me socialism is not just militant trade unionism. It is the gentle society in which every producer remembers he is a consumer too.' And Callaghan himself felt bound in 1978 to remark that 'Society today is so organized that every individual group almost has the power to disrupt it. How is their power to be channelled into constructive channels?' The question was never to be resolved in his political lifetime.

1976 had been the hottest year in recorded history and one of the most scorching in the world of British politics, so it was with relief that the government and the nation welcomed the celebrations for the queen's Silver Jubilee in 1977. It seemed as if every house had its bunting, every street its party. Callaghan, as firm a believer in monarchy as he was in every traditional institution, was delighted to be called up by the queen to share the accolades. But once the bunting was taken down, the nation was once again revealed as poor, shabby and, above all, discontented. The punk band the Sex Pistols had released 'God Save the Queen', a less than reverent celebration of her role in which she was described as being a 'moron'. It was banned by as many radio stations as could keep up with its popularity, but reached number one in the charts.

Callaghan had established a cap on wage increases of 5 per cent in order to hold down inflation. It was audacious for the time, but it held, more or less, until 25 September 1978, when the Ford workers agreed to strike. With inflation standing at 8 per cent, 5 per cent was not enough, they argued. Their action took immediate effect. From then on, strikes sprang up like toadstools after rain. Most damagingly, the public sector unions, many of them representing the least affluent, felt bound to join in. Callaghan saw his pay policy unravel almost daily, and Michael Foot, who had done so much to champion the unions and had the most right to feel betrayed, unleashed a speech of unprecedented fury at the Labour party conference. The delegates were reminded with biting sarcasm of the kind of pay policy they could expect under the Tories – it was known as 'unemployment'.

But the unions were unmoved. Indeed, with such awards dangling in front of their members, they had little choice. By the late autumn of 1978 the expression 'Winter of Discontent' was on everyone's lips. People lay unburied in coffins, with the bereaved families turned away. Lorries bringing in emergency supplies were attacked, hospitals were picketed and refuse built up into stinking slag heaps in Leicester Square, while pickets proclaimed that it was not 'a question of whether the country can afford to pay us, but of whether they can afford not to'. All of this and more contributed to a sense that the unions were fast becoming enemies of the people. It was never, of course, a general strike – most unions did not participate – but the effects hurt the public materially and emotionally, as striking became known abroad as 'the English disease'.

Towards the end of the crisis, Callaghan agreed to an interview with the political journalist Llew Gardner. Callaghan's voice was, as usual, reasonable and reassuring, his soft Hampshire accent enlivened by occasional flickers of hauteur. But his eyes were cold and furtive behind his spectacles, his finger jabbing at an imaginary chest. He had a message for the unions: 'You can't get more out of the bank than there is in it!' Asked what happened to sour relations so terribly, he answered: 'Too much responsibility has been devolved from the centre onto local shop stewards who do not fully comprehend the basic tenets of trade unionism.' 'Wasn't 5 per cent an unrealistic figure?' Gardner asked. 'The realistic figure,' barked the prime minister, 'is the one the country can afford! Not the one people conjure out of their heads.' Gently prodded on the question of talks with the trade unions, Callaghan remarked, 'There is a time for reticence.'

Reticence was the keynote in other respects. The notion of a secret ballot had already been mooted by Margaret Thatcher. Surely, she maintained, union members must be allowed to vote without fear of reprisal. Callaghan expressed an openness to this thought, but not, he emphasized, if it was made a legal requirement. And there perhaps lay the crux. For Callaghan, a union man still, the law should stay away from organized labour. Besides, he hinted, the unions were above the law, and had the means to retain that position. Moss Evans, the new head of the TGWU, did as much as anyone to ensure Callaghan's downfall, yet he understood this predicament. His message to the government was itself a melange of defiance and helplessness: 'I won't and I can't restrain the stewards.' Among the general public, meanwhile, the expression 'Social Contract' had become a swear word. 'I don't give a Social Contract about that!' was a retort commonly heard.

That the Conservatives had a quite different policy from the unions was obvious, but even the Labour party and the unions, despite their symbiosis, had separate agendas. Though people spoke of Labour as the parliamentary wing of the trade unions, they had to govern and the trade unions had to protect their members – the two programmes were bound to conflict sooner or later. In any case, although the most contentious quarrels lay between Labour and Conservative, the most bitter rivalry lay between different unions. Britain's unions were the oldest, and the most diverse, in Europe. By 1960, there were still 180. The English trade union tradition was local and particular, an inheritance, perhaps, from the medieval guilds and later from the friendly societies. Each trade, however small, had its union, and the difficulty lay in the fact that one union would find itself in inevitable competition with another. So it was that the conditions established under the Attlee consensus, and extended under the Wilson government, enabled the various unions to compete, with no legal checks upon them.

Douglas Hurd, who had been an adviser to Heath during the miners' strike, summarized the question thus: 'In a public sector dispute, the employee barely suffers. Any temporary loss of income is usually covered by the union and is in any case quickly recouped out of the eventual settlement. The employer, the actual administrator of the public concern, does not suffer at all, for his salary is secure. It is the public, and only the public, which suffers, first as consumer and later, when the bill comes in, as taxpayer. The public picks up the tab for both sides.' Paul Johnson, the historian and journalist, put the matter more vividly yet: '[The unions] did not plan the victory . . . [and] they do not know what to do with it now that they have got it. Dazed and bewildered, they are like medieval peasants who have burnt down the lord's manor.'

But surely it need not have come to this. Was there not North Sea oil, discovered in the late Sixties, to look forward to? The promise of it was to become a sticking point for the left wing of the Labour party. In the run-up to the IMF bailout they asked why the government needed to squeeze wages when North Sea oil was almost, as Tony Benn put it, 'running up our shores'. It was in this context that the far Left held the IMF responsible for the meltdown of the late Seventies. However that may be, Callaghan found himself in parliament facing a no-confidence vote and lost by a tiny margin.

And so the parties went to the country. Callaghan had personal appeal, but nothing else to offer. Thatcher might be less likeable, but she had a plan. Perhaps no one in her position could have lost. In later years she would pay tribute to Callaghan, saying that in happier times 'he would have been a very successful Prime Minister'. She even admitted that he often worsted her in the House of Commons. Still, the nation had had enough, and the Conservatives came to power, though with a surprisingly modest majority. On her way to Buckingham Palace, Margaret Thatcher addressed the nation in the words attributed to St Francis: 'where there is discord, may we bring harmony'. In years to come it became apparent that it was the working class and not the bourgeoisie that had ignited the Thatcher revolution. There had been money in union membership; there was still more in becoming an entrepreneur.

50

Here she comes

The grocer's daughter had worsted the carpenter's son; more significantly, the shopkeeper had triumphed over the shop steward. There would be no more rule by union fiat. For all its seeming goodwill, Thatcher's invoking of St Francis would have misled few who heard it. The nation knew well that it had elected a terrier with a burning torch gripped in her teeth. Not for Thatcher 'the orderly management of decline' that Sir William Armstrong had suggested was the real business of twentieth-century governance.

She began as Methodist and became an Anglican, a change of emphasis that affected her political personality. Her accent, which in moments of anger or stress betrayed the cadences of her native Lincolnshire, first hardened and then softened into the genteel warble of a suburban nanny. Although her origins were theoretically lower-middle-class, she managed to obscure the fact by marrying a highly successful businessman, Denis Thatcher. She found her personality partly by identifying with others and partly by play-acting.

Thatcher had entered parliament in 1959, three years after the Suez crisis, but she had to live with that failure all the same. The English political class, according to one historian, 'went from believing that Britain could do anything to an almost neurotic belief that Britain could do nothing'. If she ever contemplated such a thought, she quickly cast it aside. The journey from Grantham to Oxford was the first stage of her political maturity. She fought implacably to become the MP for Finchley, and once she had attained that position she solidified it with hard work and slowly made her ascent. She first became a parliamentary undersecretary, and in 1967 she joined Edward Heath's shadow cabinet, as minister for fuel and power. In October 1969, she made another leap and became shadow education minister. After the Conservative victory in 1970, she became a minister in her own right, as secretary of state for education and science. Her liberal or free-market supporters, however, might not have been particularly enthusiastic about this term of her office, in which she sanctioned 3,286 comprehensive schools and rejected 328. It could be said that she was following her statutory duties, but she performed them with a vengeance.

There began in 1971 another series of struggles between the government and the public sector unions, with Heath beginning to give ground to Rolls-Royce and the Upper Clyde Shipbuilders. In turn came the National Union of Mineworkers. These were the conditions for the irresistible rise of Mrs Thatcher. During the campaign for the Conservative party leadership she maintained her composure, but there was a large element of ambition in her remorseless advance. None of her colleagues yet knew of what material she was made. Certain traits, however, were becoming clear. Defeatism was the plague against which she fought relentlessly. Pessimism was the second curse. And Ted Heath was, in her eyes, the embodiment of both.

When it became apparent that after two defeats Heath could no longer lead the party, Thatcher expected her friend and colleague Keith Joseph to put himself forward. Ever diffident, he declined, leaving Thatcher to uphold and defend the new creed known as 'monetarism'. It remained to inform Heath of her decision; legend has it that he offered her the blunt retort 'You'll lose!' The truth was that he heard her out and said simply, 'Thank you.' On her victory for the party leadership, knocking out Heath, Whitelaw, Prior and Peyton, Thatcher remarked that 'I almost wept when they told me. I *did* weep.' Plenty more tears would follow.

On 4 May 1979, Thatcher drove to Buckingham Palace, and so began one of the more unusual periods of English history. The economy was turbulent, but she had an instinctive conviction that her financial policies were correct. This was confirmed and encouraged by her more or less permanent dissatisfaction with, and distrust for, the nascent European Community. 'They are much cleverer than us,' she said; 'they will run rings around us.' But she was also guided by what many considered to be old-fashioned nationalism. She had been happy to support the 'Common Market' when it was still referred to as such, but the creeping federalism within Europe came to unsettle and even enrage her and she referred to VAT payments to Europe as 'our money' or 'my money'.

Above all, Thatcher saw Conservatism as an ideal, not merely as a political stance. It was precisely the notion that Conservatism could be something as vulgar as a crusade that so displeased the patricians of the party, but it was to be her distinctive contribution to a party that had spent the post-war years in broad agreement with Labour. Another of her particular skills was sensing the mood of the nation, at least in her early years. 'I think,' she said in a television interview in 1978, 'people are really rather afraid that this country might be rather swamped by people with a different culture.' The remark caused intense outrage among the 'media', but not perhaps among the population as a whole.

She faced a nation directed by the fluctuations of the stock market and by the relentless drive of materialism, by the energy of popular music and the colourful panorama of television. Because of the latter medium, the nature of news and comment had an instantaneous visual impact that supplanted analysis and reflection. The country shone with screens, with flickering images lasting for no more than a few seconds. Thatcher was the ideal embodiment of such a world – if ever an ascending prime minister was willing to act as chameleon, it was she. Under the auspices of the PR consultant Gordon Reece, she doffed the faintly ridiculous hats which reminded too many of the Mothers' Union. She underwent voice training. The playwright Ronald Millar provided her with mantras: 'Let us be cool, calm – and elected' was the first. Laurence Olivier himself assisted in her voice coaching sessions. The singer Lulu and the comedians Kenny Everett and Ken Dodd were all happy to be associated with Thatcher. This was to change – in the years to come, no self-respecting 'artiste' would dream of giving succour to the lady from Grantham.

Employment in the early Eighties became of paramount importance, with lists of the most significant redundancies read out on the television news as if they were casualties in a war. But for Thatcher, these casualties were the price to be paid if inflation was to be conquered. She had inherited a tax system that could be described as either 'confiscatory' or 'redistributive' according to personal conviction. The upper rate of tax was set at 83 per cent, but it began at £20,000; it was not levied only upon millionaires. Thus it seemed as if Labour had taxed the rich to feed the poor, only to render everyone poor. It is within this context that Thatcher's 'Franciscan' exhortation should be understood.

The Labour government had proved itself unable to contain the divisions within the nation; with the Conservative government, there would be no more juggling of incompatible priorities. This was the true 'Thatcher revolution', at least in principle. Inflation was the great danger, and it must be crushed before any reforms could be contemplated. So far as she and her chancellor Geoffrey Howe were concerned, the solution was to control the money supply and let the market adjudicate in matters of price. Monetarist theory had at its heart a dictum that was simple enough: government should not spend what it did not have, and what it spent must be worth something. Thatcher and Howe had only to be thrifty, but the 'dismal science', as economics had become known, was young and inexact. They soon found themselves dismayingly close to the position of their predecessors, cramped and hobbled by circumstance. The monetarist drive in Howe's first budget ran counter to election promises that could not lightly be cast aside. To honour the latter, and to support the hundreds of thousands left unemployed by the new policy, the government found itself pouring millions more into social benefit than was sustainable under monetarism. The result was recession.

Had it all been a costly and ghastly mistake? The human price was already apparent: unemployment had reached 2 million by 1980 and was climbing. Three hundred and sixty-four economists had written to the press to testify that this revolution had no basis in sound economics. Many were predicting a U-turn, a challenge to which Thatcher offered a celebrated retort at a Conservative party conference: 'You turn if you want to; the lady's not for turning.'

Caught off guard when the conference was invaded by activists protesting at job cuts, she rose to the occasion, observing that 'It's wet outside, I expect they wanted to come in . . . It's always better where the Tories are.' Although she lacked a sense of humour, she was quite capable of wit.

Naturally, no U-turn was forthcoming. In other fields, matters were more auspicious. The 'Right to Buy', the policy by which the Tories promised council tenants the opportunity to purchase their homes, had been the jewel of the Tory manifesto, and it was set in place. The pledges to restrict secondary picketing and to establish secret ballots were likewise in the manifesto, but it would be a while before they could be tested. The top rate of tax was reduced from 83 per cent to 60 per cent, the European average. In the eyes of many, the previous rate had been one of the chief causes of the country's relatively poor economic performance. The rich could always seek other climes.

The cost of the war on inflation mounted ever higher, and its casualties began to protest. Riots broke out in the early Eighties, motivated in part by the insensitive 'sus' laws, later known as 'stop and search', and in part by mass unemployment in the black communities. They began in the depressed district of St Paul's in Bristol in April 1980, and spread to Brixton in London the next year, with burning buildings, tear gas, police charges and mob attacks. The frenzy was contagious, and riots took place in at least 58 British towns and cities. *The Times* reported that fears about the breakdown of law and order were being widely expressed in foreign centres, no doubt laced with schadenfreude. Some commentators went perhaps too far. 'The extinction of civilised life on this island,' wrote E. P. Thompson, 'is probable.' It was an opportune moment for dismay: at the end of March 1982, there was a strong warning that the Argentinian navy was about to invade the sovereign territory of the Falkland Islands.

51

The Falklands flare-up

Neil Kinnock, later leader of the Labour party, said of Thatcher that she had 'the greatest gift: the right enemies'. Certainly General Leopoldo Galtieri of Argentina was an ideal enemy. He had come to power in a coup and had ensured that some 20,000 of his compatriots 'disappeared'. Now the Falkland islanders were next on his list of internal undesirables.

It had the makings of a great naval adventure, but it played out in the eyes of a world looking for disasters. Many wanted to see the back of Thatcher and cheered on the Argentinians. Others wanted to retain Britain's influence and cheered the British contingent. It was a small turf war, but it had momentous consequences for Britain. Was it about to decline into a third-rate power? A genuine fear of failure invaded the military, as well as the diplomatic contingent, Westminster and the public at large.

As early as 1976 there had been negotiations between Britain and Argentina about the sovereignty of the islands. In early 1982, the Argentinian government formulated plans for a military solution, and the possibility of confrontation came closer when it was proposed to withdraw HMS *Endurance* from its hydrographic work in the vicinity – to the Argentinians, it appeared like the prelude to a more general withdrawal.

An Argentinian invasion fleet sailed on 28 March, with the

instruction to protect the lives of the island population. Its presence became known to the British authorities by 2 April, and five days later the first stage of the 'task force' was under way. Diplomatic initiatives, led principally by the Americans, now became vital. It was not militarily or financially feasible, the British Foreign Office suggested – it would be better to back down or to reach an accommodation. But Thatcher would have none of it: 'They wanted us to negotiate. You can't negotiate away an invasion! You can't negotiate away that the freedom of your people has been taken . . . by a cruel dictator. You've got to stand up and you've got to have the spine to do it!'

For their part, the British people confined their protests to hurling cans of corned beef at the windows of the Argentine embassy, while a BBC broadcaster conveyed something of the spirit of the time as he signed off with 'Let's just hope we win,' his tone at once gently patriotic and grimly wistful. The BBC was not always a friend to Thatcher, but here, perhaps for the last time, she found in it an ally.

The United Kingdom was not quite the lone wolf of journalistic imagination. American 'Sidewinders' proved crucial in the race for air supremacy, for example, as did the collaboration of France in sharing intelligence. Yet the odds were heavily against her. After several failed missions, the British military operation began on 1 May, when a 'total exclusion zone' had been imposed around the islands. One of the principal objects of attack was ARA *General Belgrano*, an Argentinian light cruiser that posed a serious threat to the British. A submarine was dispatched and the *Belgrano* sank, with the loss of more than 300 lives. The furore was immeasurably increased when it was discovered that it had been sailing away from the 'total exclusion zone'. Retaliation was swift: HMS *Sheffield* was attacked by an Exocet missile, and Argentinian anti-aircraft batteries injured three Harriers. More mediation followed under the guidance of the Peruvians, but it came to nothing. In Britain, Tony Benn claimed that not only had the *Belgrano* been torpedoed, but with it any chance of a settlement. He cannot have known that Galtieri could afford to climb down no more than could Thatcher. His regime, too, was at stake.

There seemed little option but to mount an armed invasion against the islands, with all the risks that the intervention implied.

The landing itself was deemed to be a success. There was some confusion in the Argentinian High Command, which meant that their attacks on the British were still sporadic. But Argentinian naval intelligence was nevertheless effective and a container ship, the SS *Atlantic Conveyor*, went down, as did six Wessex, one Lynx and three Chinook helicopters. The reaction in Britain was one of shock and incredulity. Could the nightmare materialize, and the power of Britain be threatened? Many believed in any case that Britain had become restless, irresolute and essentially weak. Could this be an apocalypse that might destroy the reputation of the nation? For the prime minister it was an ordeal by fire that could only have one conclusion. The national mood, if not exactly summoned by drums, was sounding a fiercer note.

The Battle of Goose Green was a British success, and the British moved on to Stanley with high hopes. The final assault was on 13 June, and the Argentine forces signalled their surrender on 15 June. It was a victory with many difficulties along the way and largely dependent on chance. A different season of the year, a different set of political circumstances or more reliable Argentine bombs, and all could have changed. Nonetheless, it could be claimed that English gallantry was still alive. One man to receive the Victoria Cross posthumously was Colonel 'H' Jones who, holed up by a long line of Argentine machine-gunners, roared to his men, 'Come on, A Company, get your skirts off!' and rushed out to take the enemy position, alone and in the teeth of their fire. His death gave heart to his men and dismayed the Argentines, who quickly surrendered. But the war had shown other sides to the nation, as well as to Thatcher herself. She wrote letters of condolence to the families of every British soldier killed, yet was angry to hear the Archbishop of Canterbury mentioning the Argentine bereaved as proper subjects for prayer. Her powers of sympathy were often stunted by a lack of imagination.

For Thatcher, it had been a time of constantly strained nerves, arguments and tears. She had stared national humiliation in the face and had not flinched. She kept her will intact, and faced down those who predicted failure. It was a great national and personal victory. If she had become indomitable, it could only reflect brightly on her political future.

52

The Big Bang

The prime minister realized that it would be opportunistic to call an election on the merits of the victory in the Falklands War, but there were other ways of taking advantage of the situation. In the words of her new chancellor, Nigel Lawson, 'she came to believe in the media presentation, and to act in a quasi-presidential style'. Norman Tebbit, though fiercely loyal, had to admit that 'she could be merciless'. Her bullying rose to the surface, with the gentle Howe as its chief victim. They had once been allies, sharing a methodical rigour and an insatiable appetite for work. Perhaps she saw him as her true rival in diligence. Almost supernatural qualities began to be ascribed to her. It was rumoured that she subsisted on coffee and vitamins alone, and that she bathed in an electric bath. The writer Iain Sinclair suggested half-facetiously that she was a latter-day witch.

It was in this period that Thatcher began to espouse the imprecise notion of 'Victorian Values'. There were already signs of intrigue against her. A leak from the Central Policy Review Staff suggested large budget cuts, but her landslide victory in 1983 did nothing to mitigate her zeal. Steady privatization was maintained without much comment. The sale of British Telecom was continued, and local government spending came under scrutiny. Her victory in the Falklands had increased her confidence. Her opponent, Michael

Foot, had been committed to a manifesto of socialist retrenchment so radical that it was dubbed 'the longest suicide note in history'. At the beginning of 1984, she stripped the unions at the Government Communications Headquarters (GCHQ) of their rights, imposing upon them the secret ballot and a prohibition on secondary picketing.

In the same year, she began yet another confrontation. Three years ago, she had been forced to back down in the face of a miners' strike. Now another threatened, and the National Union of Mineworkers saw nothing to suggest that they should not win again. Moreover, their leader was now Arthur Scargill, who had so triumphantly routed Edward Heath. For Thatcher, it was a fight between democracy and militant trade unionism, against an attempt to 'substitute the rule of the mob for the rule of law'. For Scargill, the aim was not merely to win, but to 'roll back the years of Thatcherism'. For Tony Benn, perhaps the only Labour politician fully to back the miners, it was Thatcher's war on the strongest union. If it was won, then the others would be cowed.

The battle took on familiar lines. The NUM refused to hold a national strike ballot and the Nottinghamshire miners carried on working. They belonged to another union and proved to be Thatcher's inadvertent and even unwilling allies – she could claim that it was miner against miner. Moreover, having learned from her predecessors' mistakes, she had enough coal to withstand any strike. At the so-called 'Battle of Orgreave', mounted police dispersed the flying pickets on which Scargill had placed such hopes. The nation watched and concluded that this was a barren cause, which brought out the worst in everyone. The strike ended on 13 March 1985, though the majority of miners had returned to work long before that. The banners of the unions flew in the breeze and brass bands played as men rejoined the ranks of those they had termed 'scabs'. Although it was not seen as a defeat, it presaged one. The Nottinghamshire miners, to whom Thatcher had sent her thanks in writing, were to lose everything they had fought for under her successor. A Conservative government would still eventually close their pits.

She went back to the first principles of privatization. Her chancellor, Nigel Lawson, had written to her in 1983 warning that the new life of the private companies would impinge upon 'the giant utilities and unprofitable companies', but nothing could stop her now. Twenty-three enterprises, including the British Gas Corporation, British Telecom and the National Coal Board, were up for sale. Half of the shares of British Telecom were put on sale in November 1984 at a low price, which rose by 43 pence on the first day and never dipped. For the first time in its history, the stock exchange seemed a benevolent institution, and it spread a sparkle over the late period of capitalism that socialists could not overcome. In effect it changed the whole attitude of the country: private and public wealth now went hand in hand. The first mobile telephone sets were sold, and the proportion of homes that were owner-occupied rose from 55 per cent to 67 per cent. It was an extraordinary metamorphosis, though it went largely unnoticed at the time. But on 27 October 1986, the fissures of the financial volcano merged and created a mighty explosion which became known as the 'Big Bang'.

53

The Brighton blast

On 12 October 1984, the Conservative party was to hold its conference at the Grand Hotel in Brighton. In the early hours of the morning, Norman Tebbit noticed the chandelier above his head swaying. Within seconds, the ceiling began to collapse. Tebbit sensed the cause in a moment. The building had been bombed. He survived, though his wife, Margaret, was left paralysed from the neck down. In later years, he would remember the friendly grip of Fred, a fireman, pulling him through the rubble and to safety.

The IRA's principal target also survived, though her bathroom was wrecked. Five people were killed in the blast, among them the wife of the chief whip, John Wakeham. After she had visited the survivors and comforted the staff, Mrs Thatcher and her husband retired to bed for a few hours. 'We said a prayer and tried to go to sleep,' she recalled. Daybreak brought two urgent questions. The first was whether the delegates should immediately return to Westminster. But though shaken and sleepless, Thatcher was unmoved. 'The conference will go on as usual,' she told the press, pale-faced and wary-eyed. A second question now arose: given that most of the bedrooms in the hotel were now crime scenes, what were the delegates, still in pyjamas and nightgowns, to wear to the conference? Marks & Spencer were prevailed upon to open their doors at 8 a.m. And so, with all immaculately dressed, the conference started at

9.30 'precisely', as Thatcher was quick to point out. She had proved yet again that she could be neither cowed nor deflected, and the nation took note.

'We do not surrender to bullets or bombs,' Thatcher had proclaimed in 1983. If she had, it would have been no wonder. The IRA had been intensifying its campaign, pressing ever harder on the nerve of British fears. Two members of the Irish security forces had been killed; a Unionist politician had been assassinated; and Harrods, the symbol of all that was affluent on the mainland, was targeted. Six people died. The IRA's campaign had intensified since the late Seventies. In 1976, in the aftermath of bombings in Guildford and Birmingham, the Labour government had withdrawn political status from those convicted of terrorist offences, a policy that Thatcher continued. 'There can be no question of granting political status,' she said. 'A crime is a crime is a crime.' The IRA was only the most famous, and not always the most brutal, of the terrorist groups in the Province, but if every atrocity was presumed to be the work of the IRA, then it had only itself to blame. Moral considerations aside, the political folly of taking 'the war' to the British mainland should have been apparent to its high command. But the IRA was still riding high on the deaths of the hunger strikers in 1981, a cause which gained it yet more funds from the United States. With the Brighton bombing, however, direct attempts on the life of the premier ended. 'Today we have been unlucky, but remember, we have only to be lucky once. You will have to be lucky always,' the IRA offered. But it was bluster.

The bombing had occurred in the midst of negotiations with the Irish Republic. While it was generally agreed that nothing should divert this process, Thatcher was in no humour for what she called 'appeasement'. Her Irish counterpart, Garret FitzGerald, was a genial, well-meaning man, but he too had the sensibilities of his people to consider. Time and again, Thatcher ruled out any talk of an executive, or even consultative, role for the Republic in the affairs of the Province. The truth was that she understood little of Ireland or of its history. On one occasion she wondered aloud whether the Catholics might not be better off moving to the Republic. Hadn't that been done before? Yes, but under Cromwell, it was pointed out. The Unionists, moreover, were largely excluded from the process, a fact that the Reverend Ian Paisley was not slow to allude to.

But still the process continued, until on 15 November 1985 the Anglo-Irish Agreement was signed. The concessions now appear cosmetic; at the time they were radical. The Irish were given their cherished 'consultative role' in the Province, while accepting that there could be no change to its constitution unless the majority of the population should desire one. That possibility seemed remote to the British, but less so to their Irish counterparts, who knew that the demographics of the Province had begun to tilt towards such an eventuality.

While Thatcher evinced little concern for the Province, her opposite number in Washington cared a great deal. Ronald Reagan had been the chief spur to the Anglo-Irish Agreement. The two politicians were very different beasts. Reagan had won his position by conjoining an easy, unaffected charm and an equally easy patriotism, but a keen intellect was not his distinctive trait. In later years, when asked why she had held in such high esteem a man whom she would never have appointed to her cabinet, Thatcher replied: 'Because Ron has an instinctive understanding of the greatness and destiny of America.' As cold warriors, they were popularly supposed to be inseparable, but here their approaches differed. For Thatcher, the West's nuclear deterrent was an indispensable guarantor of both freedom and peace. Had not the doctrine of mutually assured destruction kept the great Bear in his cage? For Reagan, nuclear missiles were at best a necessary evil. He was heard to exclaim at meetings, 'Why don't we just abolish nuclear weapons?'

Many asked the same question. One of the most effective of the anti-nuclear protests came from a group that became known as 'the women of Greenham Common', who combined the recently rediscovered authority of their sex with a fierce antagonism to nuclear weaponry. Their protest arose from the arrival in England of American cruise missiles; these were stationed at RAF Greenham Common, in Berkshire, which became the focus of mass demonstration when in 1982 the women set up an extended camp, intending to remain as long as the rockets stayed in position. On 1 April 1983, the women formed a human chain around the site, which caught the world's imagination. The camp settled into something like a mini city, with different quarters for different groups. It was a long wait, of some nineteen years, and the camp was not disbanded until 2000. In the end, the missiles were removed from Greenham Common as the result of a nuclear treaty between the United States and the then Soviet Union, but the women refused to leave until a memorial for their achievement was set up. Had they succeeded? In any direct sense, the answer must be no. But they set a new, strange and deeply English example of peaceful rejection of power.

It was Thatcher who first struck a mattock into the ice of the Cold War. In February 1984, Yuri Andropov, the ageing premier of the USSR, died. Thatcher attended his funeral, where she impressed the Politburo and the Russian people with her dignity and courtesy. She also formed a new acquaintance, one Mikhail Sergeyevich Gorbachev, a man, as she said, 'she could do business with'. It helped that Gorbachev had defied precedent by bringing his wife. Konstantin Chernenko succeeded Andropov only to follow him into the grave, and Gorbachev was appointed in his place. The empire he had inherited was vast in scope but sick with senescence. Its economy was doubly vulnerable: firstly, oil and gas accounted for half its exports. Secondly, in order to keep pace with the United States, it was obliged to spend a vast percentage of its GDP on defence. These disadvantages might have counted for less had its once legendary technological initiative not atrophied since the Sixties. In sum, having run out of ideas, the USSR was beginning to run out of money and will.

The Special Defence Initiative, better known by the sobriquet 'Star Wars', was Reagan's suggestion as to how the Cold War impasse might be broken. The intention was to spend over a trillion dollars on a satellite system that would effectively end the possibility of conventional nuclear conflict. When the subject was raised during talks over the future of mid-range nuclear weapons, it became crushingly clear that the USSR could never match such an innovation. Thus began the end of the Cold War and, ultimately, the dissolution of what Reagan had once called the 'Evil Empire'. SDI ended its days in 1993, stillborn. It was perhaps the greatest bluff in history, and a bluff all the more remarkable for being inadvertent.

The contribution of Britain to the end of the Cold War may

easily be exaggerated. Neither the women of Greenham Common nor Thatcher herself were to lift that swaying sword from its hook, but it was Thatcher who made the first overtures to the eastern bloc. For all his personal warmth and evident goodwill, Reagan was seen as Thatcher's charming guide, a guru without innate authority for the role. The enduring image of him was that captured by a new British television comedy: he was shown as hardly ever leaving his bed, his face either twisted in consternation or alight with a brainless smile. The president, along with every politician, actor, singer, celebrity, churchman, member of parliament and member of the royal family, was a latex puppet. *Spitting Image* not only lampooned the coarseness, cynicism and vulgarity of the time – in many minds it embodied it.

The puppeteers responsible were Peter Fluck and Roger Law. They mischievously altered their names to 'Luck' and 'Flaw' in the concluding credits, although alternative malapropisms had no doubt occurred to them. The humour was not so much a rifle as a blunderbuss, with shot flying everywhere and everyone wounded. If the Tory cabinet was presented as a court of nervous sycophants led by a dictator, the Labour party appeared as a crew of unelectable clowns. The voice artist captured perfectly the prime minister's laboured mellifluousness, but also let her lapse into a Lincolnshire growl when crossed. However inspired its puppets or its jokes, the show could never be accused of delicacy. The puppeteers confuted their critics with an unanswerable observation. 'People say we're too savage, but you don't hear anyone accusing Conservative Central Office of being gratuitously benevolent.'

These were the years when alternative comedy at last reached the home, though it was never domesticated. *The Young Ones* depicted four students sharing a sublimely dilapidated house. We were introduced to a hippy, a punk, a 'wide boy', a sociology student and their erratic Polish landlord. Of the four, only Mike, the wide boy, was a creation of the Eighties and yet he was the character who provoked the least laughter. For until deep into the decade, the favourites remained the old favourites. *The Two Ronnies* and *Morecambe and Wise* still set the nation laughing, as, until his death in 1984, did Tommy Cooper. Their baton was picked up by Cannon and Ball and Little and Large. The direct, apolitical and apparently artless comedy of former years never lost its hold, and many comics whose oeuvre might be thought antithetical to variety later paid tribute to that tradition.

In the Eighties, a second musical invasion occurred. After the dip of the Seventies, British pop music began once more to startle and surprise, and the American charts were soon awash with British acts. A third of all 'chart-toppers' were British; such an invasion had not been seen since the Sixties. For decades, popular music had been driven by a quest for the 'authentic', with the 'serious' musician habitually looking backwards to an heroic age of purity. In the Eighties the source of inspiration shifted: the future now issued a peremptory summons. The anthem for this change was the suggestively titled 'Video Killed the Radio Star' by the Buggles. Style was all, and it was a style in which the wildest retrogression mingled with an almost astringent futurity. The names of the groups themselves evoked this: Visage, Depeche Mode, Culture Club, the Style Council, New Order, the Human League, Spandau Ballet, Ultravox, Orchestral Manoeuvres in the Dark, Gary Numan and the Eurythmics. The alarmingly named Kajagoogoo had begun its brief life in the public eye as 'Art Nouveau'. In Adam and the Ants, the dandy had returned, but without the menace and aggression of the Fifties Teddy boys. Adam Ant was swathed in the glittering lustre of a Regency beau at a masquerade or the voluminous cloak of a highwayman. Elegance could find other manifestations: Spandau Ballet and Duran Duran performed in what seemed to be the best of Savile Row tailoring. The 'New Romantics' was the term applied to many of these groups.

The guitar, the supremely working-class instrument, now ceded place to the synthesizer, an unmistakable symbol of modernity. This portable electric keyboard provided the distinctive sound of the early Eighties with a frantic but colourless buzz. The prevalent timbre of the voices was dull and punctuated by leaps into falsetto. The old word 'band', connoting brotherhood, was replaced by 'group'; impersonal, expressive of nothing. It was a fitting reflection of the age. Indeed, with 'groups' springing up and dying back over mere months, it was small wonder that many artists, women in particular, chose to go solo. The pop musicians of the period were seldom openly gay, but it scarcely mattered; the queer ethos was everywhere. As if in reaction, groups like Wham! evoked the style of Fifties rockers in their sun-swept, if ersatz, masculinity. In one of the period's better ironies, it transpired that George Michael, the lead singer and the supposed embodiment of clean-cut heterosexuality, was himself gay.

And at a time when homosexuality had become the object of increasing hostility, gay groups were well placed to resurrect a forgotten musical genre in the protest song. Frankie Goes to Hollywood was a largely gay group whose music suffered so much tinkering in the studio that only trace elements of its members' contribution were discernible. The public cared little, however. In 'Relax', they offered a song so obviously suggestive of sex that it was taken off the air. In the video for 'Two Tribes', world leaders were shown in a boxing ring. During the Seventies, English musicians had largely eschewed the great questions of the day; even the Sex Pistols addressed them only obliquely. In any case, no focus for anger could exist when there was still a political consensus. In the Eighties, an enemy had arisen in the human shape of Margaret Thatcher. Now a spring of dissent could blossom.

By the late Eighties, the individualism of most recent music had receded before a movement whose aim, if it had one, was the dissolution of the self. 'Acid house' had arrived from the United States by way of the party island of Ibiza. It was an almost entirely electronic confection, with musicians nowhere to be seen. The dull thrum of the beat was overlaid by a still darker bass note, and within those liberal confines the 'songwriters' were free to add whatever tunes or lyrics they could lift from other artists. The effect could be mesmerizing or galvanizing. LSD was the *amuse-bouche* for early acid house. However, the drug was quickly displaced by MDMA or, when taken in pill form, 'ecstasy'. The emblem for the drug, and for the music, was a smiling face. For a time, the ravers were indeed all smiles, but the drug was still illegal. The government began to clamp down on the revellers and the concerts decamped to the countryside, where 'raves' could continue unmolested. 'House party' no longer evoked a weekend away in a stately home, but a vast open-air concert in the dead of night. There was a gathering known as the 'Second Summer of Love' in 1988, where 50,000 attended, and a third in 1989.

Initially these conclaves proved almost impossible for the law to detect. However obvious the signs of their presence – lorries, lights, stadia, music swelling over fields of sugar beet – the raves could spring up anywhere, and the organizers proved adept at luring the police into countryside cul-de-sacs. But such strategies fell victim to an ancient principle: once the crime has been committed, time favours the law. The police began to adopt the methods of their quarry and soon the illegal outdoor 'rave' became little more than a wistful memory.

The music itself was to prove yet another example of the English genius for restitching foreign fashions. In front of a solitary disc jockey mixing melodies and beats, dancers swayed and writhed as if before a priest preparing a sacrifice. Indeed, it seems more than coincidental that this movement ripened in tandem with a religious revival, one as striking as it was ephemeral. The Pentecostal movement, largely Afro-Caribbean in origin, had spread to the white suburbs and even into the city. There it became 'charismatic'. As if its meaning had not already changed enough, 'house party' could now refer to a weekend away on an evangelical retreat. There was a surge of new religious movements or cults, with Mormons, 'Moonies' and Hare Krishna devotees increasingly in evidence. The first tales of alien abduction began to be heard and garish rumours of satanic sexual abuse slid into the tabloid press. Happily, they proved insubstantial, but they too were a sign that the so-called age of consumption was avid for the wondrous, the bizarre and the unearthly.

In the spring of 1984, news came that Ethiopia had fallen victim to a famine. Even to a nation jaded by pictures of Belfast bombings, the images of suffering had the power to move and appal. One man was convinced that something could be done, and by musicians. Bob Geldof, lead singer of the Boomtown Rats, possessed an almost boundless force of will. In November 1984, he and Midge Ure of Ultravox composed 'Do They Know It's Christmas?' for famine relief, and it soon sold over 3 million records. But Geldof had only begun his mission. He appeared on television, tired, tousled and plainly impatient, addressing the camera with jabbing finger. 'If you've given your money already, go to your neighbour and bang on their door and tell them to send some too.' In 1985, he employed his formidable skills as missionary and arm-twister to cajole the great and good of the musical world to play at a concert, for free. It was to be called 'Live Aid'. Although George Harrison had established a precedent in a concert for Bangladesh in 1972, nothing on this scale had been attempted. More remarkable yet, it was all arranged within a month. Over a fifth of the world's population watched the concert and it generated many millions; as with many such feats, the purity of the original vision occluded many troublesome questions about its effects. The important thing, as Geldof proclaimed, was that something be done. The idea is with us still: good intentions are sacred in themselves. It was not quite a Thatcherite position, but it suited the climate well and set a precedent. The role of the musician was no longer to furnish entertainment; he or she was now moral instructor and spiritual guide.

Another conception of the artist as deserving beneficiary rather than paid *jongleur* was seen in the artistic community's response to Thatcher and Thatcherism. Indeed, the reaction of many artists seemed not so much emotional or intellectual as olfactory; she stank in their nostrils till they quivered. Jonathan Miller spoke of her 'suburban gentility . . . her saccharine patriotism.' How could such a one understand the aspirations and yearnings of the true artist? The hatred had at least as much to do with her policies as with her personality. Although her government spent more on the arts than its predecessor, it spent less as a percentage of GDP, which could not help but impinge upon an innately delicate realm. Particularly for those in the performing arts, labour-intensive and largely unprofitable as they must be, the smallest dip in subsidy could result in ruin; this was seen in the collapse of the D'Oyly Carte Opera Company in 1982. The answer, Thatcher reasoned, was to bring in the businessmen, which only exacerbated matters for the intelligentsia: was the holy of holies to ring with the vulgar cries of the costermonger? Moreover, the theatre particularly had a proud tradition of leftist sympathies; the values of drama and Thatcherism were thus felt to be irreconcilable.

54

Was she always right?

In some quarters of the artistic establishment, Thatcher was openly declared a fascist. Her politics were understood as 'an authoritarian dogma . . . bright with pastels'. In *Greek*, Steven Berkoff's reimagining of *Oedipus Tyrannus*, the Jocasta character refers to Thatcher as 'dear old Maggot', mentioning that her portrait is on the wall beside one of Hitler. A production of *Richard III* was criticized for failing to make a comparison between the hunchbacked tyrant and the current prime minister. An increasingly politicized Harold Pinter seemed to take it for granted that Thatcher represented a new and sinister mutation of the fascist plague. In popular culture, the notion was still more prevalent. A video for the pop group the Communards depicted Britain as a totalitarian state, with grey overcoats and menacing guards in evidence. And *Spitting Image* regularly portrayed Thatcher in the attire of a military leader who had attained power by dubious means. It may be that the word 'fascist' had lost some of its power as the generations rolled. When Enoch Powell was heckled with cries of 'fascist' and 'Nazi', he remarked, 'Before many of those accusing me of fascism and Nazism were born, I was fighting both fascism and Nazism.'

Thatcher herself was certainly authoritarian in temperament and often in address. She was deeply unpopular even among many who voted for her. She was unapologetic in her belief that the police were the guardians of law and order and should be respected as such. That she presided over more than her due share of battles between policemen and dissidents cannot be denied. In education, she imposed a national curriculum on unwilling teachers, though her influence in that sphere was far less pervasive than was generally believed. During the Falklands War, her willingness to accept help from the Chilean dictator Pinochet stained her in the eyes of many. And it may be that her very poise counted against her: she was always right.

But her regime was as liberal as any before or since; she was a lifelong foe of tyranny; she placed herself in the firing line whenever one existed; she was democratically elected three times; and she gave succour to the impulse for freedom whenever she thought it had a chance of life. The charge that she was a 'Little Englander' was harder to refute, though in truth she was more of a 'Big Englander'; she did not understand the aspirations of Wales or Scotland, and tended to construe Great Britain as no more than a greater England.

But whether a 'little' or 'big' Englander, Thatcher was hard to perceive as a European. This was not through want of effort on her part. She had been an enthusiastic supporter of the Common Market and a leading participant in the negotiations that led to the Single European Act. It may be that landslide of 1987 had lent Thatcher a new sense of confidence that rendered impregnable her notion of Britain leading Europe by its example of capitalist revolution. It was her misfortune to have as antagonist a man whose understanding of the European Community, and Britain's role in it, was quite different.

Jacques Delors had been appointed president of the Commission in part owing to Thatcher's good offices. In her eyes, he was vastly preferable to the alternative candidate, a socialist; Delors respected Thatcher as a 'rich and complex character', who had done much to accelerate the progress of the Single Market. In the aftermath of the Single European Act of 1985, a largely British achievement, they had worked well together; yet few political honeymoons have proved quite so tempestuous or indeed ephemeral. Delors, like de Gaulle before him, found it hard to distinguish between the interests of France and those of the European Community. Moreover, the brash new anglophone world forged by Reagan and Thatcher was little to his taste. And for all his energy and apparent modernity, Delors seemed the denizen of an older world, one in which France ruled the conference table just as Britain ruled the waves. On one occasion, when asked why he refused to speak in English, Delors retorted: '*Parce que le Français c'est la langue de la diplomatie . . .*' (Because French is the language of diplomacy). And in a growling undertone, he added: '*et de la civilization!*' (and of civilization).

Between two such mastiffs, each convinced of the justice of their cause, a clash was inevitable. On 6 July 1988, Delors delivered a speech in which he predicted that 80 per cent of the Community's economy and much of its social and political policy would be determined at European rather than national level. He added, two weeks later, that the 'germ' of a European government was now laid. These statements alone would have been enough to irritate and even dismay the British prime minister, but Delors then committed a more serious offence. On 8 September, he took his case for federalism to the British TUC.

Under Michael Foot, the Labour party had been almost implacably hostile to Britain's membership of the EEC. The European project was a capitalist cartel that had compromised Britain's sovereignty and would render nearly impossible the implementation of a truly socialist programme in Britain. By 1987, with the more pragmatic Neil Kinnock as leader, the party had softened its stance. Speaking quietly, Delors appeared to promise the unions a restoration of the rights they had assumed in the Seventies. 'Dear friends,' he said in valediction. 'We need you.' Almost to a member, the congress rose in enraptured applause. It says much for his powers of persuasion that even Michael Foot, seeing his beloved unions wooed, now began to support the EEC.

Not only had Delors placed himself in the vanguard of a vision that Thatcher could never accept, he was now appealing to her oldest and greatest enemies in its defence. An opportunity to make her feelings known came quickly when, in September 1988, she was invited to address the College of Europe in Bruges. Her speech began innocuously enough, as she hastened to root Britain firmly within Europe, its traditions and values. Then the tone changed: 'But we British have in a special way contributed to Europe. Over the centuries we have fought to prevent Europe from falling under the dominance of a single power. We have fought and we have died for her freedom . . . Had it not been for that willingness to fight and to die, Europe would have been united long before now – but not in liberty, not in justice.'

Up to this point, the speech had been well judged, with references to British help for Europe balanced by praise for Belgian courage. Now she directed the conference's attention to the east. 'The European Community is one manifestation of . . . European identity, but it is not the only one. We must never forget that east of the Iron Curtain, people who once enjoyed a full share of European culture, freedom and identity have been cut off from their roots. We shall always look on Warsaw, Prague and Budapest as great European cities.' The message was plain: Europe must look beyond Western Europe. But the vision, though expansive, was incomplete. Romania, Bulgaria, Yugoslavia, Albania and Russia, having nothing in the way of a capitalist tradition, simply did not count. 'Europe,' she continued, 'will be stronger precisely because it has France as France, Spain as Spain, Britain as Britain, each with its own customs, traditions and identity.' The nation state, not the Commission, should be at the heart of Europe. That this ran counter to at least some of the reforms established by the Single European Act was an irony lost on her. Nonetheless, Thatcher's understanding of a Europe run by European nations was thoroughly of a piece with her support for British membership in 1973. The term 'Eurosceptics' was not yet in currency, but even if it had been, the Bruges speech furnishes no evidence that Thatcher was of their number.

Later in the speech, she made the assertion for which the speech will always be remembered. 'We have not successfully rolled back the frontiers of the state in Britain, only to see them reimposed at European level with a European superstate exercising a new dominance from Brussels.' Perhaps she imagined that this would go down well in Bruges, a rival Belgian city, but it seems improbable. Ironically enough, the expression 'superstate' was one of the few with which none in her party, or in the Foreign Office, took issue at the time.

The free movement of peoples was all very well, she suggested, but border controls were needed if the citizen was to be protected from crime, drugs or illegal immigrants. The speech trumpeted NATO, though with a warning that member states of the union should begin to pay their share. She also invoked her bête noire, protectionism. 'We have a responsibility,' she said, 'to give a lead on this, a responsibility which is particularly directed towards the less developed countries. They need not only aid; more than anything they need improved trading opportunities if they are to gain the dignity of growing economic strength and independence.'

It was a point that was also to be raised by many on the left, for whom the European Community was an overfed giant that squatted on the smaller economies, crushing all breath from them. It was altogether a remarkable affair, but none foresaw how deeply it would alter Thatcher's reputation and her dealings with those in Europe. Howe was forthright when he read the first draft, remarking that 'there are some plain and fundamental errors in the draft and . . . it tends to view the world as though we had not adhered to any of the treaties.' It was a just point, but then Howe went further. While he agreed that 'a stronger Europe does not mean the creation of a superstate', he re-emphasized the unpalatable fact that it 'does and will require the sacrifice of political independence and the rights of national parliaments. That is inherent in the treaties.'

This Thatcher could never accept, yet Howe was right. Clause Eleven of the Treaty of Accession had made it quite clear that the laws of the European Community would supersede those of the English parliament. Thatcher's curious doublethink on the matter ended in what Howe was later to call her 'defection' from the party. Whatever the intention may have been, the speech achieved precisely the opposite of what many had hoped. Thatcher could not but intrude her own vision in a speech conceived to celebrate Anglo-European unity. Now, however inadvertently, she had opened a fissure between herself and her colleagues in the cabinet, in the party and in Europe.

55

Money, money, money

The Conservatives had been elected on a promise of economic salvation, re-elected when recession turned into a boom, and elected again because enough of the populace had become wealthy. New wealth had created new types – along with the 'yuppie' was the 'wide boy', immortalized by the comedian Harry Enfield and his catchphrase 'I've got loadsa money!' This figure marked a revolution. There had been only a few epochs in English history in which 'conspicuous consumption' was not a matter for shame; this decade was one such epoch, but with a difference. The arrivistes of the Tudor or Victorian periods had attempted to array themselves in the ermine of pedigree, but the newly rich of the Eighties had no such anxieties. They did not seek to hide their origins or to emulate the accents of the upper class. They had 'made good' and that was enough.

In tandem with the wide boys strode the Sloane Rangers, a type made famous by *The Official Sloane Ranger Handbook*. The 'Sloanes' were rich, conservative and rural in sympathy if not always in location; they dressed in tweeds and 'ate jelly with a fork'. In many respects they were thought to represent the last hurrah of old money, but this was erroneous. By the end of the decade, those who had inherited wealth still accounted for the top 57 per cent of the wealthy. 'Popular capitalism' was the term Thatcher adopted to encapsulate her vision of a property-owning democracy, an expression that had little resonance and less charm for many of the poorest.

'Care in the community', as it became known in the late Eighties, was an offshoot of the influential Griffiths Report of 1983. The report's main suggestion was that superfluous expenses might be removed if managers could oversee and correct an organization sometimes lacking in efficiency and accountability. In the same spirit, it encouraged the view that the elderly or mentally ill should receive treatment at home. Roy Griffiths believed fervently in the NHS, but he felt it could do better under something resembling a business model. Moreover, the notion that patients could be better served within their own homes seemed a more humanitarian proposition than a lifetime spent within an institution. But many could not thrive or even survive at home, and found too little around their home that could be called a community. The cumulative result was a rise in homelessness. The National Audit Office suggested that the figure in 1989 had reached 126,000.

When a little-known MP named Jeremy Corbyn rose in the House to call the soaring levels of homelessness a 'disgrace', Thatcher barely turned her head. In this case, she could not easily be blamed. By 1990, a startling 100,000 council houses stood empty, and the government was to spend £300 million renovating them. Another 600,000 private properties were similarly unused, and that was harder to remedy. Grants and other incentives to housing associations were provided by the Housing Act of 1988, but the crisis of homelessness could only be eased, not abolished.

The unions had been tamed, but another traditionally leftist foe had submitted neither to lash nor leash. For the Tories, animated by the principle that 'central knows best', local councils were a hydra of jostling irritations. The first of these, predictably, concerned money. True to her conviction that people can be trusted to take responsibility where they feel they have a financial stake, Thatcher was anxious about the seeming unaccountability of so many local councils. If, she reasoned, the rates levied on property were to be replaced by a tax on the individual, members of the public would become true local taxpayers, shareholders with the right to demand proper standards. Councils in turn would therefore have to justify their expenditure and their policies. The notion was first seriously mooted in 1983 and took some years to gestate. When at last the new tax was approved, it was given the most innocuous of titles: the community charge.

A second thistle hid within a paradox. The Tories might govern the land, but their rivals governed the cities. The consequences of this lay in education, which was the responsibility of local government and persistently overlooked by the Conservatives. Those children, the vast majority, who did not go to private schools, grew up under a right-wing government but received a left-wing education. This alone ensured that the shadow of the post-war consensus still stretched over the Thatcher government, and that years after the memory of the Seventies had dulled, Thatcher was still vilified in increasingly vague but no less vituperative terms.

In some left-wing boroughs, the children of immigrants were encouraged to read and write in their mother tongues rather than in English. *Young, Gay and Proud* was the title of a book for secondary school students. The honest impetus behind such initiatives did not protect them from attack. Indeed it was precisely the eclectic approach of such councils that led, some argued, to the Conservative victory of 1987. In its election campaign, the Conservative party placed some of the more provocative textbook titles with the question: 'Is this Labour's idea of a comprehensive education?'

Under Ken Livingstone, or 'Red Ken', the Greater London Council had proved particularly noxious to the prime minister, with its unabashed socialism, its sometimes uncritical support for fringe causes, and its wholehearted welcome of anything associated with ethnic minorities. That it was led by a true Londoner, who recognized that afternoon tea and scones had given way in the metropolis to curry and rice, did not sweeten matters. Happily for Thatcher, the GLC had its gun squarely trained on its own foot. When it transpired that the council had spent more on the advertising campaign to preserve its own existence than the money collected for the Ethiopian famine, its socialist credentials became harder to maintain.

No longer was there talk of the unions bringing down the government, but Nigel Lawson was not alone in feeling that the prime minister's renewed self-confidence in the wake of the 1987 landslide was not entirely wholesome. And this self-confidence was now deployed in an arena where the foe had grown considerably more nimble. Thatcher's last great achievement in Europe had been the Single European Act. Although it had included legislation that freed the Community from any internal trade restrictions, the act also paved the way for monetary union. It was perhaps an uneasy recognition of this that had led to the Bruges speech. But now an unsettling shift had occurred. Where before Thatcher had been at the heart of matters, pushing for ever fewer trade restrictions, she now seemed alone. It is possible that her very strength now seemed an anachronism; the new Europe, under Jacques Delors, had a warm embrace for biddable ciphers, not for those who knew their own minds, however flawed.

Unsuspected by Thatcher or Reagan, the eastern bloc had been steadily crumbling for years. The nations of central and Eastern Europe relied on Russia for their oil and gas, and on Western loans for much else. Russia itself needed Eastern Europe for raw materials. It could not continue. Eastern Europe faced bankruptcy and Hungary was the first to go, slipping away from the bloc in 1988 with so little fanfare that its pioneering defection is hardly remembered. In 1989, the harassed leader of East Germany announced that citizens from East Berlin would be allowed to cross the Berlin Wall. The Berlin Wall was first climbed before being breached and then torn down. Czechoslovakia and Poland fell next. The nations closest to Russia, culturally and politically, took longer, but by that point it scarcely mattered to the West: a great shadow had lifted. Thatcher's own contribution had been ancillary to the contest between Reagan and Gorbachev, but a midwife was still indispensable. Yet what role now for Britain in the uncertain world that had opened?

The European Community had changed too, but here also Britain's role seemed diminished. Jacques Delors had imbued the increasingly tired and sclerotic EEC with his own sharply federalist vision, in which monetary union would render national currencies obsolete. More radically yet, such a union would be followed, in time, by its political equivalent. British statesmen since Macmillan had urged their colleagues to press on with European membership in order to influence the Community at its heart, confident that it could 'steer Europe away from federalism'. To some extent, this promise had been fulfilled. On Britain's insistence, the EEC had at last begun to consider those countries behind the Iron Curtain as European. And the Single European Act was a largely British project. But as Thatcher noted, there was no hope of a retreat from the federalist course, and with the unification of Germany looming, Britain's pretensions to the status of paramount European power appeared self-deluding.

But first, the currency question had to be addressed. Both Nigel Lawson, the chancellor, and Geoffrey Howe, now foreign secretary, believed that entry into the Exchange Rate Mechanism could no longer be delayed. Thatcher was unconvinced, but the big beasts were not to be cowed. On 25 July 1989, they warned that they would both resign over the issue. The challenges had begun to mount. When they flew out for the Madrid Summit later that day, an arctic silence prevailed between Thatcher and Howe. At the summit, Thatcher surprised the rebels, agreeing that Britain should enter the ERM. A month later she removed Howe from the Foreign Office, but if she recognized that the anger she felt towards him was now being reciprocated, she did not show it.

On 26 October, Lawson resigned, a decision long in the brewing. In the end, he had been undermined by Sir Alan Walters, Thatcher's economic adviser, who questioned his judgement in an article for the *Financial Times*. Keeping sterling pegged to the fortunes of the Deutschmark had become Lawson's obsession, and even rising inflation could not divert him. It was a rare lapse: he had been responsible for lifting almost a million of the poorest out of the tax system, for sowing and irrigating growth and investment on every side. His was a remarkable talent and the prime minister could little afford the loss.

When John Major was summoned to Number Ten, in order to replace Lawson as chancellor, he found the nation's unbendable leader 'close to tears'. She had never been so outfaced, and now a frightened little girl broke through the carapace. A more superstitious woman might have begun to study the signs: 1990 was full of disquieting omens. By-election results appeared to predict a Conservative defeat. On 30 July, Ian Gow, Thatcher's former parliamentary private secretary, was killed by the IRA. Resignations, defections and conspiracies seemed to loom in the shadows. A month after Lawson's resignation in October 1989, the unthinkable happened in the form of a challenge. Sir Anthony Meyer bid for the leadership. Thatcher received almost ten times as many votes, but the tremors of dissent were unmistakable. The next of many resignations came about largely by ill luck and unthinking flippancy, when in July 1990 Nicholas Ridley resigned over a faux pas in which he had compared European Monetary Union with the Third Reich. As with so many such blunders, much depended on context.

On 5 October 1990, Major and Thatcher announced Britain's entry to the ERM. Major beamed, while Thatcher slipped on her patient smile. She had wanted inflation brought down first, while Major had argued that ERM membership would achieve that. Inflation was then running at 10.9 per cent. Nonetheless, euphoria flowered in the press and in the City. It would take only a few years for the flower to shrivel. The Rome Summit was held at the end of October. It was ragged and unsatisfactory, and Thatcher was not impressed by the Italian chair. At last, Thatcher openly opposed stage two of the Delors Report. She had envisaged the 'ecu', as it was still termed, as a currency that would run in tandem with national currencies, but now it seemed as if it would be imposed. Whatever lay over the hill could not be seen, but Thatcher saw smoke rising, and that was enough for her.

When she returned to the House, Thatcher found it in savage and mocking revolt. Baited by both Kinnock and Paddy Ashdown, she turned and bit. 'Mr Delors said at a press conference the other day that he wanted the European Parliament to be the democratic body of the Community, he wanted the Commission to be the executive and he wanted the Council of Ministers to be the senate. No, no, no.' It was intoned with utter finality. Howe, for one, was appalled. If it was hard for many to see how her position differed materially from his, it was clear enough to him. In her Bruges speech, Thatcher had spoken approvingly of the use of the ecu. Now, an unfathomably deep crevasse had opened.

On 1 November, having been effectively demoted and disparaged, Howe resigned as deputy prime minister and lord president of the council. He asked to speak in the House to explain his decision, and in soft tones began to dismantle his colleague and former ally, the prime minister. His first remarks were suffused with quiet irony. 'If some of my former colleagues are to be believed, I must be the first minister in history who has resigned because he was in full agreement with government policy.' Thatcher sat still, head cocked, an indulgent smile on her lips. 'Not one of our economic achievements,' he continued, 'would have been possible without the courage and leadership of my right hon. Friend.' Thatcher's smile did not alter. He invoked too their former collaboration in Europe, 'from Fontainebleau to the Single European Act'. Then, with the preliminary courtesies performed, he began the attack. 'There was, or should have been, nothing novel about joining the ERM.' He told the House that he and Lawson had consistently urged Mrs Thatcher to join the ERM, before assuring it that he did not 'regard the Delors Report as some kind of sacred text'. He invoked Macmillan, who in 1962 had urged the nation to take its place at the heart of the EEC. Howe protested that we should not 'retreat into a ghetto of sentimentality about our past and so diminish our own control over our own destiny in the future . . .' He went on to say that 'had we been ready, in the much too simple phrase, to surrender some sovereignty at a much earlier stage . . . we should have had more, not less influence, over the Europe we have today. We should never forget the lesson of that isolation.' A choice between a Europe of entirely independent states and a federal one was 'a false antithesis, a bogus dilemma . . . as if there were no middle way. We commit,' he urged, 'a serious error if we think always in terms of surrendering sovereignty.' He contrasted Churchill's stance with 'the nightmare image sometimes conjured up by my right hon. Friend . . . who seems sometimes to look out upon a continent . . . scheming, in her words, to "extinguish democracy", to "dissolve our national identities" and to lead us "through the back-door into a federal Europe". What kind of vision is that, Mr Speaker . . . for our young people?

'None of us wants the imposition of a single currency,' he assured the House. 'The risk is not imposition but isolation . . . with Britain once again scrambling to join the club later, after the rules have been set . . . Asked whether we would veto any arrangement that jeopardized the pound sterling, my Right Honourable Friend replied simply, "Yes." The question of the ecu would be addressed "only by future generations. Those future generations are with us today."'

Visibly warming to his theme, Howe decided that a cricketing metaphor might be apt. The chancellor and the governor of the Bank of England, he suggested, had been placed in the position of 'opening batsmen . . . only for them to find, the moment the first balls are bowled, that their bats have been broken before the game by the team captain'.

The House laughed loud and long. Nigel Lawson, in the row behind Howe, permitted himself the briefest flash of a grin. He then quoted a letter to him from a British businessman living and working on the Continent, trading in Brussels and elsewhere, who wrote that 'people throughout Europe see our Prime Minister's finger wagging and hear her passionate, "No, No, No", much more clearly than the content of the carefully worded formal texts.' A little later, Howe's reserve broke. 'Cabinet government is all about trying to persuade one another from within . . . the task has become futile.' If there had been any doubt as to Howe's real intent, it was dissolved by his final words: 'The time has come for others to consider their own response to the tragic conflict of loyalties with which I have myself wrestled for perhaps too long.' The House heard the simple words of a man honestly aggrieved. It was a reliably devastating device.

The next day, Michael Heseltine formally challenged the prime minister for the leadership. He had had a mixed career under Thatcher's rule. While he had done much to invigorate Liverpool and the Docklands area, and had served well as the government's 'ambassador' in its dealings with environmental groups, he was perhaps too flamboyant and ambitious to garner very much affection in the House. He was also a passionate Europhile at a time when such a loyalty seemed suspect. Less than five years previously, he had resigned from the cabinet over the so-called 'Westland affair', a controversy so involved and intricate that Thatcher later reflected, 'I can't even remember what the actual Westland thing was about now.' Few could.

At root, it was the tale of an ailing helicopter company that some felt needed to be rescued. Two bids for Westland had been made, one American and one European. Michael Heseltine, as defence secretary, had strongly supported the European bid. Given that it was the less 'capitalist' of the alternatives, offering far more bureaucracy than its rival, it was never likely to have Thatcher's support. In an effort to contain him, Thatcher placed Heseltine under something like a gagging order, but it proved quite ineffective. On 9 January, he demanded in cabinet that all the options be discussed, and when Thatcher refused, he swept out and announced to the press outside that he had resigned. As he gathered his papers, she said simply, 'I'm sorry.' Whether or not she was sincere, the sentiment was widely shared. Indeed, 'Tarzan', as Heseltine had become known, enjoyed far greater popularity than the prime minister herself. Moreover, he had not been idle in his five years on the back benches. He had toured constituency associations all over the country, sounding out support obliquely but unmistakably.

Heseltine's gesture dominated the headlines, but the matter of greater moment was the cabinet's agreement to approve the community charge, introduced on 1 April 1989 in Scotland and a year later in England. The choice of April Fool's day was an unhappy one; the sly, bland misnomer never caught the public imagination and it was soon replaced by 'the poll tax'. A fomenter of riots and a slayer of kings, the poll tax had brought down Richard II himself, and the attempt to implement it proved disastrous from the outset. It was formidably difficult to collect, and its manifest inequities enraged even natural Conservatives. While it might have seemed only fair that the citizen should pay for what he or she received in services from the local council, the less well-off were immediately disadvantaged. How could it be just that a poor widow should pay as much as a millionaire? A campaign of non-compliance began, under the slogan 'Can't pay, won't pay'. Kenneth Baker, architect of the tax, assured the country on television that 'the community charge is here to stay'. The bland complacency in his smile seemed to many to sum up the government's attitude to all popular discontent, and then came the riots.

On Saturday, 31 March 1990, a protest in Trafalgar Square was blocked by the police. In minutes, violence had erupted. The nation saw mounted policemen charging at civilians, but felt no sympathy for the forces of the law. Thatcher blamed 'Marxists' for the violence, and the Marxists blamed the anarchists, but behind the whole protest movement lay the Militant tendency. Thatcher's sympathies were plain: at the sight of smashed windows and overturned cars she could only exclaim, 'Oh, those poor shopkeepers!'

After her grand 'No, no, no' in the Commons, popular perceptions of Thatcher shifted. She was increasingly regarded as unhinged as well as tyrannical. *Spitting Image* presented her with the manner of a Nero or Caligula, with rolling eyes and fiddle in hand. But she was not deranged nor even deluded, merely blinkered. She was, however, alone, having sacked more ministers than any other prime minister in British history. The poll tax had put her at odds with the nation, and her position on Europe with her own party. With Whitelaw incapacitated by a stroke, and Tebbit having left the cabinet to care for his wife, she had lost both her protectors, the guard dog and the guardian angel. Like many ministers before and since, Howe resigned when there was comparatively little to resign from. As far as he was concerned, the captain seemed bent on scuttling the ship. It was a just cause for mutiny.

56

The curtain falls

In the first ballot of the leadership contest, Thatcher won her majority, and expressed almost oleaginous pleasure to the cameras. But it was a charade and all knew it; her majority was not large enough to fend off a second ballot. Had only two of Heseltine's supporters voted the other way, she would have won outright. The outcome of a second ballot was far from certain. Heseltine was not popular enough to win, but the fact that he had lost by a whisker boded no good. One by one, her ministers came to visit her. None could guarantee the loyalty of his colleagues.

On Thursday 22 November, Thatcher announced her resignation. Tebbit was to call Heseltine 'a serial Conservative assassin'. The image is not altogether apt: an assassin usually works for others. In the House, Thatcher was greeted by waving ballot papers. When pressed by the opposition on the question of betrayal, she supported her party. Privately, she was distraught. Alan Clark, a true believer, attempted to turn her mind to the glories of the past, but she could not be distracted. The nation did not mourn, but the staff at Downing Street openly wept as they presented her with a silver teapot. 'How useful,' was her characteristic response. A camera pointed at her limousine caught her leaning forward, with tears in her eyes and biting her lip.

Her vision had been refracted through prisms softer than her own, but when she spoke her mind, without filter or script, the effect was too often discordant and divisive. And towards the end, she even spoke her mind in defiance of government policy. Not Salisbury, Disraeli, Baldwin or even Sir Robert Walpole had sought so openly to remould the nation in their image. For this attempt alone, popular memory has found it hard to forgive her. Then must be reckoned the 3 million who lost their jobs in her battle with inflation, the hammer taken to the old mining communities, the disintegration of union power, her perceived philistinism, her weakness for tub-thumping, and the suspicion, shared by colleagues and country alike, that she could not listen.

In her own eyes, Thatcher had not ended the post-war settlement but had simply withdrawn it to the frontiers of the feasible. Certainly she did not turn Britain into a copy of the United States, as some suggested. In 1979, Thatcher found herself at the head of a mixed economy, and it was a mixed economy that she bequeathed, though the balance had tilted in favour of the private sector. But she did offer security, of a sort – security for the future, in bricks and mortar, in shares and investments, in a promise of wealth that could be passed on. Perhaps she would have wished the City less acquisitive, British culture less avid for pleasure, or the people less stubborn, but these were birds she had hatched. When Kingsley Amis told his heroine that his latest book concerned a Communist takeover of Britain, Thatcher advised him to 'get another crystal ball'. And indeed she proved the better seer. Yet although she contributed to the end of the Cold War, it seemed to some as if she had no real desire for a peaceful settlement. She could never quite acclimatize herself to a world without the Red Menace. It had been the enemy for so long that she found it hard to identify new enemies except in relation to old.

When she left Downing Street, the Iron Lady floated away to political oblivion. But she could comfort herself with one certainty: John Major, her appointed *dauphin*, would surely continue her work. He had defeated Heseltine and Douglas Hurd. The 'boy from Brixton', charming, unassuming but tenacious, was 'gold, just gold', she told others. If he was wanting in fierce conviction, if he appeared a little too pragmatic on European questions, he was nevertheless 'one of us'.

* * *

That John Major would succeed Thatcher in vision as well as in office was taken for granted by all save Major himself. For all his apparent mildness, Major was resolved to be a leader. The differences, both in style and in address, were legion. Some were more subtle than others. Thatcher may be called the last of the truly 'English' prime ministers of the twentieth century. She had wanted not only a nanny but 'an *English* nanny' to bring up her children. This sense of Englishness also informed her attitude to the Celtic nations. As a Londoner, John Major was only incidentally English, and his outlook was metropolitan rather than national. 'What has the Conservative Party to offer to a working-class kid from Brixton? It made him Prime Minister.' So ran the party slogan for the 1992 election. The suggestion was cunning, if not entirely accurate. His father had run a business making that most English of artefacts, the garden ornament, and his mother had been a music hall artiste. The Majors' fortunes dipped when the business ran into difficulties and the family was obliged to move into lodgings. Despite later claims, the family was more of the lower middle than of the working class, but the diligence so often associated with that group was not noticeable in the young John. He left school with only three O levels and a deep sense of shame for having let his parents down.

Once he had been elected as an MP, however, Major's progress was startlingly swift. He became prime minister after only two years in the cabinet, during which time he had been foreign secretary and chancellor of the Exchequer. This remarkable ascent was to prove a mixed blessing; he had little experience and almost nothing in the way of identifiable political conviction. His great strengths, however, were already apparent. Where other politicians would pay attention chiefly to those they thought might be of use, Major greeted everyone with unaffected warmth. If anything, he paid more attention to ordinary people, seeming happiest when chatting to elderly mothers or attendant wives. He was, moreover, famous for an almost photographic memory for names and faces, and an attention to detail which impressed all who spent even a little time in his company. It was as well that Major had already established a reputation for emollience, for the clan of which he found himself head was a bloody and fractious one. Sharply aware of this, he divided his cabinet almost equally between the left and right wings of his party.

His would be a rule by consensus, cabinet 'as it should be', as one former minister put it.

The 'flagship' of Thatcherism, the poll tax, had evoked Thatcher at her most doctrinaire, and was popularly thought to have destroyed her. Aside from its tainted association, the tax proved as unworkable as it had been unpopular. Fittingly, it fell to Michael Heseltine to put the already moribund community charge out of its misery. He replaced it with the 'council tax', a comparatively innocuous levy that is still with us. The poll tax had been in existence for less than a year, costing over £1.5 billion to set up and dismantle. In other respects, too, it proved costly. The Tory presence in Scotland took more than a generation to recover.

But before any domestic matters could be settled, the instinctively pacific John Major found himself leading a nation at war. In the previous year, a crisis had arisen in the Persian Gulf. Saddam Hussein, the bellicose ruler of Iraq, had invaded the gulf state of Kuwait, ousting its emir and redirecting its oil supplies to Iraq. The crisis came in the last stages of the Cold War, and President Bush had other reasons for bringing about a swift conclusion. The international community was supportive of the United States, and Britain, the United States' chief ally, could scarcely be seen as a laggard.

Bush invited Major to Camp David. The gesture was presented as a meeting of families as much as of war leaders, but few doubted its true purpose. The president felt it best to address the real issue immediately: Iraq had been given until Thursday, 2 November 1990 to withdraw, but the president was under little illusion that it would comply. Diplomacy would still be employed, but, 'John,' he said, 'if all this fails, we're going to have to commit our troops in battle.' Major assented. The United States could count on its ally, and it was made clear that neither cabinet nor parliament need be consulted. Like Thatcher, Major had been expecting war; unlike her, he approached it with no relish. He concealed his reservations so well that the president saw only wholehearted support. The meeting was otherwise affable and informal. Major's style was more friendly and casual than Thatcher's had been and the president warmed to him accordingly.

Saddam proved intransigent and the deadline for withdrawal loomed. War had become inevitable. On 16 January, the air attack would begin, a largely American effort intended to destroy at least 50 per cent of Saddam's airborne strength. The counterinvasion was to be termed Operation Desert Storm. Before sending his troops to possible death, Major wanted to speak to them. He had no military experience of which to boast, even in the form of national service. All the more reason therefore for him to speak and, above all, to listen. When he met the troops, he quickly discovered that uncertainty was the chief concern. When Major told them that in all probability they were to be called upon to fight, he sensed mass relief. In spite of his military inexperience, he was in his element. The troops found him approachable and good-humoured. And Major was struck, above all, by the youth of the soldiers; they were, he reflected, no older than his own children.

He had promised the troops that the nation was behind them. This was true in part, but to people in their late teens and early twenties, weaned on a progressive and even pacifist education, this was a war fought not to contain aggression but to keep the oil flowing. But if expressions of disquiet were small and even unpopular – it was not unknown for students to be jostled or even assaulted – they established a precedent that would be followed on a far greater scale. The war itself was won by the spring. As a war leader, Major had been vindicated. Now a very different kind of struggle beckoned, one which he was determined should not bear the character of a conflict.

1991 was the year in which the communities of Western Europe met in Maastricht to determine the future direction of the European project. Major described himself as neither Europhile nor Eurosceptic, but as chancellor he had made his support for Britain's entry to the ERM plain. It was at Maastricht that the strands of theory, economic expediency and political necessity were woven together. There, the European Economic Community became the European Union. Major's was among the younger, more vigorous voices, and this, combined with his tenacity, ensured that two treasured 'opt-outs' were embedded in the final document. The United Kingdom would be obliged to accept neither the Social Chapter, in which were enshrined the rights to a minimum wage and to a maximum working week, nor, in the immediate future, monetary union. But critics were quick to point out that these assertions of power placed Britain on the fringes of influence, while doing nothing to halt the federalist advance. The treaty cannot be said to have aroused much enthusiasm among the English people, but it had consequences that were overlooked in the usual partisan squabbling. The Single European Act of 1987 had turned the Common Market into the Single Market; Maastricht removed any doubt that something far more comprehensive lay ahead.

57

The fall of sterling

The journalist Simon Heffer went so far as to proclaim that 'nothing happened at Maastricht to keep Britain off the conveyor belt to federalism; indeed, quite the reverse'. This was perhaps an exaggeration, but it could not be doubted that, in obtaining the concessions it did, the Major government was implicitly offering a concession of its own. Britain could be only a rock in the midst of the federalist tide; it had no power to turn it. When Major commended the treaty to the House of Commons, he appeared to acknowledge as much, if only by omission: 'This is a treaty which safeguards and advances our national interests. It advances the interests of Europe as a whole. It opens up new ways of co-operating in Europe . . . It is a good agreement for Europe, and a good agreement for the United Kingdom. I commend it to the House.'

In the eyes of moderates across the House, quiet persistence had succeeded where intransigence had failed. Even some Eurosceptics were pleased, or at least relieved. Thatcher herself largely kept her counsel, though in a private letter to Sir Bill Cash, a prominent Eurosceptic, she expressed the belief that the new direction of the EU was 'contrary to British interests and damaging to our parliamentary democracy'. The rapture, or relief, in England was not altogether echoed on the Continent. Many were irritated by the opt-outs that Britain had secured. A federal Europe was the inevitable destination, so why did Britain insist on a back route? It should be noted that throughout the process, the mandarins of the Commission were perfectly clear in their intent. As one negotiator observed, 'It's getting tiring having to drag Britain along . . . we can lose the word "federalism" if they want, but . . .' The elision was eloquent. In the event, 'subsidiarity' was the genial obfuscation selected in preference.

It was at the committee stage in parliament that the treaty's labour pains began. Beside the Labour party, which wanted the opt-outs removed, the government had to reckon with dissent in its own ranks. At the treaty's second reading, twenty-two 'Maastricht rebels' either voted against the government or abstained. Having lost the whip for their integrity, or audacity, few among them were surprised when it was returned to them. Major had intended this as an act of magnanimity but it was interpreted as weakness. On and on the negotiations trudged, with the rebels tabling amendment after amendment. With defeat looming again, it seemed that only another election could resolve the matter, but rather than take the issue to the country, he took it to the House. A confidence motion was proposed, and Major obtained his mandate. And so, after almost two years of prevarication and obstruction, the Maastricht Treaty was passed, by forty votes, on 20 July 1993.

It is easy now to forget the comparative youth of the movement known as Euroscepticism. Unlike Enoch Powell or Tony Benn, whose shared hostility to the European project was radical and immovable, the Eurosceptics were simply Thatcherite: they wished Britain to remain in the European Community, but in a free trade association rather than as part of a single polity. Any desire to 'liberate' Britain from Europe was confined to the fringes of the Right and the Left. But the fringe was now wider and its voice far louder. The treaty had been passed in a sullen, angry mood. Only months after Maastricht, the tycoon James Goldsmith set up the Referendum party. Its stated aim was to have a referendum on the subject of Britain's continued membership of the EU, but many saw in this only resurgent nationalism. Similarly, the United Kingdom Independence Party, or UKIP, appeared in 1994 with a stated aim of withdrawing from the EU altogether. These two were regarded for a time as follies rather than parties, but they were at least 'respectable', disavowing the far right, its beliefs and all its works.

But in the early Nineties new groups were seen. Flyers began to appear on street corners and in telephone booths, depicting a skull with a Nazi helmet and urging violence against 'the Enemy'. Names never before heard began to enter the lexicon. There was 'Combat 18', whose aims were openly terrorist. The British National Party, their first patron, was too soft for them. 'Race – not nation,' they proclaimed. There were also the mysterious 'White Wolves', who eagerly claimed every murder of a minority member as their own doing. The placatory but insidious voice of extreme nationalism, the League of St George, once excused James Goldsmith for being Jewish, however, conceding that 'none of this is his fault'. Xenophobia has rarely been militant in Britain, and most of these groups soon choked on their own bile.

The election of 1992 had been preceded by a long and only intermittently optimistic Conservative campaign. The land was still in recession, and perhaps many missed in Major the ferocity and certitude of Thatcher. Neil Kinnock was the object of much affection and, being naturally flamboyant, he often had the best of Major in the House. Moreover, the Conservatives had been in power for thirteen years. On polling day, the prevalent mood was subdued. Only Major seemed buoyant as he returned to his Huntingdon seat. It was not until the early hours that the miracle became apparent: the Conservatives had won, and with the greatest polling majority ever known. Yet the 14 million votes translated into only twenty-one extra seats. The Tories had been confirmed in government, but their majority was too small to allow them to exercise power as they sought.

Neil Kinnock, so often decried as 'the Welsh Windbag', resigned with dignity – for all his achievements, he had led the party to its second defeat. Like Thatcher, he had a weakness for the soundbite. His advice to those living in a Conservative world had been stark. 'Don't be old, don't be sick, don't be ordinary, don't be poor, don't be unemployed.' For Labour, the defeat of 1992 represented a watershed. Kinnock had been both firebrand and conciliator, a leftist bruiser and a cunning statesman, but his journey was not one he could share with his party.

John Smith, his successor, was by conviction a modernizer, though in an age where cosmetic considerations were paramount, he did not look like one. With his bullet head, his spectacles and thinning hair, he recalled a dour trade union leader of the old school. But his uninspiring exterior concealed a quick intelligence, a sharp sense of humour, and a deep sense of social justice. His judgement, however, was not always sound. While the country and the City were still reeling after Black Wednesday, he launched an attack that would have been more credible had he not himself supported the move into the ERM.

Britain had entered the ERM in the last days of Margaret Thatcher's premiership. Since then, nothing had occurred to make the move seem anything but benign. Nigel Lawson had insisted that British interest rates be tied to those of Germany. Thatcher was unconvinced but when Major professed himself in agreement with Lawson, there was little that the Iron Lady felt she could do but accept. The pound, she ordained, was to be 'pegged' to the Deutschmark at 2.95. When Major, then chancellor, told his opposite number in Germany of the decision, he was told that such a matter was not one for the prime minister to decide. The rules of the EC dictated that the matter be discussed and agreed upon. That was not Thatcher's style, of course, and the rate remained. It was not a propitious start, nor, as events were to prove, a wise decision.

Entry into the ERM, touted by Major among others as a cure for inflation, had by 1992 done nothing to ease the recession of the late Eighties. If anything, it seemed to have accelerated it. One million lost their jobs. A new and virulent strain of poverty appeared, one which struck the previously affluent, and with it arrived a new term, 'negative equity', with houses suddenly worth less than the mortgages taken out to pay for them. Moreover, the high interest rate that Britain was forced to adopt brought the country back to the unhappy days of the Seventies; British exports became once more uncompetitive. Still, inflation appeared again to be shackled, as Major had prophesied. But even here, an objection could be raised. At a dinner hosted by Andrew Neil, the editor of the *Sunday Times*, Major crowed his triumph as the prime minister who had ended the threat of inflation. At this, one of the journalists present asked, 'What's the point of having low inflation if the economy is not just on its knees, but on its back?' In one form or another, the question would be repeated in the months to come.

On the Continent, within the quiet confines of the Bundesbank, troubling events had also begun to unfold. East Germany was now within the capitalist pale of the West, but the cost of its inclusion was climbing ever higher. The Bundesbank was independent of the German state and could take decisions as it saw fit. In the summer of 1992, it raised interest rates. Helmut Schlesinger, the Bundesbank president, felt bound to act according to 'what is necessary at home'. In Britain, the effect was instant. High interest rates hit the housing market, and 'For Sale' boards sprang up like nettles. By late summer, currency traders began to sell pounds and buy Deutschmarks, with the result that sterling sank to the lowest level permitted within the ERM. Once again, a British chancellor was caught in a web of irreconcilable priorities, but despite his private misgivings, Norman Lamont publicly rejected the possibility either of devaluation or of exit.

Chancellor Kohl had sent Major a letter in which he indicated that he would also like to see German interest rates lowered. Major had high hopes. Lamont was altogether less sanguine. At a meeting of national and EC finance ministers in Bath, Lamont was met by protesters demanding that Britain leave the ERM. Neither he nor his continental colleagues were reassured. There was much to be discussed, not least the vulnerable state of many currencies within the EC. For the continentals, however, the meeting was to be a cordial affair, in which delicate matters might be raised, but not quarrelled over. Lamont, however, was desperate, and was not disposed to be diplomatic. The French finance minister recalled his questioning as 'without introduction and without conclusion: quick, brutal, cutting'. Four times Lamont asked Schlesinger whether he would not lower interest rates. Schlesinger, a financial grandee unaccustomed to being berated like a scullion, recalled: 'One cannot be treated as an employee . . . one cannot accept it. I thought, "He is not my master . . . I must bring this exercise to an end."' In an obvious snub, he switched to Bavarian dialect in an aside to Waigel, the German finance minister, saying: 'I think I should go now.' It was all Waigel could do to restrain him from marching off. Lamont left empty-handed.

Worse was to follow. On 11 September, in Rome, the value of the imperilled Italian lira plummeted. Speaking on the telephone to John Major, Giuliano Amato, the warm and expansive Italian premier, had a chilling message for his British counterpart: once the traders have finished with us, they will come for you. But Major refused to devalue, just as he refused any suggestion of leaving the ERM. He was confident that his policy would survive. From Germany came the signs of a faint thaw, as Schlesinger offered to lower interest rates, should the currencies that were struggling agree to 'realign'. This, for Major, was out of the question. For Italy, however, there was no escape, and the lira was devalued by 7 per cent. Surely this would satisfy the Germans? The response was a token 0.3 per cent cut in interest rates. European solidarity appeared to be fraying by the week. For all the public assurances offered by Major and Lamont, banks, pension funds and international companies had no doubt that the pound would depreciate. The result was one of those tragically self-fulfilling prophecies that haunt international finance, a world in which perception is often the principal reality.

Perhaps Schlesinger was still smarting from Lamont's assault; perhaps he was simply putting the needs of his own country first. But when, on the evening of Tuesday 15 September, he suggested in an interview that the pound should have devalued along with the lira, he unleashed a cyclone. Schlesinger later protested that his remark had been offered unofficially, but it made no difference. Dawn had barely given way to sunrise on Wednesday 16 September when the feast on sterling began. George Soros, one of the more avid of the predators, recalled his conviction that 'the Bundesbank was egging on the speculators'. In desperation, the Bank of England entered the fray, buying sterling on a colossal scale, but £1 billion was lost in minutes. The spade drove deeper, digging further into public money. The bank would have to raise interest rates; 12 per cent was agreed by Major. Perhaps he had no choice, perhaps it was the presence of Hurd, Clarke and Heseltine in Admiralty House that swayed him. All were convinced Europhiles. But the interest hike did not deceive the speculators, who saw in it only an act of desperation, and selling increased. Kenneth Clarke's chauffeur spoke for many when he quietly said, 'It hasn't worked, sir.' The politicians had been isolated from events, caught in the tragicomic position of knowing less 'than anyone in the United Kingdom'.

Eddie George, the governor of the Bank of England, realized that 'the game was up'. Britain had to get out. Once again, Hurd, Heseltine and Clarke, the 'big beasts', were summoned. Lamont desperately urged suspension, but the others overruled him. Interest rates were yanked up once more, to 15 per cent. It hadn't worked the first time, so clearly they must try again even harder. The prime minister had mortgaged his reputation; he could not now withdraw. After a negligible rise, the pound slipped again. By the afternoon, the Bank of England had spent £15 billion in defence of sterling. Behind the scenes, the prime minister gave way. At 4 p.m., abruptly, there was silence on the trading floors as the news came that the Bank would no longer shore up the pound. The silence, one trader confirmed, lasted perhaps three seconds, before a whoop of triumph broke out. As if determined to give its audience one last flamboyant flourish, the pound dived through the bottom of the ERM. As one trader put it, 'There was a sense of awe . . . that the markets could take on a central bank and win.' Open competition had turned on its nurse.

At 7.30 p.m. on 16 September 1992, forever known as 'Black Wednesday', Norman Lamont announced Britain's suspension from the ERM. It was to be a temporary measure, he assured the cameras, to be reversed when matters were 'calmer'. The prime minister had remained uncannily composed throughout the debacle, but now he cracked. He determined to speak to Fleet Street; he wanted to reassure the chief editors that all was well and to ask them how they would present the day. But they were no more deceived than the speculators had been. Kelvin Mackenzie of the *Sun* genially informed him that he had 'a big bucket of shit on my desk . . . and I intend pouring it all over you'. Major rallied enough to give the joshing answer, 'Oh, you are a wag!'

A sense of collective responsibility ensured that Lamont remained, but he resigned nine months later. For all his outward protestations, he had never believed in Britain's membership of the ERM and would remember the involvement of Heseltine, Hurd and Clarke with some bitterness. He wondered why the prime minister was spending so much time closeted with the big Europhile beasts while, as he put it, 'we were haemorrhaging'. Major in turn insisted that since it was a question as much political as economic, the crisis was one in which the other ministers had a right to a say. For their part, the beasts felt like 'doctors being brought in to watch the death of the patient'. In truth, there was no ready scapegoat for Black Wednesday; none could have foreseen the alacrity or skill with which the markets leapt on the stricken pound.

Lawson and Major had both accepted that sterling must be 'pegged' to the Deutschmark; only later did their folly become apparent. Beneath the rhetoric of mockery and outraged patriotism, the Eurosceptics were jubilant, dubbing Black Wednesday 'White Wednesday'. Their stance had been vindicated, and by their own opponents in Europe. For amidst all the blasts and counterblasts, the quiet words of Schlesinger to Waigel were heeded. 'In 1948,' he said, 'remember, we had nothing, and look at what we have now. We achieved it by pursuing our own line of policy. We mustn't weaken now.' Thatcher herself broke her long silence to voice her agreement. 'I do not blame the Germans,' she said on 8 October. 'They have managed the new currency in exactly the way we should have managed ours. They put their country first.' And so, despite the avowals of friendship and the appeals to solidarity, the most ardently Europhile nation on the Continent had shown that if needs be it would advance its own interests over those of the European Union. So be it, mused the Eurosceptics. Perhaps the example should be followed.

58

One's bum year

'There's no such thing as Majorism,' said Thatcher dismissively in an interview, but the jibe was unjust. Major was not a revolutionary, but the time did not require such a figure. After the withdrawal from the ERM, a 'disaster' from which the economy itself recovered with ease, it was felt that the Conservative party needed some peptone in its blood, which Major provided. On 8 October 1993, he gave a speech at the Conservative conference in Blackpool that came as close as any to encapsulating his view of the world.

> The old values – neighbourliness, decency, courtesy – they're still alive, they're still the best of Britain. They haven't changed, and yet somehow people feel embarrassed by them . . . It is time to return to those old core values, time to get back to basics, to self-discipline and respect for the law, to consideration for others, to accepting responsibility for yourself and your family and not shuffling off on other people and the state.

As such, it should have been unexceptionable, but Major did not foresee the reaction of the press.

It is imprudent in any government to pose as moral guardian, but the danger here was greater yet. The 'Back to Basics' speech was quickly construed as an appeal to some potent but hazy notion of Victorian sexual probity, despite Major's own denials. It was unfortunate that the country in 1993 was falling prey to what Macaulay termed 'one of its periodic fits of morality'. In this instance, the supposed fecklessness of single mothers was the object. The more right-wing members of the government openly fanned this resentment, evoking the Victorian distinction between 'deserving' and 'undeserving' poor. The party that proclaimed itself a tower of rectitude was ripe for shaking.

The *News of the World* began the frenzy. David Mellor, a close ally of the prime minister, was discovered to be having an affair with an actress called Antonia de Sancha. Piers Morgan, then editor of the *News of the World*, remarked that 'probably every Tory MP is up to some sort of sexual shenanigans'. And so it proved. In January 1994, scarcely a day passed without a Tory MP being unmasked. One vocal supporter of the 'Back to Basics' campaign, Tim Yeo, was found to have fathered a child outside his marriage; it was, to use the period's most popular euphemism, a particularly egregious 'error of judgement'. But not all the peccadilloes were sexual in their nature. Indeed, it was the fact that so many of the scandals lay in banal cases of financial impropriety that alerted Major to a disquieting truth: the press had turned against him. The *Daily Telegraph*, once the Tories' sturdiest ally, was no more sympathetic to Mellor than it had been to Lamont. 'It is not the business of the press to protect Mr Mellor's family,' a leader tartly observed. 'It is Mr Mellor's.'

1993 had been an unhappy year in every respect. The miners had successfully challenged another set of deep pit closures, but the closures went ahead anyway. The government's probity was once more in question. That the pits closed had been the ones worked by the very miners whom Thatcher had praised during the strike of 1984 only added to the gall. Thatcher herself claimed that she would never have permitted such a betrayal.

But if 1993 was hard for the government, the previous year had been troublesome for an institution once thought unassailable. In 1992, Princess Anne divorced Captain Mark Phillips, the Duke and Duchess of York separated, Major announced the separation of Charles and Diana in the House of Commons, and Windsor Castle was devastated by fire. To these dramatic events may be added a slew of photographs, taped recordings and television revelations, all of which were damaging to the monarchy. The queen herself summed up her feelings in an after-dinner speech towards the end of the year. It had been, she said, an 'annus horribilis'.

If the Tories under Major had stinted on bread, they had been more niggardly still in providing circuses. This was to change in 1994. The English had traditionally baulked at the idea of lotteries. Now, in the aftermath of recession, the advantages both to the nation and to the Tory party seemed obvious; all was grey, and a 'flutter' might provide some much-needed gaiety. It might also provide a novel source of revenue, as its critics felt bound to remark. On 7 November, John Major inaugurated the National Lottery, and with it a custom previously thought the preserve of those unfathomable continentals. And if it was, in some measure, a 'stealth tax', it was one that benefited the arts, the sciences and the lucky few who won.

It was in 1994, too, that the last great privatization came into force. The days had long passed when the railways were Britain's boast. The system was complex beyond utility, the machinery archaic, the service indifferent. British Rail was seen as the last great nationalized behemoth and its privatization was trumpeted as a Thatcherite stroke against inefficiency and state planning. Less advertised was the fact that the move was in part the result of an EU directive. The result was a bewildering array of individual companies, each with supposedly discrete responsibilities. That the privatization would improve the rail service was doubted at the time, and the doubts remain. It seemed to many that Major could not get it right.

It was sadly ironic that this supremely conciliatory man should have presided over a cabinet more deeply divided than any in modern memory. Michael Portillo recalled telling Major that he and other Eurosceptics would accept even their own dismissal if unity could be achieved. He could perhaps have played Heseltine to Major's Thatcher but did not take the role. In any case, Major assured him, he would never sack Portillo himself.

The reputation of the Tories for economic omniscience had been damaged by 'Black Wednesday', but there was no reason for them to despair. The recession had ended, and even 'Tory sleaze', the catchphrase of the time, did the Conservatives little harm. For after all, was there any alternative? The generation that remembered the Seventies was still politically alert. The Labour party represented, it seemed, a fast-vanishing constituency. The aspirant working class had long ago settled behind the Thatcherite banner, their ardour for political change dampened by affluence. If there was to be a successful counter-revolution, it would have to find its recruits elsewhere.

59

Put up or shut up

In the election of 1983, a young barrister named Anthony Blair had won the seat of Sedgefield. The man forever associated with the modernizing wing of Labour entered parliament just as the country rejected its socialist wing. As a comparative newcomer, Blair saw that there was no future in that faith, at least not for the British Labour party. It was fruitless, he felt, merely to rail against Thatcherism. The British had elected Thatcher three times, even while rather disliking her; clearly she was getting something right. Thatcherism must be understood and learned from – even, if necessary, emulated. He knew that any change in the party must be radical; pruning would not serve. Under the leadership of John Smith, he ensured that the block vote previously enjoyed by the unions should be replaced by 'one man, one vote'. In democratizing the unions, Thatcher had demoralized them; in democratizing the Labour party at the expense of the unions, Blair sought to revivify it. It was the first of several links with Labour's past to be snapped beyond mending.

John Smith died suddenly on 12 May 1994 of a heart attack. At once forthright and subtle, progressive and 'right-wing', he was universally lauded as a 'decent man'. This is a sobriquet which tends in parliamentary circles to hint at someone ineffectual and uncharismatic, but he was sincerely mourned. Who now was to succeed him? One of the three contenders, John Prescott, put forward the choice with unusual precision. 'The Labour party has always had a socialist and a social democratic wing. I am a socialist. Tony Blair is pleased to call himself a social democrat.' The other candidate was Margaret Beckett, deputy leader of the Labour party and, like Prescott, of the Left. The result of the leadership election left the more cerebral Tories uneasy; Tony Blair had won, and with over 50 per cent of the vote.

The early Nineties were ready for him. The vines of Eastern Europe had withered before those of the New World, the pub had been succeeded by the wine bar, the public servant by the career politician, the celebrity by the 'artist', the adman by the 'creative'. At its most extreme, right and wrong became 'appropriate' or 'inappropriate'. Such curious verbal manoeuvres shadowed another movement characteristic of the time. 'Political correctness' was an American import. When not lampooned, it was assailed as 'liberal fascism', malignant and stultifying. The *Guardian* remarked in its defence that it seemed to be attacked 'nine times as often as it [is] used'. In essence, it expressed what Martin Amis has called 'the very American, and very honourable, idea, that no one should be ashamed of what they are'. Thus, 'the disabled' became 'the differently abled'. While the idiom lent itself easily to satire, the principle behind it survived and even prospered. The Tories found it hard to align themselves with the new spirit. In local elections they polled only 27 per cent of the vote and lost nearly one-third of the seats they had won in 1990.

Although no formal challenge to his leadership had yet materialized, John Major knew that his authority was being undermined by the Eurosceptic right. 'Put up or shut up' was his message to his critics. Beneath the fighting words, however, lay the old conciliatory impulse. The Right had to be appeased. In an interview he attacked the practice of begging and encouraged the public to report it to the police. A furore ensued. The shadow housing minister, John Battle, claimed that by cutting benefits for sixteen- and seventeen-year-olds, the government was responsible for the increase in young people living on the streets. Other social problems arose in Major's 'classless society'. Nicholas Scott, minister of state for social security and disabled people, admitted to having authorized civil servants to assist in the drafting of a large number of amendments to the Civil Rights Bill. In addition, Scott had talked the bill out, speaking for over an hour. Several people were arrested on 29 May as disabled people protested outside Westminster. Although called upon to resign, Scott remained in office.

In Europe, the oft-repeated refrain that Britain would be 'at the heart' was proving difficult to sustain. In June, at a European Council meeting in Corfu, John Major vetoed the candidacy of Jean-Luc Dehaene as president of the European Commission, declaring that he objected to Dehaene's 'interventionist' tendencies, and to what he had described as French and German attempts to impose their candidate on others. As the other candidates had withdrawn, this gesture was widely interpreted as sabre-rattling. Mitterrand declared that 'Great Britain has a concept of Europe completely at odds with that held by the original six member states.' It was an observation with which few could honestly disagree. In the UK, the use of the veto was seen as yet another genuflection before the party's Eurosceptics. The government's obsession with all matters European was revealed to be one that the electorate did not share. Elections to the European Parliament turned out to be spectacularly anticlimactic, with turnout a modest 36.4 per cent. In July, Major decided upon a cabinet reshuffle. Amidst other changes, he appointed a Europhile, Jeremy Hanley, to the party chairmanship and a Eurosceptic, Michael Portillo, to the post of secretary of state for employment.

The party's various 'sexual shenanigans' were damaging insofar as they came in the wake of the 'Back to Basics' campaign; the 'cash for questions' scandal was another matter. This corruption was a reproach to everything upon which the British prided themselves. Two MPs were suspended for accepting money from a *Sunday Times* journalist posing as a businessman. Later in the year, Tim Smith and Neil Hamilton found themselves having to answer similar charges. For Hamilton in particular, the struggle to clear his name would prove protracted, bruising and finally disastrous.

Other problems remained. Northern Ireland dogged Major's tenure, but now at last there seemed the possibility of a solution. John Major welcomed a statement by the IRA leadership that 'there will be a complete cessation of military operations' at midnight on

31 August 1994, but sought an assurance 'that this is indeed intended to be a permanent renunciation of violence, that is to say, for good'. The UK government had repeatedly declared that three months free from violence was necessary to confirm any IRA commitment. This the IRA proved incapable of delivering. Indeed, the surreal alternation between the IRA's earnest public pronouncements and its continuing campaign of violence led many to wonder whether the government's approach held much promise of success. On 19 September, Major said that the IRA was 'very close' to providing assurances that its currently open-ended ceasefire would be permanent. On a visit to the United States, however, Gerry Adams appeared to undercut such optimism by saying that 'none of us can say two or three years up the road that if the causes of conflict aren't resolved, that another IRA leadership won't come along'. That the two sides differed materially on the question of 'causes' was for the time being an insoluble conundrum.

In September, the prime minister gave a speech calling for a 'real national effort to build an "anti-yob" culture'. This was criticized in the press as an attempt to counter Tony Blair's declaration that he would be 'tough on crime, tough on the causes of crime', but such criticisms missed the mark. The 'anti-yob' culture was entirely of a piece with Major's world view. He understood the temptations that poverty presents, but refused to accept that they could not be resisted.

Protests grew over the Criminal Justice and Public Order Bill. It was a fitting response to a bill which restricted the right of public protest, but it had no effect. Tony Blair was a notable signatory to the bill. The *Big Issue*, a magazine set up by homeless people to address homelessness, asked Blair to explain his decision. In a smog of recrimination and impasse, one small symbolic gesture shone out. The queen visited Russia, the first of her family to do so since 1917, but the Duke of Edinburgh, in a rare denial of duty, refused. As far as he was concerned, the heirs of the Bolsheviks were the heirs of those who had 'murdered my family'.

Concerns about what had become known as 'the environment' came to a head in this decade. The 'greenhouse effect' and anthropogenic global warming had both been identified in the late Eighties, but only in the Nineties did they begin to affect policy.

A Royal Commission on Environmental Pollution was established, with the aim of reducing pollution caused by motor vehicles.

In November, John Major announced that 'preliminary talks' with Loyalists and Sinn Féin could begin, in the light of the former's ceasefire. But the discussions continued in tandem with further incidents. Feilim O'Hadhmaill, a lecturer at the University of Central Lancashire, was sentenced to twenty-five years' imprisonment for having plotted an IRA bombing campaign on the UK mainland. It was a winter of problems. In December, the government was forced to back down on a proposed VAT rise after losing a parliamentary vote; the chancellor proposed increased duty on alcohol, tobacco, petrol and diesel instead.

In the meantime, the Conservatives lost the Dudley West constituency – the haemorrhage of by-elections had begun. The Common Fisheries Policy had long been one of the more contentious terms of British membership of the EU, and in January 1995, it sparked a debate in the House of Commons. Why, it was asked, did countries with no historical claim on the North Sea have rights in it? It was a running sore, but the vote was carried. The prison population had risen from 40,000 to 50,000 under the tenure of Michael Howard. A breakout was attempted at Whitemoor Prison, with five IRA members involved. Into this and related matters, the European Commission of Human Rights issued a ruling that, if upheld by the European Court of Human Rights, would remove from the home secretary the power to determine the length of time that juveniles convicted of murder should remain in prison.

Meanwhile, Europe and its discontents rumbled on. Major declared that 'the UK should refuse to participate in a single European currency in 1996 or 1997 but might participate in 1999, subject to fresh, more stringent conditions than those already set out in the Maastricht Treaty'. On 16 February, he asserted: 'we shall retain our border controls'. A joint framework document for Northern Ireland was at last agreed but promptly leaked. The joint framework agreement included the removal of the Republic's claim on the six counties, but mooted a 'north-south body'. It was to be yet another near-win for a government that was not so much ill-managed as ill-starred.

60

The moral abyss

'A disgusting feast of filth.' 'Sheer, unadulterated brutalism.' Such were among the criticisms levelled at *Blasted*, a new play by the playwright Sarah Kane that opened in 1995 at the Royal Court. Both author and artistic director were reportedly aghast at the press reaction. By all accounts the play was not easy to watch, but it was no harder than many other productions from the Royal Court. In this light, 'a disgusting feast of filth' seems hackneyed as well as overwrought and a little suspect. And so it proved. The furore that burst from the press night was nothing more than a puckish Fleet Street plot. Newspaper theatre critics had met during the interval and agreed to make this play a *succès de scandale*. The controversy achieved what controversies tend to achieve, with full houses and long queues at the box office.

Blasted begins with the romance between a seedy, self-destructive tabloid journalist in middle age and a frightened, stuttering girl in her twenties. It is a black comedy, but any summary of the plot must remain conjectural; we never quite know how much is to be accepted as symbolism. In the first act, we are given a nasty, tender and tortured exploration of rape and, possibly, paedophilia; in the second, a homoerotic tale of male violence. Kane herself remarked that the thematic progression from rape to war was a matter of the merest logic.

Thus was inaugurated a remarkable resurgence in new writing for the theatre, compared at the time with the arrival of kitchen sink drama or with the rise of Beckett, Stoppard and Pinter. It showed an attempt to present rather than to represent. The demolition of the 'fourth wall' in Victorian theatre was here taken one phase further, in an avowed desire to make us *feel* the action in a way that even Brecht could not have foreseen. Dialogue tended to austerity; the characters to self-absorption; staging to the unabashedly violent.

Many others followed Kane, the most celebrated of whom was Mark Ravenhill, whose *Shopping and F**king* explored similar questions through the prism of Nineties commercialism. This movement, in some ways peripheral, reflected the state of England at the time in a way that was not formally accurate, but strikingly suggestive. These were the dying days of an increasingly discredited Conservative government, compromised by sleaze allegations and a perceived loss of authority in economic matters.

Thatcherism was 'in decline', but it had left its mark, and Mark Ravenhill and Sarah Kane responded with plays that traced the broken arch over a moral abyss. The violence they invoke is often so extreme as to be unfeasible. Moreover, if these playwrights knew about genuine privation in the council estates, or war, or extreme poverty leading to extreme depravity, then their plays do not show it. But then that was never the point.

In this period, the perceived purpose of radical theatre changed subtly but deeply. The Fifties and Sixties notion of theatre 'changing society' had given way during the Thatcher years to the notion of play as product. Now the theatre as engine of change was lent new life, but the new direction to be offered was never clear. The ideal had a poignant charm in its utopian belief in the power of entertainers to act as prophets.

The hard dirt track of purely political theatre was unavailable to the playwrights of the Nineties. Communism had failed, morally, politically, militarily and economically; now its alternative seemed equally barren. As a consequence, the new theatre of the Nineties had no politics in any sense that a playwright of the Sixties or Seventies would have recognized.

61

A chapter of accidents

In March 1997, John Major gave a surprisingly Thatcherite verdict on the future of the ERM. 'I do not anticipate joining [the ERM] in the lifetime of the parliament . . . Europe may be forced to return to . . . a parallel currency.' The government meanwhile completed the sale of its remaining 40 per cent share in National Power and Powergen. It had wanted to privatize the Post Office, too, but this was a treasure too dear to the hearts of the nation to squander.

The government, in many ways so successful, was cruelly jinxed or, according to taste, mercifully frustrated. Of particular concern was the status of the 'special relationship' between Britain and the United States. Inevitably, perhaps, Ireland was the chief cause of friction. Major and Clinton clashed over the visit of Gerry Adams to the United States. Major wrote a letter to Bill Clinton, but little came of it. The dream of the special relationship could be sustained under Reagan, and even advanced under Bush, but the expansive Bill Clinton and the modest John Major found that they had little in common. The chief issue was once again the unwillingness of the IRA to speak unequivocally about total decommissioning. Major visited the United States, where he found the president more friendly than helpful.

On 29 April 1995, a special conference of the Labour party voted to restore Clause IV, on the need for thorough nationalization, but the new dynamic of the party could not be halted. In the following month, the Conservatives sustained their worst local council defeat in post-war electoral history. On 22 June 1995, with the flourish that he kept in reserve for crises, Major unexpectedly resigned in order to begin a leadership contest and acquire a fresh mandate. With the leadership open, he was challenged by John Redwood, a prominent Eurosceptic and right-winger. But for all his populism, he seemed too much the mandarin. In the event, Major won the leadership contest on 4 July. His mandate in the country might be withering, but the party was his once more. A further cabinet reshuffle ensued, though it did not encourage confidence. The tally of by-election defeats lengthened further, with the loss of Littleborough and Saddleworth to the Liberal Democrats.

Elsewhere, there were riots in Luton and Leeds after rumours that police had beaten up a thirteen-year-old boy. The early release of Private Lee Clegg, a British army paratrooper serving a life sentence for murder for shooting a Catholic teenager riding in a stolen car, also led to three days of rioting. It is noteworthy that the Major government, under a man whose mission had been to unite, suffered more such disturbances than its defiantly anti-consensual predecessor. In August, 'Operation Eagle Eye' was launched in London to crack down on mugging. Sir Paul Condon, who had claimed that 70 per cent of muggers were black, said that he expected this operation to result in the arrest of large numbers of black youths. Under the most auspicious circumstances, such a move would have been controversial, but the circumstances were anything but auspicious. Memories of the death of Jamaican-born Joy Gardner, who had died while resisting deportation, were still fresh. In a manner that was to become familiar, the three officers concerned were acquitted. Riots in the city of Bradford were one result.

Meanwhile, the withdrawal of troops continued in Northern Ireland; once again there were no further concessions from the IRA. Despite Major's good intentions, it seemed to many that the Republicans were dictating terms. In September, the government began 'reviewing' its support for the European Convention on Human Rights. The ECHR had condemned the shooting of three IRA members in Gibraltar. The Convention was to prove a growing irritant to the Eurosceptic wing of the party, and even to the country as a whole. Its judgements were generally admitted to be humane and sensible, but the propriety of its attempts to overrule parliament was increasingly called into question.

In the meantime, Alan Howarth, a Tory MP, defected to Labour, citing the strengths of Tony Blair and the 'arrogance of power' he considered endemic in his own party; Emma Nicholson followed suit later in 1995, though she defected to the Liberal Democrats. The defections were enough to create unease that would soon sharpen into fear.

The phenomenon of 'benefit tourism' increasingly seized the headlines in an England where anxieties about the foreign wastrel elided easily with fears of the creeping power of the EU. The High Court ruled against two 'benefit tourists', saying that local authorities were not obliged to house vulnerable homeless nationals from other EU countries. Nevertheless, the Appeal Court was to rule a year later that local councils had a legal obligation to provide food and shelter for asylum seekers whose right to claim social security benefits had been withdrawn. The Queen's Speech in November showed itself strongly tough on crime and illegal immigrants, a transparent attempt to ape and subvert the Labour party's stated intention of being 'tough on crime and tough on the causes of crime'. The home secretary, Michael Howard, announced new measures against bogus asylum seeking. And as if to remind the electorate of the one area in which the Tories could still claim popularity, the government lowered income tax in that year's budget. But certain poltergeists seemed reluctant to depart the House; on the question of standards in public life, the government suffered a fifty-one-vote defeat. MPs would now have to declare what financial benefits they received from consultancy agreements.

In December 1995, at the Madrid Summit, the introduction of the 'euro' was announced. On majority voting and the powers of the European Parliament, the UK found itself once more isolated. The government's overall majority was now reduced to three and it found itself defeated on the Common Fisheries Policy, but the vote had no direct effect on its policy – it no longer seemed to matter that the government was worsted so often in the Commons.

1996 seemed to bring with it some reprieve, or at least some welcome distraction. In an education debate, it was remarked that both Harriet Harman and Tony Blair, supporters of comprehensive education, had sent their children to selective and grant-maintained schools. Though this was not without precedent, it reminded the House, and the nation, of the sharply bourgeois direction taken by the party of the workers.

In February, the Scott Report was published. Set up to investigate the Arms-to-Iraq affair, it was the most extensive of its kind. There had been no need, and certainly no reason, for parliament to remain in ignorance of high-quality weaponry being sold to Iraq. In mitigation, Iraq had become the greater enemy since its days as perceived bulwark against Iranian extremism. The selling of arms to a rogue nation with which Britain had so recently been at war would have raised eyebrows but little else. As it was, the government seemed intent on obstructing the judiciary at every turn. At last, though with fierce criticism of the government's conduct, the report established that no British arms had reached either Iraq or Iran 'during the conflict in question'. However, the government was perceived as at once bullying and pusillanimous, and it could ill afford such a reputation.

The IRA called off its ceasefire with a bombing in London's Docklands in which two people were killed. More bombing attempts followed, some of which were stillborn. On 15 and 18 February 1996, two other bombs were discovered. The first was defused and the second went off by accident. A hit list was subsequently discovered, including members of the royal family. In a fine display of bluster, Mitchell McLaughlin blamed the UK for 'procrastination' in its negotiations. Naturally enough, Gerry Adams said he knew nothing of the attack. On 5 April, the largest explosive device ever found on the mainland was discovered on Hammersmith Bridge. The IRA claimed responsibility for this, too, as it began a campaign of disruption targeting motorways and rail services as well as London's transport system. The IRA had by no means finished with the ancient enemy.

Over the twilight of the Major years, a shooting star appeared, barely noticeable at first. It was a book, but of the sort usually read with hunched shoulders and furtive glances to the side, for it was not 'proper' or 'real' literature. Yet somehow it caught the imagination of the pensioner, the secretary, the tea lady, the manager, the magnate and the shop girl as surely as that of the pre-teens for whom it was written. Its author's path was not smoothed by mercies. As J. K. Rowling recalled, 'I knew nobody in the publishing world. I didn't even know anybody who knew anybody.'

What followed had no precedent. The book, *Harry Potter and the Philosopher's Stone*, became a phenomenon so striking that for some it altered how books were read and even understood. The plot of the saga may be swiftly summarized. Harry Potter, the half-blood son of wizards, must overcome Lord Voldemort, his parents' killer and the would-be conqueror of the wizard realm. This realm exists adjacent to our own, but may be entered through 'Platform nine and three-quarters' at King's Cross station. The plots of the individual books amount to a system of arches, with any weakness or ambiguity handed over for the next section to carry. The result is that the eyes of the reader are always straining ahead. We see elements of Cinderella, the Ugly Duckling, the schoolboy tales of Jennings, *The Lord of the Rings* and even Christian myth. Some beasts or characters, such as boggarts, unicorns, spectres and trolls, are familiar from folklore; others could only spring from the anxieties of the late twentieth century. Thus, we meet 'dementors', spirits who plunge the sufferer into a state eerily evocative of manic depression.

Critics, commentators and scholars have puzzled over the unparalleled success of the series. At one level, the cause seems clear enough: the appeal of myth does not distinguish the child from the adult. But that in itself would not account for it. Rather, in these books, an ancient theme met a still more ancient motif. There is a secret heir, whose royalty must be concealed from the world and even from himself. A uniquely English sensibility made the translation possible. Perhaps most pertinently, *Harry Potter* united two previously disparate strands in children's fiction, the naturalistic and the fantastic. The first tends to show the child's struggle for 'self-realization', while the fantastic depicts the child taking part in a great, even cosmic, struggle. Uncertain, idealistic and orphaned, Harry Potter is a bespectacled everyman with only the urge to do right sustaining him. The age, too, was ready. In exciting without offending, the books were impeccably Blairite. They were fun, endlessly inventive and a generation was raised with them.

* * *

The Bosnian civil war had exercised Major's considerable energies, but to little avail. Among other leaders, he had stood out for his calmness and sense of purpose. He had drawn up a plan to reconcile the warring parties, but assumed that all would act from their best impulses. When David Owen drew up a plan for the partition of Bosnia along ethnic lines, the Serbs, in particular, would have none of it. Theirs was a world in which the Ottoman Empire was still in place. They referred to Muslim Bosnians as 'Turks'. A prominent Serb cleric stated that the Vance-Owen plan would 'drive the Serbs back into the hills'. It must have seemed unsettlingly redolent of the Troubles in Northern Ireland.

For all its limitations, 'Operation Irma' proved a 'light after dark', as one UN official put it. Major had been appalled by the plight of Irma, a Muslim girl rendered paraplegic by a Serb bomb in Sarajevo. He ordered an airlift, and momentum gathered for a wider operation. When his government was attacked for its perceived tokenism, Douglas Hurd, the foreign secretary, said, 'It's better to do something for someone than nothing for anyone.' The Major government's decision to impose an arms embargo upon all parties equally only served to restrict the Bosniaks, who, unlike the Serbs or Croats, had no neighbours to assist them.

Sadism and violence had been unleashed at home, too, all the more shocking for their domestic setting. In Gloucester, Fred West was discovered to have buried the bodies of countless girls, including his own daughter, in various places around his house and elsewhere. He hanged himself in prison. Rosemary West, his wife, was sentenced to ten terms of life imprisonment. Their house was razed to the ground, the only conceivable commemoration.

In the BSE crisis of March 1996 may be seen the stirrings of a wider crisis, which touched on Britain's relations with the EU and raised troubling questions of national identity. Bovine Spongiform Encephalopathy, or BSE, was a condition that affected cattle whose fodder had been adulterated with animal matter. The symptoms, which included erratic behaviour and loss of motor control, gave the condition the name 'mad cow disease'. The EU acted swiftly, voting for a ban on British beef, a decision challenged by the National Farmers' Union. Thus fell what was termed 'a beef curtain' across Europe, but the effects of the ban on the farmer could not be laughed away. Having insisted that 'we cannot continue', John Major urged a compromise, though one that required a mass slaughter of British cattle. The action was fiercely and deeply resented. Why, some asked, was the government at Westminster so bluntly indifferent to rural needs? Was Britain merely a nation of burghers? From this sense of grievance the Countryside Alliance was born, a long and near intractable thorn in the side of government.

Other divisions were evident. The armed forces minister, Nicholas Soames, informed the House that the British army would oppose any move to remove the ban on homosexuals serving in the armed forces. Four ex-service personnel planned to challenge the ban in the House of Lords, but on 9 May 1996, parliament maintained the ban, despite warning that 'action in the European Court of Human Rights would force a change in policy within three years'. Westminster once again seemed caught between the forces of modernity and those of tradition, with no rudder to guide it beyond the ambiguous influence of Brussels. The Referendum party was one of the many manifestations of a prevailing desire to cut the Gordian knot. That party, among others, spelt more local election disasters for the Tories. And the *froideur* between John Major and his predecessor intensified. Some comfort for the Tories was derived from Jonathan Aitken's exoneration of complicity in the sale of weapons to Iran.

On Saturday, 15 June 1996, the IRA ended yet another ceasefire by detonating a bomb in Manchester. As far as they were concerned, Major had broken faith in demanding the immediate decommissioning of arms. The bomb was the largest ever detonated in peacetime, yet none were killed. It appeared that this was quite deliberate; prominent buildings and government morale had been the only intended victims. The IRA had alerted the police to the bomb's presence over an hour before the explosion: enough time to remove residents and shoppers from the vicinity. Such finesse illustrated a change: together with an undimmed readiness to use force, there seemed a new willingness to spare life.

62

The unhappy year

The winds of the time blew fitful and contrary. On 15 July 1996, the Conservatives tightened asylum legislation, in spite of an amendment proposed in the Lords. In the same month, ministerial salaries rose, with attendant protest. Industrial unrest resumed with a postal dispute and a strike of underground train drivers. British Energy was at last completely privatized, with still controversial nuclear power involved.

The House of Commons Home Affairs Select Committee decided not to recommend a ban on the private ownership of guns; since a massacre had occurred at Dunblane in Scotland only a few weeks previously, the ensuing protests were as inevitable as they were extensive. The shooting of an IRA suspect in the same month only added to the unease. Restrictions on handguns were eventually tightened, but no ban ensued. John Major reaffirmed that all paramilitary activity must cease before Sinn Féin could be invited to participate in further talks. As the prospect of a general election loomed, a reduction of 1 per cent was announced in the basic rate of income tax. It was a token gesture, but the government could promise little else in the circumstances. In December, and amidst further unrest over cash for questions, the Tories lost their majority. The fragility of the government was never more obvious than in January 1997, when it brought two Conservative MPs in an ambulance to attend a vote. The same tactic had of course been employed during the Labour government's efforts to defeat a no-confidence motion in 1979, but that was in a less squeamish era.

With the loss in February of the South Wirral seat to Labour, the government was left in a parliamentary minority. The armed forces minister, Nicholas Soames, came under pressure to resign, having admitted to 'very serious failings' over the MoD's handling of Gulf War Syndrome. Nor was it a happy year for British justice. The Bridgewater Three, victims of a miscarriage of justice almost twenty years before, were at last released.

This paled beside the furore aroused by the Stephen Lawrence case. Lawrence, a black teenager, had been murdered in 1993 by a gang of five white youths. The cry of 'What, what, nigger?' uttered by the youths as they crossed the road to assault their victim might have hinted that the attack was racially motivated, but the police seemed curiously obtuse in that regard. That their own delay in arresting the suspects and their disregard for the testimony of the only witness – also black – might be construed as racist was another possibility to which they seemed oblivious. In a ghastly paradox, there was overwhelming evidence of racially motivated murder but almost no direct evidence against the chief suspects. The errors of procedure committed by the police suggested an attitude that was informed by prejudice. Neville Lawrence, father of Stephen, put it thus in a sombre judgement. 'When a policeman puts his uniform on, he should forget all his prejudices. If he cannot do that, then he should not be doing the job – because that means that one part of the population is not protected from the likes of those who murdered Stephen.' After charges against the five were thrown out, Stephen's parents embarked upon a private prosecution in 1994, but it foundered for lack of evidence. An inquest in February concluded that Lawrence's death represented 'an unlawful killing in a completely unprovoked racist attack by five white youths', but nothing came of this. It fell to the *Daily Mail*, not known for its championship of the oppressed, to highlight the injustice. The next day, on the front page were shown the faces of the five accused with the stark message 'Murderers' above. The *Mail* then challenged the suspects to sue, but they did not. Justice, of a sort, would be served in the years to come.

By March 1997, the government reeled rather than ruled. Yet its predicament was in some ways puzzling. There was no lack of talent, diligence or goodwill. Equally, however, there was no effective majority, too much self-defeating rhetoric and far too many scandals. A general election was called for 1 May 1997. The government's decision, though welcomed by the other parties, was overshadowed by the continuing controversy concerning cash for questions. Allan Stewart became the latest in a long line of Conservative politicians to resign over allegations about their private lives. Piers Merchant, however, refused to resign. It seemed as if questions of guilt or innocence were long forgotten – to stitch the tattered robes of credibility with numbed and indifferent fingers was all that could be expected. When the prison ship *Weare* arrived in Portland Harbour, recalled to ease prison overcrowding, it seemed grimly symbolic.

The issues dominating the election were the economy, the UK's future relationship with Europe, education, the NHS and proposed constitutional reform. On the economy the Tories had cause to congratulate themselves. Under Major, the country had seen the longest sustained economic growth in post-war history. He and his colleagues could only hope that the country would bear that success in mind. On all the other issues, Labour held the initiative. Having now styled themselves 'New Labour', Blair and his party found themselves subjected to a strikingly provocative advertising campaign. In one poster, the Tories depicted him with Luciferian eyes and the slogan 'New Labour, New Danger'. Less flamboyantly, the Liberal Democrat leader, Paddy Ashdown, assured his supporters at a conference: 'New Labour, No difference!'

In the last days of the campaign, the Tories received an unexpected windfall to their morale. On 21 April 1997, Jacques Santer, the president of the European Commission, delivered a 'Message to the Eurosceptics'. 'We have decided on our direction,' he said, 'so there is no point at all in keeping our feet on the brakes – it is even dangerous. Be constructive, not destructive. That is my message for the sceptics – wherever in Europe.' Whether or not it was aimed at the snarling naysayers of Tory Britain, it was certainly construed in that light. Major asserted openly that the Tories had been vindicated in their reserve towards Europe, while New Labour was incandescent. Alastair Campbell suggested that someone call Santer and ask him 'what the fuck he was playing at'. Robin Cook, shadow foreign secretary, issued a public rebuff. And the Tories, gleeful for once, released a cartoon of Tony Blair sitting on the lap of Chancellor Kohl. Was it paranoia or pooterism that led to such a storm? Mr Santer did not mention British Eurosceptics by name, and he had more proximate concerns of his own. At any rate, all political parties were publicly united in opposition to this 'attempt to interfere' in British politics.

In many ways, the election of May 1997 recalled that of 1979. But where the Callaghan government had contrived to find slivers of gold in the dark cave, the Major government saw only defeat. As constituency after constituency brought in its results, Tony Blair addressed the faithful. 'You know I don't like to be complacent,' he announced, although his beam belied him, 'but it's looking pretty good.' Indeed it was; the country had swung from Conservative to Labour by a margin of 10 per cent. For once, 'landslide' was apt; the government was buried beneath its own debris. Speaking of politics as 'a rough old game', John Major tendered his resignation as Conservative leader. Ever sanguine, he had already booked seats at the Oval for that afternoon. One party refused to take its place in the House of Commons. Sinn Féin was bound never to collude with the hated British polity. Betty Boothroyd, the Speaker, therefore issued a prohibition: since Sinn Féin had refused their seats in parliament, they would be denied their seats in the 'Commons facilities'. It was an impeccably English response.

Major's had been a troubled premiership, but by no means a disastrous one. Edwina Currie's judgement that although 'one of the nicest men ever to walk the halls of Westminster', Major should 'never have been prime minister' represents the orthodoxy but not all the truth. Others thought the government successful and its leader sly, but it could not be claimed that it had been a period marked by vision. Amidst the uncertain or ephemeral achievements, one deserves commemoration: one last onslaught on the post-war consensus had been launched in 1991 in the form of the Citizen's Charter. It had been assumed by the creators of the welfare state that those who provided state-funded services would do so with a smile; that this need not be the case was a contingency few had anticipated. Public servants were to establish charters in which their obligations to consumers would be set out. It represented a clear reversal of attitudes traditional since the Second World War, a Thatcherite initiative but one 'with a human face', as Major's supporters put it.

But the face was one of which the people had tired. Major both evoked and invoked the past, whether in his 'Back to Basics' campaign or in quoting Orwell's England of 'warm beer and cricket'. Even his status as a working-class boy made good had begun to count against him as the decade progressed. And if Major had shown that class could be discarded, Blair offered a promise of class transcended. He was, moreover, young, and his voice, emphatic and eager, seemed to carry all the certitude of youth. In place of parliamentary rhetoric, he spoke in an idiom all his own, with a blend of the company boardroom and the popular radio station. He was metropolitan to his marrow.

'Cool Britannia' was the watchword of this epoch. Like Harold Wilson, but for different reasons, Tony Blair sought to identify with the culture of the young. Wilson's courting of the Beatles was not a gimmick; he recognized the value of the common touch, but he knew also that his pipe and his age were against him. For Blair, however, inviting pop stars to Downing Street was an existential statement; in the manner of middle-class public schoolboys the country over, he believed that he could become proletarian by proxy, that ownership of a guitar and cordial relations with working-class pop stars granted him access to the world of the labouring man. A spirit of conciliation seemed to seep through his very smile, always ready to sink into a thoughtful grimace should its object fail to reciprocate. People spoke of the 'Blair effect'. He was charismatic, clearly middle class and 'trendy', although it was John Prescott, the seaman's son and well-known 'bruiser', who declared that 'we are all middle class now'. When Blair came to power, many on the Continent felt in his accession the gust of a warm wind. A fluent French-speaker, Blair was more Europhile than any of his immediate predecessors and understood the sometimes blunt, sometimes byzantine, ways of the European Union. Like Major, he saw himself as the heir to Thatcher, perhaps with more reason. More than one former colleague used the word 'messianic' to describe him.

63

The princess leaves the fairy tale

And so came about the disappearance of a prime minister who had made far less impression on the public than most of his predecessors. Yet that year was distinguished by one shocking and tragic event in the marriage of the Prince of Wales. Charles and Diana were not the best matched of couples. He was a man of strong convictions and a stubborn streak; she had come of age with only a vague idea of what it meant to be a member of the royal family. A curious snobbery informed this ignorance. Her family regarded the German-descended Windsors as parvenus; Diana was even heard to say that she felt she had married beneath her. Nevertheless, in more formal times it could have been the model of an arranged marriage, with each going their separate ways. Their holidays were taken apart; their friends seemed to have little in common. But the public was always present, with ears pricked and eyes hungry.

It soon became apparent, to those at court, that the princess was seriously disturbed. She threw herself down the stairs and used a penknife, a lemon slicer and a razor blade against herself, while her husband carried on his principal duties of hunting and fishing. The truth was that they had nothing in common but the children, but she had the gift of intimacy. There are certain people who for a brief period represent the ideals of the nation and come to embody them. She herself acknowledged this attribute when she recognized that 'you can make people happy, if only for a little while'. The 'queen of people's hearts' was the one figure who came to represent the Eighties and Nineties, principally by first defying and then by ignoring the traditions in which she had been raised.

Diana Spencer was born in 1961 in what would have been the best of circumstances, had she not been the classic 'third girl' and had her parents not argued constantly until they separated in 1967, a traumatic episode that did not leave her. She was to all appearances an ordinary girl, but ordinariness can be one of the most effective disguises. She was talkative, with a marked tendency to giggle, but she was enormously afraid of the dark. When her father suggested that she should be dispatched to a boarding school, she is supposed to have said, 'If you love me, you won't leave me.'

She failed her O levels and in the same period began to suffer from bulimia, but she also began a series of meetings and encounters that began to suggest what a royal marriage might entail. The ears and eyes of the public grew larger. The queen herself played no part in guiding or advising the young couple, although by Diana's own account, the publicly unresponsive Prince Philip did. It seems that destiny or, in this instance, fate, was to make its own progress.

The narrative of the next few years has been retold a thousand times. 'The pack' were at her heels, chasing every move she made. In a mood of deep despondency, she told her sisters that marriage would not be possible. 'Bad luck,' they said. 'Your face is on the tea towels.' It was on the mugs too, with 'my prince', as she called him, supporting Diana with one arm, and her head cocked at an angle. Her reception within the palace elicited feelings of anxiety and betrayal, while her loneliness was compounded by disappointment. It has been said that while a man fears a woman's future, a woman fears a man's past; and so it proved in this instance. Another love still held sway over the prince. There were confidential interviews with 'friends', and books, authorized or unauthorized. 'I never thought it would end up like this,' she told one friend. 'How could I have got it all so wrong?' Their separation was announced in the early months of 1996, and their divorce soon after.

An impulsive and unselfconscious person, Diana rarely calculated the effects of her actions on others, but nothing could have averted the final disaster. She was in Paris with her companion, Dodi Fayed, when they entered the Pont de l'Alma road tunnel and their speeding car crashed. At four in the morning of 31 August 1997, she was declared dead. The press took a morsel every hour, as if watching the collapse of a stock market. At one point, Diana was struggling, at another she was said to be recovering. The nation awoke to news of her death.

Her death released a torrent of tears. These were shed for her smile, for her work with the victims of AIDS and of landmines, for her status as a free spirit and wronged wife. And inevitably she was mourned in mythic terms, as fearless martyr and sacrificial lamb. The shock of her demise in Paris was compounded by the fact that her two young sons were still in England; her former husband hardly seemed to enter the nation's sorrow. Her relative youth was one cause of dismay, but it was her sudden and brutal absence that provoked the greater mourning. Something seemed to have torn out the heart of Britain, recognized even in the overwhelming wave of grief that dominated the days after her death.

It soon seemed as if England had become moist in mind as well as in soul; some universities began to include 'Diana studies' on their curriculum. When the singer Elton John adapted his song 'Candle in the Wind' to celebrate Diana, the nation bought the record by the million. So promiscuous an outpouring of grief inevitably provoked satire. A cartoon in *Private Eye* showed a frightened householder being menaced by two men in dark glasses with the reproach 'We have reason to believe you haven't bought "Candle in the Wind".'

It was Blair who coined the expression 'the people's princess'; it may be that he saw himself in the role of 'people's prince'. But for all the later calumnies, New Labour was not a one-man show. At the apex of the new government stood a triumvirate of equals. Blair brought his charm and Brown his brain and his industry, while Peter Mandelson offered his skills as a strategist. He became known as 'the Prince of Darkness', but the jibe was as frivolous as it was unjust. Like many in the new government, he had abandoned the strict socialism of his youth only with intense misgivings. Mediating the 'message', as it became known, was Alastair Campbell, Blair's press officer. He had been editor of the *Daily Mirror*, and the knowledge accrued there served him and the government well. Under his auspices, ministerial pronouncements became subject to strict censorship; to be 'on message' was all.

Having clawed at its cage for eighteen years, Labour bounded out with teeth bared. If the economy seemed serviceable, little else did. Haste was needed. Under Gordon Brown, the Bank of England was permitted to set its own exchange rates, a concession that effectively granted it independence. It was a move widely praised, even in the Tory press. The government also sought to discard the image of Labour as the party of the cloth cap, backward-looking and aggressively masculine, by bringing 101 female MPs into parliament. The jibe of 'Blair's babes' soon acquired currency, though the term was swiftly dropped. Its mocking successor, 'Tony's Cronies', would take longer to exorcise.

For Blair, Europe represented a wound that would turn septic if not addressed. Major had opted out of the Social Chapter. Blair accordingly opted in, accepting the Maastricht Treaty in all its fullness. Signs of future conflict were nevertheless apparent when, after a particularly difficult set of discussions, the normally ebullient prime minister offered the bleak observation 'We can't do business like this.' With such an imposing majority, Blair could perhaps afford some latitude in respect of parliamentary procedure. In a move widely seen as presidential, he reduced the amount of time allowed for Prime Minister's Questions. There was, he assured everyone, too much to be done.

Devolution for Scotland and Wales had long been on the new movement's agenda. 'Central knows best' had been the damning slogan ascribed to the Tory administrations of the past decade; such an impression of arrogance must be avoided at all costs. Therefore, and in another break from the party's roots, unity would now encompass diversity. In 1997 the government announced referenda on the question of devolution. The Scots had been chafing for some such concession for years, while the Welsh, having spent the best part of two millennia in a struggle with the English, were more blasé. Scotland was given back its parliament, and Wales was offered an assembly.

These were the halcyon days for the government. Even airy talk of a political 'third way', under which New Labour would inaugurate an era of apolitical politics and harness capitalism to serve the common good, found eager listeners. The twin extremes of trade union hegemony and unfettered monetarism were alike disposable. 'Social-ism', as Blair put it, was the new watchword. There was nothing original to this initiative, but it proved a useful soundbite.

In the spring of 1998, the spirit of devolution took a new turn. It was determined that a new London Assembly should be set up, at once a nod to the former Greater London Council and a rebuff to its connotations. Ken Livingstone was not deterred by the fact that his name lay at the root of those connotations. After much internal wrangling, he was expelled from the Labour party for running against Frank Dobson, the official Labour candidate for Mayor of London. Blair had warned against Livingstone, saying: 'I can't think of Ken Livingstone without thinking of Labour's wilderness years . . . I think he would be a disaster for London.' Livingstone went on to prove that the New Labour consensus was not universally shared. Speaking as the newly elected Mayor of London, he began, 'As I was saying, before I was so rudely interrupted sixteen years ago . . .'

Blair's government developed a taste for what came to be known as 'humanitarian intervention', one of the more revealing euphemisms of the period. Robin Cook, the foreign secretary, had spoken of Labour conducting 'an ethical foreign policy', but how could such a policy be maintained? There can be little doubt that some of the causes selected were deserving. Under Slobodan Milosevic, Serbia had already made itself a pariah during the Bosnian civil war. Its subsequent repression of the largely Albanian province of Kosovo led in 1999 to a bombing campaign sponsored by Britain. This had the effect of forcing a Serbian withdrawal but also of imbuing the Serbs with something like the spirit of the Blitz. In Belgrade, posters were unveiled that alluded to this irony. 'We're following your example' was their message.

Less obviously 'ethical' was Britain's support for George W. Bush's bombing of Iraq in 1998. In Sierra Leone, too, the British government intervened; violent rebels had threatened the legitimate government, not to mention vital British interests. Perhaps as a result of this injection of realpolitik, the British venture was successful, but this 'humanitarian' approach to military action divided conservatives and socialists alike. The question of the propriety of invading another nation because one disapproved of its rulers was one that did not deter the new administration. If a minority was oppressed, they were right in every respect, and come what may.

Legislation throve in those fecund years. The Human Rights Act of 1998 was passed and thus the European Convention on Human Rights became 'native'. The National Minimum Wage Act, passed in the same year, was opposed by Tories on the grounds that it would lead to unemployment. It did not, and this failed prophecy did little for the Conservatives' reputation. Welsh and Scottish devolution brought about another, unintended, change. Blair was fond of invoking 'the British people', but with the reassertion of Celtic identity came something like a crisis of Englishness. The West Lothian question remained; it was an anomaly and, some said, an injustice. The Scottish, Welsh and Northern Irish MPs were allowed to vote in the British parliament on purely English affairs.

The matter of the euro had bedevilled the government of John Major. Publicly, Blair expressed himself in favour of the currency, but his chancellor was less enthusiastic and proclaimed five 'tests' for Britain's entry into the eurozone. The crucial ones were whether economic convergence with other European nations could be achieved, and were they flexible enough? The answers remained doubtful, and therefore the euro was rejected. Gordon Brown's Five Tests, it is worth noting, were Thatcherite in inspiration. Despite this, the Tories affected scorn as their response.

It cannot be doubted that in one respect Labour fell short. Where the Tories had been able to mine a rich and colourful seam of scandal, involving sexual indiscretion, bribery and perversion, New Labour could offer only a dusty bundle of financial improprieties. There were some exceptions, of course. In January 1998, the son of the home secretary Jack Straw received a police caution after admitting to possession of cannabis. Straw himself had recently declared that he would not support the drug's legalization. Most scandals, however, were of the 'Geoffrey Robinson' type. Robinson, the Paymaster General, was accused by the Conservatives of hypocrisy after it was revealed that he had failed to register an offshore trust, having abolished tax relief on savings over £50,000. It was a dreary effort. The revelation that Robin Cook had been conducting an affair was more tragic than comic. Meanwhile, the Conservatives under William Hague set new procedures for the election of the party leader; whereas the decision had rested solely with the parliamentary party, the new rules gave all party members the vote, which inevitably led to a swing to the right.

The problem of restricted opportunity had to be addressed and so the welfare-to-work scheme was launched, intended to lift the unemployed out of welfare dependency. In a similar spirit, the March 1998 budget promised 'work for those who can, security for those who can't'. Behind the soundbite lay nothing that Thatcher herself would not have approved. However, disaffection still flourished. In the spring, 200,000 joined the Countryside Alliance on a march on London. The Alliance had arisen partly as a response to a private member's bill to outlaw hunting with hounds, but also to the government's perceived indifference to the concerns of the countryside. There were to be many such public protests during the Blair tenure. The Alliance rarely won its battles, yet its very existence was an omen. The old divide between the metropolis and the land was to become not narrower but wider in succeeding years.

In September 1998, foreign affairs remained to the fore. The government confirmed that it would grant full UK citizenship to 100,000 citizens of the remaining British dependencies. Asylum applications were shown to have risen by 6,000. In a small but resonant echo of the new influx of women to parliament, Marylebone Cricket Club voted to admit women to its membership. At so early a stage, any government would be obliged to pour out a stream of promises; nonetheless, such announcements were evidence at least of excellent intentions.

1999 was as frenetic a year as its predecessor. In January, Paddy Ashdown stepped down as leader of the Liberal Democrats. Robin Cook's ex-wife wrote a book, serialized in *The Times*, in which she wrote of his having felt that he had 'sold his soul to the devil' by abandoning his socialist principles in favour of the Blair regime. Buckingham Palace announced the engagement of Prince Edward to Sophie Rhys-Jones, photographs of whom frequently showed her in poses and styles reminiscent of the late Princess of Wales.

The decline of manufacturing gathered pace, with *The*

Economist reporting that manufacturing employment was 57,000 lower in July than in February 1996, the biggest single loss being British Steel's decision to shed up to 10,000 jobs. The last tin mine closed, at South Crofty, thus ending 3,000 years of tin mining in Cornwall. It was reopened in 2001, having been bought by a Welsh mining engineer, and was once again Europe's only remaining working tin mine. Crofty aside, the mining industry in England could boast of no amelioration. The Annesley-Bentinck coal mine, the oldest in the UK, was closed. Elsewhere, too, the signs were bleak. Fujitsu announced it was to close its Newton Aycliffe semiconductor plant. The TUC urged the government to take 'remedial action'. Blair was sympathetic but made clear that he could not help the 'twists and turns' of world markets, instead promising to 'help the hurt'.

For those with eyes to see, some modest gains were apparent. British Aerospace took over the Marconi defence electronics arm of the GEC, becoming Europe's biggest defence and aerospace company. Signs of progress emerged elsewhere, too. The government again voted to lower the age of sexual consent for homosexuals. Other liberal measures were assured of a similar progress. The death penalty was formally abolished for all offences, in accordance with Protocol 6 of the European Convention on Human Rights.

In February 1999, the Macpherson Report on the Stephen Lawrence case was published. The report became famous for its controversial use of the term 'institutional racism' to describe the workings of the Metropolitan Police, though a close reading of the report reveals something more circumspect:

> It is vital to stress that neither academic debate nor the evidence presented to us leads us to say or conclude that an accusation that institutional racism exists in the MPS [Metropolitan Police Service] implies that the policies of the MPS are racist. No such evidence is before us . . . It is in the implementation of policies and in the words and actions of officers acting together that racism may become apparent.

The expression referred to a culture in which even black officers were by their own admission often complicit. Clearly something had floated up between the cracks of policy.

The government suffered three defeats in the House of Lords over plans to abolish the hereditary component of the upper chamber. Blair himself expressed a certain affection for the sanctuary of ermine and scarlet, but remarked, 'I just don't see what it's got to do with Britain today.' The House of Lords Act of 1999 reduced the number of hereditary peers to ninety-one; thus the great reform of the upper house was at last achieved. But if Blair or his successors imagined that an elected house would be more pliable than a hereditary one, they were quickly disabused.

Nonetheless, many born to privilege were tottering. Jonathan Aitken, whose hubristic lawsuit against the *Guardian* newspaper had backfired, was forced to plead guilty in 1999 to two charges of perjury. Accused of corruption by both the *Guardian* and *World in Action*, he had sued them, armed with imprudent clichés about the 'sword of truth', before the sword duly turned on him. Like Oscar Wilde, he went to jail and wrote a ballad, and, like Profumo, he began a lifetime of penitence.

Social amelioration proceeded apace. A £60 million government campaign to halve the incidence of under-eighteen pregnancies by 2010 was announced; single mothers must be protected, but underage pregnancies avoided. Somehow, a Cromwellian politics could coexist with cavalier liberty. Like Margaret Thatcher, Blair wanted a Britain that would suit his own personality.

Much that was odd or wayward died in this time, though much of the same strand was born. Screaming Lord Sutch of the Monster Raving Loony party gave up his anarchic ghost. And yet a Carnival against Capitalism broke out in the heart of capitalism itself, the City of London. It was, by later standards, a happy affair, with a spoof edition of the *Evening Standard*, the *Evading Standard*, printed and circulated. In similarly quixotic fashion, Tony Blair announced his bill to ban hunting with hounds in July 1999, as the Countryside Alliance had predicted, even though they could not have foreseen the forum for that announcement, on the television programme *Question Time*. It was also a busy month for relations with the Continent. The European Commission formally lifted its ban on beef imports from Britain. The great matter of Europe impinged in other respects. Forty, mainly religious, independent schools confirmed that they would appeal to the European Court of Human Rights against legislation banning corporal punishment in all UK schools. The irony of such an appeal was lost on them.

In December 1999, the Good Friday Agreement, signed in 1998, came into force. For thirty years, the Troubles had blighted Northern Ireland; over 4,000 lives had been lost. How could a tourniquet to the bloodletting be applied? Somehow, irreconcilable demands must be respected and met. Under the government of John Major, a 'three-strand' solution to the problems of the Province had been mooted. Under Blair, this was now implemented. The central suggestion was radical indeed. Northern Ireland would remain a part of the United Kingdom, but only for as long as the majority of its citizens wished it so. The 'Good Friday Agreement', as it became known, would not have been possible without careful movements in the wings of power. Two taoiseachs, three prime ministers, a president of the United States and the leaders of both the nationalist and Unionist communities of Northern Ireland all brought about the conditions for a devolved Assembly and Executive, for 'north-south' cooperation between the north and the Republic, and for 'east-west' cooperation across the Irish Sea.

It almost collapsed. Deadlines for agreement came and went. Ian Paisley's Democratic Unionist party wanted nothing to do with the whole affair. It was made acidly clear to the prime minister that his presence was needed if any sort of deal was to be reached. 'This is not the time for soundbites,' he declared before setting out. 'Let's leave them at home. I feel the hand of history on our shoulders.' He was much mocked at the time, yet after only three days the warring parties laid down their fears, prejudices and hatreds. The Republic gave up its constitutional claim to the six counties, while England repealed the act of 1920 that had formally divided the island. While both nations therefore retained their interests in the affairs of the Province, they had in a sense withdrawn from it.

Blair was perhaps more fortunate than his predecessors. His allies and delegates were more emollient; he inherited happier conditions; above all, the Province longed for air, as the referenda on the agreement made plain. And Blair was obviously sincere in his desire for a settlement that would benefit all. In the end, only the Democratic Unionist party refused to accept the treaty, and the overmastering pull of peace drew the scattered filings together. The agreement was to undergo many vicissitudes in the new millennium. For much of its first decade it was suspended due to disagreements over policing and decommissioning. There were inevitable casualties. David Trimble, the hard-bitten leader of the Ulster Unionist party, had committed his followers to the agreement on the understanding that the IRA would surrender its weapons, and, when it did not, he and others like him were obliged to cede place and power to more radical elements. In England, the news was received with a blend of hope and weariness – most had grown wary of the 'new beginnings' promised in breathless headlines. For those who cared, Northern Ireland had been retained for the Union, but on entirely new grounds. The future of the Province now rested with the people of Northern Ireland rather than with the parliament of the United Kingdom. In constitutional terms nothing of substance had changed, except for the underlying principle.

The land of prophecies and dreams was silent as the new millennium approached. The only prophecy to exercise public concern was dismally prosaic; it was rumoured that a 'millennium bug' would cause computer software to collapse unless it could be aligned with the coming date, but the problem was largely resolved in advance. And so England awaited the new age much as it always had. It may be that the quiet revolution of Blairism had assuaged what longing there had been for change. Despite its roaring for flesh, the English lion is often content with a simple bone.

Still, the millennium had to be marked somehow, and its central image was to be the Millennium Dome. Intended to recall a vast and imposing spaceship, it seemed to many a giant, bloated beetle. It had, in fact, been the brainchild of the previous government: Michael Heseltine had seen an opportunity to reclaim toxic land in Greenwich.

British politics seemed to have come to an end. Post-war dogma had been replaced by Thatcherite dogma. This new orthodoxy was massaged under Blair, but any changes were cosmetic. The once mighty Liberal vote had retreated, and the party itself renamed as the Liberal Democrats, though each of its new leaders assured the nation that they were still a force to be reckoned with. By early 2000, polls revealed that Blair's reputation for trustworthiness stood at 46 per cent, no small achievement for an incumbent prime minister. It might have been higher had his promises not proved difficult to fulfil.

After years of Thatcherism, a more 'progressive' mood could be detected. In 1997, the British Social Attitudes study recorded that 75 per cent of the people said they favoured tax rises for public service improvements. Polls revealed a populace far less exercised than it is now by questions of ethnicity. Concern about immigration lay at 3 per cent in 1997, while interest in foreign affairs stood at 2 per cent. Asylum seekers and economic migrants were no longer a bugbear. The wealth divide grew, although all incomes rose. A benignly self-centred nation emerged.

The Nineties have been called the decade of 'spin', but the novelty lay in the prominence of the spin doctors, who had taken the place of trade union leaders as the most important national figures outside government. The collapse in voter turnout reflected a government adept at soothing the populace; as a result, parliamentary discourse acquired the attributes of a patois: 'tackle', 'raft', 'package', 'deliver' and the suggestive 'meaningful'. Is it uncharitable to suggest that when John Major left Downing Street, he took the English language with him? It may be that he took pragmatism with him, too. He could not match the wild-eyed millenarianism of his predecessor, while Blair was nothing if not a believer. 'The eyes of the world', 'the hand of history', 'the right thing to do': resonant banalities of this sort were his demesne, and for five years they worked.

And so, with many bangs and flashes of fireworks, the twentieth century ended. No bug had bitten, no rapture had occurred, and the frost added glitter to the great white marquee. In accordance with the spirit of the time, the Dome enshrined the future. Yet the past seems to gain in allure as modernity cloys. It may be that as the millennium progresses, the English will recover what was once their glory in that most precious and fugitive of instincts: a capacity for awe.

The End

Bibliography

Books

Addison, P., *The Road to 1945: British Politics and the Second World War* (London, 1977)

——, *Churchill on the Home Front, 1900–1955* (London, 1992)

Aldcroft, D. H., & Richardson, H. W., *The British Economy, 1870–1939* (London, 1969)

Ashworth, W., *An Economic History of England: 1870–1939* (London, 1960)

Barnett, C., *The Lost Victory: British Dreams, British Realities, 1945–1950* (London, 1995)

Bartlett, C. J., *A History of Postwar Britain, 1945–1974* (London, 1977)

Beaven, B., *Leisure, Citizenship and Working-Class Men in Britain, 1850–1945* (Manchester, 2005)

Beckett, A., *When the Lights Went Out: Britain in the Seventies* (London, 2009)

——, *Promised You a Miracle: UK80–82* (London, 2015)

Beer, Samuel H., *Modern British Politics: A Study of Parties and Pressure Groups* (London, 1965)

Benson, J., *The Rise of Consumer Society in Britain, 1880–1980* (London, 1994)

Bentley, M., *High and Low Politics in Modern Britain: Ten Studies* (Oxford, 1983)

Blake, R., *The Unknown Prime Minister: The Life and Times of Andrew Bonar Law, 1858–1923* (London, 1955)

——, *The Conservative Party from Peel to Major* (rev. edn.) (London, 1997)

Blythe, R., *The Age of Illusion: England in the Twenties and Thirties, 1919–1940* (London, 1963)

Blythe, R., *Private Words: Letters and Diaries from the Second World War* (London, 1991)
Bogdanor, V., & Skidelsky, R., *The Age of Affluence, 1951–1964* (London, 1970)
Bower, T., *Broken Vows: Tony Blair: The Tragedy of Power* (London, 2016)
Boyd, F., *British Politics in Transition, 1945–1963: A Short Political Guide* (London, 1964)
Bradford, S., *King George VI* (London, 1989)
——, *Queen Elizabeth II: Her Life in Our Times* (London, 2011)
Brown, C. G., *The Death of Christian Britain: Understanding Secularisation 1800–2000* (London, 2001)
Brown, K. D., *Labour and Unemployment, 1900–1914* (Newton Abbot, 1971)
Bullock, A., *The Life and Times of Ernest Bevin* (vol. 1. *Trade union leader, 1881–1940*; vol. 2. *Minister of labour, 1940–1945*; vol. 3. *Foreign secretary, 1945–1951*) (London, 1960–83)
Burnett, J., *A Social History of Housing, 1815–1985* (2nd edn.) (London, 1986)
Butler, D., & Butler, G., *Twentieth-Century British Political Facts, 1900–2000* (Basingstoke, 2000)
Butler, D., & Stokes, D. E., *Political Change in Britain: Forces Shaping Electoral Choice* (London, 1969)
Campbell, J., *Edward Heath: A Biography* (London, 1993)
Camps, M., *European Unification in the Sixties: From Veto to the Crisis* (London, 1967)
Cannadine, D., *The Decline and Fall of the British Aristocracy* (New Haven, 1990)
——, *Class in Britain* (London, 2000)
——, *Margaret Thatcher: A Life and Legacy* (Oxford, 2017)
Carlton, D., *Anthony Eden: A Biography* (London, 1981)
Channon, H. (ed. R. R. James), *Chips: The Diaries of Sir Henry Channon* (Harmondsworth, 1970)
Churchill, R. S., *Winston S. Churchill, The Official Biography*, vol. 1. *Youth 1874–1900* (London, 1966); vol. 2. *Young Statesman 1901–1914* (London, 1967)
Clarke, P. F., *Hope and Glory: Britain 1900–1990* (London, 1996)
Clegg, H. A., & Fox, A., & Thompson, A. F., *A History of British*

Trade Unions Since 1889 (vol. 1. *1889–1910*; vol. 2. 1911–*1933*; vol. 3. *1934–1951*) (Oxford, 1964–94)

Coleman, T., *Thatcher's Britain: A Journey through the Promised Lands* (London, 1987)

Collier, J., *Just the Other Day: An Informal History of Great Britain Since the War* (London, 1932)

Cosgrave, P., *The Lives of Enoch Powell* (London, 1989)

Cowling, M., *The Impact of Labour, 1920–1924: The Beginning of Modern British Politics* (Cambridge, 1971)

Crafts, N. F. R., *The British Economy Since 1945* (Oxford, 1991)

Dangerfield, G., *The Strange Death of Liberal England* (London, 1936)

Daunton, M. J., *Meanings of Modernity: Britain from the Late-Victorian Era to World War II* (Oxford, 2001)

Dilks, D., *Neville Chamberlain* (Cambridge, 1984)

Donoughue, B., *Prime Minister: The Conduct of Policy under Harold Wilson and James Callaghan* (London, 1987)

Dyson, J., *Against the Odds: An Autobiography* (London, 1997)

Egremont, M., *Balfour: A Life of Arthur James Balfour* (London, 1980)

Feiling, K., *The Life of Neville Chamberlain* (London, 1970)

FitzGibbon, C., *The Blitz* (London, 1957)

Floud, R., & McCloskey, D. (eds.), *The Economic History of Britain Since 1700* (vol. 2. *1860–1939*; vol. 3. *1939–1992*) (Cambridge, 1994)

Foot, M., *Aneurin Bevan: A Biography* (vol. 1. *1897–1945*; vol. 2. *1945–1960*) (London, 1962–73)

Foot, P., *The Politics of Harold Wilson* (Harmondsworth, 1968)

Ford, B. (ed.), *The Cambridge Cultural History of Britain* (vol. 9. *Modern Britain*) (Cambridge, 1992)

Foster, R. F., *Modern Ireland, 1600–1972* (London, 1988)

Fussell, P., *The Great War and Modern Memory* (London, 1981)

Gallagher, J., *The Decline, Revival and Fall of the British Empire: The Ford Lectures and Other Essays* (Cambridge, 1982)

Gardiner, J., *The Thirties: An Intimate History* (London, 2010)

Garnett, M., *From Anger to Apathy*: *The British Experience Since 1975* (London, 2007)

Gifford, D., *Run Adolf Run: The World War Two Fun Book* (London, 1975)

Gilbert, M., *Winston S. Churchill, The Official Biography*, vol. 3. *1914–1916* (London, 1971); vol. 4. *1917–1922* (London, 1975); vol. 5. *1922–1939* (London, 1976); vol. 6. *Finest Hour 1939–1941* (London, 1983); vol. 7. *Road to Victory 1941–1945* (London, 1986); vol. 8. *'Never Despair' 1945–1965* (London, 1988)

——, *The Second World War* (rev. edn.) (London, 1990)

——, *The First World War* (London, 1994)

Grainger, J. H., *Character and Style in English Politics* (Cambridge, 1969)

Green, E. H. H., *The Crisis of Conservatism: The Politics, Economics and Ideology of the Conservative Party, 1880–1914* (London, 1995)

Green, J., *All Dressed Up: The Sixties and the Counter-Culture* (London, 1998)

Green, M., *Children of the Sun: A Narrative of 'Decadence' in England after 1918* (London, 1977)

Grigg, J., *Lloyd George* (vol. 1. *The Young Lloyd George*; vol. 2. *The People's Champion 1902*–1911; vol. 3. *From Peace to War 1912–1916*) (London, 1997)

Gunn, S., & Bell, R., *Middle Classes: Their Rise and Sprawl* (London, 2002)

Guttsman, W. L., *The British Political Elite* (London, 1963)

Halsey, A. H., *British Social Trends Since 1900: A Guide to the Changing Social Structure of Britain* (Basingstoke, 1988)

Harris, J., *Unemployment and Politics: A Study in English Social Policy, 1886–1914* (Oxford, 1972)

Harris, K., *Attlee* (London, 1982)

Harrison, B. H., *Seeking a Role: The United Kingdom 1951–1970* (Oxford, 2009)

——, *Finding a role? The United Kingdom 1970–1990* (Oxford, 2010)

Haste, C., *Rules of Desire: Sex in Britain: World War I to the Present* (London, 1992)

Hately-Broad, B., *War and Welfare: British POW Families 1939–45* (Manchester, 2009)

Hattersley, R., *David Lloyd George: The Great Outsider* (London, 2010)

Havighurst, A. F., *Britain in Transition: The Twentieth Century* (Chicago & London, 1979)

Hennessy, P., *Ruling Performance: British Governments from Attlee to Thatcher* (Oxford, 1987)
——, *Having it So Good: Britain in the Fifties* (London, 2006)
Hibbert, C., *Edward VII: A Portrait* (London, 1976)
Hilton, M., *Consumerism in Twentieth-Century Britain: The Search for a Historical Movement* (Cambridge, 2003)
Hoggart, R., *The Uses of Literacy: Aspects of Working-Class Life* (new edn.) (London, 2009)
Hollowell, J. (ed.), *Britain since 1945* (Oxford, 2003)
Hopkins, E., *The Rise and Decline of the English Working Classes 1918–1990: A Social History* (London, 1991)
Horne, A., *Macmillan: The Official Biography* (vol. 1. *1894–1956*; vol. 2. *1957–1986*) (London, 1988–9)
Hynes, S., *The Edwardian Turn of Mind* (Princeton & London, 1968)
——, *The Auden Generation: Literature and Politics in England in the 1930s* (London, 1979)
——, *A War Imagined: The First World War and English Culture* (London, 1990)
Jackson, A. A., *Semi-Detached London: Suburban Development, Life and Transport 1900–39* (London, 1973)
Jalland, P., *The Liberals and Ireland: The Ulster Question in British Politics to 1914* (Brighton, 1980)
James, R. R., *The British Revolution: British Politics, 1880–1939* (vol. 1. *From Gladstone to Asquith, 1880–1914*; vol. 2. *From Asquith to Chamberlain, 1914–1939*) (London, 1976–7)
Jay, R., *Joseph Chamberlain: A Political Study* (Oxford, 1981)
Jenkins, P., *Mrs Thatcher's Revolution: The Ending of the Socialist Era* (London, 1987)
Jenkins, R., *Asquith* (London, 1964)
——, *Mr Balfour's Poodle: Peers vs People* (London, 1999)
——, *Churchill* (London, 2001)
Johnson, C., *The Economy under Mrs Thatcher, 1979–1990* (Harmondsworth, 1991)
Johnson, W., & Whyman, J., *A Short Economic and Social History of Twentieth Century Britain* (London, 1967)
Keegan, W., *Mrs Thatcher's Economic Experiment* (London, 1984)
Kennedy, P. M., *The Realities Behind Diplomacy: Background Influences on British External Policy,* 1865–1980 (London, 1981)

Kershaw, I., *To Hell and Back: Europe, 1914–1949* (London, 2015)
King, A., & Crewe, I., *The Blunders of our Governments* (London, 2013)
Koss, S. E., *Asquith* (London, 1985)
Kynaston, D., *Austerity Britain 1945–51* (London, 2008)
——, *Family Britain 1951–57* (London, 2009)
——, *Modernity Britain: A Shake of the Dice 1959–62* (London, 2014)
Levin, B., *The Pendulum Years: Britain in the Sixties* (Cambridge, 2003)
Lewis, J., *Women in England 1870–1950: Sexual Divisions and Social Change* (Brighton, 1984)
——, *Women in Britain since 1945: Women, Family, Work and the State in the Post-war Years* (Oxford, 1992)
Lloyd, T. O., *Empire, Welfare State, Europe: History of the United Kingdom 1906–2001* (Oxford, 2002)
Lockhart, R. H. B., *Your England* (London, 1955)
Longden, S., *Hitler's British Slaves* (Moreton-in-Marsh, 2005)
Lowe, R., *The Welfare State in Britain since 1945* (Basingstoke, 1993)
McDermott, G., *Leader Lost: A Biography of Hugh Gaitskell* (London, 1972)
McDonald, F., *Britain in the 1920s* (Barnsley, 2012)
Mackay, R. F., *Balfour, Intellectual Statesman* (Oxford, 1985)
McKenzie, R. T., *British Political Parties: The Distribution of Power within the Conservative and Labour Parties* (London, 1955)
McKibbin, R., *The Ideologies of Class: Social Relations in Britain 1880–1950* (Oxford, 1990)
——, *Classes and Cultures: England 1918–1951* (Oxford, 1998)
——, *Parties and People: England 1914–1951* (Oxford, 2010)
Mackintosh, J. P. (ed.), *British Prime Ministers in the Twentieth Century* (vol. 1. *Balfour to Chamberlain*; vol. 2. *Churchill to Callaghan*) (London, 1977–8)
McSmith, A., *No Such Thing as Society: A History of Britain in the 1980s* (London, 2010)
Maillaud, P., *The English Way* (London, 1945)
Marquand, D., *Ramsay MacDonald* (London, 1977)
——, *Britain Since 1918: the Strange Career of British Democracy* (London, 2008)

Marsh, P. T., *Joseph Chamberlain: Entrepreneur in Politics* (New Haven, 1994)
Marwick, A., *The Deluge: British Society and the First World War* (London, 1973)
——, *Women at War, 1914–1918* (London, 1977)
——, *British Society Since 1945* (Harmondsworth, 1996)
Masterman, C. F. G., *The Condition of England* (London, 1909)
——, *The New Liberalism* (London, 1920)
——, *How England is Governed* (London, 1921)
——, *England After War: A Study* (London, 1922)
Medlicott, W. N., *Contemporary England 1914–1964* (London, 1967)
Middlemas, K., *Diplomacy of Illusion: The British Government and Germany, 1937–1939* (London, 1972)
——, *The Life and Times of George VI* (London, 1974)
——, *Politics in Industrial Society: The Experience of the British System Since* 1911 (London, 1979)
——, *Power, Competition and the State* (vol. 1. *Britain in Search of Balance, 1940–61*; vol. 2. *Threats to the Postwar Settlement: Britain, 1961–74*; vol. 3. *The End of the Post War Era: Britain since 1974*) (Basingstoke, 1986–91)
——, *The Life and Times of Edward VII* (London, 1993)
Middlemas, K., & Barnes, A. J. L., *Baldwin: a Biography* (London, 1969)
Monk, R., *Bertrand Russell: The Spirit of Solitude* (London, 1996)
——, *Bertrand Russell, 1921–70: The Ghost of Madness* (London, 2000)
Montgomery, J., *The Twenties* (London, 1970)
Moore, C., *Margaret Thatcher: The Authorized Biography*, vol. 1. *Not for Turning* (London, 2013); vol. 2. *Everything She Wants* (London, 2015)
Moore, J., *Portrait of Elmbury* (London, 1957)
Morgan, K. O., *Keir Hardie* (London, 1967)
——, *The Age of Lloyd George* (London, 1971)
——, *Consensus and Disunity: The Lloyd George Coalition Government, 1918–1922* (Oxford, 1979)
——, *Callaghan: A Life* (Oxford, 1997)
——, *Twentieth-Century Britain: a Very Short Introduction* (Oxford, 2000)

Morgan, K. O., *Britain since 1945: the People's Peace* (3rd edn.) (Oxford, 2001)
——, *Michael Foot: A Life* (London, 2007)
Mosley, O., *My Life* (London, 1968)
Mowat, C. L., *Britain Between the Wars, 1918–1940* (London, 1955)
Muggeridge, M., *The Thirties: 1930–1940 in Great Britain* (London, 1940)
Nicol, P., *Sucking Eggs: What your Wartime Granny Could Teach You About Diet, Thrift and Going Green* (London, 2009)
Nicolson, H. (ed. N. Nicolson), *Diaries and Letters* (3 vols.) (London, 1966–8)
Orwell, G. (ed. P. Davison), *The Complete Works of George Orwell* (20 vols.) (London, 1998)
Osgerby, B., *Youth in Britain Since 1945* (Oxford, 1998)
Overy, R. J., *The Morbid Age: Britain Between the Wars* (London, 2009)
Parker, J., *King of Fools* (London, 1988)
Pearce, M., & Stewart, G., *British Political History, 1867–1990: Democracy and Decline* (London, 1992)
Peden, G. C., *British Economic and Social Policy: Lloyd George to Margaret Thatcher* (Oxford, 1985)
Pelling, H., *Modern Britain, 1885–1955* (London, 1969)
——, *Britain and the Second World War* (London, 1970)
——, *A Short History of the Labour Party* (London, 1972)
Percy, E., *Some Memories* (London, 1958)
Perkin, H. J., *The Rise of Professional Society: England since 1880* (London, 1989)
Phillips, M. G., & Phillips, T., *Windrush: The Irresistible Rise of Multi-Racial Britain* (London, 1998)
Pimlott, B., *Hugh Dalton* (London, 1985)
——, *Harold Wilson* (London, 1992)
Plowden, W., *The Motor Car and Politics, 1896–1970* (London, 1971)
Pollard, S., *The Development of the British Economy, 1914–1990* (4th edn.) (London, 1992)
Ponting, C., *Breach of Promise: Labour in Power, 1964–1970* (London, 1989)
Priestley, J. B., *English Journey: Being a rambling but truthful Account of what one Man saw and heard and felt and thought during a*

Journey through England during the Autumn of the Year 1933 (London, 1934)
——, *Margin Released: A Writer's Reminiscences and Reflections* (London, 1962)
Pugh, M., *The Making of Modern British Politics, 1867–1939* (Oxford, 1982)
——, *State and Society: British Political and Social History, 1870–1992* (London, 1994)
Ramsden, J., *The Age of Balfour and Baldwin, 1902–1940* (London, 1978)
Raymond, J., *The Baldwin Age* (London, 1960)
Read, D., *Documents from Edwardian England, 1901–1915* (London, 1973)
——, *Edwardian England* (London, 1982)
Reynolds, D., *Britannia Overruled: British Policy and World Power in the Twentieth Century* (London, 1991)
Rose, J., *The Intellectual Life of the British Working Classes* (New Haven & London, 2001)
Rose, K., *King George V* (London, 1983)
Rosenthal, M., *The Character Factory: Baden-Powell and the Origins of the Boy Scout Movement* (London, 1986)
Sampson, A., *Macmillan: A Study in Ambiguity* (London, 1967)
Sandbrook, D., *Never Had It So Good: A History of Britain from Suez to the Beatles* (London, 2005)
——, *White Heat: A History of Britain in the Swinging Sixties* (London, 2006)
——, *State of Emergency: The Way We Were: Britain, 1970–1974* (London, 2010)
——, *Seasons in the Sun: The Battle for Britain, 1974–1979* (London, 2012)
Seaman, L. C. B., *Life in Britain between the Wars* (London, 1970)
Skidelsky, R., *Politicians and the Slump: The Labour Government of 1929–1931* (London, 1967)
——, *Britain since 1900: A Success Story?* (London, 2014)
Smith, S. B., *Diana: The Life of a Troubled Princess* (London, 1999)
Stevenson, J., *British Society, 1914–45* (London, 1984)
——, & Cook, C., *The Slump: Society and Politics during the Depression* (London, 1977)

Stewart, M., *The Jekyll and Hyde Years: Politics and Economic Policy since 1964* (London, 1977)
Strange, J.-M., *Twentieth-Century Britain: Economic, Cultural and Social Change* (Harlow, 2007)
Sykes, A., *Tariff Reform in British Politics: 1903–1913* (Oxford, 1979)
Symons, J., *The Thirties: A Dream Revolved* (London, 1960)
——, *Between the Wars: Britain in Photographs* (London, 1972)
Taylor, A. J. P., *The Origins of the Second World War* (London, 1961)
——, *The First World War: An Illustrated History* (London, 1963)
——, *English History, 1914–1945* (Oxford, 1965)
——, *The Second World War: An Illustrated History* (Harmondsworth, 1976)
Taylor, C., *Return to Akenfield: Portrait of an English Village in the Twenty-First Century* (London, 2006)
Taylor, D. J., *Orwell: The Life* (London, 2003)
——, *Bright Young People: The Rise and Fall of a Generation, 1918–1940* (London, 2007)
Thompson, F. M. L. (ed.), *The Cambridge Social History of Britain 1750–1950* (vol. 1. *Regions and Communities*; vol. 2. *People and Their Environment*; vol. 3. *Social Agencies and Institutions*) (Cambridge, 1990)
Thomson, D., *England in the Twentieth Century, 1914–63* (Harmondsworth, 1965)
Thorpe, D. R., *Alec Douglas-Home* (London, 1996)
Tiratsoo, N., *From Blitz to Blair: A New History of Britain Since 1939* (London, 1997)
Todd, S., *The People: The Rise and Fall of the Working Class, 1910–2010* (London, 2014)
Tomlinson, J., *Problems of British Economic Policy, 1870–1945* (London, 1981)
——, *Employment Policy: The Crucial Years 1939–1955* (Oxford, 1987)
Turner, A. W., *Rejoice, Rejoice! Britain in the 1980s* (London, 2010)
——, *A Classless Society: Britain in the 1990s* (London, 2013)
Vincent, D., *Poor Citizens: The State and the Poor in Twentieth-Century Britain* (London, 1991)
Vinen, R., *Thatcher's Britain: The Politics and Social Upheaval of the Thatcher Era* (London, 2009)

Vital, D., *The Making of British Foreign Policy* (London, 1968)
Walton, J. K., *The British Seaside: Holidays and Resorts in the Twentieth Century* (Manchester, 2000)
Wells, H. G., *Mr Britling Sees It Through* (London, 1916)
Williamson, P., *National Crisis and National Government: British Politics, the Economy and Empire, 1926–1932* (Cambridge, 1992)
Wilson, J., *C.B.: A life of Sir Henry Campbell-Bannerman* (London, 1973)
Wilson, T., *The Downfall of the Liberal Party, 1914–1935* (London, 1966)
Winterton (Earl), *Pre-War* (London, 1932)
——, *Orders of the Day* (London, 1953)
Woodham, J. M., *Twentieth-Century Design* (Oxford, 1997)
Woodward, E. L., *Short Journey* (London, 1942)
Young, J. W., *Britain and European Unity, 1945–1992* (Basingstoke, 1993)
Youngson, A. J., *The British Economy: 1920–1957* (London, 1960)
Ziegler, P., *Wilson: The Authorised Life of Lord Wilson of Rievaulx* (London, 1993)
Zweiniger-Bargielowska, I., *Women in Twentieth-Century Britain* (Harlow, 2001)

Articles

Articles relating to twentieth-century English history published in the following journals:

Cambridge Historical Journal (London, 1923–57)
English Historical Review (London, 1886–)
Historical Journal (Cambridge, 1958)
History (London, 1912–)
Journal of British Studies (Chicago, 1961)
Past & Present (Oxford, 1952–)
Transactions of the Royal Historical Society (London, 1872–)

Index